COLUMBIA COLLEGE
720.222B919A   C1   V 0
ARCH

YO-ATB-096

Columbia College Library
600 South Michigan Avenue
Chicago, IL 60605

720.222 B919a

Bucher, Francois.

Architector

DATE DUE

MAY 2 0 1998		
APR 1 3 2000		
OCT 0 7 2004		

DISCARD

GAYLORD   PRINTED IN U.S.A.

ARCHITECTOR

ARCHITECTOR

The Lodge Books and Sketchbooks
of Medieval Architects

Françcois Bucher

Volume 1

LIBRARY
CF
COLUMBIA COLLEGE
CHICAGO ILLINOIS

ABARIS BOOKS • NEW YORK

F-Ph-A 720 .222 B919a

Bucher, Franpcois.

Architector :

In Memoriam

Hans R. Hahnloser

Copyright © 1979 by Abaris Books, Inc.
International Standard Book Number 0-913870-47-1
Library of Congress Card Number 77-086233
First published 1979 by Abaris Books, Inc.
24 West 40th Street, New York, New York 10018
Printed in the United States of America
Ari N. Josephy Production

This book is sold subject to the condition that no portion
shall be reproduced in any form or by any means, and
that it shall not, by way of trade, be lent, resold, hired out,
or otherwise disposed of without the publisher's consent,
in any form of binding or cover other than that in which
it is published.

Contents

Acknowledgements

This series was inspired in 1954 by my mentor Hans R. Hahnloser and sharply refocussed in a discussion between Robert Branner, Paul Frankl, Erwin Panofsky, and myself on the "Ideal Gothic Structure" at the XXth International Congress of the History of Art in September 1961. My thanks are addressed first to the teacher-architects and masons of Barcelona, Cologne, Esslingen, Haarlem, Regensburg, Santo Domingo, Strasbourg, and Ulm, among them especially Juan Bassegoda Nonell, Walter Supper, Rudolf Triebe, and my friend Arnold Wolff.

My research was greatly encouraged by John Harvey, Hans Koepf, Werner Mueller, Josefa Weitzmann-Fiedler and in Austria by Ernst Bacher, Hofrat Walter Koschatzky, Alphons and Wanda Lhotzky, Alice Strobl, and M. Zykan. In Germany I received additional suggestions from Paul Booz, Edith Chorherr, Goetz Fehr, Konrad Hecht, Hans Stehkemper, and especially from Peter Pause, Anneliese Seeliger-Zeiss and Elke Weber, as well as the staff of the Staedel Gerhard Ringhausen, M. Stuffman, S. Malke, and Mr. Anton. In the United States I owe warm gratitude to my friends and colleagues James Ackerman, Sumner McK. Crosby, John Fitchen, Kurt Forster, Creighton Gilbert, John Hoag, Walter Horn and Henry Millon. I greatly enjoyed the lively critiques from Carl F. Barnes, Bert Hansen, Robert Mark, and the rich spectrum of ideas offered by Daniel and Judy Williman. The series was to be jointly published with Lon Shelby whose publication of Roriczer's and Schmuttermayer's booklets proved most helpful. Conversations with friends such as Jean Gimpel, Rudolf and Esther Guyer, John James, Luc Mojon, Walter Ueberwasser, Philippe Verdier and Jacques Vicari were as seminal as the insights of Lawrence Durrell, William Golding and Ernst Juenger. I also acknowledge with pleasure the support received from André Corboz, Louis Grodecki, Rowland Mainstone, Franz Meyer, Roland Recht, Marcel Thomas and the pleasant visits with Michael Stettler. Above all students and friends in Princeton, Binghamton, and Europe provided for a continuous discussion of evolving problems. Eugene Kleinbauer, Helen C. Kaplan, Katherine Little, Andrea Mathies, Christa von Preussen, Nina Saller, and especially John Zukowsky were delightful and sharp critics at all times.

Finally I owe thanks to Walter Strauss and Margaret Barlow who nurtured the typescript during my stay at the Florida State University Campus in Florence.

F.B.

Preface

An art historian attempts to follow closely the creative processes of architects and artists and the genesis of their work. He proceeds to examine the progress, completion, and effect of their creations. He tries to recreate the cultural and visual world of the artist and traces the cross-currents between intellectual endeavors and visual phenomena of a given period. He is therefore a cultural biographer delving into a given period, and participating in the emergence of works of art on the basis of written, visual, and oral documents. He finally charts the overall impact of creative efforts within a historical perspective, a privilege only rarely accorded the artist. This series deals with the principles and methods used by medieval architects.

In it I hope to describe and interpret the personal sketchbooks of several architects. Some of these became the property of the workshop or lodge, while others were intended for printing. They follow a tradition established in ancient Greece and continued by the Roman architect Vitruvius in his *Ten Books on Architecture*. Like his later colleagues, Vitruvius dealt largely with the realities of building. He discussed the nature of the site and the perception of solids, voids, color, and texture from the point of view of stationary and moving observers. He noted the optimum size, weight and strenght of materials such as brick, wood and stone. In addition, he dealt with the effects of light on buildings and the optical corrections these might necessitate. He stressed the need for careful composition and pattern repetition in facades and the principles of symmetry in the rhythm of masses and intervals. He analyzed the acoustic properties of spaces in theatres and clearly defined the three main orders of columns which he adapted to specific building programs. Like his followers he believed in the correctness of structural and aesthetic systems which are founded on a theory of proportions, and which he justified by comparison with musical scales. Like later Renaissance architects he mainly suggested numerical multiplications of a module resulting in relationships which can be expressed in rational numbers. The graeco-roman architects stood in sharp contrast to the Gothic masters who relied heavily on a geometric generation of basic shapes resulting in irrational numbers. For Vitruvius all elements together created *Eurythmy*, i.e. total clarity and coherent balance.

None of the medieval architects left us a similarly sophisticated and systematic statement. Seen together the sketchbooks published here give us the basis for a Gothic architectural theory which will be summarized in the concluding volume. The booklets reassert the requirements of Vitruvius who demands that the architect be versed in all the arts as well as in other fields such as music, medicine, law, astronomy, optics, arithmetic, and geometry. His emphasis on machinery for building and for war is echoed by Villard de Honnecourt's catapult whose design came from treatises such as Philip Moench's *Book on War* (figs. 38 b, c). Villard also designed furniture and sculpture, areas in which other sculptor-architects such as Arnolfo di Cambio and members of the Pisani and Cosmati families excelled. Some of the other treatises published here deal with lettering, water-proofing, carpentry, sundials, and projective geometry. Numerous terms enlarge our knowledge of medieval architectural terminology and are analyzed in the glossaries. The sketchbooks and the loose leaves from lodge compilations cover all aspects of secular and religious architecture of the Gothic age.

Checklist of Documents

For technical reasons the manuscripts could not be grouped in chronological order. The following brief checklist of the manuscripts and printed treatises establishes their physical makeup, location, authors, dates, content, and purpose. Each document is preceded by an introduction. Their common importance and the essence of the architectural theory they contain is summarized in the concluding volume.

VOLUME I

1. The Lodge Book of Villard de Honnecourt

Designation: V. Paris, Bibliothèque Nationale, ms. fr 19093.
Author: Villard de Honnecourt, c. 1175-1240, Northern France.
Entries c. 1215-33. Parchment, 66 pages. 240 x 160 to 235 x 154 mm. Some losses in the section on carpentry. His book contains 96 architectural and machinery drawings, 94 figural, and 43 animal sketches. Some theoretical material and Latin titles were added by another person, Master 2. End of active use c.1240. Purpose: Organization of materials for didactic use.

2. The Frankfurt Lodge Book of Master WG

Designation: WG. Frankfurt-am-Main, Städelsches Kunstinstitut und Städtische Galerie, 8-494.
Author: A mason and subcontractor for Abelin Jörg in Stuttgart. Begun c. 1560, completed 1572. Paper Bavarian (1541-61). 316 pages. 201 x 149-153 mm. Drawings and cut-outs based on pre-existing sketches. 222 projects among them 23 windows, 147 vaults, 28 vault schemata, 6 theoretical sketches, and sundials, mullions, stairs and gables. Range: Bavaria and Würtemberg. Purpose: Memorial volume summarizing previous work, and possibly used for vault contracting.

3. Hans Boeblinger, Leaf-Pattern Book of 1435

Designation: H.B. Munich, Bayerisches Nationalmuseum.
Author: Hans Boeblinger, mason, c. 1412-82, completed, probably in Constance, 1435. Paper, 20 pages. 216 x 154 mm. French (Montpellier?) watermark (1428-54). Purpose: Probably part of Boeblinger's apprenticeship work as a leaf cutter. Use: In ornamentation of the West tower of the Frauenkirche, Esslingen, 1440, and especially in the Octagon of 1479. Importance: Precedes famous graphic examples of ornamental leaves by Schongauer and others, stressing importance of architecture as a pioneering discipline.

VOLUME II.

4. The Lodge Book of Wolfgang Rixner, Jerg Reiter and Others

Designation: W.R. Vienna, Albertina, Graphic Collection, Cim Kasten, Fach 6 Nr. 55.
Authors: Wolfgang Rixner, c. 1445-1515, Jerg Reiter from Zeil, c. 1540-1599 (or 1608). 292 pages. Paper. 152 x 208 mm. Datable 1467-68. The architectural cut-out patterns were recently mounted separately. Rixner's entries cover the years c. 1467-1500, Jerg Reiter's contribution reaches to 1599. The early material covers the area around Stuttgart and stands in the orbit of Abelin Jörg and Peter of Koblenz. The later material in Franconian dialect points to Zeil near Bamberg. There are 83 vaults, 27 traceries, 26 decorative and sculptural motifs, 39 theoretical problems as well as stairs, templates, machinery and gables. The 207 images are complemented by a monotonous, technical text dealing with measurements, proportions, and medical advice. The manuscript became a lodge book handed down from one master to another with material accumulating over a century and reflecting varied stylistic concerns.

5. The Dresden Sketchbook of Vault Projection

Designation: DR. Vienna, Oesterreichische Nationalbibliothek, Cod. Vind. Min. 3. Paper: Dresden c. 1560-70. 30 pages, 374 x 253 mm., one folio 490 x 370 mm. Contents: 32 vault designs with their projection procedures and two distillation furnaces. Some vaults are north-eastern German and Bohemian. Purpose: A basic summary of vault projection methods including complex vaults with interpenetrating ribs and balconies with doubly curved elements.

6. The Treatises of Lorenz Lacher (Lechler) 1516, and of Jacob Facht von Andernach, 1593

Designation: LL, JF. Historisches Archiv Cologne W 276.* Paper: 124 pages, 245 x 355 mm. Authors: The first text by the noted Palatinate mason, fortress designer, sculptor and gunsmith Lorenz Lacher (Lechler) was written for his son Moritz in 1516. Lacher (c. 1460-1516) worked in Esslingen, Heidelberg, Speyer and in the Palatinate, specializing in "micro-architecture". His manuscript contains 9 pages of illustrations culled from Matthaeus Roriczer's booklet on finials (see below) as well as a mullion, vault patterns, studies of proportions and 37 pages of text ranging over a series of architectural principles and practical advice. The important treatise by Jacob Facht (Feucht, Voygh, alias Kruell) from Andernach near Koblenz is dated 1593 and contains 9 pages of text which include a building ordinance (pp. 24-26) and 42 pages of vault patterns with their projections. In addition there are 10 theoretical drawings, stairs, a console and two Renaissance columns. Purpose: handbook for Gothic architects.

VOLUME III

7. Mathes Roriczer, *Puechlen der fialen gerechtikait,* Regensburg, 1486
Mathes Roriczer, *Aus der geometrey,* Regensburg, c. 1487-88.
Hanns Schmuttermayer, On Finials and Gables, Nuernberg, c.1488

Designation: MR, HS. The first tract on finials by Roriczer (died 1492) consists of 20 pages measuring 235 x 154 mm. The "geometrey" which deals with simple geometric constructions and the design of a gable has 10 pages measuring 209 x 152 mm. Hanns Schmuttermayer's booklet on finials is clearly related to Roriczer's *Puechlen* and gable presentations. The Nuernberg copy (Germanisches Nationalmuseum, 8° Inc. 36845 K 497) has 10 pages measuring 209 x 152 mm.

The following are later texts or do not relate centrally to Gothic architectural concerns and will be treated briefly:

8. Rodrigo Gil de Hontañon, Simon García, *Compendio de Architectura y simetria de los templos,* Salamanca, 1681.

Madrid Bibl. Nacional, Mss. 8884. The book contains 66 pages with plans derived from designs by Rodrigo Gil de Hontañon (c. 1500-77) and includes a theory on structural computation discussed by G. Kubler and J. Hoag.

9, 10, 11. Three loose-leaf, dismantled sketchbooks

12. Late treatises such as the vault projection theory by the Danzig architect Bartel Ranisch must be seen in connection with South German seventeenth and eighteenth century designs related to the Gothic survival. Several fragments and the lost *Von des Chores Masz und Gerechtikait* as well as ancillary manuscripts such as Mariano Taccola's *De Ingeneis* and Philip Moench's *Book on Strife* complete the list of technical manuscripts written by or available to the medieval architect.

VOLUME IV   COMMENTARY

ABBREVIATIONS USED IN VOLUME I

H.B.	Hans Boeblinger, Leaf-Pattern Book of 1435
V	The Lodge Book of Villard de Honnecourt
WG	The Frankfurt Lodge Book of Master WG

Introduction

Ars sine scientia nihil est.
[Art without theory is nothing]
Jean Mignot, Consultant to the Fabric of Milan
Cathedral, 25 January 1400.

This compendium of illustrations and commentary is comprised of the personal notebooks of medieval architects. As such, they represent a remarkable source of information on medieval architectural theory and methods of construction. They record practical problems which came up in the day-to-day practice of the builder's profession, desired and actual commissions, and theoretical problems. The notebooks were often handed down from one generation to the next, either personally or within workshops, thus becoming lodge books. The most important of these remained with the guilds. Others were discarded as they became obsolete. In several instances the carefully organized notes and sketches of some architects were printed.

Although we may now deduce theory from them, in origin the notebooks were essentially practical. They provide a representative view of Gothic building practices from the early thirteenth through the sixteenth centuries. From the more mundane specifications for foundation building, through roof construction and surface decoration, and sometimes offering tips on how to secure commissions, the notebooks span the entire range of architectural interests. They include procedures for building cisterns, furnaces and machinery of all sorts, as well as methods for approaching the complex geometry of plans and elevations. However, their primary concern is with the central problem of Gothic architecture: the creation of the carefully profiled tracery windows and vaulting, and visually exciting supports and buttresses which were the essence of its skeletal structures. The ribs with which the Gothic architect met this challenge provided both the support for a light, fire-resistant vault and a visually potent decoration. The aesthetic quality of late Gothic architecture was enhanced by increasingly complex and structurally ornamental rib patterns, and eventually through double curved ribs and hanging keystones.

Moreover, the sketchbooks demonstrate the omnivorous curiosity of the Gothic architects and the variety within their profession. Many builders were also interested in lettering, sculpture, carpentry, goldsmithing, military architecture, weaponry, and in designing furniture, fountains, reliquaries and altars. Some even dabbled in medicine and alchemy. Their industry and wide ranging curiosity demonstrate an instinctive and primary Western drive to leave a visible mark on civilization through carefully ordered, monumental accents — the Gothic towered cathedral as much as the pyramids — imposed upon the unstable environment of nature.

All effective architectural systems rely on a small number of geometric shapes. These can be combined to produce numerous efficient and handsomely proportioned structures. The major design methods used to create fine buildings have varied little in Western architecture, from Greece through the nineteenth century. They often interconnect two major systems, one harmonic, the other geometric. Harmonic or musical proportions are based on the tones of the octave and were decisively used in the Renaissance, as demonstrated in R. Wittkower's *Architectural Principles in the Age of Humanism* (London, 1962). The ratios generated by a string or monochord include the octave, 1:2; the fourth, 3:4; the fifth, 2:3; etc. A room based on these modules would therefore measure six by twelve feet, its height being eight feet. The ratios 1:2, 2:3, and other simple sequences were commonly employed in the Middle Ages, especially during the Romanesque period. The standard, considerably more

Introduction Figures

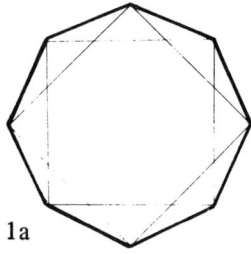

1a

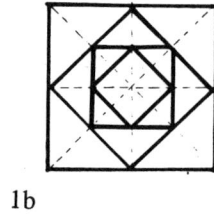

1b

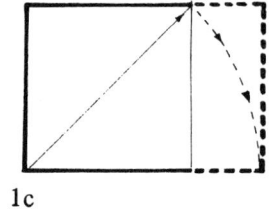

1c

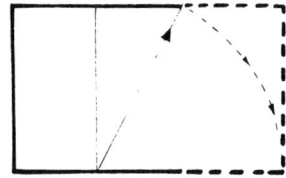

1d

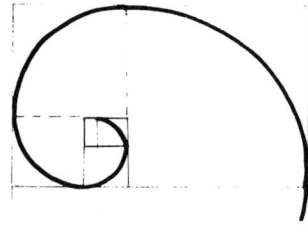

1e

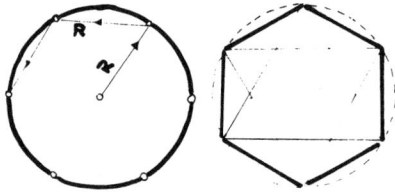

2a

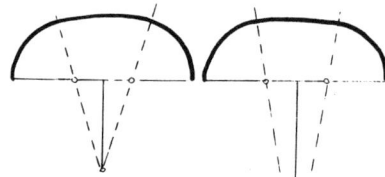

2b   2c

3a

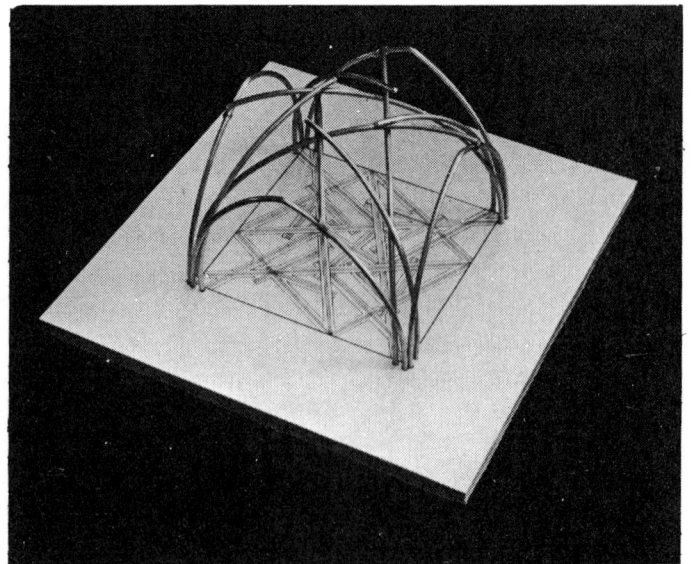

3b

dynamic Gothic method involved purely geometric configurations and little arithmetic.

The most important of these configurations is the square and its derivations, used in superimpositions and rotation. A square can be rotated around itself by 45°. When connected by lines, the corners will form an octagon (fig. 1a). The most important method in determining many—if not all—of the component parts of a Gothic plan consisted in rotating successively inscribed squares (fig. 1b). The side of the first inscribed square will measure $\sqrt{2} \times \frac{a}{2}$, while the side of the next square is $\frac{a}{2}$ and its surface a quarter of the original square. The procedure is repeated until we arrive at a very small square. Luc Mojon, in *Der Münsterbaumeister Matthäus Ensinger* (Bern, 1967), has proven that the elements of the minster in Bern were obtained through this method. The same procedure was also applied to the magnificent plans for Vienna's cathedral towers, which will be discussed in another volume. Two other shapes based on the square were also frequently used to create predictable and quickly constructed rectangles. In the first, named *diagon* by Kenneth Conant, the diagonal of a square is used to form the long side of a rectangle (fig. 1c). In the *auron,* or golden section rectangle, the square is equally halved. A diagonal drawn within one half of the square is projected downward until it meets the baseline, thus defining the long side of a rectangle (fig. 1d). By topping the *auron's* long side with a square, a larger golden section rectangle is created, etc. By using a quarter-circle in each square of the series a false spiral emerges, which appears in medieval engravings in stone (fig. 1e).

The triangle is a frequently used configuration, especially in later Gothic design. Rotated 180° around its center, an equilateral triangle will form a six-pointed star whose points, when connected, result in a hexagon (fig. 2a). A hexagon can be constructed even more easily by transferring the radius of a circle around its periphery, where it fits precisely six times. Pentagons and heptagons were more rarely used since their construction, as explained in Roriczer's booklet, was more complex.

Segments of the circle were used for the construction of arches and rib systems. Accurate construction was dependent on templates, so ovals and ellipses which would have required overly long pattern boards were avoided. Instead, false ellipses were devised by dividing a baseline into three equal parts (figs. 2b, 2c). Half the baseline—or in flatter arches, the whole—was projected down at a 90° angle from the midpoint of the baseline. Two lines rising from the new bottom point were drawn through the thirds of the baseline. The distance from the thirds to the end of the baseline then served as the radius of a segment of a circle intersecting with the diagonals rising from the bottom point, from which a connecting arch is drawn. The arch is either raised (fig. 2b) or flat (fig. 2c), depending on the radius determined by the bottom point.

Finally we must turn to the vault-projection method which determined the actual lengths and curvatures of complex ribs making up star and net vaults. The method has yet to be explained theoretically, but it works perfectly as a series of models (fig. 3b) proves. The fact that rotational projection was not mathematically understood did not bother the builders, just as today's architects need not understand all the engineering calculations behind pre-stressed concrete. A plan from the *Dresden Treatise on Vault Projection (folio 2v)* shows a net vault with a central, four-pointed star (fig. 3a). The main intersections and shapes, such as the inner star, the lengths of the diagonal broken ribs, as well as the radii for the ribs of the inner star, are determined by the rotation of three inscribed squares. Let us explain the procedure by which the exact lengths and curvatures of each rib were determined.

Step one consists of measuring the main diagonal "breakoff" rib from its springing at the right bottom corner to its intersection with the semicircles. This distance from zero to one is transferred to the top edge of the square beginning at the left top corner. From this point line 1 is drawn vertically. Returning to the plan we now follow a quarter-circle, that is, a double curved, twisted rib, springing from point 1. We transfer the actual *squared* length of this rib to the top line also, moving to the right from line 1 to a new line designated as 2. Third, we transfer the *squared* length of the rib springing from point 2, forming a quarter-circle, and reaching the apex 3 once more on the upper edge from point 2 and thus obtain line 3. From point 3 close to the corner of the top edge we now draw a quarter circle using a radius consisting of all major added rib-lengths from the springing of the vault to its apex. We thus obtain a quarter-circle which gives us both the true interior, or *intrados,* lengths of each rib, and the consistently equal curvature. In other words rib 1, which springs from the bottom of the vault and rises sharply, is much longer than ribs 2 and 3, which lie nearly horizontal. The outer quarter-circle on the drawing indicates the thickness of the rib. The construction of models and the actual observation of existing Gothic vaults have shown that in most cases all ribs follow a single radius, a fact which is difficult to understand without the model shown in fig. 3b. If there ever was a "secret" of the masons—which is doubtful—it must have been the ability of a mason to interpret the technique developed for the precise prefabrication of numbered ribs on the ground, which, when hoisted to the vault level, fit precisely into a complex configuration.

These exercises are all relatively simple, and were therefore easily explained to the working masons. The final product is just as easily checked for accuracy. The principles enumerated here form the basic rules of Gothic architecture and were also applied to designing much smaller tabernacles, altars, and monstrances. They are part of the knowledge shared by Villard de Honnecourt, the Parlers, and even Brunelleschi, who had begun his career as a goldsmith. These artists first memorized the Gothic canon and then tested it, over and over again, in actuality. Some scholars, notably G. Lesser (1957), have equated the medieval design methods with philosophical speculation. Others have seen in them Pythagorean and Platonic perfection. I see the Gothic canon as a practical, immensely efficient tool for achieving a given aim as rapidly as possible. It became a canon from which only the great architects dared to depart. I have found no evidence of any symbolic or numerological meaning in any of the documents. The search for hidden and universal meanings fell then, as it falls now, within the realm of symbolists, mystical theologians, and interpretive historians, as will be discussed in another volume.

Except for a rough influence on the total concept, actual measurements did not enter the design phase until the last moment, when the precise size of the commission was determined. Among the approximately 5000 preserved medieval architectural drawings, less than a dozen contain actual indications of size, and some seem to have been added as an afterthought. Most designs were developed geometrically, and thus were workable for large and small structures alike. The determination of actual size was therefore reserved for written contracts. Both Mies van der Rohe and Le Corbusier would have understood this well. They shared with the great architects of the past the belief that architecture must contain time-tested proportional systems.

With the notable exceptions of Roman imperial and ecclesiastical commissions, some medieval royal projects like the palaces of Theodoric at Ravenna and of Charlemagne at Aachen, a few pilgrimage churches such as St. Sernin in Toulouse and Santiago, and, finally, the basilicas of the Order of Cluny, the majority of early medieval constructions in the Latin West were local undertakings. Most mason-contractors of the day, guided by an experienced master and by clerics such as Bernward of Hildesheim, were capable of erecting just about any structure with little trouble. The timber ceilings on vertical arcaded walls, and even small, monolithically perceived domes, presented few problems. Stone vaults were abutted with massive, over-engineered walls. Thrust problems were not sufficiently understood. The enlarged clerestory of Cluny III led to its collapse in 1125 *A.D.*, and the great windows of Vezélay resulted in dangerous structural distortions. The surviving designs, which remain to be published, are correspondingly rough and often tentative.

With Abbot Suger's introduction of the skeletal Gothic system in the choir of St. Denis on June 11, 1144—in which vault thrusts are guided down to slender supports—we finally enter an era requiring the presence of highly trained architects. The curtain-wall cathedrals with their ever-higher vaults, their vertiginous buttressing systems, and huge expanses of glass are closely related to modern skyscrapers in terms of cost, precise pre-planning, and construction logistics. The use of stone, with its great compressive but slight tensile strength, required a high sophistication in the understanding of structural dynamics, and a spirit as dynamic and ambitious as in thirteenth century society. Churches, city halls, and civic projects, as well as private commissions, had to appear large, refined, and expensive. The cathedral in particular had to fulfill stringent demands and uniquely complex specifications. It had to satisfy deep-seated religious and emotional specifications through immense interior spaces streaked by the continually changing glimmer of stained glass. At the same time inordinate civic pride expressed itself through daring, oversized roofs and increasingly monumental towers—such as that of Freiburg, which measures 380 feet, or Jan Vast's crossing tower at Beauvais, which he completed in 1569 and which reached 497 feet. The building had to physically accommodate much of the city's population and had to possess efficient circulation patterns for the throngs of pilgrims visiting the relics on feast days. It also needed good acoustics for organs and choirs, and essentially became a total artistic, cultural, and religious center. Smaller churches were designed for similar functions. Smaller communities such as Kutna Hora, Dinkelsbühl, or Schwäbisch-Gmünd often made an even more extraordinary effort to rival the impact of the immense structures of neighboring cities. Unable to finance size, they asked for an emphasis on daring structural innovations, high refinement of architectural, sculptural, and painted decoration and, often, incredibly sophisticated tabernacles, stalls, altars, and reliquaries.

It seems obvious that the responsibility for such costly long-term projects, involving all segments of the population on a high emotional level, would not be offered to a person of mediocre ability. Instead, the greatest talents and most highly recommended specialists were sought, talents such as the planner of Bourges, who was one of the foremost engineer-architects since the construction of Hagia Sophia by Isidorus of Miletus and Anthemius of Thralles. Another was the designer of Beauvais, who constructed 154-foot-high vaults over an almost completely glazed choir between 1225 and 1272. Robert Mark and Stephen Murray (1976) have established that the Beauvais designer was not responsible for the collapse of the seventh bay in 1284, which also brought down the western parts of the chevet (see *The Thirteenth Century, Acta, 3,* 1976, pp. 17-52). This and other events of a mainly economic nature contributed to the end of Gothic gigantism. Interest shifted toward parish churches and innumerable secular works, from richly ornamented houses to crossbow clubs and other projects of varying refinement, size, and cost, including works of civil engineering and weaponry. The last fell within the purview of architecture and ranged from the design of a catapult by Villard de Honnecourt (ca. 1220) to the manufacture of cannons and guns by several late-Gothic German architects.

The architect and the art of masonry.

After 1200 architecture was increasingly governed by a clearly defined set of theories based on geometry and written empirical rules. The transfer of this knowledge fell within the domain of the art of masonry, which by 1300 A.D. had become one of the most independent professions. Tightly organized and internally regulated, it even included masons' courts. The assumption that the medieval architect was an inspired amateur is therefore applicable only in rare cases when learned bishops or powerful nobles oversaw the construction of usually unsophisticated projects. Even Bernard of Clairvaux found it necessary to send his favorite builder, Achardus, as far as Flanders and Germany to instruct abbots in planning and construction and to supervise some of their twelfth-century monastic building campaigns. We know the names of many early builders and at least one pre-Gothic masons' organization, the Comacini, originating in Lombardy. After 1200 a massive, largely unpublished body of material provides information on the names and often the activities of as many as 2000 Gothic architects and masons. The contracts are rich and precise accounts of construction, and frequently characterize the master of the works as *architectus, architector,* or *ingeniator.* These *magistri* are often awarded extraordinary praise in contracts or in inscriptions on their tombs. As successors of Daedalus, the great builders were named or portrayed in large labyrinths laid into the floors of cathedral naves. Jean de Chelles, architect of a mid-thirteenth century campaign in Notre Dame de Paris, was praised in a large inscription on the south transept. Pierre de Montreuil's tomb declares him to have been a *doctor lathomorum,* a professor of stone masonry. We have more portraits and self-portraits of architects and masons than of any other medieval professionals except clergymen. At this time even the Creator himself was shown mapping out the universe with an architect's compass. So central was the architect's position in society that he became a symbol of arrogance in a sermon by Nicolas de Biard around 1260. The elegant, gloved builder, giving orders to masons while never touching a stone, was compared with the most obnoxious and lazy cleric. His statement is belied by the frenzied pace at which cathedrals were erected. The main work at Chartres, begun 1194, was completed in twenty-seven years; the eastern half of Bourges took nineteen years; and in Cologne a choir bay is supposed to have been ribbed within one week. The documents show that medieval society not only rewarded the great builders with respect and admiration, but also with considerable salaries, often including fringe benefits such as free lodging, heating, lighting, and even food and clothing.

The architect began his career as a mason's apprentice. For three to seven years, depending on the period and the country, he learned to dress stone under strict supervision. On occasion, a badly carved stone was carried on a stretcher by two apprentices and buried, while the mortified apprentice, following the "bier," was whipped a prescribed number of times. The *compagnon* or *Geselle* then had to leave the master for a year of travel. During this time he would visit other lodges and acquire additional know-how and practice. Eventually he would pass a master's examination, which usually required completing a work within a limited time as well as solving standardized but difficult design problems such as spiral staircases, a vault over an irregularly shaped room, pier and jamb designs, and profiles. Upon passage of this ordeal the young mason was certified as a master and given his registered mason's mark, which would usually identify him and his work for a lifetime. Thousands of these marks are known, and remain uncatalogued. They will be seen in several of the sketchbooks.

Depending on talent, intellectual ability, engineering acumen, social grace, and just plain luck, the master mason would sometimes obtain a large commission and thus be launched on a career which would often involve him simultaneously in large commissions and well-paid consultant's work. He would read and write, travel a great deal between jobs, and sometimes change his citizenship according to the requirements of a large commission. Sometimes he would marry the daughter of another architect, take on his sons and others—usually a maximum of two or three—as apprentices and thus create an architectural dynasty. One of these was the ubiquitous Parler family, the so called "Junker von Prag," who dominated Gothic architecture and some projects in civil engineering throughout the Holy Roman Empire from the 1350s well into the fifteenth century. A famous name and solid connections could not however, overcome a lack of talent within the stringently competitive building market. Mathes Roriczer, whose book on finials appears in this series, and who was the son of a well-known architect failed to satisfy the demands of a commission in Nuremberg, and was dismissed to become a builder of small monuments.

Many architects of lesser talent opened workshops in smaller towns and persevered to obtain commissions. They built chapels, market halls, public monuments; designed machines, stalls, tabernacles, drainage systems, bridges and, above all, houses. Except for England, where the trade of carpentry was regulated, they also branched out into timber constructions, especially spires. They worked stubbornly and reliably on buildings and objects of smaller scale. As tested and often accomplished craftsmen, they became the burghers' architects. They did not shape the overpowering spiritual and governmental monuments or the large defense systems. Instead, they provided the visual and qualitative base of the environment: places of business, interesting facades with oriels, complex gables and staircase turrets, complete with sculptural elements. Theirs was the cognitive system which gave the town its manifold and varied identity. Their sketchbooks demonstrate how they kept up with changing trends and updated their styles according to the initiatives of the great masters. They noted concepts, results of discussions, and practical advice. Their sketchbooks also included arranged designs which could be shown to a private patron, a parish priest about to commission a church, or a citizens' building committee.

The documents

Medieval architectural compendia or treatises on specific problems such as vault-projection methods or the construction of finials—be they manuscripts or published booklets—began as personal sketchbooks. Some were annotated and enlarged by other masons; many were entirely reworked by the authors in order to cover specific aspects of construction and theory. Most deal with architectural principles and specific design problems. Only one deals exclusively with architectural sculpture. Several, in part, foreshadow handbooks and catalogues used by today's contractors for information, exchange of ideas, and the sale of items such as vault patterns, more or less complex mullions, and the different types of staircases for secular or clerical patrons. All sketchbooks save one are signed either by name or with the mason's mark.

With the exception of the *Dresden Treatise on Vault Projection,* we have no sketchbooks from a major master. The most famous architects left and were often contractually obliged to leave their designs with the large lodges they had headed. Like the jealously guarded and numbered templates cut to determine the profiles of architectural members, their designs were needed for further work and repairs. A large portion of this splendid material, which the Vienna Cathedral fabric possessed, has been published by Hans Koepf (1969). We therefore have two large and distinct bodies of medieval architectural drawings. The first, which will be touched upon in a later volume, consists of loose parchment and paper leaves and actual 1:1 tracings connected with a particular site. The sketchbooks, the second source, are infinitely more personal, tentative, and experimental than the show plans submitted to building commissions and other practical designs having a definite purpose. Some of the books were broken up and have come down to us as fragments or loose leaves. The most outstanding of these approximately 400 examples—especially if they reflect the style of a great master—are illustrated at the end of this work.

The convenient size and format of these books, averaging eight by ten inches or smaller, enabled the architect to jot down ideas or make a quick sketch of anything which struck him as useful for future projects. He could also record his own work or fill blank sheets with explanatory drawings for a recalcitrant mason or an uninformed patron.

The sketchbooks serve a double role: as repositories of existing, often much older, practices and theorems; and as intimate reflections of the actual creative process. We often see ideas and stylistic changes as they are formulated, for example Villard's increasing tendency to narrow proportions of windows and to refine tracery patterns. They also offer us a unique catalogue of design choices available to the architect-mason within a tightly defined theoretical system.

In their own time these sketchbooks served varied purposes: to accumulate information useful in theory and practice, to establish a file of designs and techniques to educate younger masons, to establish a base for discussion with colleagues and patrons, and to organize and prepare the material for eventual publication, and to systematize it for use by a successor or lodge.

Nomenclature

The general terminology used by the masons is summarized in the Glossary on page forty. A sketchbook is understood as a personal compendium of an architect without any intent to publish, be it in manuscript form or in print. A treatise means a specific theoretical work addressed to a defined problem of Gothic theory and/or construction. Lodge book signifies a personal sketchbook reorganized into rubrics such as carpentry, theory, figural drawing. Usually reshaped for or by a successor, it eventually served a lodge and was, at least temporarily, deposited there.

The loss of the majority of these compendia makes it likely that sketchbooks were deposited in the lodge headed by an architect and discarded when the material became outdated. With luck, an antiquarian, cleric, or relative of the original author, would pick it up and thus preserve it. In the case of Villard de Honnecourt this would have been a clerk, the so-called "Master 3," whose architectural knowledge did not go beyond pious curiosity.

The fact that most masons whose sketchbooks survived cannot be connected with major surviving structures gives us at least a hint about the psychological bind of the less secure and more stationary master. It is he who needed broad guidelines and who, lacking large commissions, had the time to mull over architectural questions. But above all he hoped to secure his posterity through written documents. From Vitruvius to Ranisch we deal with masters from whom we do not have a single major structure conceived and constructed by them. A certain insecurity shows through the writings of these builders in their concern for an almost encyclopedic accuracy—the very element traditionally absorbed, but then changed and even disregarded, by genius. Without these precise notes, often hurried drawings by harried master masons, our task of establishing a fully-documented medieval architectural theory would have been made infinitely more arduous. For in the end, they also attempted to create maximum diversity with a minimum inventory of geometric shapes, developed with the dogged precision required by their craft.

"Don't marvel that all science lives only by the science of geometry. . . There is no tool to work with that has no proportion. And proportion is measure, and the tool or the instrument is earth. And geometry is. . .the measure of earth, wherefore I may say that all men live by geometry. . . You shall understand that among all the crafts of the world. . . masonry has the most notability and most part of its science is geometry."—Adapted from The Constitutions of Masonry (ca. 1400).

Villard de Honnecourt

c. 1175-1240

Designation: V

Recent research on Villard de Honnecourt has yielded new information about his life and architecture. Among the findings are a clearer understanding of his education, stronger indications of his participation in the construction of Vaucelles and in the planning of Cambrai and St. Quentin, the fact of his work as a subcontractor at Reims, and, marginally his endorsement of cannabis for medicinal purposes.

Villard emerges first as a craftsman, yet at the same time as an intellectual with a keen sense of observation and a strong awareness of posterity. He was a lively, versatile mason-contractor and, like other medieval architects, may have occasionally worked as a sculptor and furniture designer. He delighted in machinery and gadgets. This variety of interests was not uncommon for the medieval builder, nor for that matter, for architects from Vitruvius to Frank Lloyd Wright. Above all, Villard is our most direct visual witness to the expansive attitude of the first three decades of the thirteenth century. He was eager both to preserve tradition and to keep up with improvements and discoveries. His lodge book reflects the optimism underlying the immense drive necessary for the construction of some of the most sophisticated and dynamic stone structures in Western architecture.

The purpose of this study is to present interpretations of the comments and iconography in Villard's sketchbook, identifications of the buildings and machinery pictured, and the artists who drew them. Earlier scholarship was summarized by Hahnloser in 1972. Hahnloser never completed the introduction he planned for this section of the volume. Other new insights would have been impossible without the exacting efforts of scholars from Félibien to Branner. The purpose of our tentative biography of Villard de Honnecourt, eight centuries after his birth, is to introduce the architect as a sensitive, searching personality caught up in the artistic and intellectual life of his times.

A tentative biography

Wilars de Honecort, as the author calls himself on page 2 (V2) of his sketchbook, was born circa 1175 at Honnecourt-sur-l'Escaut. It was then a bustling town not far from the great centers of Gothic building which Pierre le Chantre characterized as the *libido* and *morbus aedificandi* in 1190 (see fig. 1). The Escaut river loops around the town on its way north to Cambrai, Tournai, and Ghent. It provided the young Villard with views of mills, bridges, half-timber and stone houses, as well as glimpses of the rich fauna of this wooded region of the Arrouaise. The town was dominated by the fortified Benedictine abbey of St. Peter, rebuilt after 1095 and containing a school, library, and hospital. The second storey of its massive tower displayed a large, mid-twelfth century "Christ in Judgment" and the *voussoirs* of the inner portal held scenes of the "Second Coming."

Villard normally would have acquired a foundation in the *artes liberales* at the local school. Although his French was vivid and accurate, he was not a Latinist. Most of the Latin comments in his sketchbook were made by its second owner, a master whose knowledge of that language was less than perfect. One can find echoes of the trivium in Villard's precise grammar, his rhetorical verve and his dialectical reasoning. The quadrivium left potent marks in the form of his preoccupation with arithmetic and geometry. Partially drawn in cooperation with the second master, V39-40 contain general precepts on design and construction, including plans for a wooden screw and a spiral. We find an example of this latter scratched into the upper surface of a capital at Chartres. The two masters' interests in surveying recalls texts based on the Roman *agrimensores* and the *Cromatici Veteres* which also appear in the Wolfenbüttel sketchbook, Gerbert of Aurillac's *Geometria incertis auctoris,* and the Abbot Eberhard and Sigiboto's *Practica geometria* written circa 1160/68. Some of these texts urge the surveyor to hug the ground precisely in the manner of the figure on V40.

Not unusual for architects of the period, there is no trace of astronomy or music in the book. The inquisitive young man was more interested in construction machinery and in the visual arts. If Villard was born circa 1175, he could not have avoided visiting the huge building project at the abbey of Vaucelles. Destroyed by fire in 1190, the new church was begun immediately. It was to measure 137 meters in length, have a 24 meter wide nave and a transept 60 meters wide. Adjoining communities could not have ignored a project which required enormous amounts of stone and timber needing to be transported by barge and carts. Moreover, it established a demand for large numbers of skilled and unskilled workers, including masons, carpenters, wheelwrights and smiths. Judging from his later entries in which the Cistercian theme reappears, Villard must have taken part in the construction activity, probably first as a journeyman (a day laborer) at about age fifteen.

The master and apprentice system had not yet been codified, but, no doubt, there was a mandatory learning period of from three to four years during which Villard's gifts of observation and imagination would have served him well. The main structures at Vaucelles were nearly complete in 1216, and the church was consecrated in 1235. Villard's book is permeated with entries on Cistercian architecture, including the only medieval graphic definition of the then antiquated Bernardine plan on V28. At Vaucelles this Bernardine schema "made up of squares" had been replaced by a more sophisticated ambulatory plan with radiating chapels which Villard copied from an existing plan on V33 (see fig. 24). At Vaucelles the western most apsidial chapels angled off toward the nave, an arrangement which deeply colored Villard's concept of the "ideal" choir, a principal focus of thirteenth-century design.

Among others, it preoccupied Pierre from the nearby town of Corbie, with whom Villard discussed an ambitious double ambulatory chevet on V29. As it stands, the unsophisticated drawing is an expanded version of Vaucelles with the apsidial chapels arranged radially. They contrast sharply with those of St. Quentin where Villard may well have designed the chapels opening onto the side aisles (see fig. 22e). The "ideal" plan shows square Cistercian chapels filling the spaces between the circular chapels, and the rib patterns of the exterior ambulatory are cleverly simplified. It was to this expanded plan that Panofsky (1951) attributed the scholastic demand for "unity gained through variety." In contrast to the plan of Cambrai on V28, the drawing on V29 is hesitant and most likely dates from c. 1216 when the major work at Vaucelles had been completed. If our chronology is correct, Villard, by now a master mason with thorough, but local experience, may have encountered a lull in building activity. It was then, we believe, that he began his sketches. They were intended both as a personal record and as proof of his drafting abilities. The book was also an illustrated compendium demonstrating his wide range of experience at various, and in part major, sites. The sketches testify to his understanding of complex construction techniques. They also establish his interests in a variety of fields concerning the medieval architect, including architectural and sculptural theory, furniture design, machinery, and carpentry.

The plan of Meaux on V29 directly below the "ideal" plan is among the earliest entries and accurately includes the window mullions indicated by short lines. It was certainly based on a plan kept in the lodge (see fig. 19). Meaux was a good three days' ride south of Honnecourt-sur-l'Escaut via St. Quentin, where foundation work on the choir began in 1195. I believe Villard ignored the more direct route via Noyon, Soissons or Senlis, but chose a detour through Laon, a day's ride from St. Quentin. The cathedral there, nearly 350 feet long, had been completed in the third building campaign circa 1190/1215. The apsidial choir had already been torn down in 1205 to be replaced by a rectilinear chevet then under construction. The building was simultaneously new and under reconstruction.

On V18 Villard expresses his touchingly naive amazement at the sight of the façade by saying, "Nowhere have I seen a tower as fine as that of Laon." More importantly, for the first time, Villard applied the fundamental Gothic layout procedure. In this plan, he clumsily used the quadrature which consisted of a design based on a 45° rotation of successively inscribed squares (see fig. 14 and caption to V18). On the opposite page he sketched one of the western towers. The tendency to elongate elements such as the large upper-storey lancet was to become one of his hallmarks. He also emphasized sculptural details like the oxen. These may have recalled an earlier miracle referred to by Guibert of Nogent concerning the death of an ox pulling a cart with building materials. It was miraculously replaced by another ox who then disappeared at nightfall. Another story tells of a persevering ox who pulled a relic cart on a fund raising tour as far north as Winchester and Exeter, and finally collapsed upon its return to Laon. These quaint accounts reflect the importance of beasts of burden in cathedral construction, especially in Laon with its exceptionally steep hill.

It seems likely that Villard then made another day trip to Reims where he was intrigued by the joining of the responds to the piers by means of a joggled joint, which he sketched for reference on V30. This sketch is rougher than the corresponding drawings of the Reims pillars on V63 which I believe date from the late 1220s. Bypassing Braine and Soissons, where according to Barnes, work on the choir directed by a master from Chartres may have been completed by 1212, Villard would have proceeded through Château Thierry to reach Meaux. Although St. Etienne in Meaux was completed in 1082, it was already undergoing major repairs since 1198. From circa 1175 to 1215/20 its choir was reconstructed. Villard's plan on V29 is accurate, includes the ribs, and reveals in detail the original layout of the choir before the addition of two chapels (see fig. 19).

It seems inconceivable that Villard missed St. Denis and Paris on his way to Chartres, but neither place is referred to in his manuscript. Since the rose window of Chartres is on the back of the leaf showing Meaux, he may have stopped in Paris for only a short time before proceeding to Chartres. It is possible that he reached the famed pilgrimage center at about the time when the scaffolding was removed from the west facade revealing the rose window. In any event, it was surely before the two more progressive north and south windows were constructed. This would have been between 1215 and 1220, dates given to the glass by Louis Grodecki (1950, p. 120) and others. The Chartres rose is drawn with some hesitancy on V30, as if Villard were confronted with an unusual problem. The changes Villard imposed upon the original rose window will be analyzed later (see figs. 21, 22). The style of the drawing must be contrasted with the less rigid, self-assured technique used for the Lausanne rose shown opposite on V31. It differs markedly from its prototype and represents a mediocre design concept of a lesser architectural talent (see fig. 23).

The appearance of the Chartres rose in the sketchbook suggests the final destination of Villard's first long trip. In 1217/18 construction was still going on in the upper regions of the cathedral. It would be tempting to consider Villard among the many subcontractors identified by John James in his 1977 work.

Had Villard remained at Chartres for one or several seasons we could more easily explain the drawings of "Humility" and "Pride" on V6 which were sketched from reliefs on the south porch, according to Sauerlander (1972) dating from the 1220s. James prefers to think that these reliefs date from the first decade of the thirteenth century which would have made a second trip by Villard to Chartres unnecessary. The sketching of the figures is accurate but stiff. They too are in Villard's early style. Assuming that his stay began in 1217, the problem remains of the labyrinth on V14. It is a mirror image of the labyrinth on the nave floor of the cathedral (see fig. 12). This in itself does not prove the sketch was not inspired by the floor pattern of uncertain date. The labyrinth may have been made at the same time as the floor, shortly after 1194, or it may have been added later. However, V14 more likely shows the influence of books such as the twelfth-century *Liber Floridus* by Lambert de St. Omer which depicts a fiercely comical minotaur within the labyrinth. This labyrinth, a likely prototype for the floor pattern, may have been discussed in Villard's presence. At this time, I see nothing to contradict Villard's possible presence in Chartres around 1217 and tend to accept James's early dating of the jamb figures on the basis of style. As to Villard's participation in the building activities, it must be kept in mind that every cathedral was an architectural matrix for accomplished master masons acting as subcontractors under the aegis of the architect in charge. They usually remained for at least one if not several building campaigns.

Villard's presence at projects that had either been recently completed, or were still under construction is the connecting link in his choice of monuments. To put it simply, the pattern of his travels is that of a master mason striving to keep up with the new, while looking for honorable and interesting short-term contracts. This, we believe, is the reason for the exclusion of St. Denis, Noyon and Nôtre Dame of Paris which could only interest antiquarians or historians but not a practicing architect who wanted to keep abreast of the new, rapidly evolving style, and, at the same time, worked to plan his future and ensure his stature for posterity. If Villard returned to Honnecourt via Senlis it would have impressed him as antiquated. In one more day he could have reached Noyon whose nave had been completed in 1205, and whose unimaginative west façade was at that time still under construction. Presumably he then returned to Honnecourt, and may have contracted to work on the choir of Vaucelles (consecrated by the Archbishop of Reims, Henri de Dreux, in 1235). In that year Vaucelles housed 111 monks and 180 *conversi* or lay brothers. After 1238, its population reached 540.

At this point in our tentative, sequential biography of the thirteenth-century builder and master mason several related matters will have to be considered: (1) The immobility and slow pace of pre-industrial society are a misconception. According to veterinarians, a good horse could have carried its rider a distance of 30–33 miles a day. The Tennessee quarter horse will do from four to six miles an hour, nearly twice the speed of the smaller medieval mount. Except for the journey to Chartres, which an excellent horse and rider could have accomplished in four or five days, and the trip to Hungary discussed below, Villard's trips to other sites were mere excursions. Just half a day's walk would have brought Villard to Cambrai or St. Quentin. (2) The builders' and masons' trade was highly seasonal. Between November and February exterior construction slowed down, however, interior work such as the preparation of building elements and timber, the carving of sculpture, and furniture making could continue, often by candle or torchlight. (3) The sudden cancellation of contracts was not unusual. Lack of funds, political unrest, changes in patronage or management, and natural calamities were all liable to have this effect. (4) There was much competition among the first-rate masters for major commissions.

These factors have to be viewed with Villard's mediocre design talents in mind. His enthusiasm and often grandiloquent advice (V28,60) sometimes exceeded his originality. But, as for most of his colleagues, there were ample opportunities for a good mason, foreman, subcontractor, or consultant at one or several of the numerous construction sites in northern France. Like most architects, he must have longed for the once-in-a-lifetime commission. It was denied to him; instead, he worked as a subcontractor at Reims, and may have played a role in the design of the choir of Notre Dame at Cambrai. More likely, he helped plan and possibly construct parts of the choir of St. Quentin which was heavily dependent on Reims.

We lack solid evidence indicating that Villard had full responsibility for a major and original structure, but no one, including this author, has taken a close look at small surviving parish churches and chapels built between 1210 and 1235 in the Cambrai and St. Quentin region. Had he been an architect in charge of a major project, Villard might not have traveled as unsystematically and his sketchbook no doubt would have contained experiments in original design and more creative applications of architectural theory.

Despite these less than inspiring developments, we must stress that Villard was an architect of varied talents and professional integrity. To recall but a few of the architects who were involved in more than a single discipline, we name Vitruvius in Rome, Anthemius of Thralles and Isidorus of Miletus in Constantinople, Daniel Heintz in Bern, Boeblinger, Rixner, and Lechler in southern Germany, Brunelleschi and Michelangelo in Italy, and Frank Lloyd Wright in America. Their many interests included painting, sculpture, metalwork, optics, hydraulics, civil engineering and geometric theory. Of particular interest to Villard and to the later fifteenth century architects was weapons design (see V59). The history of architecture is replete with great minds that actively expanded what might have been a narrow profession. Consequently, I was not overly surprised when Le Corbusier remarked to me in 1969 that posterity would remember him as a painter. Ultimately each architect must consider himself a visual humanist in charge of total manmade environments.

It is possible that at the end of the 1210s or early 1220s, Villard resumed work at Vaucelles, became involved with smaller commissions, and acted as a consultant in Cambrai and St. Quentin. Between 1216 and 1225 he may again have traveled to Reims to sketch sculpture (V54-55). Almost certainly he visited goldsmiths' shops and foundries in the north during the fallow winter weeks. As a border region, Picardy looked south to the Ile-de-France and north to lower Lorraine, the diocese of Liège, the large principality of Luxembourg and what was to become the dukedoms of Flanders and Brabant. Following the Escaut river, Villard would have passed Cambrai and Tournai to arrive in Ghent. Travelling along the Sambre he would have met the Meuse. Upriver were Dinant, Oignies, Verdun; downriver, Liège. These towns were the homes of renowned gold- and silversmiths, including Nicolas de Verdun, and the locations of some of the best foundries. Villard may have seen the lectern, handwarmer, and metal lamps in Dinant, and the *cantepleure* and perpetual motion machine in Liège, a city famous for the manufacture of gadgets (see V13, 17, 34 and figs. 8, 9, 13).

The superb "Crucifixions" on V4 and 15 (fig. 3) suggest that he visited the shops of metal sculptors like Master Gerardus of Flanders and Hugo of Oignies, a scribe, illuminator and goldsmith whose workshop produced a chalice and a processional cross of ca. 1225, now in the Victoria and Albert Museum in London (see Belli, 1969, p. 108). Villard drew some of his images from books. He probably visited the libraries of Reims and Laon which gave him the quaint city view on V7, and perhaps some of the classicizing figures from an astronomical or a calendar manuscript (V7, 22). From ivories he may have copied the circus scenes (V52, 53) and perhaps the "Pagan Tomb" on V11. Villard might have visited libraries along the old northern cultural routes. Egbert of Liège had described the taming of lions in 1023 A.D. and Thomas of Cantimpré near Cambrai was to begin work on his *Liber de natura rerum* in 1239. It was based on bestiaries and the *Liber floridus* of Lambert de St. Omer which were available to Villard, and which he copied on V1, 7, 35, and 48, as discussed in the captions.

The intense cultural ferment of the first decades of the thirteenth century was so remarkable that no thinking man could escape the influence of its vitality. Among the web of famous institutions exploring theology that was to engender the philosophy of Thomas Aquinas and which colored the search for truth of the peripatetic scholars from Chartres to Paris and to Cologne, there were innumerable lesser intellectual centers pursuing an encyclopedic range of studies. The assumption that Villard was a clerk because of his many interests is inconsistent with the contagious atmosphere of the expansive quest for knowledge during the first decades of the thirteenth century.

VILLARD DE HONNECOURT

Villard de Honnecourt may have been in Vaucelles or St. Quentin when he received an invitation to travel to Hungary, where, as he says on V30, he stayed for "many a day." In order to establish the time of this journey, dates of the following must be taken into account: the marriage and death of Elizabeth of Hungary; the side aisles of Reims; the western towers of Bamberg; the rose window of Lausanne; the building campaign at Reims from circa 1225/33, and the ongoing construction of the choir at St. Quentin. Our conclusions are necessarily tentative.

There is no question that medieval builders undertook extensive journeys. As early as 1063 Bishop Meinwerk of Paderborn dispatched Wino of Helmarshausen to Jerusalem to measure the Holy Sepulchre which he intended to copy. A Parisian mason versed in *architectiae artis* was summoned to Wimpfen in Tal, near Heidelberg, to construct a church in the "French style" between 1268 and 1278. In 1287 Etienne de Bonneuil was called to Uppsala in Sweden to become the architect of the cathedral. In the same year John the Mason from St. Dié in the Alsace traveled to Transylvania to repair the cathedral at Gyulafehérvar. Seventeen years earlier Peter and Albert were "brought from Lombardy" to supervise the construction of the tomb of Queen Margareta of Hungary on Fisher's Island. Bishop Bartholomew of Pecz, a friend of St. Elizabeth's father, Andrew II (1205/35), hired masons from Cluny to decorate his cathedral. (See H.358, n. 39.) The increased construction activity of the Cistercians in Bosnia, Serbia, and Hungary brought many additional French builders into the region beginning in the year 1200. The heroic aspects of Villard's trip are only slightly diminished if we note that everywhere he went he met compatriots.

On V20 Villard notes that he drew one of the new side aisle windows in Reims Cathedral, "while on my way to Hungary" and adds: "I had been sent to the land of Hungary when I drew it because it pleased me most." Since this part of the cathedral was under construction from circa 1220 onwards, Villard could have left only after that date. This may have been his second, and crucial visit to Reims, leading to a subcontracting engagement there after his return. Villard's trip was prompted either by the demand for a construction consultant for a Cistercian abbey in Hungary, or else at the invitation of Elizabeth of Hungary who attained European prominence by her marriage in 1221 to the wealthy Louis IV, Margrave of Thuringia. Her legendary largesse began at that moment and included a liberal donation to Cambrai around 1230. After her husband died in 1227 she was forced to seek refuge with the Bishop of Bamberg before moving to the Franciscan convent in Marburg in 1228. She remained a patroness until her death in 1231. In the year of her canonization in May 1235, a choir chapel at Cambrai was dedicated to her. If Elizabeth had anything to do with Villard's trip, her summons would have come after 1221 and her influence would have stopped abruptly in 1231. Elizabeth's contact with Cambrai makes a connection with Villard plausible. It would place his departure sometime between 1222 and 1225. It is worth remembering that the major work at Vaucelles had been completed by 1216, although the choir remained under construction until 1235.

Villard took his sketchbook with him on his journey. He would use it for teaching, making visual notes, and as a kind of professional license proving his knowledge as a mason and attesting to the range of his interests. Traveling through Reims, he probably took the easier northern route via Metz, Trier, Mayence, Frankfurt and Bamberg, possibly stopping at major Cistercian abbeys along the way, notably Otterberg near Mayence. Proceeding east he would have visited Eberbach. Its chapterhouse of 1345 with a star vault may have inspired Villard's drawing on V41 with "eight bosses." The present vault rests on a central pier which reused a Romanesque foundation and may replicate an earlier star vault.

The church of Ebrach near Bamberg was begun in 1200 and completed in 1282. It has six nave bays, a double rectilinear ambulatory and measures 87 m. Cîteaux II, Morimond and Ebrach come closest to Villard's Bernardine plan on V28 where he drew a church to be built or under construction for the Cistercian order. If we interpret the sketch as having developed out of a discussion similar to that held between Villard and Pierre de Corbie, Ebrach would have provided an excellent setting.

It is appealing to imagine Villard passing through Mayence and Bamberg for several reasons. Villard may have wanted an audience with Elizabeth of Hungary who had fled there in 1227 and who was known to support religious construction. In Bamberg he would have met sculptors and builders, some of them Frenchmen from Reims and Chartres. He might have discussed his drawings of Reims sculpture, and shown his sketches of the Laon towers. They are sufficiently detailed in plan and in elevation to have been useful for the completion of the west towers which had not progressed beyond the height of the transept gables at that time. According to Winterfeld (1972, pp. 153, 195 ff.), Frederick II made a large donation for the *opus ecclesiae* in 1225. The west choir abutting the tower stumps was completed in 1231; the towers themselves were finished in 1237. Villard's arrival around 1227 could explain the abrupt changes in the design of the towers at Bamberg which radically shift from late Romanesque to the Laon style. A plan and elevation for only the upper storeys was needed around 1227-30 and this is exactly what Villard could have provided. The actual construction reflects the basic plan which used the rotation of the square to determine the octagon and the thickness of the wall. However, the elevation was more timidly handled and adjusted to match the other eastern towers of Bamberg. Instead of tying together the two upper storeys with a single narrow lancet window, they returned to the traditional repetition of three approximately equal storeys topped by a triangular gable. The total effect is a regression from the bold concept of Laon and a shift from French to German architectural techniques. We cannot suggest that Villard participated in the completion of the towers; his subsequent activities would have made this impossible. But it must be recalled that he would have visited Bamberg during the time when the deliberations over the completion of the towers took place and that he carried with him contemporary drawings of Laon. At Bamberg, Villard had to leave the safer and more comfortable river routes along the Main to reach the Danube at Regensburg. His sketchbook contains no trace of Magdeburg whose francophile Bishop Albrecht also contemplated a Laon-type elevation for his own church until 1230 when the design was changed. The sculptors preferred continuing in the tradition of the north portal of Notre Dame in Paris and in the Strasbourg style. The last monumental copies of the Laon towers appear in Naumburg. According to Frankl (1962, p. 107), they were designed by French or French-trained architects after 1237, that is, shortly after the completion of the Bamberg towers.

From the thriving imperial city of Regensburg, Villard probably followed the Danube to Vienna from where he would have continued by barge to Budapest, a popular mode of travel in medieval times. A short day's ride would have brought him to the capital of Hungary, Estzergom, also the seat of the primate of Hungary since 1198. However, there seems to be no record of any of these sites in his book, except for the paving tiles on V30 which he declares he saw in Hungary. They reappear in the Chapel of St. Nicholas in St. Quentin (fig. 20). László Gerevitch (1971) found identical designs in his excavations of the Cistercian monastery of Pilis near Estzergom. Pilis was one of four Cistercian abbeys founded by Bela III (1173/96) and was under construction well into the middle of the thirteenth century. The church, built on the simplest Bernardine plan, had been completed before Villard's arrival. Gerevitch believes that the leaves at the bottom of V10 were copied from the tomb of Gertrude of Merân, (†1213).

There is no evidence that Villard visited any of the other Cistercian buildings under construction during his stay. We must reject the idea of Villard's participation in the construction of the church of St. Elizabeth in Kaschau, originally postulated by Henszelmann (1846) for reasons of date. Gal (1929, p. 242) sees Villard's hand, and based on Möller, his mason's mark in St. Jaák and Zsámbék. However, these buildings are too far removed in style and date to be associated with Villard. Because of the lack of buildings, statuary and wooden architecture from medieval Hungary in Villard's book, we assume his stay was a short one. His sketchbook contains only two designs that might be seen as possible commissions undertaken there. He might have designed and supervised the execution of the choir stalls on V54 and 57. The drawings are accurate, and seem to be customer oriented designs for an elaborate and a cheaper version of similarly proportioned stalls. Secondly, Villard may have designed and/or participated in the construction of the tomb of Gertrude of Meran, wife of Andrew II and mother of Elizabeth of Hungary. The fragments found by Gerevitch may well date to the 1220s, but they are not numerous enough to indicate the work of a given artist.

Upon his return, Villard may have followed the northern route as far as Linz or Regensburg and then veered off toward Bodensee to follow the Roman road as far as Avenches, Payerne and Lausanne. Alternatively he might have visited Lausanne earlier, taking the Rhine route through Mayence. If so his visit might have coincided with the construction of the rose window (Gal, 1929) in the south transept at Lausanne around 1226, which he crudely rearranged in his sketch on V21 (see fig. 23). He might also have taken the much more arduous southern route leading him through Vienna, Graz, Marburg and Laibach to Venice, where he may have seen the extraordinarily non-French looking clock tower on V12. There, he might also have seen the reliquary cross made in 1206 by Gerardus of Flanders for Henry of Flanders who lived in Constantinople. In any case, a cross very similar to the one presently in the treasury of St. Mark inspired his drawing on V15 (fig. 3).

Proceeding from Venice through Vicenza, Verona and Brescia, sites replete with "pagan" monuments like the "tomb" on V11 and nude statuary which may have inspired V22, 43, he would have reached Milan and continued over the St. Bernard Pass. The monastery at the top of the pass still houses a thirteenth-century, northern French hand warmer in the shape of a sphere. It has only three gimbals in contrast to the incredible six gimbals of Villard's design V17. (H. ills. 194-95). He would have continued through St. Maurice to reach Lausanne by boat around 1228. There he would have met several Frenchmen, among them Jean Cotereel, *magister operis* in Lausanne, 1227-36, and Pierre d'Arras, a glass painter who established his shop in 1217 and worked there until 1234/5.

Beer suggests that the rose window at Lausanne was under construction in 1227. The transept was completed around 1226 and roofed before 1232 at which time the relics were transferred back into the cathedral (Biaudet, Meyland, Beer and others, 1975, pp. 45-48, 221, 249). If we place the visit of Villard ca. 1227, then we can see the free but inaccurate sketch of the rose on V31 as an alternate solution based on discussions of the precise design of the window under construction (fig. 23). The use of trilobes and quadrilobes within the circle, and the rotation of the whole design by 22½° combines to make it one of Villard's least sensitive drawings and confirms our observation of his singular lack of design ability. At the same time it points out that Villard, while aware of the quadrature as basic design method, having used it in his earlier plan of the Laon tower on V18, still had not accepted it as the standard practical approach (Bucher, 1968). This fact alone would indicate a stay in Lausanne sometime before the 1230s, after which date Villard no longer ignored the organizing principle of quadrature, using it in the face and the fighters on V38.

The well known Aristotelian, Boniface of Brussels, a friend of Godefroi de Fontaine, Bishop of Cambrai (1220/1237), was installed as bishop in Lausanne in 1231, probably after Villard's visit. Boniface himself was succeeded by Gui de Laon (1238/47). With these connections it is not surprising that the massive southwest tower of Lausanne Cathedral is yet another "copy" of Laon. Villard's drawing may again have influenced the choice of the design of this tower which had been under construction from circa 1210, and whose upper storeys, inspired by Laon, were completed no earlier than 1232.

Villard presumably returned to France by way of Dijon, Troyes and Reims, where work had progressed during his absence. Villard reappeared in St. Quentin or Honnecourt by 1227/28, surely supplied with stories of harassment, unpredictable food, dirty hospices and other details of his journey. Even for the usually well traveled medieval architect the journey to Hungary was arduous, especially if Villard used the more dangerous southern route. Among the many difficulties he might have encountered were language barriers, toll collectors, robbers, dangerous roads, overloaded ferries and a host of diseases such as dysentery, typhus, malaria and rabies. In view of these hazards, Villard's medicinal advice on V65 gains greater relevance. His recommendation of cannabis may reflect illness, but also the psychological rigors that confronted the sick foreign traveler. Villard's trip to Hungary covered at least 3700 kilometers. This meant about four months in the saddle and on crowded barges. Considering the inevitable delays occasioned by bad weather, sickness and sightseeing, connected with discussions, consultations and the hope of securing a large commission, Villard was probably absent for at least one year. Longer stays at Bamberg, Estzergom, Pilis, possibly Venice and certainly Lausanne would have lengthened Villard's trip considerably. It might well have taken a total of two years, probably 1226-28. After circa 1228 Villard was involved with his last projects, namely subcontracting work in Reims and a careful study of the fabric. After 1233 he may have assisted in the planning or participated in the construction of the choirs of Cambrai and St. Quentin, both based on Reims.

The construction of the new cathedral of Reims began on 6 May 1211 and the *chorum novum* was first used by the chapter on 7 September 1241. Major work on the choir is assumed to have taken place in 1227. The project was large and sophisticated, creating work for many subcontractors. James (1977) has shown that highly qualified master masons worked on assigned parts of the structure through one or several building seasons, probably supervising preparatory carving in the lodge sheds during the winter months. Reims could be reached in two days ride from Honnecourt. The side aisle window on V20 which Villard drew on his way to Hungary around 1226 attests to his acquaintance with the architect and subcontractors of the fabric. Despite the precision of this drawing in which he added a section through the middle mullion with its two attached colonettes, he significantly left out any masons' mark (see fig. 42). As mentioned earlier, I believe that he returned to Reims around 1228 following his trip to Hungary.

On V60-63 of his sketchbook, Villard drew specific elements of the eastern fabric and included the marks of at least six masons working on various parts of the structure. These included the cornice below the triforium of the choir, the colonettes of the triforium (V60), extensive details for tracery of the side aisle windows (V62) and working drawings for mullions identified in the caption accompanying V63. I can only interpret the masons' marks as work assignments. Earlier Villard studies were handicapped by not recognizing him as a minor builder, a mason-contractor ready to take on major supervised commissions as well as small projects of his own, especially towards the end of his career. Interestingly enough he shares his secondary status with most of the other builders discussed in our volumes. For several seasons Villard was a secondary master working under the aegis of the cathedral architect. The drawings on V60-63 must therefore be viewed as location sketches, considerably reduced templates, and precise descriptions of parts of the structure in his charge. In turn, he assigned these to masons whose marks he entered on the corresponding architectural elements, thus keeping a log of every worker's personal responsibilities. These masons' marks are similar to those from St. Denis, published by Crosby, and to those of Chartres recorded by James (1977). Villard took visual notes on interesting procedures such as the complex construction of piers on V63. These elements and the reduced templates on V41 do not contain masons' marks. As a secondary master and foreman he would have been informed of the ongoing work and would have participated in discussions about elevations and the design of the buttressing system of the choir illustrated on V64. His repeated verbal stress of the need for crenellation seems to reflect his personal taste. He may have tried to impose this upon the architect in charge who, however, seems to have favored the lofty balustrades which were to top the chapels designed after 1236. The touching addition of a measuring and triangulation cord which could double as a plumb line on V63 seems to beg future readers to consider his participation in the construction. Translated into words, his statement might read: "I also built here." Considering the dates of the parts bearing masons' marks it is most likely that Villard joined the Reims campaign of 1220/33 directed by Jean le Loup. According to the controversial sequence of architects summarized by Stoddard (1966), Jean's campaign included the triforium of the chevet, advancing work on the transept, the addition of two more bays to the nave's existing three eastern bays and twelve nave piers. By 1233 the chevet was ready for vaulting, work on the north transept and eastern nave was proceeding, and the earlier facade design had been revised (1228/30). The upper and lower cornices for the side-aisle roof were in place as shown in the left margin of V62. The bases of the buttressing towers, including the floor of the passageway presumably had advanced to the stage also shown on V62. On the other hand, the schematic angels would not yet have been in place. The outer turrets of the buttressing system of the choir shown on V64 (figs.44-45) were to have an extended narrow opening reaching to the level of the upper fliers. The inner tower contains a passageway at the bottom which was retained in the final execution. Another decorative opening between the lower and upper fliers was deleted and replaced by solid masonry. Moreover, the existing system adopted very large outer aediculae and much heavier finials adorned with crockets. The fliers were even more vertically staggered than originally planned. These design changes most probably occurred during the fallow period, 1233/36. In 1233 some burghers, financially harrassed by the bishop, killed his marshall, besieged the canons, and erected barricades which included stones from the fabric. On November 8, the canons fled and returned in January 1236. R. Branner in "Historical Aspects of the Reconstruction of Reims Cathedral 1210-1241" in *Speculum* (1961) documents these events which were violent enough to have led to a near total disruption of work. It was only under the architect Gaucher of Reims (1236-54) that the chevet was vaulted and readied for use in 1241. Villard's drawings indicate that he no longer participated in this phase since the most elevated architectural member provided with a mason's mark on V62 is a cross rib below the internal cornice crowning the nave wall. I feel that Villard's drawings must be taken largely at face value. They show the state of completion of the eastern parts of the nave and the buttress stumps, as well as the planned elevation of the choir buttressing system as they existed in 1233. Furthermore, I believe Villard subcontracted for the sculptural traceries of the sideaisle windows, the chevet triforium including its base cornice and blind arches, the *tas de charge* of the nave vaults and the first elements of the eventually discarded nave ribs. Consequently he would have been at Reims from about 1228 to 1233.

Villard's probable participation in the Reims lodge as a subcontractor would have given him the prestige necessary to obtain his last commissions, probably as consultant or designer of the Cambrai choir chapels, and as designer of the choir of St. Quentin from at least 1233.

Referring to V61, Villard states on the opposite page "you can see the elevation of the chapels at Reims as they exist. In such a manner those at Cambrai must be made, if done correctly. The upper entablature must form crenellations." On V28 he mentions the choir of Cambrai "as it rises from the ground" and adds that in his book one could find the now lost interior and exterior elevations, drawings of the chapels, walls and flying buttresses. The disappearance of these designs is a major loss. In fact, the plan on V28 is the only accurate working drawing in the book except for the more general sketch of the choir of St. Stephen in Meaux on V29 (see fig. 18), and it corresponds closely to Boileux's plan of 1779, published by Le Glay in 1825.

Cambrai was detached from the diocese of Reims in 1169 and the choir of the huge metropolitan church, begun in 1227, was to reach a length of 136 m. By 1230 the construction of the choir had proceeded far enough to include the chapel of St. Nicholas, followed in 1239 by the chapel commemorating Elizabeth of Hungary. Villard's mention of the rising foundations of V60 corroborates dating his stay at Reims to the late 1220s and stresses not only the close planning similarities between Reims and the large, now destroyed choir at Cambrai (see caption V28), but also indicates Villard's cooperation in the project. Construction was slow and there may have been a stoppage between 1234 and 1235. In 1243 a chapel was dedicated to St. Blasius; the choir walls were completed around 1246 and the vaulting was finished by 1251. The vaults differed from Villard's design and the upper structure was strongly influenced by elements of Amiens which Villard probably never saw.

Cambrai was located less than half a day's ride from Honnecourt, so it is likely that Villard helped in the planning, and after 1233 perhaps even in the construction of the choir and semicircular transepts of Cambrai. The transepts were begun in 1227 and seem to have risen more rapidly than the choir. If he had been involved in this construction, it would not have been for very long since neither his wishes nor his advice were followed after 1240.

It seems likely that Villard was involved in the planning of St. Quentin both before and after his stays in Hungary and Reims. From its very inception in 1195 the Collegiate Church of St. Quentin was a huge project. Its nave was to measure 12.35 m. in width, and reach a height of 35.20 m. compared with the only slightly larger Reims, whose respective dimensions are 12.8 m. and 37.60 m. The clerestory windows completed in the fourteenth century in accordance with the original design measure 13 m. and are among the largest in France (fig. 40). By 1220 the outer elements of the choir were nearly finished and a chaplaincy was founded in one of the radiating chapels. In 1228 the relics were removed from the crypt. According to Héliot (1967, pp. 38-40), this meant more active construction. On 2 September 1257 in the presence of St. Louis, the relics were transferred into the largely completed choir. Villard surely could not have ignored building activities centered around a large workshop less than a half day's ride from Honnecourt on the road to Laon and Reims. In 1867 Pierre Bénard assumed that Villard was the first architect in charge of the structure. Because we believe Villard was actively present at Reims until 1233, and in view of the lack of any signs of Gothic stylistic developments after this date, we must modify this theory.

Bénard had published a graffito—a full scale design carved in drying plaster—which he found in a radiating chapel and attributed to Villard. Recently we rediscovered the supposedly lost graffito, a rose probably destined to adorn the choir windows, 0.8 m. above the floor on the wall of the northernmost radiating chapel. As Bénard and Hahnloser had stated, a reconstruction of the damaged low relief rosette strongly evokes the sketch of the Chartres rose on V30 (figs. 21-22). By placing the polylobed rosettes into the spandrels of the arches, the graffito harks back to the original Chartres concept, albeit changing the proportions to a 1:1:1 ratio of the radii of the circles and by keeping the lobed rosettes oriented radially instead of vertically as at Chartres. In addition, the chapel of St. Michael in the west tower completed circa 1215, contains a tile floor with star motifs and other patterns framed by narrow slabs of stone (fig. 20). The six-pointed stars are thrown slightly off axis like the stars drawn by Villard in Hungary which are on the same V30 as Villard's Chartres window. This double coincidence has led me to the conclusion that Villard's sketchbook and presumably Villard himself were present at St. Quentin after his return from Hungary. This occurred at the crucial moment of increased building activity in St. Quentin around 1228 (see Bucher, 1977).

In an attempt to reconstruct Villard's life, one must keep in mind that Villard had a thorough knowledge of Reims. His influence may explain the close relationship between the Reims and St. Quentin choir elevations, as seen in fig. 40. Both choirs are in an approximate 3:8 vertical proportion, but St. Quentin has lower ambulatory arches, a busier tripartite triforium instead of twin arcades, and narrowed lancets. The elevation thus corresponds to Villard's tendency to force verticalization and to thin out vertical elements. I believe he remained in Vaucelles until circa 1216 at which time he traveled to Chartres before leaving for Hungary. This means he had ten possibly contract-free years before his presumed departure, during which time he could have continued to work in Vaucelles. On the other hand, he might have joined the lodge of St. Quentin and the *épure* might be as early as 1220 when a chaplaincy was established in the new choir. It is equally possible that he was called in as a consultant during his stay at Reims. Since work in St. Quentin proceeded slowly, it is much more likely that he became involved with the Collegiate Church after his return from Reims. It is even possible to defend his presence as *maître d'oeuvre* from 1233 onward

Héliot compares the elements of the ambulatory with St. Rémy in Reims, Auxerre, St. Yved de Braine and Soissons, buildings which were either finished or near completion around

1212/16. Were Villard the architect in charge, his tenure was brief since his sketchbook contains no indication of any architectural advances beyond 1233. The buttressing system and the treatment of the transepts of St. Quentin, still under construction in 1248, presuppose knowledge of Amiens or of the stunning elevation of St. Nicaise at Reims, begun in 1231 and undoubtedly important to an architect like Villard for whom *modernitas* meant so much. If he had been connected with St. Quentin in any important capacity, we would have to assume that he resigned his commission or that he died shortly after accepting it.

Villard probably spent his last years, presumably his late 50s and early 60s, as a consultant and perhaps as an occasional subcontractor at Cambrai and St. Quentin. Multiple commissions and consultant's engagements were not unusual for the medieval architect. Looking back upon a satisfying but not highly distinguished career, Villard organized his drawings with the help of Master 2. He did this in the hope that they would be useful to others. He neglected stylistic advances to concentrate on the mechanical and theoretical additions of the 1230s. Villard never visited Amiens, begun in 1220, whose nave was completed circa 1233/36 nor did he ever see Beauvais, begun in 1225. Both towns were only a few days traveling from Villard's center of activity.

Having worked closely with his sketchbook for many years and having visited many sites which he knew well, Villard strikes me as a busy man who may never have realized his professional limitations. His youth in the bustling town of Honnecourt was punctuated by visits to the nearby site of the abbey at Vaucelles which remained central to his architectural conceptualization. He delighted in wrestling (V28), interesting faces (V18) and animals. Villard's general scholarly interests prove that he remained in contact with intellectuals, be they his Benedictine teachers in Honnecourt, the Cistercian community at Vaucelles, military engineers, and last, but not least, the architects, subcontractors and sculptors of Reims. His curiosity remained that of a clever, slightly wide-eyed provincial, constantly trying to improve his knowledge in the hope of obtaining a major commission. The relatively restricted radius of his travels in northern France and Brabant, with the exception of his trips to Chartres and Hungary, makes it very likely that he had a family in Honnecourt and established a shop there. There would have been enough work for a good mason: repairs on the abbey, bracing of houses as seen in V45, the construction of roofs as in V34 and the building of bridges and machinery along the Escaut river (V39, 44, 45). In a small town he would have been a respected member of the community, a respect which translates itself into the occasional self assured statements of his sketchbook. His trip to Hungary which he mentioned so insistently was surely the great adventure of his life, and we can well imagine the interest accorded him and most foreign travelers in medieval times. His deepest aesthetic experience as an architect was Reims, its sculpture and its building, in which he seems to have participated as a sub-contractor.

Still dependent on the genius of others, even at the height of his career he tried to impose Reims, his ideal, on Cambrai, and probably also St. Quentin. The interior of its choir became an attenuated copy of Reims. His interests and conviviality show in his discussion with Pierre de Corbie mentioned on V29. Above all, they come across in the wide variety of subjects he chose for his drawings (see figs. 13, 31, 32; 38). He was undoubtedly in contact with the leading minds of the Picardie and Brabant during the first decades of the thirteenth century. In the late 1230s these contacts may have discouraged his interests in more modern gadgets and procedures, and directed him toward a deep concern for his profession. He became interested in the theory of architecture, and began to worry about the survival of his principles and his reputation. He wanted his sketchbook to become a text others would consult, in short a lodge book. At that point, he reorganized it. He labeled and reformulated his ideas and professional experience in the hope to transform them into a pictorial treatise on architecture and the related arts. By overstating his own participation in the Gothic architectural drama through comments such as "you will see from this book" or "in this book one can find good counsel" (V2, 18), he constantly asks us to overlook his tragic flaw, namely his lack of original and creative design talent. Villard was probably never given a major commission.

In the tightly knit, competitive world of medieval masonry Villard must have heard of the bold new experiments going on around him. The transept and nave of Amiens were completed in the early 1230s. The reckless curtain wall of the Beauvais choir was begun in 1225, completed up to the eastern piers of the crossing in 1272, and collapsed on the evening of Thursday, 29 November 1284. Villard never saw Bourges which was begun a year after Chartres, nor probably Rouen whose nave was finished in 1235. If Villard's desire had been to keep up with the latest trends, surely there would be traces of these sites among his sketches. His lack of awareness of stylistic changes after the early 1230s indicates that he may not have lived long enough to see them. Too old to accept the rigors of long rides, and no longer interested in the rapidly changing pace of Gothic architecture, he straightened out his affairs. On the introductory page of his book he wrote in the firm script he had learned from the Benedictines: "Wilars de Honecort greets you and asks all who will work with these aids to pray for his soul, and to remember him. For in this book one can find good counsel on the great art of masonry and carpentry constructions. And you will find in it the art of drawing which the principles and the discipline of geometry requires and teaches."

The humanist architects

Before 1048 Poppo, the Abbot of Stablo, called Thietmar a "master of carpenters and masons whom he loved for his expertise in his art" (Lehmann-Brockhaus, Nr. 3036). Villard's contemporary, Gervase of Canterbury (died 1210), characterized the architect of Canterbury Cathedral, William of Sens, as *in ligno et lapide artifex subtilissimus,* a most subtle craftsman in wood and stone. These are only two of many statements demonstrating the varied abilities of the medieval architect, whose life and status has been discussed by Pevsner, Hahnloser (345-46), Harvey, von Schlosser, de Lasteyrie, Frisch, and others.

Beginning in the middle of the thirteenth century, the architect was considered a master of several trades. For Joinville they were the *Maistres Engignierres* or *Engignours.* Jean de Liège, architect to the Dukes of Savoy, is described in an inscription on the stalls of the Lausanne Cathedral (1387) as the *Architectus* and "outstanding sculptor of this multifaceted work." He is portrayed nearby holding a divider and level (H. 345). Architects were highly paid, traveled extensively, and were honored with inscriptions, portraits, and tomb effigies such as those of Hugues Libergier (died 1263) and Pierre de Montreuil called a "doctor of masons." The strict definition of the activities allowed masons, stone cutters, and plasterers in the *Livre des Metiers* by the Provost of Paris, Etienne Boileau, in 1258 cannot be taken too literally. Boileau described the architect's profession as a trade requiring a six-year apprenticeship, with fixed working hours, taxes, fines, and discussed the role of the master of the guild. Many examples show that the architect often transgressed his assigned role and was often deeply involved in all facets of construction and other visual arts, including painting. Pierre de Chelles, an architect of repute, was in charge of the tomb of Philip the Bold between 1298 and 1307 (Sauerländer, p. 122), just as Villard may have designed the tomb of Gertrude of Meran (died 1213) in Pilis. Even a builder as intent on architectural graphism as Daniel Heintz, for four years in charge of the construction of the vaults of Bern Cathedral, was given a sculptural commission by the Amerbach family of Basel in 1578.

The heterogeneous quality of Villard's booklet reflects the wide interests of architects of many periods, earlier and later masters including Arnolfo di Cambio, L. Lechler, Brunelleschi, Michelangelo and Le Corbusier. In the exciting decades of the early thirteenth century, most minor architects must have kept notebooks, just as did the painters of the Freiburg, Wolfenbüttel, Reun, Venice, Icelandic and Pepysian codices, and, most masterfully Albrecht Dürer. The sketches and designs of major architects in charge of long range projects were filed in and remained in the lodges for consultation during the architect's directorship. There they could be studied side by side with larger, more precise plans and elevations such as those preserved in the palimpsest showing façade projects and other details of Reims Cathedral. (Hahnloser 1933; Branner, 1958). Some of the later manuals such as Roriczer and the *Dresden Sketchbook of Vault Projection* are exceptionally sterile when compared to other treatises such as Juan de Arfe y Villafane's *De Varia Commensuracion para la Esculptura y Architectura* of 1585.

Villard excerpted *(estraites)* from his world everything he thought might be of future use, and in addition things new, strange and whimsical. He used painters' pattern books, bestiaries, encyclopedias, copied templates and noted new inventions and construction methods. He accumulated an immensely entertaining catalogue of visual aids. One gathers from his sketchbook that Villard was both a *sage et courtois* professional and a person who enjoyed his work tremendously, whether straightening a sagging house or devising playful theories of proportion and quadrature, in short a true *architector*.

Appendix I: Physical description, purpose and history.

Villard de Honnecourt's book is now in the Bibliothèque Nationale, Paris (*Ms. fr.* 19093). The book was rebound in leather in 1926. Its parchment leaves originally measured nearly 255 x 180 mm. They were trimmed down to the present 235-240 x 154-160mm. no later than the fifteenth century. Half of the manuscript's pages are of thick and barely bleached parchment. More formal drawings, such as the nude figure with washes on V22 were done on thinner sheets of polished parchment.

Sixty-six pages remain from the original book. From Hahnloser's reconstruction of the original gatherings (H. 282-87) and from a study of the pagination done at varying periods, one concludes that eight pages have been lost since the fifteenth century, among them a view of the transept of Reims, and an elevation of the catapult mentioned by Villard himself. Félibien still counted 40 leaves or 80 pages. It is likely the manuscript originally had six quaternions equalling 96 pages. We must assume a minimum loss of at least eight leaves which would have brought the original total number of pages to a minimum of 82. The heaviest losses occurred in the second and the last gathering which contained drawings of animals and, presumably, of the synagogue, two drawings of Cambrai referred to on V28 and V60, and figure studies which are partially preserved in the gutters. There seem to be major losses in the chapter on carpentry and in the area of vault design.

Villard's original purpose was mnemotechnical. He traced the architectural drawings with a needle to indicate the main horizontal and vertical axes, paying special attention to cornices. He used a lead pencil for the actual drawing. A few sketches may have been inked. He used parchment leaves measuring circa 53 x 18 cm, a number of which may never have been bound into the volume. Around 1216 he had some of the existing leaves and blank parchment bifolia bound into a book initially destined for his personal use. In the tradition of Vitruvius and others he must soon have decided that his booklet could be helpful in discussions with patrons and colleagues, and useful for the instruction of younger masons. Later in his life, presumably around 1233 Villard decided to expand and edit his sketches. The drawings were inked, inscriptions were added where necessary, and, with the help of the second master the theoretical parts were expanded. On V2 he firmly defined the purpose of the manuscript as a treatise on masonry, machinery, carpentry and principles of geometry which underlie the drawings of figures and architecture. The book was already on its way to becoming a systematic architectural treatise, an intention haphazardly pursued by the second master who translated the French text into Latin and added theoretical drawings of his own (see V29, 39, 40). The manuscript gives "sound advice," mixing theory with practice, and enriching the content with famous *exempla*. Villard transformed his personal notebook into a lodge book. He is therefore not unjustly called a "Gothic Vitruvius" (Frankl, 1960, p. 37).

I believe the first sketches date to circa 1215 and the last ones were completed before 1235. Therefore, they would not include his apprenticeship and only cover his twenty year career as a master and mason-contractor. This assumption is consistent with our later observations on the testamentary nature of most personal notebooks which the architects began to visualize as the sum of their vast experience. This knowledge was meant to be handed down to their successors. Apparently, the only contemporary use of the manuscript took place in Reims between circa 1228-1233 and during the planning stages of St. Quentin from 1220 to 1228.

It seems likely that the second master and inheritor of the treatise prepared some entries in Villard's presence. According to paleographic evidence established by Daniel Williman, he may have been older than Villard. His comment that the idealized *bresbiterium* [sic] was designed by Ulardus de Hunecort and Petrus de Corbeia *inter se disputando,* his mislabelling of St. Etienne of Meaux as St. Faron (V29), plus his emphasis on "correct" joints of piers, the importance of gargoyles and the quick identification of Chartres (V30) recall Villard's thinking. He was a middling latinist and a cataloguer who would add the gratuitous title: "This is a clock housing," in faulty French right above Villard's more correct wording (V12). His double labelling of the figural section in faulty Latin and French on V35, his pale titles (V25) and mistaken identification of drawings copied, presumably under Villard's personal guidance (V39-41) reveal his pedantry. On the other hand, his excellent understanding of machinery, his attempt to organize the treatise and to clarify it by erasing some of Villard's drawings (V39-40) show him to have been a less creative but generally more systematic theoretician than Villard himself. His texts and drawings on V12, 25, 29, 33, 35, 39, 41, 44-45 clearly identify him as a Picard and as an orderly epigone. It seems most likely that he was an older didactic mason who may have minded Villard's shop during his absences, and who survived him by only a few years. His notations were followed by those of a third owner called Master 3. His recipes on V42 are in the practiced hand of a scribe. He was apparently the type of person some authors have seen in Villard, namely a clerk, an architectural and iconographic buff who was more interested in commentary than substance. He tended to be neat and expressed *horror vacui* by filling up empty spaces. On V33 he mislabelled the prostrate St. John or St. Peter based on a Byzantine Transfiguration as the Lord's Fall. But on V6 he correctly identified Pride and Humility. His recipes for a watertight vessel made of Roman brick, lime and linseed oil and for a depilatory containing quicklime further attest to interests beyond architecture. However, we must keep in mind that advice ranging from mortars and balms such as Villard's own potion on V65, to the distillation apparatus in the *Dresden Sketchbook* are natural adjuncts to architectural treatises from Vitrivius through the Renaissance. Even more incredibly, we find a balm against hair loss in the Rixner manuscript over two and a half centuries later.

The lack of professional additions in Villard's book after 1240 also explains the survival of the lodge books. By the time Master 3 made his entries, the formal vocabulary of Gothic as exemplified by Beauvais, the nave of St. Denis or the Sainte Chapelle in Paris had become infinitely more subtle. For someone like Pierre de Montreuil, or even the educated third owner, the booklet had lost architectural actuality and had already entered the realm of historical quaintness. It is therefore likely that it was integrated into a clerical library, possibly that of Master 3. The early fourteenth century addition of sketches showing a crucifixion and an ornamental plaque on V15 attest to academic ownership. The next owner may have added a pagination which runs from a to t (see H., 282-87). The entry, "Amen, I say" is underlined four times and intends to corroborate the success of the perpetual motion machine on V9. The error of fact, the biblical provenance of the Latin phrase, and the addition of two irrelevant lines on the axle indicate continued clerical ownership. In the 15th century the book entered the possession of J. Mancel who paginated the remaining 41 leaves. It then belonged to an equally unknown Jehanne Martian (V66). In the course of time lines and dots were added like the dots over the swan's eye on V7, the lines under the figures on V28, 43, and the juvenile pagination letters on V4-5.

At some time, perhaps as early as the ownership of Master 3, the manuscript was brought to Chartres where it came into the enthusiastic possession of a member of the Félibien family around 1560. The owner identified with Villard and claimed him as an ancestor by faking an inscription at the left of the devil on V1 in which he states that "In this book you can find the machines of my ancestor the good Sire Alessis Fellibien who is known as Sire de Montgognie. Remember him and all the generations of engineers. 1482." This text, which paraphrases Villard's introduction was 'confirmed' on V46 where the knight mounting a horse is none other than "*li sire de mengognie aiel de honnecort.*" The family connection between Félibien and Villard is further stressed by an implied verbal tradition attesting to the fact that the warrior on V3 is none other than de Honnecourt "as he presented himself in Hungary." The whole matter culminates with the addition of the Félibien arms to the shield of the rider at the right on V16. The date of 1560 found under a lock of the former binding indicates a repair of the manuscript, and possibly the regularization of the pages through marginal cutting which is most clearly visible on V9, 19, 21, 33, 44-45, 49 and 52. This unbounded enthusiasm for the Middle Ages coincided with the nostalgia evident in sixteenth century Gothic sketch-books which also reflects a conscious Gothicism directed against the Renaissance in the north. It was evident in the works of Benedikt Ried in Prague and its environs. Whatever the murky family connections between Villard and the Félibien family may have been, their interest assured the survival of the lodge book which was transmitted by another Félibien, *Sieur des Avaux et de Javercy*, a high government official in Chartres, to his son André Félibien. The latter took it to Paris where he became the official historian of Louis XIV in 1666. As a scholarly man and secretary of the *Académie*, André was probably responsible for erasing falsifications of his ancestor on V1, which now can only be read under ultraviolet light. In the fourth of his *Entretiens sur les vies et les ouvrages des plus excéllents peintres anciens et modernes* (1669, 528), he mentions a *vieux livre de parchemin* of a twelfth [*sic*] century author which "fell into his hands." Its numerous figures impressed him deeply enough to elicit his statement that at the time of Cimabue "the taste of design in France was as good as that found in Italy." The exquisitely refined constructions *selon l'ordre Gothique* encouraged by Henry IV and the even more important, neo-gothic construction of the transept and facade of Orléans Cathedral undertaken by the architects of Versailles, combined with the possession of Villard's manuscript to make Félibien deeply sensitive to the Middle Ages. In his *Dissertation touchant l'architecture antique et l'architecture gothique*, posthumously published in Paris (1707), he praised Gothic vaults as Vasari had done a century earlier by comparing them to a baldachin of leaves.

One of his two sons, either Francois the architect, or more probably Dom Michel gave the lodge book to the Abbey of St. Germain-des-Près. There it was catalogued as *Ms Sancti Germani* lat. 1104. In 1795 it was entered into the *Fonds Latin* of the Bibliothèque Nationale and provided with the stamp on V1. In 1865 it was transferred to the *Fonds Français* and given its present designation, *ms. fr.* 19093.

Appendix II

Contents, style and iconography

The number of illustrations and figures varies depending on the observer. Where Hahnloser finds 163 human and sculptural representations, I find only 94.

The general division of Villard's sketches by subject is as follows:

Animals, including decorative use of beasts (H:63)	43
Plans, elevations, architectural details	44
Furniture, decorative elements, city view etc.	19
Machines, gadgets, lectern, weapons	13

Theoretical drawings, quadrature, triangulation	37
Carpentry, excluding losses	6
Total	256
Original total based on estimated losses	341-425

Drawing procedures and architectural designs

Together with ornaments, carpentry, machinery and gadgets, the architectural category includes 129 subjects. There are ninety-four figures and forty-three animal portraits. Certain drawings were made before the book was bound, for example, the "ideal plan" and the plan of Meaux (V29) are found in the same gathering as Vaucelles, the roof constructions (V33-34), the amateurish Passion scenes probably traced over a manuscript (V53-56) and the Martyrdom of Saints Cosmas and Damian. The double leaf on V54-55 shows three figures from the north portal of Reims. The circus scene in silverpoint was followed by the stalls. When Villard had this leaf bound in his book, he chose to show the stalls and the Passion scenes right side up, to improve the Martyrdom by outlining and to spare the lion's tail. In this manner he kept the better drawing intact. Villard's clumsiness with faces is apparent on V2,15 and 21. V2 is the earliest of the three. The shading applied to the dragon on V21 may have led to the washes on V22 if the washes are not thirteenth century additions, possibly by the draftsman who added sketches on V15. I presume V17 was a loose leaf with the gamblers and the animals preceding the hand warmer and cantepleure, both of which Villard decided to show right side up and to describe in detail, thereby giving them preference over the figures. St. Peter's (?) head on V35 was another earlier sketch around which he drew figural schemata while strengthening the outlines of the portrait.

The architectural problems discussed and illustrated by Villard and Master 2 range from *exempla* such as the towers of Laon, and the side aisle windows and choir solution at Reims, to questions of construction and architectural theory. The third gathering probably contained several pages depicting Cambrai and St. Quentin.

The bevelling of an oblique springer without a template, the representation of a negative template which can slide along a curved rib segment, the constant insistence on a precise determination of angles, and the use of masons' marks for the purpose of work assignments are all architectural devices to assure precision and to save time in the complex Gothic building process (V41,63). Villard is again within the tradition of architects like William of Sens (before 1178) who designed *formas quoque as lapides formandos* or Lorenz Lacher, who in 1516 mentions the types of *Bretter* or templates necessary for the correct carving of cornices and elevation members (Shelby, 1971).

In his architectural "portraiture" Villard often softens the angular lines of the Gothic, elongates and lightens the members, and generally tends to heighten overall proportions such as those of the Reims nave on V62. The Reims window and the templates for its roses and mullions (V20,63) are drawn more precisely, as if for actual use in construction. The same can be assumed for the catapult on V59 (figs. 38, 39) which could be easily dismantled and might have been either a commission from Louis IX whose campaign against the Albigensi was completed in 1229, or perhaps a local commission, in view of possible incursions over the northern border of the increasingly centralized Kingdom of France. The lectern on V13 and the stalls on V55 and 57 are also drawn precisely enough to have been intended as working drawings for the execution of these objects. Villard's interest in the unusual is apparent in his sketches of a pagan tomb, a clock—or more accurately the bell tower, decorative leaf-heads, and a plan for the construction of an unsupported middle arch (V11,12,40,43). His impulse to change existing models is most apparent in his modification of the proportions and disposition of the Chartres west rose and his unsuccessful changes imposed upon the design of the Lausanne transept rose discussed in the captions to V30-31 (figs. 22-23).

As regards Gothic theory, Villard and Master 2 discovered the quadrature, and witnessed its—possibly not yet fully conscious—application in the important plan of the Laon tower and in the trilobe with an inscribed equilateral triangle used as the base for a lectern (V13, 18, 38-39, figs. 8, 14, 25). Villard's formula for spatial recession is subtractive. For example, an arch angled at 45° will be cut by one-quarter on the near side, or less if the angle is wider (V12, 18, 60-61). Villard stressed the need for solidity, and workmanlike quality. Admiring the advanced star vaulted room on V41, he says, "This is good masonry." He judged the Laon towers to be the most unique he had ever seen and wrote about a Reims side aisle window, "I drew it because I liked it best." His drawings and statements add up to create an image of a builder completely secure in his aesthetic and professional environment.

Tips, machinery and gadgets

Architectural primers often include collections of practical tips and descriptions of gadgets. In contrast to most other cultures including Byzantium, western technological fantasies were limitless, often playful, and advanced steadily from the mid-twelfth century onward. Automata, revolving halls, immense structures with transparent floors under which one could see monsters and talking robots are only a few of the ideas presented by the writers of the *Pélerinage de Charlemagne*, the *Roman de Troie, Flore et Blancheflore*, the *Marienlob* and by authors as different as Heinrich von Veldeke and Albrecht von Scharffenberg.

Villard offers a deep insight into this feverish interest in improvements. These range from practical tips on the construction of floors with short timbers, the manufacturing of storm lanterns, and the straightening of sagging structures, to the strengthening of hoisting wheels (V39, 44-45, fig. 34). His machinery includes a catapult, a screw jack, an underwater saw, an automatic saw mill with a reciprocal drive (V44-45, 59, figs. 31,38). The gadgets are indicative of the lively contemporary lateral thinking which made serious inventions possible. They include a hand warmer with gimbals, an eagle reading along with a priest, a cantepleure based on the siphon principle, a clockwork turning an angel pointing at the sun, and a whimsical perpetual motion machine which was derived from Indian and Arabic sources and which, ironically, could serve as an efficient brake (V9, 17, 44, figs. 13, 32-33). The more theoretical tools and instruments include triangulation methods, a crossbow with a wired arrow, and a procedure by which a pear can be made to fall from a tree onto an egg placed on the ground (V39, 41, 44, fig. 27). Finally we find medical and other recipes originally based on Dioscorides' *Materia medica* and on the writings of Odo of Meung (V42, 65), and for transferrals from one dimension to another. The halving of a square by inscribing in it another square at a 45° angle is applied to two cylindrical vessels, one of which contains twice the volume of the original container (V39).

Villard's curiosity attests to the inventive spirit of the thirteenth century and to the ease with which the western mind approached technology. The pattern continued and inspired Cardinal Bessarion to write to Constantine Palaeologos in 1444 urging him to send young men to the West for a superior technological education, which could help prevent a takeover by the Turks.

Human figures, statuary, animals and figural geometry

Villard's unhampered professional approach to architecture and machinery does not apply to his figural studies and the often contrived schemata imposed upon them. Most of his animals are taken straight from bestiaries and manuscripts except for the frontal lion which is based on an aquamanile (Cf. V7,48 and fig. 5, 35). The vigor of his grasshopper, fly and dragonfly recall the other fundamental zoological treatise of the thirteenth century, Frederick II's *De arte venandi cum avibus*.

Human figures, statuary and animals.

All silverpoint sketches of figures and animals were reworked in ink, see the frontal Virgin Mary and the sheep on V20, 36. Villard's figural sketches display considerable uneasiness which is to be expected from a professional builder. It was this insecurity which encouraged Villard to adopt the geometric "overlays" which he stressed in his chapter on "portraiture."

Most human figures, drawn with varying degrees of success were based on sculptures, reliefs, a reliquary and manuscripts. They range from the awkward Passion scenes, the tinted nude and insecure Ecclesia (V8, 22, 56) to sketches done with great verve such as the Sleeping Apostle or the refined classical figures on V46, 58. Villard felt more comfortable with drawings for architectural sculpture such as the wrestlers, ornamental dragons (V12, 21), and drawings for church furniture like the reliquary of Henry of Flanders (?) and the diagram of the lectern (V13, 15, figs. 3, 8). More successful are figures, presumably copied from smaller metalworks, and the Seated Christ which is related to the Andrew Philactery of Hugo of Oignies, (V21, 32, fig. 16). The drawings of the circus scenes, presumably based on ivories (V52, 53) and even the frontal sketch of a lion, almost certainly based on an aquamanile (V48), are more convincing than the somewhat ponderous sketches from full scale sculpture. Except for the dramatic group of reliefs for Pride and Humility from Chartres (V6, fig. 4), the monumental sculpture, copied mostly from Reims shows awkwardly parallel hairpin folds and disorganized pleats. The proportions of the figures under their heavy drapery are clumsy, especially in the early examples of *Ecclesia*, the seated king and the group from the north portal at Reims (V8, 49, 54, 55).

Villard clearly realized his limitations when he explained his schemata from which figures, faces and animals can be drawn. In his introduction to what is probably the only fully preserved chapter of his book he explains on V36 that "the method of drawing as taught by the discipline of geometry facilitates work" (*por legierement ovrer*). His theoretical schemata defining human and animal proportions are a mixture of tentative and more precise rules. For instance, the second figure in the top row and the last figure in the second row of V37 are derived from Villard's most valid schema for the construction of frontal figures. Twice the diameter of the head gives the width of the shoulders. A rectangle measuring five heads high is then drawn. The two bottom corners of the rectangle are connected with the top corners through two diagonals. Two additional lines drawn from the bottom corners to the center point of the upper edge of the rectangle will define the chest, and the outer, lower lines, the spreading legs. The knees are located three head diameters below the shoulder line (see fig.).

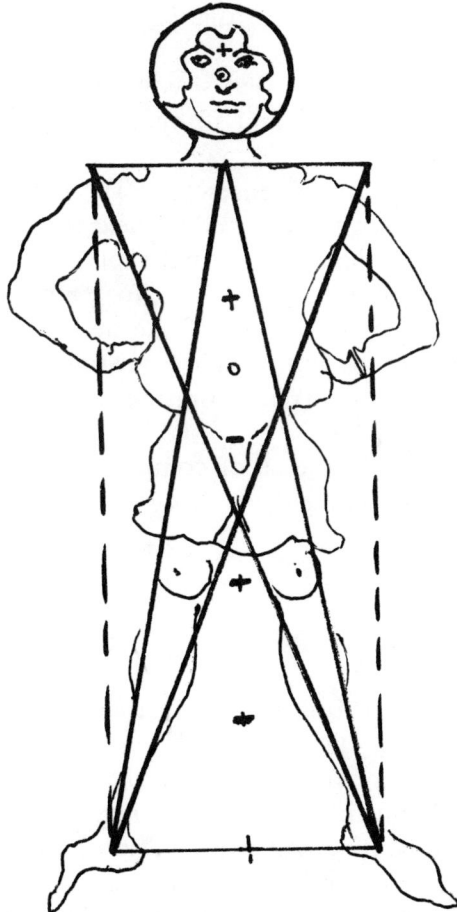

VILLARD DE HONNECOURT

This schema resulting in a 1:6 proportion for the human figure is rough and imprecise. Nevertheless, it will assist in the rapid construction of frontal figures (see H. ills. 127-139). It cannot be compared with the more refined classical and Renaissance canons, as is apparent in the standing nude on V43 which display a 1:6½ proportion. By comparison with the Alexander bronze illustrated by Hahnloser (H. ill. 139a), the awkwardness of the figure is apparent.

The heads on V36 are divided into horizontal thirds and they reappear along with other schemata used by Villard in German treatises on drawing: Hans Lautensack's *Des Zirkels und Richtscheyts. . .Underweysung* completed in Frankfurt in 1563, Erhard Schoen's *Unterweisung* of 1538, and Hans Hoesch's *Geometria Deutsch* (H. ills. 111-122). It is interesting to note that later authors referred back to the dynamic swastika pattern underlying the galloping and kneeling knights on V37, a mnemotechnical arrangement of axes rather than a design. Except in the case of a few animals taken from a bestiary such as Oxford, Bodl. Libr. Ms. Ashmole 1511 (V7, fig. 5) the geometric schemes imposed upon animals on V35, 36 are less than convincing. The pentagram laid over the heraldic eagle seems of little use.

For the most part, Villard's chapter on figural geometry is a highly planar conception of living forms. If we extend this awareness to three dimensional figures such as the frontal and side views of horses or the lion (V16, 46, 48), we recognize how shallow Villard's volumes are.

The architect felt more comfortable with geometric grids, but his use of the pentagram for two trumpeters and of the quadrature for two wrestlers is somewhat gratuitous (V37). More precision and ease are shown in the quadrature underlying the four masons, a Gothic decorative device used for instance, in the Cistercian abbey of Maggenau, in the quadrature defining the fighters, and in the frontal head consisting of 16 squares. The nose is placed at a 1:3 and the eyebrows at a 1:1 level while the width and height of the head comprise half the square. The neck which should have flared to two squares unfortunately thickens to 2½ squares at the bottom.

It seems Villard did not take note of previous canonical studies of figural composition such as those found in Vitruvius. He probably had heard of such treatises, and stubbornly tried to reinvent one responsive to the architect's needs.

The same paucity of invention characterizes Villard's iconographic interests. The most fascinating groups such as the king with his courtiers, the two lovers, the nude musician confronting a lady (V25, 27, 51) lack the clear identification given his architectural sketches. To the chagrin of contemporary historians they are not specific enough to allow for precise identifications. Lions fascinated Villard, and he gives details on the taming of the beast, (V47). He did identify Pride and Humility (V6) correctly, but he and Master 2 mistook the prostrate figure on V33, Peter or one of the Apostles from the Transfiguration, for the "Fallen Lord."

Villard's figural studies are interesting, but do not transmit the ease of comprehension and the quick interest which he gave his architectural drawings and gadgets, his *exempla* of existing monuments, and his architectural *dicta*.

Conclusion

Although the ultimate importance of Villard's sketch- and lodge book will be further discussed in my concluding volume, let me briefly summarize its impact. His manuscript was embedded within the tradition of architectural treatises. Villard, like many authors of later handbooks, used educational *exempla* such as Laon and Chartres. He identified closely with nearby structures such as Vaucelles, Cambrai and Reims in whose planning and construction he may have participated. He recorded building technology as it existed and was fascinated with new inventions. His interest in furniture is by no means exceptional while his numerous drawings of sculpture may indicate sculptural commissions. More likely however, they are visual witnesses to an architectural concept which was generalized in the thirteenth century, namely, a total integration of sculpture within architecture. In retrospect, it may be difficult to realize that facades dominated by sculpture such as that of Reims, which also was to possess a sculpted internal facade, must have confronted the architect with intensely exciting design challenges and organizational problems of the most complex nature. Therefore Villard tested several methods leading to a streamlining of figural programs in architectural design. He drew the angels on top of the nave buttresses of Reims as abstractions (V62) and tried to devise schemes for the quick rendering of figures.

Like all architects before and after him, he studied existing buildings and designs. He changed them, overemphasized elements and selected whatever he thought could be of further personal or general use. He offered alternatives to the plan of Vaucelles, the windows of Chartres and Lausanne, and even to the proportions of the Reims nave elevation. He understood the tenets of Gothic architectural theory which were codified and generalized only after his death in the late 1230s. The philosophical base of Gothic such as the light theory of Dionysius the Areopagite held little interest for him nor did he care for numerological details. Instead, he involved himself in the drama of ever more precise and streamlined construction methods. Like other intelligent and creative participants in an exciting humanistic age, he was aware of his role in history, even if he seemed to know he might never be counted among the very great. He did not share the fame of Winihard, a "Daedalus"; William of Caen, *petrarum summus in arte;* or Pierre de Montreuil, *doctor lathomorum.* Nevertheless, the survival of Villard's lodge book seems allied to his strong will to transmit to posterity a clear imprint of his activity.

The importance of his primer lies in his participation in the mainstream of early thirteenth century architecture. It is not an isolated expression of a genius ahead of his time. It is a highly competent and often inspired compendium of much that he found important enough to transmit to his successors. His sketches and notes are moving witnesses to the curiosity of an alert early thirteenth century *architector.*

BIBLIOGRAPHY FOR VILLARD DE HONNECOURT

For this first critical edition of Villard de Honnecourt in the English language since the publication of R.W. Willis' facsimile of 1859, a large number of books and essays had to be consulted. Highly specialized texts mentioned in the captions which accompany the plates are not included in this bibliography.

Ackerman, James S. 1949. "Ars sine scientia nihil est," Gothic Theory of Architecture at the Cathedral of Milan, *Art Bulletin* vol. 31 (June), pp. 84-111.

Aubert, M. 1947. *L'architecture cistercienne en France,* Paris.

Barnes, C. F. 1972. The Gothic Architectural Engravings in the Cathedral of Soissons, *Speculum,* vol. 47, pp. 60-64.

Beckwith, J. 1964. *Early Medieval Art,* New York.

Belli-Barsali, I. 1969. *Medieval Goldsmith Work,* London.

Bénard, P. 1864. Recherches sur la patrie et les travaux de Villard de Honnecourt, *Travaux de la société académique des sciences, arts, etc. de St. Quentin,* 3e série, vol. 6, pp. 66, 260-280.

Beer, E. 1952. *Die Rose der Kathedrale von Lausanne,* Bern.

Biaudet, J. C., Beer, E. *et. al.* 1975. *La Kathédrale de Lausanne,* Bern.

Biebel, F.M. 1950. The Angelot of Jean Barbet, A.B. 32, pp. 336-44.

Bowie, T. 1957. *The Sketchbook of Villard de Honnecourt,* Bloomington.

Branner, R. 1957. A Note on Gothic Architects and Scholars, *Burlington Magazine,* vol. 99, pp. 372-3.

———. 1957. Three problems from the Villard de Honnecourt Manuscript, *Art Bulletin,* 39, pp. 63-66.

———. 1958. Drawings from a 13th century Architect's Shop: The Reims Palimpsest, *JSAH* vol. 17, pp.9-21.

———. 1960. Villard de Honnecourt, Archimedes and Chartres, *JSAH* vol. 19, pp. 91-96.

———. 1961. Historical Aspects of the Reconstruction of Reims Cathedral, 1210-1241, *Speculum,* vol. 36, 23-37.

———. 1963. Villard de Honnecourt, Reims and the Origins of Gothic Architectural Drawing, *Gazette des Beaux Arts,* Vol. 61, pp. 129-46.

———. 1973. Gothic Architecture, *JSAH,* vol. 32, 327-33.

Brunel, C. 1960. L'origine du mot ogive. *Romania,* vol. 81, pp. 289-95.

Bucher, F. 1960. Cistercian Architectural Purism, *Comparative Studies in Society and History,* vol. 3, pp. 89-105.

———. 1968. Design in Gothic Architecture, *JSAH,* vol. 27, pp. 49-71.

———. 1968. Medieval Landscape Painting, *Medieval and Early Renaissance Studies,* Chapel Hill, pp. 119-168.

———. 1973. Medieval Architectural Design Methods, 800-1560, *Gesta* vol. 11, No. 2, pp. 37-51.

———. 1976. Micro-Architecture as the "Idea" of Gothic Theory and Style, *Gesta,* 15, pp. 71-89.

———. 1976. The Beauvais Collapse and 13th Century Art; *Acta,* 3, pp. 1-16.

———. 1977. A Rediscovered Tracing by Villard de Honnecourt, *Art Bulletin,* vol. 59, 315-319.

Burstall, A. 1965. *A History of Mechanical Engineering,* Cambridge.

Cahier, C. and Martin, A. 1851-1856. Pierre de Beauvais, bestiaire en prose de Pierre le Picard, *Mélanges d'archéologie, d'histoire et de littérature,* Paris vol. 2 (1851) pp. 85-232, vol. 3 (1853) pp. 203-80, vol. 4, (1856) pp. 55-87.

Cardwell, D.S.L. 1974, *Turning Points in Medieval Technology,* New York.

Colombier P. du. 1953. *Les chantiers des cathédrales,* Paris.

Crombie, A.C. 1959. Medieval and Early Modern Science.

Crosby S. Mc. K, 1966. Masons' Marks at St. Denis, *Mélanges offerts à René Crozet,* Poitiers pp. 711-17.

Daumas, M, 1964. A History of Technology, New York.

Deneux, H. 1925. Signes lapidaires et épures du 13e siècle à la cathédrale de Reims, *Bulletin Monumental,* vol. 84, 109-17, Paris.

Deshoulieres, M. 1920. Meaux. *Congrès Archéologique de France,* pp. 140-70, Paris.

Dimier, M.A. 1949, 1967. *Recueil de plans d'églises cisterciennes,* 2 vols. Grignan and Paris.

Enlart C. 1895, Villard de Honnecourt et les Cisterciens, *Bibliothèque de l'Ecole des Chartes,* vol. 56, pp.1-20.

Eydoux H.P., 1952. *L'architecture des églises cisterciennes d' Allemagne,* Paris.

Feldhaus F. M. 1931. *Technik der Antike und des Mittelalters,* Potsdam.

Félibien A. 1669. *Entretien sur les vieset ouvrages des plus excéllents peintres anciéns et modernes,* 2nd ed. Paris.

——. 1707. *Dissertation touchant l'architecture antique et l'architecture gothique,* Paris (posthumous).

Ferber, S. 1975. *Islam and the Medieval West,* Binghamton.

Ferguson, E.S. ————. The Mind's Eye. Nonverbal Thought in Technology, *Science,* vol. 197, Nr; 4306, pp. 827-833.

Fett H. 1910. En islandsk Tegnebog, *Videnskabs-Selskabéts Skrifter, 2 Hist. Filo. Klasse,* Vol. 191, No. 2. pp. 3-29

Fitchen, J. 1961. *The Construction of Gothic Cathedrals,* Oxford.

Fraenger, W. 1922. *Die Masken von Reims,* Erlenbach, Leipzig.

Frankl, P. 1960. *The Gothic,* Princeton.

——. 1963. *Gothic Architecture,* Baltimore.

Frisch T. G. 1960. The Twelve Choir Statues of the Cathedral of Reims, *Art Bulletin,* vol. 42 (March) pp. 1-24.

———. 1971. *Gothic Art 1140 - c.1450, Sources and Documents,* Engelwood Cliffs.

Gal, L. 1929. *L'architecture religieuse en Hongrie du 11e au 13e siècle,* Paris.

Gerevitch, L. 1971. Villard de Honnecourt magyaroszágon, *Müvészettörténeti, Ertesito, Akadémia Kiadó,* pp. 81-104 Budapest.

Gerstenberg, K. 1966. *Die deutschen Baumeisterbildnisse des Mittelalters,* Berlin.

Gimpel, J. 1976. *The Medieval Machine,* New York

Glay A. le. 1825. *Recherches sur l'église metropolitaine de Cambrai,* Paris.

Grimme E. G. 1972. *Goldschmiedekunst im Mittelalter,* Cologne.

Grodecki L. 1950. *Le vitrail francais,* Paris.

——. 1958. Chronologie de la cathédrale de Chartres, *Bulletin Monumental,* vol. 116, pp. 91-119.

Hahnloser, H.R. 1972. *Villard de Honnecourt, Kritische Gesamtausgabe des Bauhüttenbuches ms. fr. 19093 der Pariser National Bibliothek,* 2nd edition, Graz-Austria.

——. 1933. Entwürfe eines Architekten um 1250 aus Reims. *Résumés des communications présnetées au 13e Congrès International d' histoire de l' art,* Stockholm p. 260.

——. 1971. *Il tesoro di San Marco,* Florence.

——. 1968. Das Gedankenbild im Mittelalter und seine Anfänge in der Spätantike, *Accademia Nazionale dei Lincei,* vol. 105 pp. 255-66, Rome.

Harvey, J. 1972. *The Medieval Architect,* London.

Hecht, K. 1968 and 1969. Mass und Zahl in der gotischen Baukunst. *Abhandlungen der Braunschweiger Wissenschaftl. Gesellschaft* vol. 31 pp. 215-325 and vol. 32 pp. 105-263.

Héliot P. 1956. La nef et le clocher de l' ancienne cathedrale de Cambrai, *Wallraff Richartz Jahrbuch,* vol. 18, 93 ff.

——. 1959. Chronologie de la basilique de St. Quentin, *Bulletin Monumental* vol. 117, pp. 7-50.

——. 1967. *La basilique de St. Quentin et l'architecture du Moyen Age,* Paris.

——. 1971. La cathédrale d' Arras, *Archeologia,* vol. 39, pp. 56-59.

Hinker, D. 1967. *Studien zum Wortschatz der gotischen Architektur in Nordfrankreich.* (Dissertation) Vienna.

Horn W. 1966. The ''Dimensional Inconsistencies'' of the Plan of St. Gall and the Problem of the Scale of the Plan, *Art Bulletin,* vol. 48, pp. 285-307.

James, J. 1977. *Chartres, les constructeurs.* Chartres.

James, M.R. 1922-1923. *An English Bible Picture Book of the Fourteenth Century,* The Walpole Society, vol. 11, London.

———. *The Drawings of Matthew Paris,* The Walpole Society, vol. 14, London.

Katzenellenbogen, A. 1964. *Allegories of the Virtues and Vices in Medieval Art,* New York.

Kletzl, O., 1940. *Peter Parler, der Dombaumeister von Prag,* Leipzig.

——. 1935. *Titel und Namen von Baumeistern der deutschen Gotik.* Munich.

———. 1939. *Planfragmente aus der deutschen Dombauhütte von Prag in Stuttgart und Ulm,* Stuttgart.

Knoop D. and Jones G. P. 1967. *The Medieval Mason,* reprint New York.

Koepf H. 1969. *Die gotischen Planrisse der Wiener Sammlungen,* Vienna.

Kubler, G. 1944. A Late Gothic Computation of Rib Vault Thrusts. *Gazette des Beaux-Arts,* vol. 26, 134ff.

Kurmann, P. 1971. *La cathédrale de Saint Etienne de Meaux,* Geneva.

Lassus J.B.A. and Darcel A. 1858. *Album de Villard de Honnecourt, architecte du 13e siècle, manuscrit publié en fac-similé, annoté, précédé de considerations sur la renaissance de l'art francais au 19e s. etc.* Paris, Imprimerie Impériale.

Legner, R. 1972-1973. *Rhein und Maas, Kunst und Kultur,* 2 vols. Cologne.

Lehmann-Brockhaus, O. 1938. *Schriftquellen der Kunstgeschichte des 11, und 12. Jahrhunderts für Deutschland, Lothringen und Italien,* Berlin (See Nr. 3036).

Lesser, G. 1957. *The Gothic Cathedral and Sacred Geometry,* London.

Matthews, W.H. 1970. *Mazes, Labyrinths, Their History and Development,* New York.

Mathies, A. 1976. *Wooden Vaulting in English Ecclesiastical Architecture,* M. A. Thesis, S.U.N.Y. Binghamton.

Mortet, V. 1911. *Recueil de textes relatifs à l'histoire de l'architecture et à la condition des architectes en France au moyen-âge, 11e-12e siècle,* Paris.

——— and Deschamps, P. 1929. Recueil ———. vol. 2. 12e et 13e siècles Paris.

Meulen J. van de. 1965. Histoire de la construction de la cathédrale de Notre Dame de Chartres apres 1194. *Bulletin de La Societe Archeologique d'Eure et Loire,* vol. 23, pp. 81-126.

Mitchell, S. 1965. *Medieval Painting,* New York.

Omont, H. 1906. *Album de Villard de Honnecourt, Architecte du 13e siècle,* Paris (Bibl. Nationale ed.)

Panofsky, E., 1927. Ueber die Reihenfolge der vier Meister von Reims, *Jahrbuch für Preussische Kunstwissenschaft,* p. 55.

———. 1921. Die Entwicklung der Proportionslehre als Abbild der Stilentwicklung, *Monatshefte für Kunstwissenschaft,* pp. 188-219.

———. 1951. *Gothic Architecture and Scholasticism,* Latrobe.

———. 1960. Renaissance and Renascences in Western Art, Copenhagen.

Pevsner, N. 1942. The Term Architect in the Middle Ages, *Speculum,* vol. 54, pp. 549-62.

Prager F. D. and Scaglia, C. 1972. *Mariano Taccola and his Book de Ingeneis,* Cambridge (Mass).

Quicherat J. 1849. Notice sur l'album de Villard de Honnecourt, architecte du 13e siècle. *Revue Archeologique,* lère série, vol. 6 pp. 65-80, 164-88, 211-26.

Reinhardt H. 1963. *La Cathédrale de Reims.* Paris.

Rowland, B., 1973. *Animals with Human Faces,* Knoxville.

Sachs, H. 1964. *Mittelalterliches Chorgestühl von Erfurt bis Stralsund,* Heidelberg.

Sauerländer, W. 1972. *Gothic Sculpture in France, 1140-1270,* London.

Salet, F. 1967. La chronologie de la cathédrale de Reims, *Bulletin Monumental,* vol. 125, pp. 347-94.

Scheller, R. 1963. *A Survey of Medieval Model Books,* Haarlem.

Schlosser, J. von 1925. *Kunstliteratur,* Vienna.

Schnitzler, H. 1965. Die Elfenbeinskulpturen der Hofschule, *Karl der Grosse,* Aachen pp. 309-359.

Schoen, Erhard, 1542. *Unterweisung der Proportion und Stellung der Possen,* 3rd ed. Nürnberg (ed. by Baer, L. Frankfurt, 1920).

Sené, A., 1970. Un instrument de précision au service des artistes du Moyen Age: l'equerre. *Cahiers de la Civilisation Médiévale,* vol. 13, pp. 349-58.

Shelby L., 1961, 1965. Medieval Masons' Tools, *Technology and Culture,* vol. 2, pp. 127-30, vol. 6, pp.263-48.

———. 1964. The Role of the Master Mason in Medieval English Building, *Speculum,* vol. 39, pp. 387-403.

———. 1971. Medieval Masons' Templates, *JSAH,* vol. 30, May, pp. 140-54.

Singer, C. 1957. *A History of Technology,* Oxford.

Stoddard, W. 1966. *Monastery and Cathedral in France,* Middletown.

Swarzenski, H. 1954. *Monuments of Romanesque Art,* London.

Ueberwasser, W. 1928-30. Spätgotische Baugeometrie, *Öffentliche Kunstsammlung Basel,* vols. 25-27, pp. 79-122.

————./1935. Nach rechtem Mass, *Jahrb. der preussischen Kunstsammlungen.* vol. 56 p. 250 ff.

————. 1939. Der Freiburger Münsterturm "im rechten Mass", *Oberrheinische Kunst,* vol. 8, pp. 25-36.

Velte, M. 1951. *Die Anwendung der Quadratur und Triangulatur bei der Grund- und Aufrissgestaltung der gotischen Kirchen,* Basel.

Viollet-le-Duc, E. *Dictionnaire raisonné de l' architecture francaise du lle au 15e siècle,* 10 vols. Paris. (see vol. 5).

Villafañe J. de Arfe y. 1558. *De varia Commensuracion para la Esculptura y Architectura.* Seville.

White, L. n.d. *Perspectives in Medieval History,* Los Angeles.

White, L. and Keller A. G. 1962. *Medieval Technology and Social Change.* Oxford.

White, T. H. 1960. *The Bestiary.* New York.

Winterfeld, D. von, 1972. *Untersuchungen zur Baugeschichte des Bamberger Domes,* Bonn.

Willis, R. 1859. *Facsimile of the sketch-book of Villard de Honnecourt from G. B. Lassus, translated and edited with many additional Articles and Notes by the Rev. R. W.* London.

Wittkower, R. 1962. *Architectural Principles in the Age of Humanism,* London.

Wixom, W.D. Tne Greatness of the so-called Minor Arts, *The Year 1200,* F. Deuchler, ed. vol. 2, pp. 93-132. New York.

Wood, C. E. and Fyfe, M. 1961. *The Art of Falconry of Frederick II of Hohenstaufen.* Stanford.

Zinner, E. 1954. Aus der Frühzeit der Raederuhr, *Abhandlungen, Deutsches Museum,* vol. 22, 'hen, vol. 22 pp. 7-38, 46-71. Munich.

GLOSSARY FOR VILLARD DE HONNECOURT

This glossary is highly selective and includes only the most important architectural terms used by Villard, M2 and M3.

acainte	side aisle	*force*	art, knowhow	*piet*	foot
afaire	work	*forme*	frame	*piler*	pillar
aguile	spire	*fust*	beam	*plom*	plumb bob
angle	angel, angle	*geometrie*	geometry	*pont*	bridge
arc, arkes	arch	*glize*	church	*portrait*	drawing
areste	pier, buttress	*grosse*	thickness	*portraiture,*	design, plan
art	discipline, science	*haut*	above	*purtraiture,*	Art of
bas	wooden beam	*hautece, hauture*	height	*porturature*	drawing
boteret	flying buttress	*huge*	chest, box	*poupee*	poppet
bresbiterium		*ierloge, orologe*	clock	*quare*	square
presbiterium	choir	*imagene*	picture	*quint point*	five point
cantepleure	birdshaped syphon	*iometrie*	geometry		arch
capele	chapel	*justicier*	calibrate	*recoper*	cut precisely,
chapiele		*kaus*	lime		dress
capitel	chapter house	*keuvre*	copper	*rederscir*	re-erect
carpentrie	carpentry	*largece*	width	*roonderround*	
chavec	chevet	*legier*	light, simple	*reont*	pier
ciercle	circle	*letre*	text	*ruee, roe*	wheel
ciment	cement	*letris*	lectern	*salir*	stick up high
cintreel	round arch	*livel*	level	*scere*	right angle
ciziel	chisel	*loison*	joint	*sepouture*	tomb
clef	keystone, moulding	*lonc*	long	*soir, soore*	saw
clostre	cloister	*lons*	distant	*sole*	base, ground
coen	corner, corner stone	*maconnerie*	masonry	*sorvol*	blind arch
conble	roof	*machonnerie*			(above an arch)
combe		*maillet*	mallet	*suel*	sill
conpas	arc, circle	*maison, maizon*	house, housing	*taillier*	to cut, chisel,
contrefaire	drawing, copying	*maniere, manine,*	manner		subdivide
contrepois	counterweight	*manire*		*tiirc*	Tiers point
copresse	bracing work	*matere, materia*	example, instructions,		arch
corde	rope, cord		introduction	*tor*	tower
coste	side	*mesure*	measure	*toral*	pillar for
covertic	roof	*metre*	put, lay		tower
creste	ridge	*miliu*	middle	*torner*	turn
creteus, cretal	crennelation	*moitie*	half	*dorner*	
crues	hollow	*molle, mole*	profile, model	*tourete*	
cuin	corner	*montee*	elevation, rising	*torete*	little tower
deseure, desor	above		masonry build up	*trait*	basic line
desos	below	*nef*	nave	*travecon*	cross beam
droit	horizontal, correct	*nokere*	gargoyle	*tumeie*	cross section
enbracement	frame	*ogive*	diagonal rib	*tyeule*	tile
engieng	engine, apparatus	*orbe*	blind (arcade)	*vassel*	vessel
entaulement	storey	*ovrer*	to work	*verge rod*	bar, turnpike
entreclos	separating wall	*pan, plain*	wall panel	*veriere, vesrire*	Glass window
erracement,		*penel*		*verrere*	
erracenment	springing of vault	*part*	side	*vies*	old
esligement	plan	*pavement*	pavement	*vif argent*	mercury
esscandelon	scale	*peignon*	gable	*vive kaus*	quick lime
estage	storey	*pendant*	hanging	*vis*	screw
estancon	stanchion		arch or	*voie*	corridor, ambulatory
estor	window		vault	*volser*	to vault
fenestra,	window	*pendre*	lean	*vosor*	voussoir
fenestre		*persoir*	press	*vosoir*	
fillole	turret, finial	*piere*	stone	*vosure*	arch
fons	ground, bottom	*pire*		*windas*	windlass

Villard de Honnecourt's Lodge Book

Captions

The illustrations are placed in the same sequence as that of the original manuscript, and are accompanied by a brief commentary. In addition, we adhered to the often clumsy style and punctuation of the inscriptions which frequently differ from previously published interpretations in order to approximate the basic fabric of the original.

The abbreviation H refers to the 1972 H. R. Hahnloser edition. M2 designates the second master, and M3 the third owner who possessed and participated in the creation of the book. Additional references are as follows: V refers to Villard, B to Bénard, and D to Dimier.

V1 Heraldic Pelican

According to Vincent of Beauvais' *Speculum Naturale,* vol. 16, chapter 127, Isidore of Seville and the *Physiologus,* the pelican is a symbol of Christ because it lacerates its breast to feed its young. Thomas of Cantimpré, a compatriot and contemporary of Villard states in his *Liber de naturis rerum* that the pelican kills its offsprings in anger, then resurrects them through its blood. This image was commonly used in paintings and reliefs.

V1 Seated Bishop or Abbot

Countless portrayals of seated clerics appear in paintings and in sculpture, especially in such archivolts as those of the Calixtus portal at Reims, circa 1225-30.

V1 Owl

A day-shunning bird who is compared to Judaism.

V1 Magpie

It greets the Lord with unseemly chatter. Appears in the Reun pattern book, in Vincent of Beauvais, and bestiaries.

V1 Crouching Devil

From the style, it seems to be one of the late entries.

V1 Inscriptions

Sancti Germani a Pratis, lat. 104 refers to the eighteenth century ownership of the lodge book by St. Germain des Près, Paris. The stamp indicates the transfer to the Bibliothèque Nationale in 1795. The semierased fake inscription of circa 1560 at the bottom left was entered by Sire Félibien who claimed Villard as his ancestor. See our introduction.

H 5-9, ills. 1-4, binding ill. 6 and Sauerländer 1972, ill. 243.

V2a Twelve Seated Apostles

"Here you can find the figures of the twelve seated Apostles." The figures were drawn freely from a Gothic portal comparable to that in St. Yved de Braine.

V2b Honnecourt's Greeting

"Wilars de Honecort greets you and asks all who will work with these aids (engiens) found in this book, to pray for his soul, and to remember him. For in this book one can find good counsel on the great art (force) of masonry and carpentry constructions. And you will find in it the art (force) of drawing which the principles and the discipline of geometry requires and teaches." On page 29 the author calls himself Vilars while M2 uses Ulardus de Hunecort. H also reads Uilars which is closest to the original pronunciation. We would prefer Vuillard but will adhere to Villard. The word engien derived from the latin *ingenium* will be translated either as invention, machine or construction, depending on the context.

The text is a formularized table of contents. The deep respect for the arts of masonry and of geometry echoes through all lodge books and proves that there was little change in the definition of the architects' professional qualifications and responsibilities. Throughout the age of Gothic and to this day these range widely.

In addition to the apostles we seek a monk conversing with a nun who holds a book, and the powerfully elegant "dancing" Salome, who is represented almost identically in the St. John portal, Rouen Cathedral (fig. 2).

H 9-18, Nn. 1-6, 100, 113, ill. 4. Sauerländer 1972, ill. 182.

V3a   Footsoldier

Villard displays the newest in armour such as chain of mail leggings tied at the back of the calves and an early chapeau de fer or "iron hat", a novelty to which the warrior points. He also carries a shield, lance and a club. The inscription "de honnecor as he presented himself in Hungary" was added by Félibien and is discussed in our introduction. The ineptly sketched snail is a later addition, an iconographic pun referring to the cowardice of a knight fleeing or being startled by a hare.

H 18, N. 118.

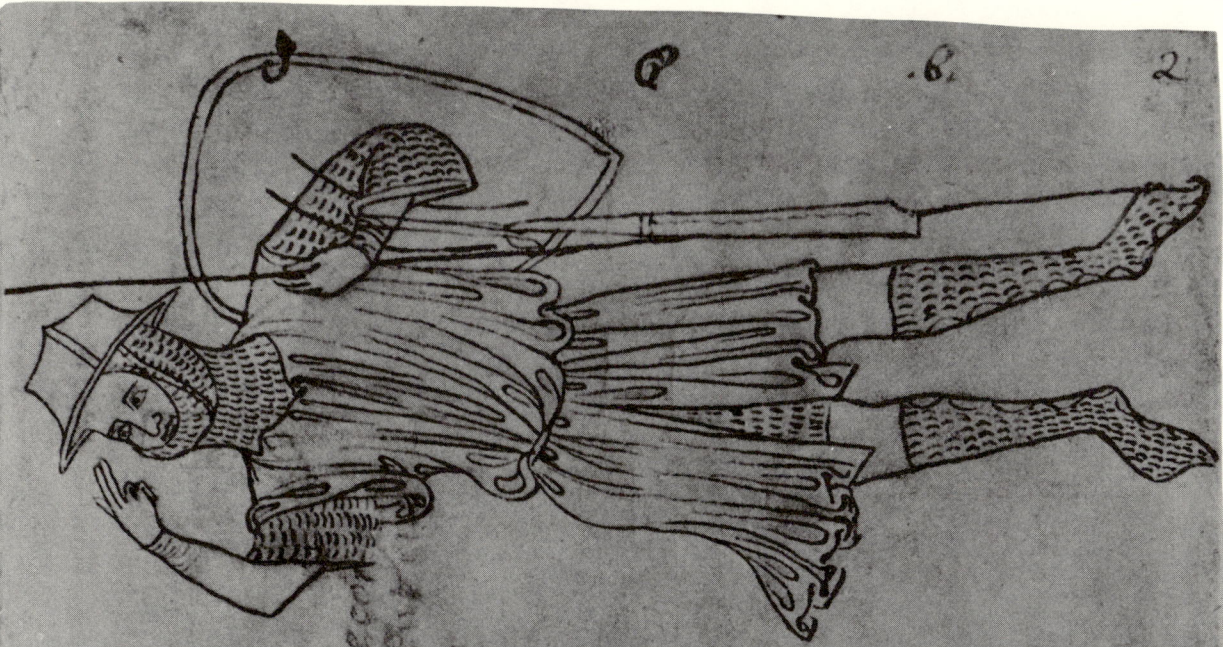

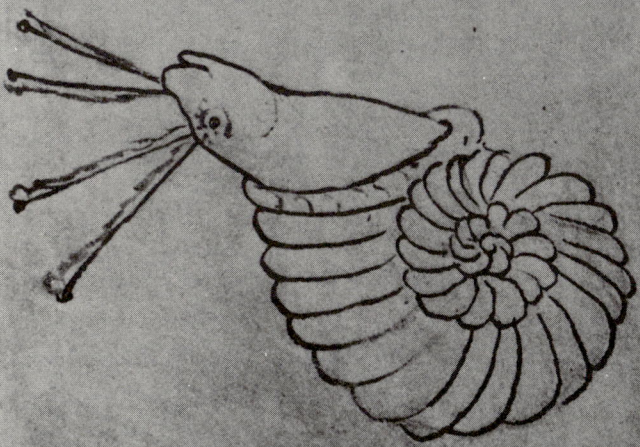

V4   Crucifixion of Christ

The stylistically advanced sketch is Villard's westernized version taken from an early thirteenth century Byzantine reliquary cross on V15 (fig. 3). The hill, the cross in the halo and the skull are probably by the same juvenile hand which was responsible for the unblotted, paginated letters.

H 19, N. 15, ill. 33a, Missal from St. Corneille in Compiègne. See also discussion V15.

V5 Fragment of the Cross

In the gutter not shown here, there remains a fragment of the arm of a large dressed figure. The inept copy of the cross on V4 is accompanied by an uncouth seventeenth-century sketch of a vase or pilaster with ionic volutes.

H 19, N. 116.

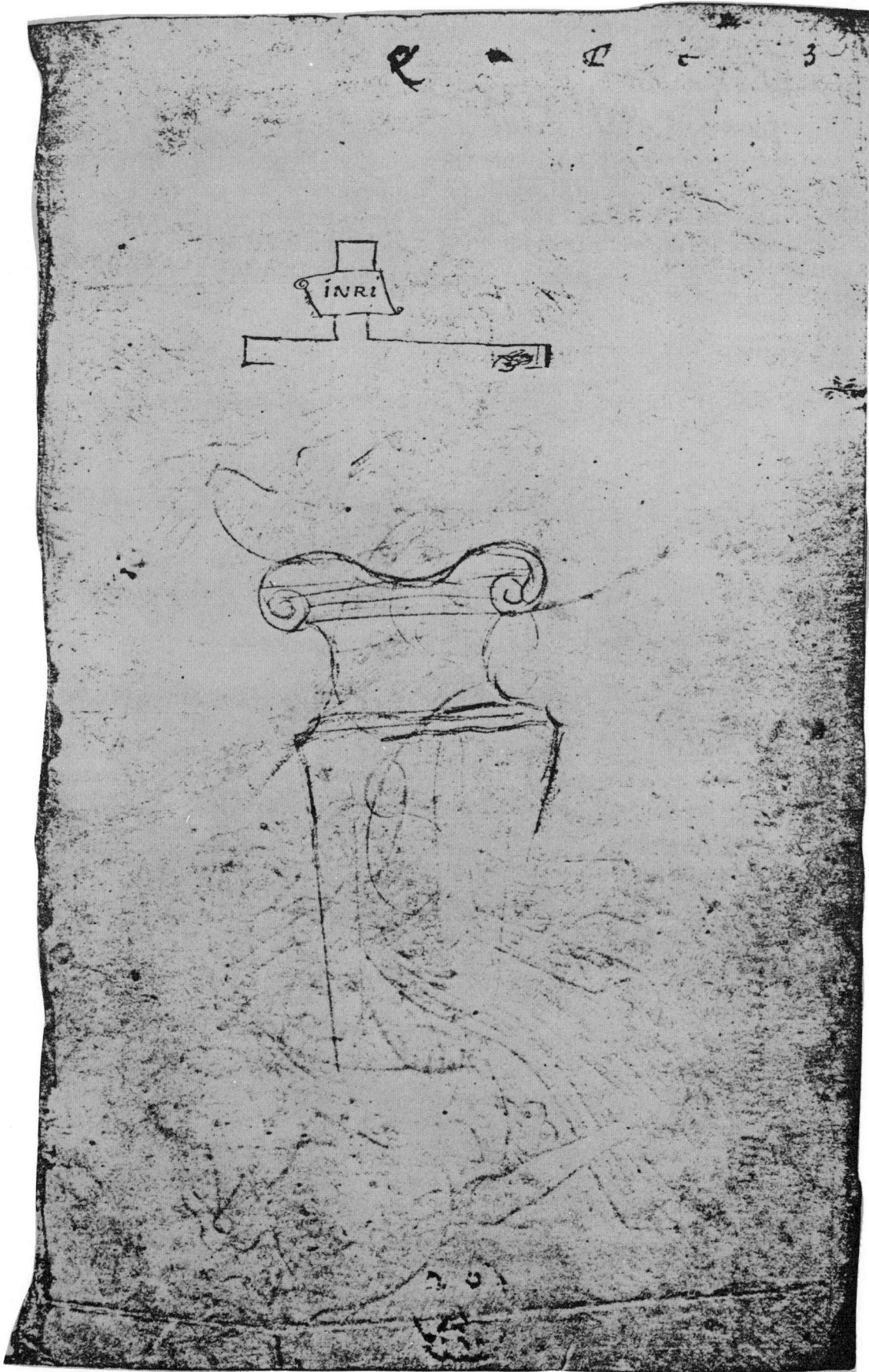

V6 "Pride as it Falls," "Humility"

Inscription by M2. Deriving from the early fifth century, Prudentius describes in his *Psychomachia* the spiritual weapons available to Christians to combat the forces of evil. These representations of personified virtues and vices became popular in manuscripts, paintings, reliefs and stained glass. "Humility" holds a disc depicting a bird which looks more like some kind of predatory bird than the dove it professes to be. Pride shows a fop falling from his horse. Aside from their slight changes, both drawings are copied from the reliefs of Faith and Pride in the south porch of Chartres Cathedral of circa 1210-30 (fig. 4). Similar reliefs are found in Amiens (circa 1225-30), Auxerre (1230), and Paris (circa 1220) where the Virtues also hold discs. H suggests that Villard may have used the pattern book which served the sculptors of Chartres. This would explain the switch from Humility to Faith.

H 20, Nn. 7, 102, ills. 48, 50-51. Katzenellenbogen 1964, 83-4, ills. 72-76. Sauerländer 1972, ills. 125, 151, 162.

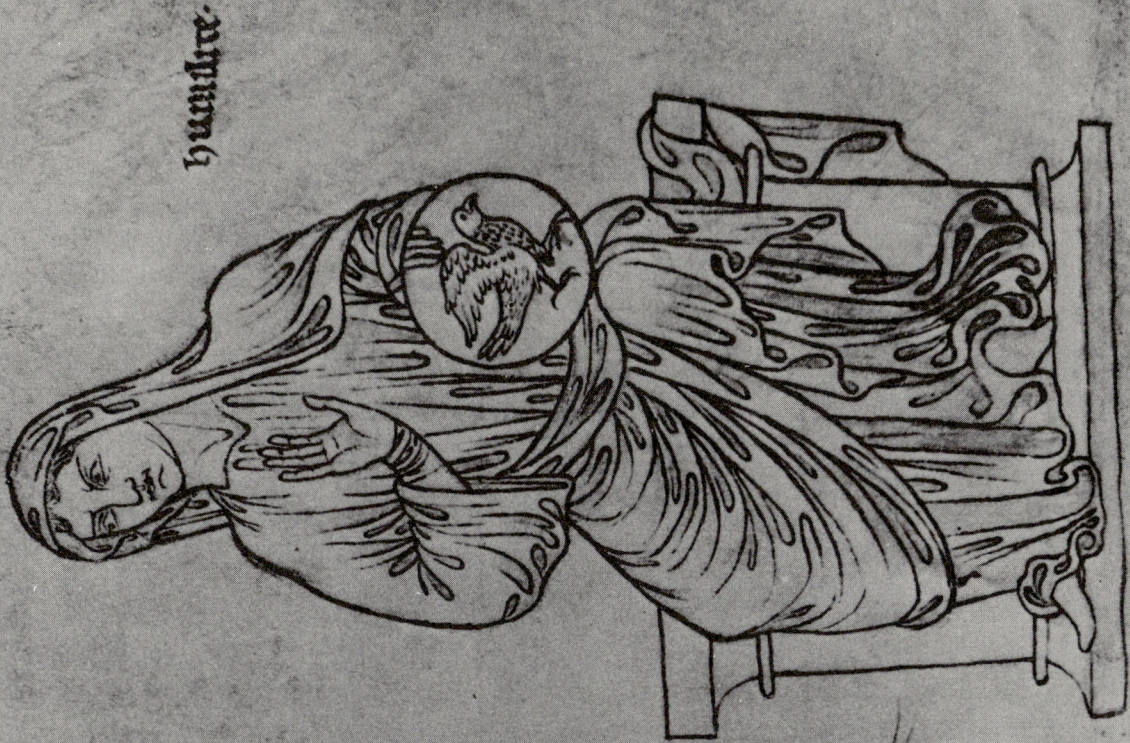

V7 Bear, Swan and Palace

The male bear was both a symbol of lust (luxuria) and brute force in the late twelfth century work *Hortus Deliciarum*. Bears heal themselves eating herbs and ants. They copulate upright and sleep for three months and are therefore considered slothful. The female bear licks her pulpy cubs into shape. Nature is thus shaped by beauty and instruction. This image was even used by Titian who chose a female bear as his emblem adding the motto: *Natura potentior ars*. The swan on the other hand sings sweetly with the help of its long neck. It prefers the accompaniment of lute players and brings luck to sailors. When angry, it reveals fortitude in its wings.

These two animals are clearly copied from one of many bestiaries. The irate swan resembles the one in the Oxford, Bodl. Libr. Ms. Ashmole 1511 fol. 71 of circa 1200 A.D. It is displayed in the reverse in our fig. 5. Villard, who was familiar with dancing bears, swans and other animals (see V14), chose not to sketch "al vif" but preferred to use a manuscript, possibly a precursor of an illustrated Cantimpré (see V1). The drawing representing a palace was taken from a ninth to eleventh-century manuscript from Reims or Echternach, or from an ivory such as those of Reims and Metz. Not only was Villard educated in the arts at Reims, but he was also sensitive to anything quaint; this includes the crennelations he stressed repeatedly in his studies of Reims Cathedral. The scalloped line in the swan's wing is a later addition.

H 21-23, White 1960, pp. 45, 118. Vincent de Beauvais 16, chapt. 50. Rowland 1973, 31-35. Cahier vol. 2 1851, 85-100, 106-232, vol. 3 1853, 203-80, vol. 4 1856, 55-87. Palace: see Beckwith 1964, ills. 38-40, 44, 58.

V8 The Church Triumphant

Ecclesia holds the banner of Christ and the chalice of the Last Supper. Usually She was juxtaposed with a blindfolded Synagoga whose staff is breaking. In medieval terms, this figure is akin to Mary made by the Visitation Master for the Reims west portal (fig. 37a). Similarities include the pleated right sleeve, the strongly detached elbow, the right leg bent in a contrapposto, the mantle used as a hood and the veiled left hand with a pronounced thumb from which She gathers a lively fall of folds. Above all, both figures wear a round medallion affixed to the border of their collars, and both are covered abundantly with hairpin loops. Perhaps we are dealing with a lost figure by the Visitation Master. However, it seems more likely that Villard transformed the famous statue by adding a crown, chalice and banner. We shall discuss similar transformations on V54-55. The very elegant Ecclesia of Strasbourg, which Sauerländer dates around 1230 also is more advanced in style.

H 23, ills. 7-8, Sauerländer 1972, ills. 132, 193, 199.

V9 Perpetual Motion Machine

"For many days the masters debated how to make a wheel which turns by itself. Here is one which can be made with an uneven number of hammers or with mercury." Above the wheel an underlined fifteenth century statement: "Amen I say." H and this author remained fascinated by the device which we perceived as a light wheel driven by pivoting hollow hammers filled with mercury. Each hammer, flipping over near the top, was supposed to keep the wheel in motion. A model built by Anthony Costagliola in 1976 showed the gadget to be an efficient braking device in that the wheel once set into rapid motion stopped immediately. In his notes and illustrations H discusses the machine from its known beginnings in the texts of the Hindu astronomer and mathematician Bhaskara circa 1150 to sketches which show tightly spaced mercury filled tubes, or triple hinged wooden rods which were to drive the wheel with such force that it could set a bucket hoist in motion. More interesting is the Picard provenance of the brilliant Pierre de Maricourt whose *Epistola Petri Peregrini de Maricourt ad Sygerum de Foucaucourt militem* of 1269 A.D. is rightly famous for its studies of magnetic forces. Already around 1260 he had designed a perpetual clock, an *ingenium* driven by the end of its magnetized hand. This and other treatises are too late to have influenced Villard. They nevertheless prove that sophisticated work on magnetism and mechanics was being undertaken in the region. It is noteworthy that this is the first of many energy saving devices which appear in lodge books, and which continued to interest architects and fortress engineers into the Renaissance. Among them were Giovanni da Fontana, and Mariano di Jacopo known as Taccola whose famouse treatise of 1433, *De ingeneis,* survives in many copies, and Philip Moench's *Book of War* of 1476.

H 24, N. 8, ills. 175-79. Prager, Scaglia 1972.

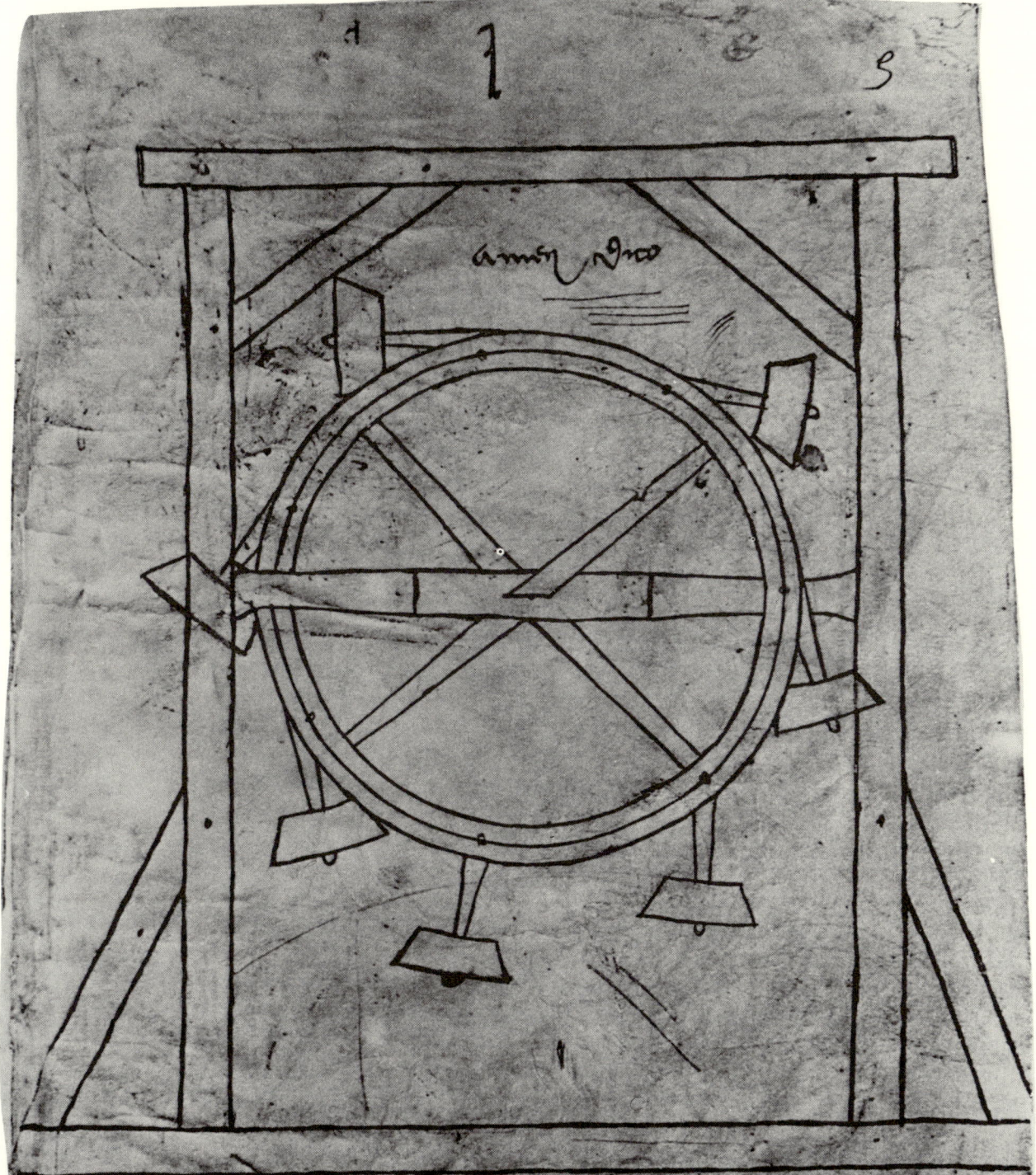

Maint ior se sunt maistre despute de faire tor ⁓ ner une rue
par li seule uel en ci co en puet faire par maillet uouperes
par ufargent.

V10 Leaf Faces, Voussoir, Branches

On V42 similar heads are called "testes de fuelles." H illustrates a head sprouting leaves from an Estoire de St. Aedward, and many leaf bound figures are found in mosaics, ivories and in marginalia. The leafy heads in fig. 6 also appear in sculpture from Constantinople to France. Above all they are also present as corbel heads on the choir and as consoles for some ribs at Reims Cathedral. This explains the extrusions from the head at the right and the strange neck lines.

V10b Decorated Voussoirs

At Reims there are many splendidly decorated voussoirs which could have inspired the volute patterns in the second drawing which probably refers to one of the arches above a choir window, just as the fig leaves may have appeared on a chapel cornice. Another, more interesting provenance is suggested by Gerevitch who found a similar pattern in the spandrels on the tomb of Gertrude of Meran, buried in 1213 in Pilis, Hungary.

See H 25-6, Nn. 9, 118, ills. 21-24. Fraenger, 1922, ills. 28-9. Sauerländer 1972, ills. 251, 257. Gerevitch 1971, 81-104.

V11 Pagan Tomb

"Of such a style was the tomb of a pagan (sarrazin) which I once saw." The insecure treatment of the figures in contrast to—for instance—Pride and Humility, or the Apostle on V7 and 40 shows Villard's hesitancy in the treatment of nudes which was overcome by his keen and continued archaeological interest. He might have seen a similar monument in Reims, where the Cerunnus-stele and the so-called Mars Gate still stand. The term "qio vi une fois" could also indicate his Hungarian trip which led him through Northern Dalmatia and the Danube region where similar tombs still exist. The two lower figures display gestures of acclamation. A beardless consul or emperor sits enthroned, backed by a curtain and two nude victory figures who hold a crown above his head signifying his apotheosis. On the other hand the gallo-roman use of the hammers, the lily sceptre, the fact that the gable which should have topped the structure is at the bottom, and the erroneous use of the curtain indicate that Villard copied a very late diptych, or even more likely a Carolingian manuscript imitating a Roman imperial apotheosis. H's comparison of the Probianus diptych of circa 400 A.D. with the Congarium of Marcus Aurelius and the Lararium in the Clercq collection indicates possible sources. The term Saracene is not unusual for Roman monuments as exemplified by the Tours Sarrazins in Antibes.

H 26-29, N. 10, ills. 36-38. Schnitzler 1965, 320.

De tel maniere fu li sepouture dun
sarrazin q̃ io ui une fois

6

V12 Housing for a Clock

Letter "S" in Form of a Dragon. "This is the housing for a clock." M2: "Whoever wants to make a clock housing can observe one here which I once saw. The first lower storey is square (and) has 4 gables. The storey above it has 8 panels, and then a roof and then 4 gables. Between two gables there is a wide space. The uppermost storey is square with 4 gables and the spire has 8 sides. Here is a drawing of it." Medieval weight-driven clocks were often elaborate structures inside the churches. The size and porportions of our hypothetical reconstruction (fig. 8) corresponds to the free-standing restored late thirteenth-century clock in Beauvais Cathedral and to the astronomical clock of 1574 in Strasbourg cathedral which are further mentioned in the text to V44. The face may have been located in the "wide space." The lower storeys may have been reserved for automata or a planetarium indicating the phases of the moon which were essential for planting. The interior may have housed a carillon. Since the style is akin to late ·Rhenish Romanesque, the turret might have housed a water-clock which were still in use to some extent until the eighteenth century. It is possible that the *horologium*—so named by Hugo of Oignies, a compatriot of Villard—was weight driven and controlled by a brake and a flywheel, but certainly not yet a foliot balance as that discussed in V44 and figs. 32*a* and 32*b*. Villard's use of perspective is discussed in our introduction.

Letter "S" in Form of a Dragon is the first example of other letters found in lodge- and recipe books. In its coiled energy and mannered distortion, it resembles the initials in the Bible of Savalo de Valenciennes, Valenciennes Bibl. Municipale ms. 4 and those of the Missal of Noyon.

H 29-32, ills. 23-4, 29. See also V44 and Mitchell, 1965, pl. 71.

cest u masons

don orologe

ki uelt faire le maison dune
rerloge uesent a une q̃ to
ui une fois. La p̃mier̃
estages de desol est q̃uareſ
a iiij peignonciaus.
li estages de seure est
a viij penia̅ſ z pu̅ſ
couertie z puiſ iiij
peignonciaus entre
ii peignouſ i
espasse d̃uit.
li estages tos de sevre
sest q̃res a iiij peig
nonciaus z li cobleſ
a d̃uiij costeſ d̃es
aluec le portrait.

VILLARD DE HONNECOURT

V13 Lectern

"Whoever wants to make a lectern on which one reads the Gospels, see here the best solution known to me. First on the ground there are 3 dragons and above them a platform with 3 lobes. And above them 3 dragons of another kind. And columns as tall as the dragons. And above them 1 triangle. After that you well see how a lectern is made. Take a look at the picture. In the center of the 3 columns there must be a stem which carries a pummel on which sits an eagle." The description is precise, omitting only the three nonstructural branches on which stand acolytes swinging insense vessels and the three evangelists at the top (fig. 8). The trefoil is inscribed in an equilateral triangle and is quickly constructed with a compass and a straight edge by bisecting the sides of an equilateral triangle and using the midpoints of the sides as the centers for three circles which touch the three bisecting lines. The elegant shape is used throughout the Gothic age and the early Renaissance. It can be rotated successfully by 180° (see fig. 9). This is Villard's first important use of High Gothic geometric principles. The final elegance of the shape is corroborated by the fact that the sides of the remaining small triangles equal the radii of the circles!

The lectern is a fairly typical example of brass or wrought iron reading stands, for which the area of Dinant, south of Namur and well within Villard's orbit was rightly famous (see map, fig. 1). The cast lectern given by Bishop Lotgar to Liège Cathedral in 980, and another example from St. Jean in Tirlemont were provided with eagles moving their wings. This admirable possibility was taken up by Villard on V44. H illustrates a fifteenth century lectern from Venray, but we prefer Jean Joès' exquisite eagle lectern of circa 1370 which stands on three lions, instead of the three dragons of Villard, has three dragons on a trefoil base and four more dragons below the eagle. Though more architectural in form, the brass lectern from Dinant, which now stands in the Collegiate Church of Tongres, closely adhered to Villard's iconography.

H 33-37, Nn. 13, 69, ill. 81. Legner 1972, p. 72.

V14   Locust, Cat, Fly, Dragonfly, Lobster, Cat, Labyrinth

In all pretechnological societies there is a deep bond between humans and animals. In the rapidly changing culture of the thirteenth century, the magic properties assigned to beasts began to wane and were replaced by scientific observation (see V21). As an architect, Villard reflects these changes by representing animals with the practical curiosity which would allow him to advise customers on the ornamental use of beasts in decorative ensembles such as stalls. The animals on this page are taken from bestiaries. But some, such as the fly, the locust and the dragonfly also reflect observation. Except for the graphic quality of emblemata like the eagle on V36, Villard shows no visible interest in the symbolic lore connected with animals. However, his clerical customers knew that according to Isidore, the locust resembles man in search of spiritual nourishment, and according to Konrad von Megenburg the heads of the larvae looked like horses' heads. The fly appears in the Leningrad bestiary and in the plague illustrations of the Old Testament, most spectacularly in the late twelfth century Pamplona Bibles. The dragonfly is not mentioned in bestiaries and may have come from the studies of nature pursued in Cambrai by Cantimpré for one. The crab, on the other hand, loves oysters and will block their shell with a pebble and eat them. This behavior equates them with a deceitful person. It was well known that crabmeat attracted scorpions. The figure at the bottom which was drawn with the help of a compass, has stubbornly been called a dog. It is not, however; it is a cat licking its privates, and is very similar to one in the Pepysian model book in Cambridge (fig. 10). The cat, of course, has luminous eyes which penetrate the darkness. In this, it is like Lucifer, but it also symbolizes freedom and female lechery.

The labyrinth is an archetypal architectonic ideograph which came to the Middle Ages through Rome. It could be seen in remains similar to that in the Roman baths at Verdes, Vienna, Cormerod, Orléans etc. It also figures in manuscripts such as the famous *Liber Floridus* of Lambert de Liège or St. Omer of circa 1120 where Daedalus appears in its center. Hrabanus Maurus has it and so does the Hereford Map of 1276–83. It even appears later in an Icelandic pattern book, in almost exactly the same way Villard represented it. Above all it appeared on the floors of churches in Pavia, Ravenna, Rome, Lucca, and Cremona. In St. Germain des Près and in Piacenza, it still contained the minotaur, the snarer of the world. With the increased importance of the architect in the Gothic age, there is a shift from the inhabitant to the builder of the Cretan labyrinth: Daedalus. Like Moses and his "pupil" Euclid, he gained access into the medieval pantheon of the fathers of architecture. The labyrinths became larger, from 12′ in the chapter house at Bayeux, to 30′ in Sens and 42′ in Amiens whose labyrinth originated circa 1288. There were others in Poitiers Cathedral, two in Cologne and in St. Etienne in Caen it was named "The Road to Jerusalem" implying a symbolic pilgrimage. Most importantly, we find labyrinths which were sometimes called "Daedales" in the vicinity of Honnecourt. The labyrinths in Arras, the church of St. Bertin in St. Omer and the probably restored example in St. Quentin (fig. 11) all measured 34½′. The "lieu" in the nave of Chartres of circa 1220 measures 40′ and it takes 150 yards to reach "heaven." It is this labyrinth Villard copied (fig. 12). The labyrinth at Sens measuring 30′ and that of Auxerre are copied from Chartres. In Reims (circa 1240) and in Amiens the "Maison de Dédale" became monuments to the founding bishop and the succession of the main architects who were represented in the corners. According to the chronicler Lambert of Ardres, a Count Arnold asked Louis de Bourbourg, a carpenter, to build a labyrinth "with a skill in carpentry nearly equal to that of Daedalus . . . he made a nearly inextricable labyrinth containing recess within recesses, turning within turning."

H 37–40, Nn. 14, 118, ills. 39–42. White 1960. Bucher 1970, pl. 109. Fett 1910. Matthews 1970.
For the Reims Labyrinth see Branner and Reinhardt.

V15 Crucifixion with Mary and John, and Two Later Plaques

The page originally contained an architectural drawing which Villard erased. The inscriptions are Villard's interpretation of Greek letters (cf. V58). They state: Jesus Christ, Christos, St. Mary, John the Theologian and "hel" which could refer to *helios*, the sun, or Helena who found the True Cross. The drawing is closely akin to the lower section of a reliquary of the Holy Cross in the treasury of San Marco in Venice which had been created by Master Gerardus for the new Latin Emperor of the East, Henry of Flanders (fig. 3). If the reliquary was indeed the prototype Villard saw before it was sent off, he modernized it by updating the drapery and by reversing St. John's contrapposto to create a more stringent symmetry. The body of Christ is made weightier by the increased downward angle of the arms, and by the scrolls which end in volutes, not in points. Metal crucifixions were not new in the West, but their number increased after the conquest of Constantinople in 1204, and some assume strong Byzantine characteristics. Some noteworthy crosses Grimme mentions are those of Engelberg, Clairmarais now in St. Omer (1255-50), Cosenza (before 1222), Aachen (1230-40), and St. Trudpert now in Leningrad (circa 1280). A Mosan window of the crucifixion in Châlons-sur-Marne of circa 1160 is also very closely related to Villard's sketch and was discussed by Verdier.

The two drawings on the plaques were added circa 1320 and show yet another stylistic updating of the crucifixion which Villard himself had already undertaken on V9.

H 41-3, N. 15, ills. 32-33a, 162, and Florence 1971, pl. 117. Grimme 1972, ills. 19, 24-27, pp. 53-55. Verdier 1977, vol. 1, 259-263.

V16   Two Armed Riders

The horse at the left is being held back by the rider from whose shield protrudes a possibly later broken lance. The horse at the right is shown trotting. It is likely that the figures were copied from a hunting scene, and may be a visual note which was meant as a representation of discord. If so, it must be compared with the drawing of the wrestlers with very similar heads on V37. Secular scenes, which of course could also be used in a religious context, appear in pattern books such as that in the Augustinermuseum in Freiburg, Germany. The two coats of arms are later additions; the one at the right is that of the Félibien family which claimed ancestral connections with the author of the manuscript, see V1, 3, 46.

H 42, N. 16, ill. 156.

V17a   Checker Players

See illustration p. 75

The checker players with a 64 square board are probably taken from a Passion cycle showing the soldiers gambling for Christ's robe, or from a series leading up to discord. H ill. 5 shows a similar scene with dressed players gambling for the clothes of the Lost Son in a window of Chartres Cathedral. In Chartre's Maison du Cloître Notre-Dame which also contains wrestlers, we find another example, perhaps from the same pattern book. The wavy ground line is a later addition.

V17b   Boar, Hare or Rabbit

The wild boar was known for gross savagery and rudeness. The rabbits and hares are as cowardly as they are prolific. Both pictures are derived from a bestiary.

V17c   Tantalus Cup, Cantepleure

"See here a sing-and-cry (cantepleure) which can be made in 1 bowl in this manner: In the middle of the bowl there must stand a turret, and in the center of the turret a duct which reaches down to the bottom of the cup. The pipe must be as long as the bowl. And in the turret there must be near the bottom of the cup 3 transverse conduits so that the wine can run from the bowl into the duct. And over the turret there must be a bird with its beak held so low that it drinks when the cup is full. Then the wine will flow through the tube and through the foot of the bowl which is double (walled). And remember well that the bird must be hollow." The gadget is a gravity syphon which will operate once a vent pin in the beak or between the legs and the body of the bird is discreetly removed. The wine will flow under the base of the turret and push up into the hollow space, thus displacing air which leaves the bird through a whistle. Figs. 13a, b, and c show how the liquid rises in tube A and is then syphoned off through a corresponding duct into the hollow foot. Fig. 13a shows the air leaving the stationary bird through a whistle in the beak while the castle "rises" from the wine. Fig. 13b shows

the bird "drinking" wine. Seeing the liquid escape from its grasp, and due to decreasing air pressure it will utter an increasingly plaintive cry. Villard's drawing seems derived from sketches showing two differing wing positions. Thus it corresponds to the toys in the *Pneumatica* of Heron of Alexandria, which were still described by Angelo Vegetius in the mid-sixteenth century. Fig. 13c shows a light bird hinged at point C. Its buoyant head floats down with the vanishing liquid and it "drinks" only to a pre-determined level. Then it "strains" trying to reach the vanishing wine while emitting a heart rending cry which comes from the whistle B. Bowls with vanishing liquid were used in antiquity and throughout the Middle Ages. A Lombard example was bought in Ypres by Charles the Good, Count of Flanders, as early as 1127 A.D. They were also used as centerpieces on tables and in this way, the cantepleures literally sang while they cried. Invented as ingenious automata, they became replete with mythological, and above all moralizing overtones.

V17d   Warming Apple

"Should you wish to make 1 hand-warmer, make it like a copper apple with 2 fitting halves. In the copper apple there must be 6 copper rings, each of the rings has two pivots. The pivots must alternate in such a manner that the brazier always remains upright. For one pivot connects with the other, and if you do it right as explained in the text and in the drawing, you can turn it to whichever side you want, the embers will not spill. This apparatus is suitable for a bishop, he can heartily partake in the High Mass, for inasmuch as he holds this device in his cold hands, he will not be cold as long as the fire lasts." "There is no better device. This device is made in such a manner, that whichever way it is turned, the brazier remains upright."

The warming apple consists of two half spheres which are hinged and held together by a clasp. The lower sphere contains six gimbals, pivoting on axes which are at right angles to each other. A compass, traveling inkwell or in this case a pan with a piece of charcoal or a hot iron ball will remain horizontal. The gadget would have worked well with two gimbals. Their multiplication may indicate Villard's preoccupation with fire precautions mentioned on V62. H discusses warming apples used from the eleventh century onward including a "pume de cuevre dorées" listed in the Cambrai inventory of 1359, and a hand warmer of circa 1230–40 in the monastery of the Great St. Bernard Pass. This warmer comes from the Maas region and it contains three gimbals, a removable iron egg and was grasped with a handle. Other examples exist in St. Riquier, three in the Vatican of which two contain three rings, in the Bargello in Florence and other locations.

H 43–49, Nn. 17–20, 113, ills. 84–87, 182–86, 193–195.

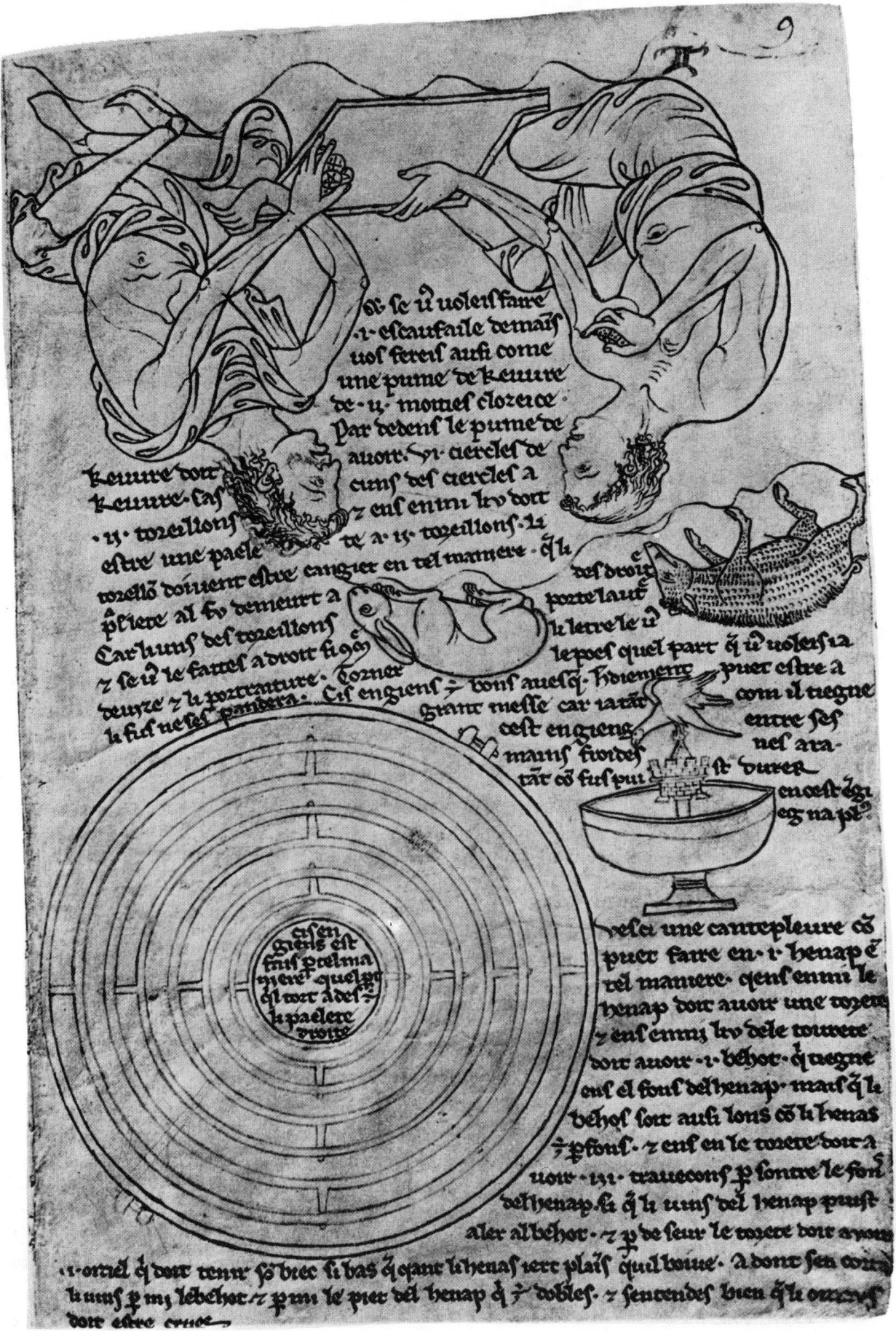

VILLARD DE HONNECOURT

V18a   Laon Cathedral, Plan of Tower

"I have been in many lands, as you can gather from this book, but no place have I seen such a tower, like that in Laon. Observe (the plan of) the first storey at (the level of) the first windows. At this level the tower is surrounded by 7 buttresses, there are 4 square turrets (supported by four bundles) of tripled columns. Then come small arches and entablatures, and turrets with 8 columns. And between two columns there is one ox each. Then come small arches and entablatures. Over them are 8 sided roofs, on each side there is a narrow arch to provide light. Observe (the drawing) before you and you will see much of the principle (manière) and the whole construction, and above how the turrets change. And if you consider building a tower with great gabled buttresses you will need them of sufficient depth. Take care in your work so that you will become wise and prudent." This translation differs from several previous publications, "...and the whole construction" refers also to V19.

The towers of Laon were completed around 1225 and received immediate admiration. In terms of Krautheimer's "medieval copy", the towers served as the model for the imitations in Bamberg Cathedral, where even the oxen appear, in Naumburg, Limburg-an-der Lahn, Lausanne; and in their constructional concept were pursued even at Reims. Villard's enthusiasm may have had deeper intellectual roots. With the exception of the base of the lectern (V13 and our fig. 9), the Laon cross section is the most exacting geometric exercise in the book. The labored sketch contains erasures and some irregularities, such as the exaggerated length of the lower left buttress, all of which are analyzed in fig. 14.

As Velte, Hahnloser and Ueberwasser demonstrated, Villard was experimenting with the quadrature or rotation of the square which was fast becoming the canon, or basic principle of the Gothic proportional series. Villard's reference to the manière—in Italy the maniera—and "to wisdom and prudence" intones similar statements found throughout medieval architectural practice. It also emphasizes the importance Villard himself attributed to the drawing. The plan is therefore the most important architectural document in the lodgebook and must be closely scrutinized according to its deliberate geometric steps. They reflected the still experimental construction and design principles, simultaneously used in several locations, roughly from Laon to Frederick II's Castel del Monte.

The geometric progression as shown in fig. 14 has been controversial for reasons I cannot perceive. It was based on the following eight squares which were inscribed within each other, and rotated by 45°. Squares B and C are also used, and square D equals square E. The plan is straightforward and more predictable than most. The following squares shown on fig. 14 determine these major elements:

A   Outer faces of buttresses
B   Master square. Outer body of tower, and prolonged to A the short eight faces of the buttresses
C   Same as B. Total width of buttresses and auxiliary functions
D   Diagonal panes of interior space, position of eight colonnettes
E   Same as D. Rectilinear interior wall panes of what has become an octagon derived from two equal squares, one of them in rotation. See the introduction fig. 1b.
F   Auxiliary
G   Outer width of jambs of large windows. Used as control square G2, it determines the angles of the embrasure
H   Equals length of the interior wall panes. Possibly used for the outer width of the openings through the diagonal panes of the octagon
I   Auxiliary. By geometric coincidence it equals the lengths of the diagonal faces of the buttresses
K   Diameter of the keystone

The left half of the drawing shows all squares needed for the design, the right half only the major progressions. Since all the measurements are geometrically interrelated, as in all effective architecture, several squares can be used for alternate purposes which gives the reader the opportunity to develop the design.

Continued on p. 78

Jan este en nilt de tieres
Si coil pozes trouer en cest lui
en aucun liu onges tel tor ne vi con
est cele deloo ues enr ci le preni es ligement si con des pmiere fenest
res Acest el ligement est li trois tornee a hvui arestes sen se les ms
fittoles ou parees seur colonbes de trois puis si uienent arker zen
taulemens se re sunt les fittoles puies a vun colonbes zctre n
colonbes saur uns bues puis uienent arker z en taulemens p
de seure sunt li conble a vun crestes en casrune espase a une
arkiere por auoir clarte esgardes deuant il sen uerele nilt
dele maniere z torte le montee z si co les
fittoles se cangent z si penses car seruoles
bien ouer denz grans pilers soikies il
couient a uoir q ases aiuent cal prendes gard
en uostre afaire si feres q sages z q cortois

V18b   Tabernacle

The tabernacle with a trefoil arch is lighter than those of Laon, and heavier than those of Reims (fig. 42). The sketch may represent the only record of an intermediate design of the upper parts of the Reims choir, that is between the heavily articulated buttressing towers shown on V64 and the present solution. Most likely this is an addition from the late 1220s. The pentagram may express perfection , but is more likely a mason's or placement mark derived from the elevations echoed on V60-61 which contain numerous marks.

See illustration ·p. 77

V18c   Bearded Male Head

The head preceded the text which has to be seen in conjunction with V19. According to Lassus it shows a beggar. It may have been drawn from life.

H 49-55, Nn. 21-24, ills. 75-79.

V19   Elevation of the Upper Three Storeys of the Tower at Laon Cathedral

The elevation begins right above an arcaded gallery which is flanked by two aediculae supporting the tabernacles topped by pyramidal spires. Since the verso page contains two later drawings, it seems likely that a more complete elevation was cut both at the top and at the bottom, leaving only the three most interesting buttressed storeys. Compared with the present structure the "montée" seems to have been derived from the existing monument and not from a design (fig. 15). The proportions of the lowest visible storey are nearly correct except for the hand of which there is no trace. The two upper storeys are elongated by the severe, practically grotesque "narrowing" of the central opening. The three colonnettes of the sketch were merged with a heavier shaft. The four small spires and the central, probably octagonal stone helmet have disappeared. They were adorned with crockets along the ridges, with an advanced motif used for St. Nicaise of Reims circa 1229, and again for the tomb of its architect Hugues Libergier.

H 49-55, Nn. 21-24, ills. 76-6. Colombier 1953, 66.

V20a   Christ and Mary

The drawing embodies the slightly melancholic and lyrical mood characterizing thirteeth-century poetry addressed to the Virgin Mary. Reinhardt 83–89 suggests a lost group from the Reims portal, using Mary as a prototype. We and H assume it was an adoration of the Magi, perhaps as a painting.

V20b   Window from Reims Cathedral

"Here is one of the windows (frames) of Reims from the spaces (bays) of the nave as they appear between 2 pillars. I had been sent to the land of Hungary when I drew it because it pleased me most."
If our dating of Villard's trip to Hungary is correct, he must have seen and admired the window around 1226. Branner, Barnes and others have pointed out that the capitals of the transverse arches spring from a lower point than that indicated by Villard. In addition, the proportions of the lancets were changed from 1:3.75 to 1:5 (fig. 42). According to Reinhardt the six eastern bays of the north sideaisle were undertaken by Jean d'Orbais who was dead by 1228. The tracery is still quite simple and must be compared with Le Mans, begun circa 1217 and Amiens' transept windows of perhaps 1233–1236 which depend on Reims, but have an increasingly more complex tracery.

H 55–58, Nn. 26–28, ills. 209–10, Branner 1963, 129–46.

V21   Blessing Christ with Book

This is the first of two large portraits of Christ in Majesty. It precedes the sketch on V32 and is more conservative and ultimately more Byzantine. It follows the sculptural tradition developed in St. Benoît-sur-Loire in circa 1200 (fig. 66 in Sauerländer 1972). H points to similarities with an initial in the Noyon Missal now Harvard College Library Ms. Typ 120 H. Even more categorically he compares it with Hugo of Oignies's phylactery of St. Andrew in Namur of the 1230s (fig. 16).

V21   Dragon for a Stall

The dragon sits menacingly on the wooden volute of a stall whose complexity lies between the designs shown on V54 and V57. This is a late entry sketched with a nearly dry pen. The quick lines give the impression of shading and increase the aggressive impact which was not present in the more graphically treated dragon on V12. The dragon was considered earth's largest monster. Its strength lay in its potent tail which could create ardent winds which would kill anything in proximity. It could strangle an elephant with its tail. Only the devil could appear in the shape of an even more enormous reptile, and in this way mislead sinners whom he would strangle with his tail and throw into hell.

H 58-59, N. 101, ills. 14-17, 24, 29-31, 167.

V22   Nude Male Before an Altar

Villard went to great lengths to bring the figure to life through the use of washes which were employed in other pattern books such as the Wolfenbüttel and Freiburg manuscripts. The figure is most likely based on an astronomical manuscript such as the early ninth century *Aratus* in the University Library in Leiden (Voss lat. 79), which originated in Reims or St. Omer. It could stem from a gemini or aquarius image or from a calendar picture such as that showing *annus* enthroned among the seminude seasons in a Fulda Sacramentary (Tübigen, Univ. Libr. Theol. lat. 192). We already suggested Carolingian or Ottonian prototypes for V7c and 11, and must remember that the rich libraries of Reims and St. Omer were within Villard's reach. Above all we must recall that the fortified abbey in Honnecourt-sur-l'Escaut itself was known for its rich holdings.

H 59-60, N. 30. Swarzenski 50, ill. 156. Panofsky, 1960, vol. 2 fig. 12. La Voix du Nord, 17 May 1974, Z-39.

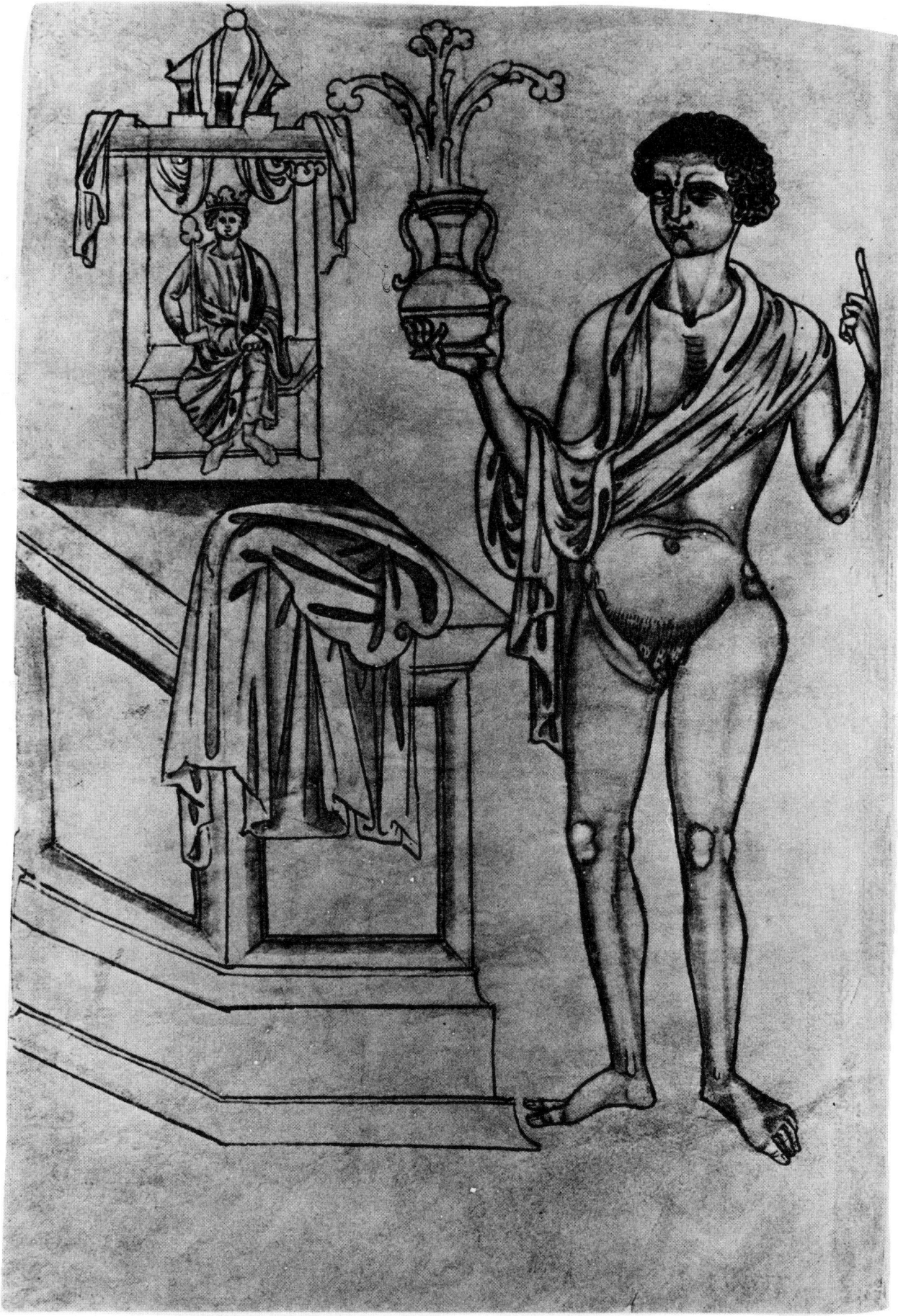

VILLARD DE HONNECOURT

V23   The False Mother from the Judgment of Solomon

"Here is one of two maidens who stood judgment before Solomon because of their child, which each claimed as her own." One would like to connect the elegant drawing with the king seated in judgment on V49. The false mother is often represented in Biblical illustrations as standing and arguing, and less so in monumental painting and sculpture. H suggests a stained glass prototype and several manuscripts among them, with two examples in the Credo of Joinville in Paris, Bibl. Nat. ms. lat. 11907, 213 v. The free flow of lines and the cavalier use of hairpin loops seem to place the drawing among the late entries in the book. The style has shifted beyond the Reims Visitation Master toward the more mannered and slender figures which were to culminate in the Ecclesia and Synagoga from the south transept of Strasbourg Cathedral, circa 1230.

H 60–61, Nn. 31–2, ill. 13. Sauerländer 1972, ill. 133.

Sefei lune def · ij · damoizeles
de q li iugemenf fu faif deva
salemon de leur enfant. qcascu
ne uoloit auer

V24   Seated Knight, Bishop, King

The knight, dressed in a fur lined robe is seated in judgment. The figure could be based on the Massacre of the Innocents, a martyrdom scene, or one of many secular frescoes. Similar representations are seen in a Mosan reliquary of circa 1220–30 and in a triptych in Mettlach of the same date. The source for the standing bishop cannot be pinpointed. The same is true for one of the three Magi from an adoration scene who points to the star of Bethlehem. He appears in textiles, manuscripts, and paintings from Spain (frontals of Llusà, Cardet) to very similar representations in Scandinavia.

H p. 25. Hoffmann 1970, 98-101, 137, vol. 2, ills. 136, 137.

V25   King at Court

"This is a king and these are his men and his retinue." The courtiers stand at the left, two of them exchanging a whispered conversation. The enthroned king, holding a magnificent lily sceptre gestures toward a supplicant kneeling before him, while two standing figures seem to argue a point. The scene is precise but cannot be as clearly identified as, for instance, Daniel judging one of the two Elders, or Urias before David. A secular, perhaps English, source is possible.

H 62–63 relates the style to the circle of Matthew Paris. See James 1925–26, vol. 14, pl. 22.

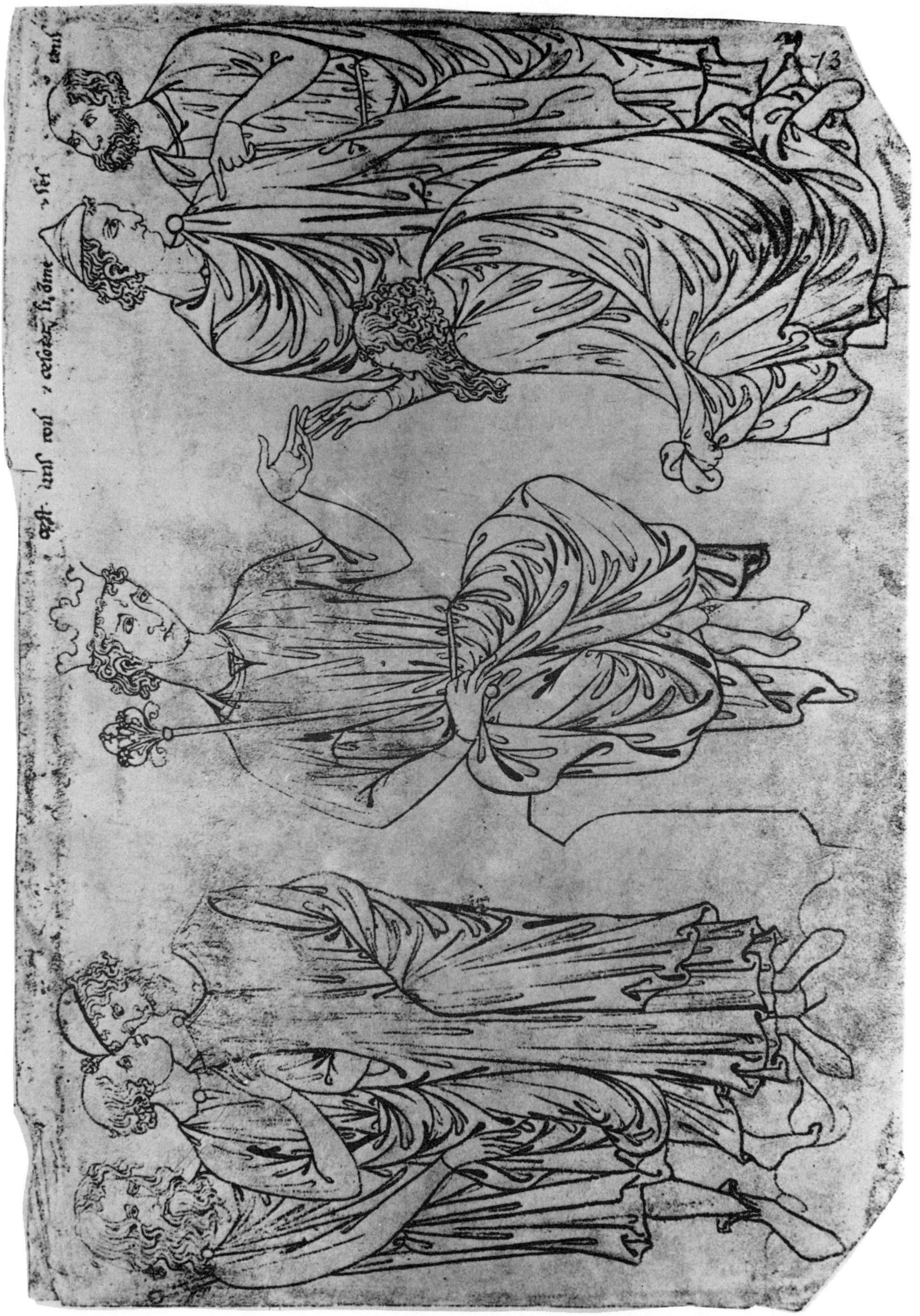

V26   Descent from the Cross

Christ is being lowered from the cross by three men, the figure on the ladder is Nicodemus. Mary at the left kisses Christ's hand, Joseph of Arimathea collects His blood. John the Apostle mourns at the right. The scene is a rich but standardized Descent. Other examples show the three Marys, the skull of Adam under the cross and additional attendants. The iconography is derived from Byzantine sources such as Nerezi of circa 1164 and objects which reached the West after the conquest of Constantinople in 1204.

V26   The Symbols of Mark and Luke

H attributes the lively and formidable treatment of the symbols of Mark and Luke also to Siculo-Byzantine and Italian examples found on medallions of crosses. This page gives an indication that Villard may have reached Hungary through upper Italy, Venice and Dalmatia where he would have been confronted with works of similar complexity and energy.

H 63-64. See *The Year 1200*, p. 272 (adaptation of Byzantine source), vol. 2, ills. 243–44 (Descent from the Cross). James 1922, pl. 15, identifies the figure collecting Christ's blood as Adam.

V27   Lovers Seated on a Chest

This is a typical aristocratic courting scene showing an elegant dandy with his hunting falcon on his gloved right hand in conversation with a formally robed lady. Scenes of such lyrical animation are found in many ivories and manuscripts such as the Manesse Codex in Heidelberg (Univ. Libr. Cod. pal. germ. 818) dated a century later.

H 64, N. 29.

V28   Wrestlers   *See illustration p. 97*

See illustration p. 97

The theme of conflict appears frequently in Villard's manuscript. It ranges from classical circus scenes on V52-53 to echoes of the Hyberno-Saxon ribbon animals on V12, to fights on V38. Human conflicts were usually allegories. The virtues attacking the vices in Tavant, Jacob's encounter with the angel, or lions, symbolic of the devil, devouring men in Oloron-Sainte-Marie, St. Gilles and Speyer symbolize the struggle between good and evil. Discord can be represented by men pulling each other's beards as in the Grossmünster in Zürich, or downright mayhem based on Biblical or historical events. In contrast to these images, Villard's wrestlers carry the benign overtones of a genre scene based on a very popular sport. The shorts with heavy cloth belts reinforced by leather thongs and the skull caps preventing hair pulling are typical for wrestlers used ornamentally such as a drawing in the *Historia Maior* by Matthew Paris which may illustrate a contest held in London in 1222, or the group of wrestlers on the choir stalls of Lausanne Cathedral, or the later wrestlers in Queen Mary's Psalter. The two figures shown here are compositionally defined by a rough circle whose center lies slightly above their knees, and whose circumference determines their backs and the meeting point of their heels. Villard took a slightly different approach to the same theme on V37.

V28 (below, left)   Ideal Cistercian Plan

"Observe a church made up of squares which was planned for construction by the Order of Cîteaux." Schematic or ideal plans could consist of lines without any indication of wall thickness. This is the case for the plans of churches in the Holy Land in Adamnanus' *De locis sanctis*, the famous early ninth century plan of St. Gall and many later examples. The plan reflects a doctrinaire Romanesque square schematism. The nave and chevet consist of six squares, the transepts comprise one and a half square each, thus establishing a 6:4 proportion. The sideaisles may have been considered as a continuous ambulatory and form a linear succession of squares measuring one quarter of the crossing. The juxta-position with Cambrai heightens the sense of Cistercian simplicity in planning expressed in the Bernardine ideal church which was to be an "officina," a workshop for prayer. We discussed in previous publications the rules of purism underlying Cistercian architecture and the churches most likely to have inspired Villard's sketch. H suggested Pontigny II of circa 1140–70. But its proportions were different and its semicircular ambulatory was built circa 1185–1210. I consider two others more likely candidates: Morimond built 1155–70 seems to have been subject to few changes and Fontaine-Jean founded 1190 and consecrated in 1233 (fig. 17). The small diagonal lines emerging from the piers may indicate groin vaults rather than ribs which are pencilled into the radiating chapels of Cambrai discussed below. The width of the wall buttresses equals one half the width of the side aisles, surely an arbitrary design device indicating geometric progression. Only the carrying members are two dimensional.

Continued on p. 96

V28 (below, right)   Choir of Cambrai Cathedral

"Observe the plan of the chevet of Our Lady Saint Mary of Cambrai as it rises from the ground. Above in this book you will find the inner and outer elevations and all kinds of chapels and also of the nave walls and the types of flying buttresses." The wrods chavec, boteres or buters (Master 3) are still in use as chevet and buttresses. Villard refers to his chevet elevations of Cambrai which are now lost. They would have been of special interest since the plan is the most precise architectural drawing in the book and presupposes a larger working plan which he copied in the lodge. A. Boileux's plan which was completed in 1779 and published by A. le Glay shows slightly heavier walls, lighter buttresses and piers with four full shafts (see fig. 18). Villard states that the building is "rising" from its foundations. He thus stresses the buttress foundations and heavy bracing walls and omits stairs, doors and windows. His chapel vaults are tentatively sexpartite while the completed vaults consisted of a narrow quadripartite bay to which a sexpartite hemicycle was attached. He therefore must have seen an uncompleted chevet.

The Metropolitan Basilica was begun in 1227. The chapel of St. Nicolas was founded in 1230. Another chapel was dedicated to St. Elizabeth of Hungary who had contributed to the funding in 1239, that is after her canonization on 27 May 1235. The choir followed the Reims model and was begun in 1211. It was of the same length and only 6.2 m. narrower, and may have reached completion in 1246. The main vaults supposedly reached 41 m over a length of 136 m. From the work of Boileux, a model of 1695 formerly in Berlin, and a drawing by van der Meulen, we know that the choir was provided with single flyers and that the decoration of the main apse integrated elements from Amiens. The church was destroyed 1796-97. Quicherat attributed the building to Villard, which geographically fell within his radius of action. The fact that he left the rib configuration open indicates that the design of the chapel vaulting had not been resolved. We therefore assume that Villard saw Cambrai in the state reported by him between circa 1227-35 when the slow construction was rising above the foundation level. At that time he had reached professional maturity and certainly participated in design discussions as is clearly indicated on V60 where he states that the chapels of Cambrai would have to be like those of Reims "if done correctly." As in St. Quentin we believe that Villard was called in as a design consultant. In Cambrai his advice, if he proffered any, which V60 seems to indicate, was ultimately neglected. In St. Quentin it seems to have been accepted. (See V30.)

H 65-69, Nn. 33-37, 87, 104, ills. 62-64, 110, 123-26, plan p. 357. Biaudet 1975, 109-11. Horn 1966, vol. 48, 285-307. Dimier, vol. 1, 116, vol. 2, 108, 203. H, N. 34 disagreed with me in regard to the plan of Morimond, which I had published in 1960. Glay 1825. Héliot 1956, vol. 18, 93 ff. with discussion of sources.

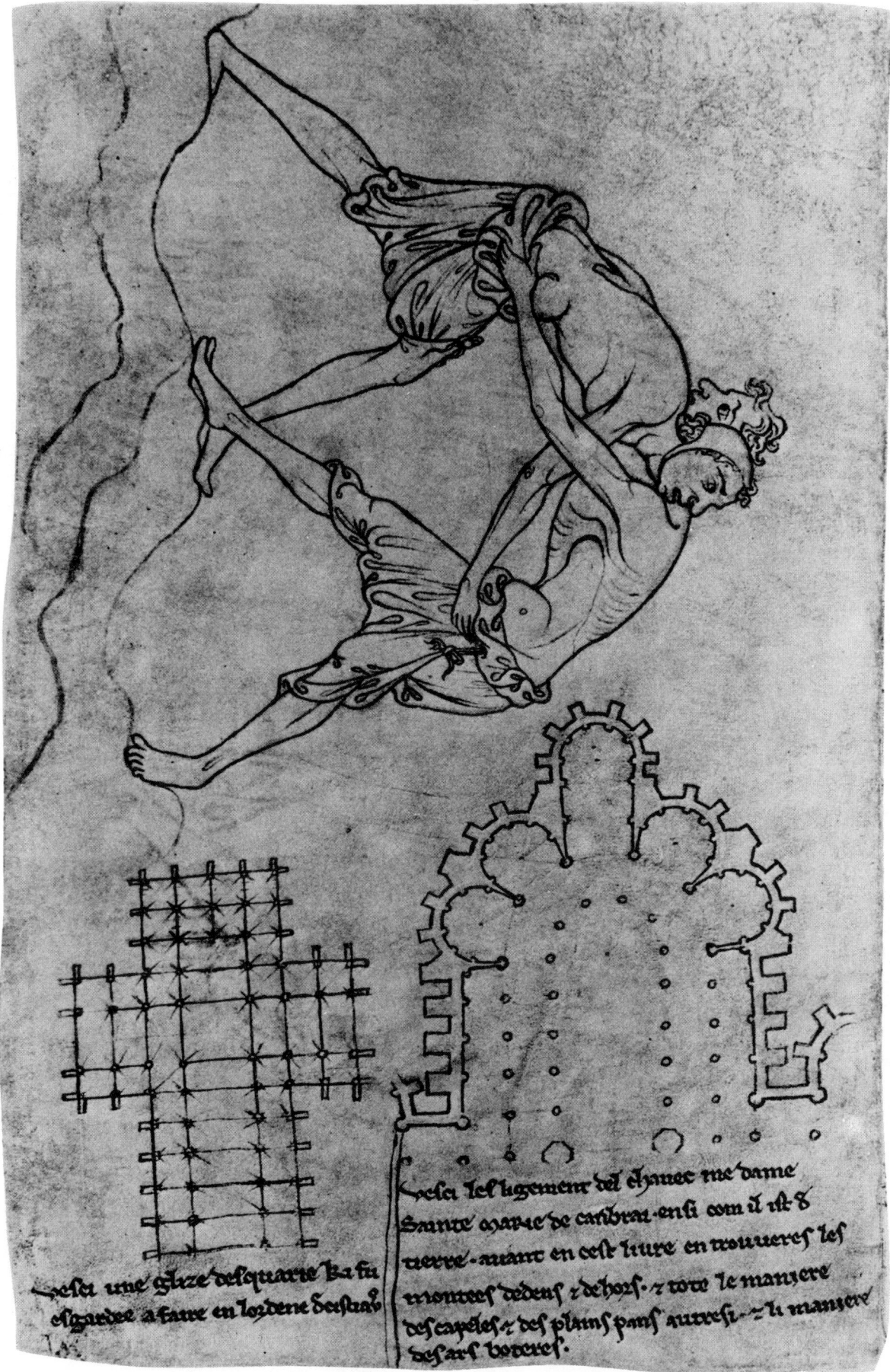

ꝑ cell les lagement del chinee me dame
Sainte marie de cambrai. ensi com il ist g
uerre. auant en cest liure en trouueres les
mouuees dedens ꝛ dehors. ꝛ tote le maniere
des capeles ꝛ des plains pans autresi. ꝛ li maniere
des ars boterex.

ꝑ esci une glize descquarie ba su
esguedee a faire en lordene decistaus

VILLARD DE HONNECOURT

Inscriptions:

M2 in Latin in the upper plan: "This choir was developed by Villard de Honnecourt and Pierre de Corbie in common discussion."

M2 in Latin in the lower plan: "This is the choir of St. Pharaon in Meaux."

Villard, bottom in French: "Observe the plan of the church of St. Stephen of Meaux. Above it is a church with a double ambulatory, which *vilars de honecort* and Pierre de Corbie designed." The italics represents one spelling of Villard's name. The term "trova" at the end of the sentence literally means: invented. M2's inscriptions are deferential, but he mistakes St. Stephen for St. Faron in Meaux which was torn down in the nineteenth century.

V29   "Ideal" Plan

The upper plan maps out a large structure. But it is less sophisticated than Cambrai and is neither innovative nor modern. The choir has a double "charole," the outer one with an alternate vault arrangement such as in Senlis, St. Martin-des-Champs in Paris and other examples. The semicircular chapels are antiquated and the size of the three square chapels which was to allow for a clearly spaced placement of three altars seems uncouth. Panofsky stressed the scholastic nature of the plan and saw in it a *questio* leading to an arrangement of homologous parts and parts of parts, and combining "all possible Sics . . . with all possible Nons." We see it as a learning piece of Villard's which combines the concept of a large Gothic basilica with a Romanesque isolation of attached parts. In this respect the plan is even less advanced than that of Vaucelles on V33 which probably inspired the discussion between Villard and Pierre from the neighboring Corbie. Perhaps they both worked at Vaucelles, and wanted to show how the existing plan could be changed to maximize space with a minimum amount of wall. Discussions and consultations among architects were part of their active lives, and we have several verbatim reports from meetings of architects called in for consultations which took place, for instance, in Beauvais, Verona and Milan.

V29   Chevet of St. Stephen in Meaux

Meaux was completed in 1198 when the tomb of Mary, Princess of Champagne was placed there. In 1213 responds were added to the piers. In 1253 a restoration was planned and in 1298 the chapter decided to reconstruct the chevet. In 1322 two radiating chapels had been placed between the original chapels and in 1331 two lateral chapels were added to the outer aisles which thus joined the westernmost earlier chapels. The plan is that of St. Stephen Cathedral and is amazingly close to the thirteenth century layout established by M. Deshoulières and J. Formigé. (See fig. 19.) It was so close in fact that it must have been copied from an existing design kept in the lodge. Villard narrowed the ambulatory and thus slightly shortened the walls between the chapels, then corrected this development when he reached the aisle bays and simply drew two diagonal walls. Lambert suggested that the "ideal" plan could be dated 1216 (?), and saw precisely the same relationships between Vaucelles and the "ideal plan" which we discussed above. Kurman dates the plan 1215. We agree with an early date but only on the basis of the style which indicates an early entry.

H 69-73, Nn. 38, 107, ills. 65-67. Panofsky 1951, 87. Deshoulières 1920, 140-70.

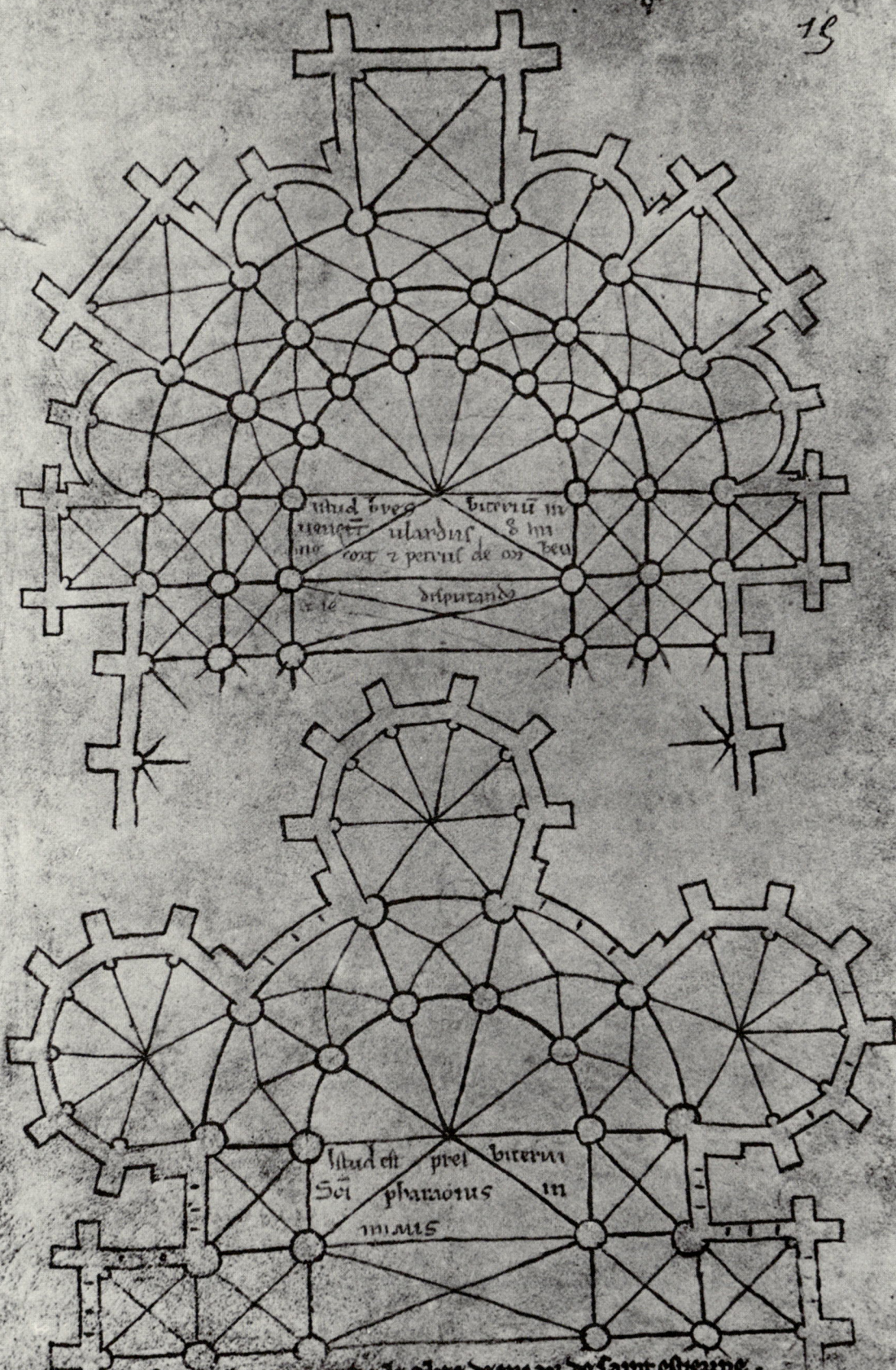

itud bueg   biteriu in
uendt ularduf   g lm
ine crt z perul de on beu

diſputando

itud eſt preſ biterni
Soi pharioruſ in
mimis

veſci lef ligement de le glize demuay de ſaint eſteune .
Deſeure eſt une glize a double charole . Karlarf dehoneocrt troua pie
reſ de corbie .

V30a Hungarian Pavement

"I was once in Hungary where I spent many a day. There I saw the pavement of a church done in this manner." The terracotta tiles seem to be those found by Lázló Gerevitch in the Cistercian abbey of Pilis near Esztergom. For a series of reasons outlined in the biography, Villard's trip probably took place between 1226-28. The circular rose pattern is not frequent in thirteenth-century France. The slight shifts in axes and the use of stone borders are unique, and seem to have been repeated only in the chapel storey in the tower of the Collegiate Church of St. Quentin where we also find the graffito of a rose derived from Villard's Chartres drawing (fig. 20). It must be stressed that Villard does not speak of more than a year spent in Hungary. His trip may have been rapid which explains the lack of any major monuments he might have seen either in Hungary or on his way, except for Lausanne on V31.

V30b Joining of a Pillar

"Here you may take advice on how to place a pillar with the right joints." The inscription is by M2. The pillar is connnected with the first construction phase of Reims. The same pillar with its core divided into halves appears in Villard's more explicit drawings of Reims on V63. Villard was intrigued by the joining of the responds to the piers by means of a joggled joint.

V30c Chartres Rose Window

"This is a window in the large church of St. Mary of Chartres." The Latin inscription is by M2, and the word "templum" implies a large size. Figure 21 shows the actual Chartres rose window at the bottom, Villard's changes at the center, and finally the graffito of St. Quentin at the top. Villard changed the proportions to lighten the outer circumference of the rosettes, and added quadrilobes in the spandrels of the arches. In his graffito he changed the axis, shifted the rosettes back so that they are lodged between the spandrels and not above the apex of the arches and equalized the three elements so that they are in a 1:1:1 proportion. The cusped base for the columns remains eliminated. The trefoils and quatrefoils may have remained but can no longer be seen on the graffito shown in figs. 22a, b, c. In this way, he changed a heavy design, completed around 1220, into a more airy tracery pattern corresponding to the slender architectural members he may well have suggested for the choir of St. Quentin in circa 1225-35.

H 73-76, Nn. 39, 117-8, ills. 52-54. Summary: Bucher 1977, vol. 59, 315-19. Gerevitch 1971. See V10.

chi pourres matter don piler
metre adroite leskons

Jestoie une fois enhongrie la v iemes maiir
loz la uiio le pauement dune glize desi faite
ogaiuere.

Par chu fenesbra in uielo ses marie cannon

VILLARD DE HONNECOURT

V31   The Rose Window of Lausanne Cathedral.   An Observer

"This is a round window in the church of Lausanne." Same text in Latin by M2. Villard passed through Lausanne on his way to or from Hungary before 1232. He must have met his compatriots Pierre d'Arras who worked there from 1217-34, the architect Jean Cotereel recorded there between 1227-1236 and perhaps the metal worker Hugh of Cambrai who is mentioned in 1205. The window of the south transept measures 8.7 m. and was presumably completed in 1226 or at the latest in 1232. Villard based his sketch on eight axes and used the compass extensively. He reduced the width of the outer frame, rotated the tracery by 45° and changed the outer square into an anemic star with awkward trefoils inscribed in triangles, and trefoils and quatrefoils strewn into the spandrels (see fig. 23). I believed earlier (1968) that these major shifts were inadvertent. I now assume that he would have judged the window to be very archaic, and unsuccessfully tried to modernize the tracery. The fact that he neglected to use the quadrature for this so eminently suitable example is of major stylistic importance in establishing a date for the solidification of the Gothic quadrature canon.

It has been suggested that the seated man contemplating the window is Moses taking off his footwear.

H 76, 77, Nn. 40, 106, ills. 56 and p. 358. Biaudet, Beer 1957, 159, 224. Beer is unclear about the use of the quadrature geometry. Bucher 1968, vol. 27, 52.

Cest une reonde veriere de le glize de losane.

Ista est fenestra in losana eclia

V32   Christ in Majesty

Possibly one of the earlier sketches which was completely reworked at a later date showing the tight security Villard acquired through his studies of the dressed figure. H connects it with objects such as the Andrew Philactery of circa 1238 by Hugh of Oignies from Namur (fig. 16). The Majesty is unthinkable without the flow of Byzantine objects to the West after the conquest of Constantinople in 1204.

H 77-78, Nn. 99, 101, ills. 14-17, 167.

V33a "This is the choir of Saint Mary of Vaucelles, a church of the Cistercian Order"

Inscription by M2. Vaucelles stood about an hour's walk from Honnecourt and was central to Villard's architectural formation. The abbey was founded in the diocese of Cambrai in 1132 by Hugo of Oisy. It was a daughter of Clairvaux and was joined by a younger brother of St. Bernard. By 1204–38 it ho housed 111 monks and 180 conversi. The large church, now destroyed, was begun circa 1190. The nave and transept were completed circa 1216 and the choir was consecrated by Henry of Dreux, archbishop of Reims in 1235. The length, 132 m., indicates it was a major construction site which Villard must have visited as a young man. He may well have worked there as an apprentice. If our tentative bi-ography is correct, he had probably reached a professional status by 1216 when the choir was begun. Excavations prove the plan to be accurate including the first two radiating chapels which were angled off toward the nave. (See fig. 24). The same solution is found in St. Yved-de-Braine and Troyes. There is no proof that he participated in the designing process. But it is clear that the plan was seminal in his thinking and affected his "ideal" concept on V29, his interest in Meaux and Cambrai V28–29, and and his clear perception of Cistercian modular planning on V28. Finally, the influence on the design decisions for the archaically angled western ambulatory chapels of the Collegiate Church in St. Quentin can also be attributed to Villard.

V33b "This is a picture of Our Lord as He Fell"

More likely this sketch shows a sleeping apostle on the Mount of Olives, and can be compared with a similar sleeper on V46. It might also stem from a Transfiguration. A Byzantine motif used in St. Mark in Venice was transferred to manuscripts such as the *Hortus Deliciarum* of Herrad of Landsberg of 1187 A.D. If we can judge from the copies, the style of the design shared some of the awkwardness of Villard's drawing.

H 78-81, Nn. 41-2, 100, ills. 11-12, 18-20, 65-66. Dimier vol. 1, 312. Lambert 1947, *Bulletin de la Société Nationale des antiquaires de France* (July session) asserts that Villard received the commission to build the choir in 1216. Aubert 1947, vol. 1, 225 states that Villard worked at Vaucelles and "peut-être en assuma la direction."

1717

ıtud eıt preſbıterıum beate marıe uacelleuſıs

ecolıe ɜrouıit cıstercɪɪ̄

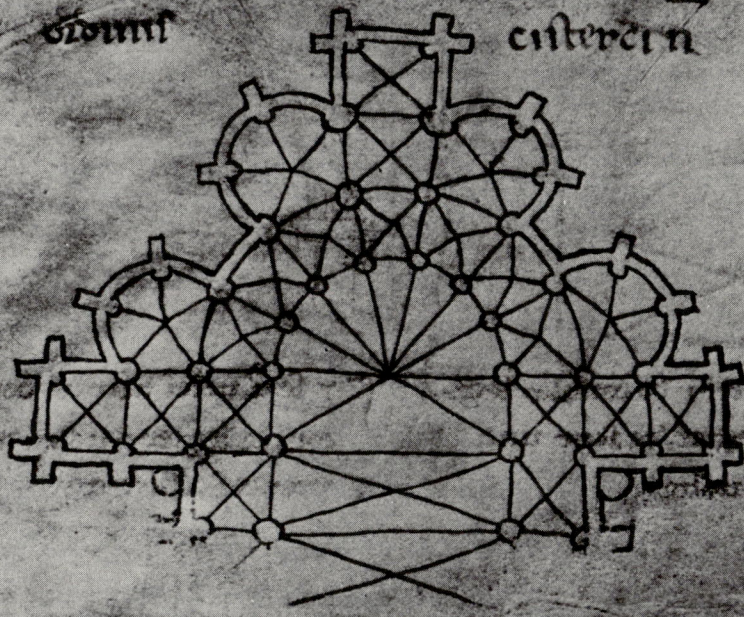

Ce eſt un ımaıe deın ſıenme ıl eſt theus.

VILLARD DE HONNECOURT

V34   Roof Trusses and a Storm Lantern

V34a   "Now you may see a light roof truss (which) fits over a vaulted chapel." This is the only surviving page of a chapter which dealt with carpentry. The drawings are rapid notations which stress joints and dowelling. The obvious, such as wall plates and purlins are left out. The first roof truss with an elevated tie beam was supposed to fit snugly over the vault, thereby lowering the height of the roof. A similar construction exists over the transept of Pontigny. The semicircle below seems to be form work, supported by two full width diagonal beams which would offer a practical solution for small spans. A measuring cord used to establish the curvature of the vault is seen at the bottom.

V34b   "If you wish to see a good light roof (for) a wooden vault, then take heed." This is an excellent saddleback roof with arched braces which will accommodate a vault. H mentions examples in Sainte Marie des Anglais near Lisieux, the wooden vault of Montiér-en-Der, and Rouen Cathedral dated before 1240. According to Deneux the dovetail joints disappear after that date.

V34c   "Observe the trussing of a strong side aisle." Villard surely meant a strong truss which the drawing does not seem to show, for the hammerbeam is not braced. H therefore assumes that the rectangle attached to the beam at the left represents a plate resting on the vault itself.

V34d   "Observe a lamp good for monks, who (want to) carry their lit candles. You can make one if you know how to turn." This is not a turning light (Bowie) but a wooden storm lantern doubling as a heating device which was turned on a lathe. These lanterns were usually made of copper.
    Between V34–35 a fragment of a leaf shows drapery, leaf ornaments or parts of an angel's wing.

H 81–84, Nn. 43–44, ills. 2 and p. 360, the Wimperti Church in Quedlinburg with a 13th century truss and a wooden vault. Matthies 1976.

Or poes veir · i · bõ conble legr
por herbegier de seur une
chapele auolre

Se vu voles veir · i · bon
conble legier auolre de fust
prendes a luer gars

Vesci une esconse q̃ bone
est amones por los candelles
porter argans · faire le pos
se il faues torner

Vesci le carpenterie
dune fort acainte ·

VILLARD DE HONNECOURT

V35   Head of St. Peter (?), Figures defined by Geometry.

"Here begins the treatise on drawing." Inscription by M2, in fact a correction of Villard's misplaced text on V36.

V35a   Bearded Head

Very likely the head of St. Peter of 1220-25 in the north transept at Reims. According to Panofsky, it may itself be derived from a portrait of Antoninus Pius.

V35b   Mary with Child

Shows a typical, forced geometrization consisting of a square and four triangles.

V35c   Stag

Unsystematic geometrization derived from a bestiary.

V35d   Two Standing Nudes

The two figures were first drawn in silverpoint and the two interlocking triangles were adaptively imposed upon them.

V35e   Ruler with Lily Sceptre

Based on a 1:2 triangle, cf. with figure on V31.

V35f   Thresher

The bend of the body is controlled by two interlocked triangles which reappear in the man with a scythe on V37. Some of the figures were used for Zodiac representations. The inscription which refers to a section on drawing submitted to geometric principles underlying the human figure is discussed in the introduction.

H 84-88, N. 46, ills. 127-32, and p. 361. Panofsky 1960, vol. 2, figs. 35, 36.

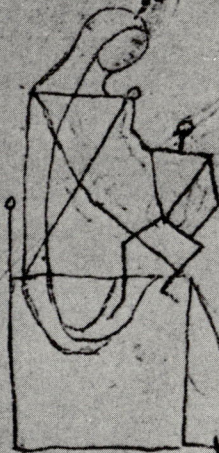

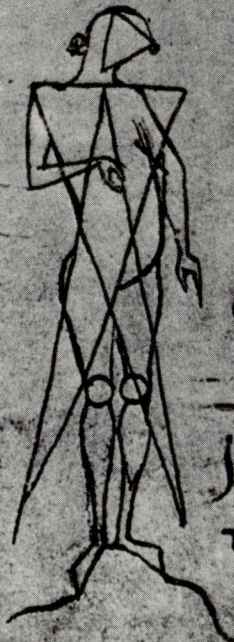

Ou commence le mare de la portraiture

Incipit materia pictuature

VILLARD DE HONNECOURT

V36   Geometric Discipline for Figures

"Here begins the art of the lines (methods?) of drawing as taught by the discipline of geometry which facilitates work. And on another leaf are those (principles) of masonry." M2 summarized and shifted this statement to V35. The page contains the ideograph of a castle with a portal whose gable is determined by a pentagram. Its proportions from the base of the arch to the horizontal roof line are identical with those of the arch and cornice of the tabernacle on V18 under which also appears a pentagram. The rectangles, triangles and half circles inscribed in, or grafted on the profile heads of a horse, a man, a jumping dog, a gloved hand and a sheep are doubtful superimpositions, as is the square with unequal thirds defining the upper female face. The male face in a circle is subdivided into nearly equal thirds: top of the head, eyebrows, lips, chin. The upper bearded face contains a pentagram, the lower male face two interlocked triangles. In each of these three cases, the geometric construction defines major points or intersections. The "stretched" pentagram in the heraldic eagle and the intersecting circles defining the necks of the ostriches complete the experimental geometrization of figurative designs which must be paralleled with a search for the Gothic architectural canon. In the end they must also be placed within the classical tradition transmitted by, among others, Boethius.

H 88–93, N. 46, ills. 101–106, 111–122. Panofsky 1955, 55–107.

Ci comence li force des trais de portraiture si con li ars de jometrie les ensaigne por legierement ourer. Et en laure fuel sont cil dele machonerie.

VILLARD DE HONNECOURT

V37   Silverpoint Sketches of Figures, Animals and Plants

Seven figures including the double lioness are constructed with the help of triangles. The top figure at the left was to be doubled. The man with the scythe is constructed like the thresher on V35 and the man who stands with his arms akimbo follows the system developed for the two bottom figures on V3. The armed man in the top row contains fine measurement lines which show that the diameter of the head, when doubled, establishes the width of the shoulders. Further, the same distance projected vertically down gives the location of the navel. The man with his arms akimbo represents Villard's main and most precise figural schema: the figure is seven heads tall, his shoulders two heads wide. The upper and lower triangles are three heads high and cross at the crotch. The schema does not allow for a neck which Villard tried to gloss over by stretching the two lines connecting the base of the lower triangle with the Adam's apple. The trumpeteers, useful for stalls and other decorative reliefs, are accurately based on a pentagram. The wrestlers at the right conform to three segments of circles, seemingly chosen as an afterthought, and are less tightly controlled than the wrestlers on V28. The quadrature superimposed upon the wrestlers at the left is a fascinating and useless transfer of an architectural principle upon figures, and speaks for Villard's architectural conceptualization. The geometry underlying the seated Virgin makes little sense. The pentagram in a leaf and the six lines in a simplified flower may be taken as mnemotechnical aids. The same is true for the kneeling figure of one of the Magi(?) top right, and the heraldic, riding knight below which prepare the viewer for the much more sophisticated and dynamic rotational games on V38. H points out that the riding knight appears in seals and a floor tile from St. Omer. The figures are all purpose figural patterns which can be integrated into secular, symbolic and religious contexts.

H 93-7, Nn. 46, ills. 110, 123-39, 144-46.

VILLARD DE HONNECOURT

V38 Overlap Figures, Facial Proportions, Pattern Figures

"On these pages are figures (taken) from the art of geometry. But to know them one must exercise great care, so that one may know the specific use of each." This leaf consists of very rough, probably reused parchment, and concludes the somewhat artificial "chapter" on figural geometry. The two figures at the bottom were drawn with reddish brown ink and were added as conclusive examples. The helmeted head and the boar are only tangentially involved with geometry. The triple fish sharing one head is most commonly found on Cistercian stalls and in marginalia where many other pictorial games uniting several bodies with one head are found. The three remaining figures are more relevant since they show the transfer of the quadrature, the rotation of a succession of inscribed squares from architecture to figural art. The kneeling masons sculpting their opposite (?) number's foot are determined by four squares in rotation, beginning with an outer square defined by the knobs on the leather caps (see fig. 25). A similar grid pattern—with the outermost square missing—determines the main axes and knee joints of the fighters at the lower left of the page. The most portentous drawing shows a face under a grid of 16 squares. The face could be constructed through the use of the four equal vertical and horizontal segments. The square angled at 45° could be said to provide a very rough positioning of the head. More importantly it shows an increasingly canonical approach to precise figurative geometry which is carried over, we believe, from architectural design methods. We are witnessing the slow crystallization of a unified design theory. After antiquity Villard is among the first to systematize these interrelationships which lived on into the Renaissance. Roriczer's finials, Hans Hösch's *Geometria Deutsch* of 1472 and other architectural treatises must be seen in common with Erhard Schoen's *Unterweisung* of 1538–42, and with the theories of Ghiberti and even Juan de Arfe y Villafane's *Commensuracion* of 1558, which covers architectural and body geometry.

H 97–104, Nn. 47–48, ills. 100, 100a, 119–22, 147–54, with the overlap figures from Maggenau, Heiligenkreuz and especially a warrior pursuing himself in a stall from the Trinity Church in Vendôme. Schoen 1542. See also V37.

en ces · iiii · fuelles adestfigures de
lart de romerrie · mais al conoistre
conuent auoir grãt esgart kl sauoir
uelt de ǫ cascune doit ouirer

V39   Problems in Architectural Geometry, Surveying and Engineering

The drawings are analyzed horizontally from left to right. H attributes the page to M2. I believe that Villard and the second master cooperated closely on this and the two subsequent pages. This is corroborated by Villard's drawings on the bottom half of V40 which follow those of M2 in the top half.

V39   "In this manner one determines the thickness of a column which is only partly visible." An open divider is held to the shaft and a stick centered between the legs touches the column as well. The three points are transferred on a surface, and one can determine the radius as shown on the next sketch.

V39   "In this manner one finds the center of a circle through a segment." By using a segment of a circle one finds its center by connecting the three equidistant points, bisecting the two lines, and drawing two lines at right angles from the half points to the center. This and other statements would be difficult to understand by anyone else but masons. The search for the center of a circle remained a standard problem and reappears in Hösch, Roriczer, Dürer and even Lautensack in 1618.

V39   "This drawing was misunderstood because *molle* which reappears in the bottom inscriptions of V63 was translated as "model" instead of "profile." Meant is a six foot arch with a three part moulding. The template—lined up with the center—serves to continuously check the widths and depths of the mouldings.

V39   "In this manner one vaults an arch centered toward the sky." The irregular "voussoirs" may represent wooden centering boards. The template calibrates the thickness of the vault.

V39   "In this manner one makes an apse with 12 glazed windows." The six dots were multiplied by two. Actually they add up to four double and one triple lancet on a wider axial wall, or a total of eleven windows.

V39   "In this manner one cuts the springer of an arch." The term used is "erracenement" or "rooting." The first voussoir is turned upside down and checked with a voussoir square which is a permanent template calibrated for a certain number of voussoirs and a specific arch type (see fig. 26). The upper, long edge of the square gives the angle of the upper joint, the short side should correspond to the height of the intrados. The tapered edge or voussoir square works only for special cases and was almost completely disregarded in late Gothic architecture. Had it worked it would have facilitated work considerably.

V39   The text of the center drawing belongs at the left: "Thus one cuts voussoirs from round masonry." We deal with four voussoirs. The triangular pieces obtained with a saw then have to be cut back to the small intersecting lines. The "hole" and the star may indicate imperfections in the stone.

V39   The text at the left refers to the center drawing: "Thus one brings together two stones in one point if they are not too far apart." To place a keystone completing an arch under construction one has to check the levels and to determine the widths, heights and angles of the opening. Assuming that the keystone is shaped like a wide funnel, it can be placed from the top. If it fills the whole thickness of the arch or vault it must be shifted into place along a horizontal axis, which would establish it immovably.

Continued on p. 120

ar chu trouom le point en mi on canpe a conpas

ar chu tailom le mole don grant arc de dens iiii. pies de tere

ar chu fait om on cauece a xii. uesrires

par cu prent om la grosse done colonbe que on ne uoit mie tote

ar chu uosom une arc le centreel de uers le ciel

ar chu tailom erracenmens

ar chu fait om cheirdeus pires a un point si lons neseront

ar chu tailom uosure destor de machonerie won de

ar chu tailom uosure belloge

ar chu fait om on point de tor one ajue de fus de xx. pies s lonc

ar chu fait om on clostre autretant el uoies com el pra es

ar chu prent om la lagece done ajue sens paseir

prent om ... ar chu la largece done senestre ki est lonc

ar chu assier om un esent bon clostre sens plonc es sens liuel

ar chu partis om ona pire que les ii. moities sont greies

ar chu tor tom le uis don persoir

ar chu fait om ii. uasias que li ontient ii. tant que li arre

ar chu tailom uosure riulere

totel cel figures sunt estraites de geometrie

VILLARD DE HONNECOURT

Continued from p. 118

V39   "In such a way one cuts an oblique voussoir." We agree with Willis and Lassus who see the drawing as an oblique opening, often used in fortifications. The angle is determined by a 3:4 right triangle, checked by means of a voussoir square. The difficulties of carving a keystone with oblique faces has been exaggerated. One cuts a stone which is a parallelogram in plan, adjusts the faces, cuts two planes along the centerline and chisels out the arch which is checked with a template.

V39   "In such a way one makes a bridge over water from 20 foot long beams." Villard's youth on the Escaut river certainly awakened his interest in bridges. The 40 foot (?) span as reconstructed by Viollet-le-Duc (H. ill. 83) seems inefficient since the truss work would tend to pull away from the ashlar anchors on both sides. This would happen to a lesser degree if the construction followed the design of the right side. The two vertical loops represent wood or stone arches.

V39   "In such a way one makes the galleries and the garden of a cloister." This fundamental drawing shows the practical use of the rotation of the square. The inner square consisting of half the surface of the outer square was first inscribed into the outer square at an angle of 45°, then turned back 22½°. See fig. 1b in introduction.

V39   "In such a way one measures the width of a course of water without crossing it." This problem of triangulation was important for bridge building and warfare and is reiterated on V40k and V44b. One moves two sticks on parallel connectors sighting a post on the opposite bank and fixes them in position. According to Vitruvius, Gerbert of Aurillac and the early geometricists one can calculate the distance mathematically, or more simply by turning the trapezoid around and sighting the distance along two converging strings. Dürer and others suggested the same method based on Africanus, but insisted on a 90° angle on one side of the trapezoid. A more precise method was developed circa 400 A.D. by Nipsus and Africanus. It consists of a wide base for a triangle on one side of a river, the sighting of a point on the other side from the left side of the base, and alignment with the point on the right side of the base. In this way one obtains a visual triangle which is flipped over 180° and reproduced on the ground (see fig. 27).

V39   "In this manner one measures the width of a distant window." The boards of the graphometer are reversed, the two outer edges are lined up at right angles with the jambs of the windows. Similarly a distance can be transferred across a river or a moat. The method is unreliable since it depends on distance. The further away it is, the more inaccurate the results.

V39   "In this manner one determines the 4 corners of a cloister without plumb line and without a level." This is the classic method for the layout of a square or rectangle with the help of four movable posts or stones shown as dots. One side is laid out, then the others are approximated. The diagonals are then measured and must be identical in order to produce right angles. The added but unnecessary control is a check on the central intersection of the cords, which for a square, must result in four right angles.

V39   "In this way one partitions a stone so that its two halves are square." It is an expensive way to produce two stones of equal shape and surface. In fact, this is the practical explanation for the geometric result of the rotation of inscribed squares. The pythagorean theorem already used by Vitruvius simply states that a square inscribed at a 45° angle into a larger square contains one half the surface of the original square (see fig. 1b in Introduction). A full understanding of this principle is basic for the perception of Gothic architecture. But it would be impractical to cut a square stone by shaving off four outer triangles.

V39   "How to turn (on a lathe) the screw of a press." This is a stereometric problem applied to a wooden cylinder. Three strings, one of which is shown at the right, are attached to equidistant points of the cylinder. They are then wound around it forming three spirals. Next the diagonally notched board would be drawn along the triple thread to produce equidistant threading. The string can be glued to the cylinder, or lines can be incised along their paths and the turning or cutting can begin. The same technique was used into the seventeenth century. Wooden screws were used for many purposes, among them wine presses—one of which is illustrated in Rixner's sketchbook— or hoists such as the large jack shown by Villard on V44.

V39 "In this manner one makes 2 vessels, of which one holds 2 times (the content of) the other." This is a mathematical *exemplum* from Euclid presupposing cylindrical vessels of the same height. The inner circle is determined by a square inscribed in the outer circle. The same doubling of mass is achieved through the rotation of the square shown in the illustration of the partitioning of a stone V390. Ueberwasser suggests that this method was useful for tapering of piers. Dürer used it for the construction of a capital in 1508 (London, Brit. Mus. Add. Ms. 5229 fol. 155 b) and by Alberti and Juan de Arfe y Villafane as late as 1585.

V39 "In this manner one carves a regular voussoir." Two voussoirs, probably for two arches with differing radii but with the same intrados height are placed upside down below a cord. The drawing at the left repeats sketch h (second row, center) on the same page.

V39 "All these figures are extracted from geometry." Other pages equally rich with information are V40, V41 and V38.

H 104-114, Nn. 49-56 and ills. 83, 91-99.

Several interpretations of the drawings herein and on the next two pages, we challenged. See Branner 1957, Bucher 1968, Lassus 1885-68, Ueberwasser 1939, Velte 1951, Viollet-le-Duc 1858-68 and Willis 1859. For architects' squares see Gerstenberg *Die deutschen Baumeisterbildnisse des Mittelalters,* Berlin 1966.

V40   The Practical Use of Angles, Spiral, Surveying of Heights

At one time this page contained five drawings in the top row. They included a pentagon, a badly drawn spiral under the present one, and a pentagon under the cross of the spire. They have been studied by H (ill. 199), Branner (JSAH 1960) and by the author. Except for the top row and the retouching of the two drawings at the left in the second row, I believe all sketches are Villard's. The comments were written by M2, almost certainly in Villard's presence. The drawings are analyzed horizontally from left to right, top to bottom.

V40   "In this manner one cuts regular pendants. Place it upside down." Hinker and H (N. 57b) assume that Villard deals with a webbing stone for a vault which had to be carved rapidly and adjustably.   Since the intersecting lines are not parallel with the sides we tentatively assume that the internal lines determine the angle of the joints of the adjoining stones.

V40   "Thus you encase (take into) a round shaft with a square and you will obtain its thickness (diameter)." The short side of a square whose long side rests against the wall allows for a reading of the diameter, preferably with the help of another square or a plumb bob.

V40   "In this manner one makes a keystone of a tiers-point (arch and) determines an angle." The arc of the semicircle must be halved, and the half point connected with the center. One thus obtains a quarter circle with a right angle at the center. A simpler way to achieve the same result is shown in our fig. 28. It shows that when the intersection of any two equal arcs which have their centers at the outer points of the diameter connects with the center of the circle, it creates a right angle. The "tjirc"—today tierce or tiers-point arch—was a common Gothic term and is used for an arch whose base line is divided into equal thirds. The points at the thirds serve as centers for two arcs whose midpoints form ample pointed arches. The second drawing shows a keystone in the proportion 1:3 which would complete such an arch. The small horizontal lines probably stand for 1:3 (fig. 29).

V40   "In this manner one cuts a keystone of the fifth point (arch)." Still called a "quint point" arch, we can obtain this slightly more pointed arch by dividing the baseline into equal quarters, thus obtaining five points. The arcs are swung from the second and third points and produce the *quinto acuto* still used by Giovanni Gherardo da Prato, Ghiberti and Brunelleschi. The four small horizontal lines indicate the 1:4 proportion of the triangular keystone (fig. 29).

V40   Spiral of Archimedes. This is not a true spiral but an easily constructed alternative. First the diameter of a semicircle is extended to form a long line. The diameter of the half circle then serves as the radius of an adjoining half circle whose center lies in the lower intersection of the original half circle with the now extended diameter line. The original center of the first half circle is used for the next adjoining half circle swung to the right of the center line, etc. (fig. 30). Other possibilities to construct a "spiral" consisting of a sequence of semicircles and based on a tracing on a capital at Chartres have been published by Branner and Cox, are summarized in H's ills. 201-205 (see fig. 1e in introduction).

V40   "In this manner one makes a square pier with good joints". The drawing clarifies the use of odd shaped stones joined together to form a square pier. The joints of the next course have to be turned 45° to assure the stability of the masonry.

V40   "In this manner one cuts a voussoir according to scale." Two diagonals with scales, the upper in relation to the lower in a proportion of 4:3 serve to establish fanlike lines which could determine the extrados and intrados of the voussoir. If this is so, the drawing lacks precision.

Continued on p. 124

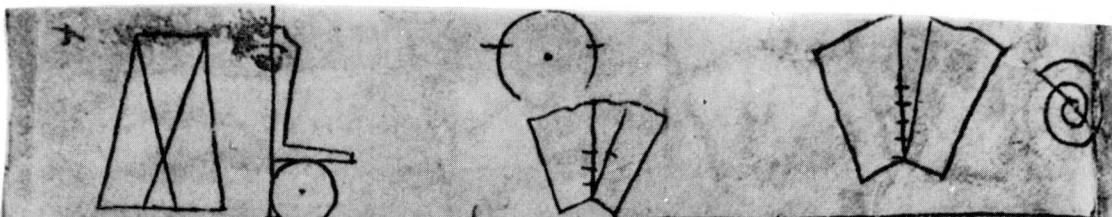

Par chu tail on peu
dant riules mete
le bas el haut.

Ensi prendes one
roonde en on
agle sen arefle
are

Par chu fait on one
clef del tirc rriusti
ce one scere.

Par chu tail on one
clef del quint point

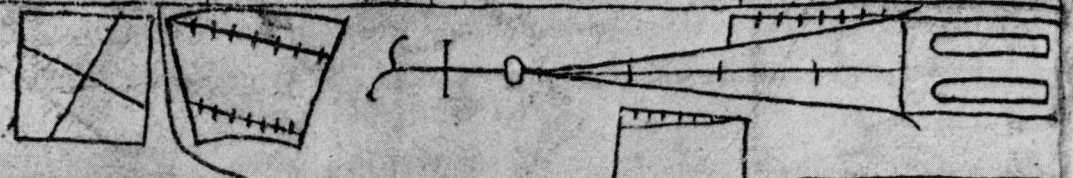

Par chu fait on on pi
ler de quatre cuins
venir aloisson

par chu tail on uolous
par escandelon

Par ceste raison montom laguile
done roor r taille les moles.

Par chu tail om
uosure pen
dant

Pa chu prn
tom le haute
ce done roor

Par chu montom
dous pilers done
hautece sens plom r sens liuel

V40   "By this method one raises a spire of a tower (and) cuts the templates." The method arrives at the height and tapering angle of a spire by multiplying the base line by four and using a triangular 1:8 template. An alternate 1:7 (?) template is shown below.

V40   "In this manner one cuts the voussoir of a hanging arch (pendant)." Constructively the two arches actually form a single arch with a "hanging" keystone which is temporarily supported by a small, truncated tree trunk. The angles of the joints are determined with a string fixed to a nail halfway between the ground and the crown of the wall. The formwork is not shown and was presumably in the section on carpentry. A similar double arch without a capital appears in Lausanne (Biaudet, 1975, V96).

V40   "In this manner one measures the height of a tower". The information is needed for scaffold construction and for military purposes. The hypotenuse of a right triangle is aimed at the top of the tower, the cosine at the base. The height of the measuring device must be subtracted from the result as indicated by a line connecting it with the tower. Triangulation was used from the time of Vitruvius to Dürer and reached the Middle Ages through the tracts of the Roman surveyors or *Agrimensores,* the *Geometria incerti auctoris* of Gerbert of Aurillac who became Pope Sylvester II and Arab mathematicians. H stresses the solution of Epaphroditus Rufus found in the Wolfenbüttel *Gromatici Veteres* which stems from the sixth or seventh century and is closely related to the method used by Villard, as is a text of 1160-68 found in a *Practica Geometriae* from Prüfening, now in Munich, State Libr. Hs. Clm. 13021.

V40   "In this manner one erects pillars of the same height without plumb line or level." A hinged post located at the half point between the columns touches the top of the column at the left and is swung over to check the height of the column at the right.

The discarded figures in palimpsest were the following: Sketches of voussoirs in draft form. A spiral turning counter clockwise. The second row contained an experimental construction of a pentagon which may be related to the plan of the tower which reappears on V41. The idea for the construction was based on a 22½° rotation of a square within a circle, but was unsuccessful and therefore erased. For a satisfactory solution see Roriczer's *Geometria* which is to follow.

H 114-21, Nn. 57-60, ills. 88-90, 92, 196-205 pp. 366-68. R. Branner, Villard de Honnecourt, Archimedes and Chartres, JSAH 19, 1960, 91-96 with response of L. Cox JSAH 20, 1961.

V41   Star Vault, Trajectory, Pentagram, Construction Procedures

The drawings are by Villard, the inscriptions probably by M2. The drawings are analyzed horizontally left to right, top to bottom (see illustration p. 127).

V41   "In this manner one constructs the capitals of eight columns with a single one, it is by no means that complicated, this is good masonry." A typical, somewhat hesitant mason's statement which an educated observer could have expressed more elegantly: In this manner one vaults a square room lightly by connecting eight bosses to a single central column. Within the development of rib systems from quadri- and sexpartite designs to more complex solutions this sketch is basic. The star vault with eight bosses, engaged wall shafts and a single central column was probably destined for a sacristy or a small chapter house, or even a baldachin. The vault can be compared with Candes, or the Toussaint church at Angers of circa 1232-35, both of which have quadripartite vaults centered on columns, but no star vaults. If there is a true architectural stroke of genius in the manuscript, it lies in the inclusion or invention of this vault which goes along with early English experiments such as Lincoln, in which the rib was used simultaneously as a support and as an ornament. (See our discussion of vaults in our treatment of WG's sketchbook below). In contrast to the formidable English experiments, Villard's vault was probably for a very small structure, if we assume the measuring board to be an indication of scale. The same boards appear in surveying sketches on V39 and 41, and would probably not have measured more than six feet.

V41   "In such a manner one places an egg under a pear so that through measurement, the pear falls on the egg." The fact that M2 understood the drawing proves that it was either a current mathematical *exemplum*, possibly derived from Hugh of St. Victor's (†1141) *Eruditionis Didascalion,* vol. 2 chapter 14, or that M2 followed Villard's instructions regarding vertical projection. Two measuring rods or surveyor's boards are placed in the same plane with the pear and a line is then scratched into the ground. The system is then turned 90°, lined up with the pear once more and an egg (erased) is placed on the crossing point of the two lines. The projection game could have been used for the erection of scaffolding against a crumbling wall from which no plumb bob could be lowered. But it seems more likely that it was used as a trick to impress a patron, if not an example of erudition.

V41   "In this manner one traces a tower with 5 buttresses (arestes)." This drawing repeats the erased sketch at V40g. Villard tries to construct a pentagon through multiple 22½° rotations of a square. A series of steps can establish an approximate regular pentagon through the quadrature, but the method is not as clean as Roriczer's construction on p. 3 of the *"Geometria"* shown below.

V41   "In this manner one finds the points (centers) of a cut voussoir." Villard means the center of the vault which is established by two strings which prolong the joints downward. The method is also used in V40i, and perhaps in the bottom row of V39.

V41   "In this manner one gives the voussoir its form without (a) template." This badly understood drawing seems to deal once more with a keystone as derived from two voussoirs. The width is indicated by the two small lines at the top, the angle might then be determined by a template.

V41   "In this manner one bevels (bevum) the oblique springing stone for one (each?) member without a template." This misunderstood drawing simply shows a "negative" template, that is a board with a profiled hole which one can slide along curving parts, mindful of continued radial precision.

V41 "In this manner one cuts a kneeling voussoir." The misunderstood "engenolie" refers to the lopsided, asymmetrical template. Anthropomorphic terms and designations taken from nature abound in masonry language. The top of a finial was and still is called "Ries" or giant, a roof truss *forêt* or forest.

V41 "In this manner one makes three kinds of arches with one compass opening." This simple sketch shows a semicircular tiers point and two point arch, into which one can of course inscribe an equilateral triangle (See fig. 29). To increase visual clarity the top two point arch at the right was erased. The dots may fix a 3:7 proportion.

H 121-127, Nn. 61-63, 89, ills. 200, p. 369. Angers Chanoine Urseau, Ancienne eglise Tousaint, *Congres Archéologique de France*, 77 Paris 1911, 222-25. Didascalion: *Patrologia Latina*, vol. 177, col 757 L.R. Shelby, Medieval Masons Templates, *JSAH*, vol. 30, 1971, 140-54.

chu

Pa chu met om on capitel diut colon
bes a one sole. seu nest mjes si en con
bres fest li machonerie bone

Par met om on oef des sos one
poire par mesure. que li poire
chice soz luef

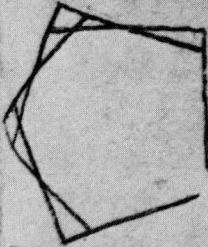

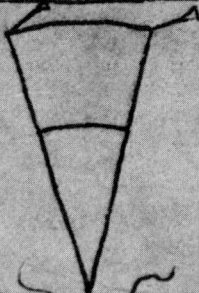

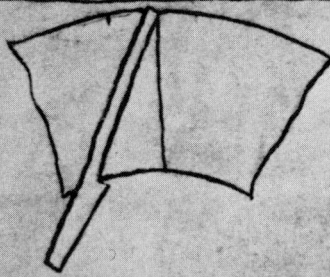

Par chu portrait om one
tooz achine arestes

Par chu tro
nom les poius
done uosure taillie.

Par chu do nom on
uosoir se turneie. sens
molle

Par chu beuum erracement
sagiis sens molle. par on
membre

Pa chu tail om uosu
re engenolie

Par chu fait om
trois matures
dart a conpas
ourir one foiz

VILLARD DE HONNECOURT

V42 The Wheel of Fortune, Recipes for Waterproofing and Hair Removal

"See here 2 heads of leaves." This inscription refers to V43.

"Here below are the figures of the wheel of fortune, all 7 images." The six states of fortune, usually from king to beggar are transformed here into an enthroned and fallen king with a broken sceptre. This iconographically full schema with *Fortuna* again as a seated royal figure, her feet balanced on the fickle sphere, can be compared with representations in manuscripts and more significantly with large executions in relief. A huge wheel adorns the north transept of the cathedral in Trento, others are in St. Etienne, Beauvais and the Basel minster. In addition machines existed which imitated the changing human fortunes. One of these was in Fécamp and is described around 1100 A.D. by bishop Baldricus from Dôle. Brunetto gives the six texts of an identical allegory with a king who states: *Sum sine regno, spes, regno, regnabo, timor, regnavi, dolor.*

"One takes lime (and) ground up Roman tile, you will take of the one about as much as of the other, a little more of Roman tile so that its color may overshadow the others. Soak this cement with linseed oil, then you can make a vessel to hold water." This inscription by M3 describes a mixture which hardens into a tough, cementlike substance which could be used for wells or cellar floors.

"One takes quicklime (and) mixes it with sulfuric arsenic (orpieument), lays it into boiling water (and) oil. This ointment is good for the removal of hair." M3. Medieval recipes are found in many treatises from Theophilus Presbyter to Cennino Cennini. Another recipe using cannabis appears in Villard's manuscript V65. Amazingly, a recipe for hair treatment also appears in Rixner's sketchbook, and will be discussed below.

H 127-30, N. 64. For watertight floors see Bucher 1957, p. 97, n. 3.

Ves la .ij. vesvel de fueilles.

Vesci desos les figures de le rvee d'
fortune. totes les .vij. imagenes.

On prent kaus z theule muliie de paieus. z fetesrume. autre tant
del une cu del autre. z un poi pluis del theule de paieus. taunt come
ses color uainke les autres. destemprez ce ement doile de limuse-
sen poez faire un uassel pur euge tenir.
Ou prent unie kaus bolere z orpieument se letner on en euge bol-
lans z oile.   Cist unnemens est bon por pail ostier.

V43   Leaf-Heads, Seated and Standing Male Nudes

The seated male nude is very likely based on a Roman statue, perhaps a bronze. In contrast to the dressed lover on V27 the microcephalic, barrel-chested nude is made up of a multiplicity of parts. The same feeling of novelty also characterizes the standing nude with chlamys which H successfully compares with a small Alexander bronze (H ill. 139a). Seeing the difficulties with which a contrapposto is handled. one marvels at the elegant ease with which the contemporary Reims sculptors resolved their revival of a classical approach to the figure. Compared with the nude of V22, Villard seems to have become acutely aware of the existence of a classical canon.

The leaf-heads are mentioned on V42. Anthropomorphic animals and plants appear, as we stated in our discussion of V10, in manuscript drôleries, in stone and especially in wood sculpture. The transformation from a humanized leaf to a firmer, leafy head was completed on V10 where we stressed the relationship between Villard's heads and bosses found in Reims Cathedral (see fig. 6).

H 130-33, Nn. 9, 65, 92, ills. 21-26, 139-40. See also Hahnloser 1968, 255-66.

V44   Advances in Thirteenth Century Technology   *See illustration p. 133*

The drawings on this page are essential for the history of medieval technology. The drawings are by Villard, the texts were added by M2.

V44   Automatic Saw

"In this manner one makes a saw which saws by itself." In our reconstruction, (fig. 31) the undershot waterwheel, which runs in the wrong direction in Villard's drawing, is built like most surviving treadmill cranes. The axle has spikes instead of the ineffectually large, spike studded wheel of Villard. The log is thus moved more slowly toward a horizontal, or with slight changes, a vertical sawblade. Rotating fixed levers run over trip cams which draw the saw to the right, or in Villard's drawing, downward. A bent branch attached to the blade with an adjustable bolt snaps the blade back. Our sketch was kept as close as possible to Villard's design including the hefty axle which might move the tree forward too rapidly. If so, Villard's spiked wheel must have been free of the axle and could be connected to its movement by means of a board turning with the axle and a strong peg which would be slipped into a hole in the wheel which then would drive the log forward until the peg was removed. White called the saw the first industrial machine with an automatic reciprocal action. A twig applying adjustable pull was not new. It had been used by turners since antiquity and became popular once more in the mid-thirteenth century. It is the combination of elements which is extraordinary.

V44   Surveying Crossbow

"In this manner one makes an unfailing crossbow." The funnelike shape could be an aiming device or a bell target. One of the uses of the powerful weapon which had been outlawed by the Lateran Synod and an edict of Innocent III of 1139, was its function as a device to measure distances quickly and precisely. The term "ki ne fau" confirms the accuracy afforded by the string, which attached to a heavy arrow would follow its trajectory.

V44   Clockwork

"In this manner one makes an angel who always points his finger at the sun." Behind this innocent statement lies the thorniest problem of the Villard research. If an angel, who would have been affixed to the vertical axle at the right, had indeed daily followed the movement of the sun, it would have had to be driven by one of the earliest illustrated weight powered clock mechanisms with wheels. As it is, Villard's drawing would not work, for the rope is strung between two spokes of the flywheel. This would only produce a momentary forward motion before there was a brief oscillation, and a complete halt. If the flywheel as shown had been used to wind the rope around the axle on both of its sides, the two weights would have set the wheel into increasingly rapid motion and would have stopped. We have reconstructed the machine with two almost equal weights and a single, shortened rope wound around the axle of the flywheel, whose spokes it avoids (see fig. 32). The two, possibly metal, rings attached to the vertical axle and resting on the horizontal beam are friction plates which can be added or removed depending on the length of the day. The flywheel would have had to be used nightly as a winch which raised the driving weights. Figure 33 shows a simplified system without friction disks, but with a heavier flywheel. The weights were of course easily adjustable. In spite of this, the mech-

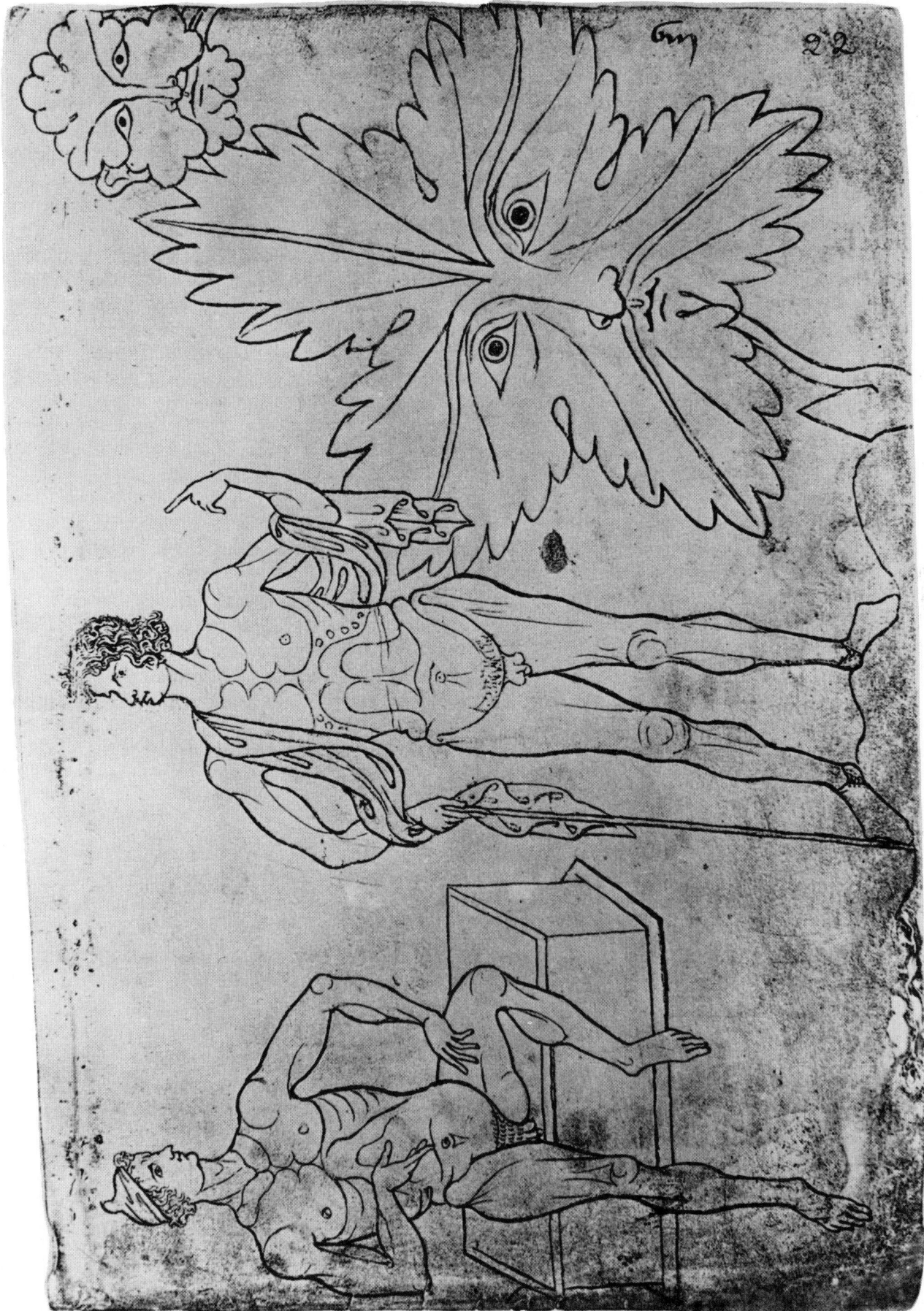

anism would have been less reliable than with an adjustable brake. The lack of any gear wheels, foliot and verge escapement clearly indicates a continued search for an accurate time measuring device. The clock housing on V12 (see fig. 7), the earlier mechanical clock of Gerbert of Aurillac (999-1023), the striking trains for bells in Canterbury (1292), Paris (1300), Salisbury (1386), the *horologium* mentioned by Hugo of Oignies after 1250, the clock of Beauvais and finally that of Strasbourg (1354) were presumably all weight driven mechanisms with *fusées*. The *fusée* was a tapered conical pulley which produced uniform torque, and may in fact explain the tapered shaft of the flywheel in Villard's drawing. It is only in the late thirteenth century and especially with Giovanni di Dondi's clock of 1348-64 that we begin to have sophisticated clocks with foliot balances, verge — and finally crown wheel escapements. One of these clocks adorns the image of Temperance in Christine de Pisan's *Epitre d'Othea* (fig. 33) of circa 1450 (Oxford, Bodleian Libr. Ms. Laud. Misc. 570 fol.28). This clock which has a foliot balance and possibly the first known and illustrated pendulum at the lower left of the housing contrasts sharply with Villard's simple mechanism. It was, after all, only the substructure of one of the robot angels which graced the roofs or towers of St. Pierre du Dorat (circa 1250), Chartres, St. Paul's London (1344), the Sainte Chapelle in Paris and the castle Mehun-sur-Yèvre. Villard's apparatus is the most important of his gadgets, and only one of the wondrous thirteenth century robots which stand in the tradition of the *Mirabilia Urbis Romae*.

V44   Hoist

"In this manner one makes one of the strongest engines there is for lifting loads." The vertical jack of very considerable size, if we assume that the levers were turned by human beings, consists of a one piece lever slipped through a hole, of a smooth axle topped by a screw, and a metal plate with iron hooks. The jack would work more efficiently upside down since it would give two men turning the screw an unobstructed radius of action. As it is the lever has to be retracted and therefore lengthened to initially bypass the load. Screw presses were well known. Another one appears in Rixner's lodge book. They are shown in many manuscripts, as well as used in construction. Gervasius of Canterbury praises a screw-driven "ingenious" hoist with which the architect William of Sens loaded and unloaded cement and stones from ships around 1175-78.

V44   Fake Automaton for Lectern

"In this manner one makes an eagle which turns its head toward the deacon when he reads the Gospels." It has been assumed that both an external and internal screw were needed to move the head of this uninspiring gadget. In fact the deacon only needed to pull the cord to turn the eagle's head to the left. Releasing the weighted rope he would have the eagle turn its head to the right. By pulling the rope back and forth, the eagle also could "follow the lines" read by the deacon from a large choir book which rested on the wings of the eagle. H mentions a lectern commissioned by Foulques, abbot of Loches in 971. This eagle would spread its wings to carry the Gospels and "artfully move its neck, as if he were listening while uttering a cry." Here we are dealing with a bellows, a whistle and a weight which presumably could move down into the body of the lectern. Villard's complex lectern on V13 doesn't seem to have contained any such mechanism. (fig. 8.)

H 133-38 Nn. 13,67-69, 101-02, 113, illus. 192, 187-89, 195. My thanks to Profs. D. Williman and B. Hansen for assistance in the interpretation of Villard's machines. Biebel 1950, 336-44. Burstall 1965, 126-32. Cardwell 1972, 12-19. Crombie, vol. 1, 210-13. Dumas 1964, vol. 2, 284-305. Ferguson, vol. 197, 827-33. Gimpel 1976, 130-131, 147-68. Schlosser 1925, 42ff. Singer 1957, vol. 3, 648-60. White, 23. Zinner 1954, 7-38, 46-71.

Burstall, *A History of Mechanical Engineering*, Cambridge, 1965.
Cardwell, D.S.L., *Turning Points in Medieval Technology*, New York, 1972.
Daumas, M., *A History of Technology*, New York, vol. 2, 1964, pp. 284-305.
   The drawings are by Villard, the texts are by M2.

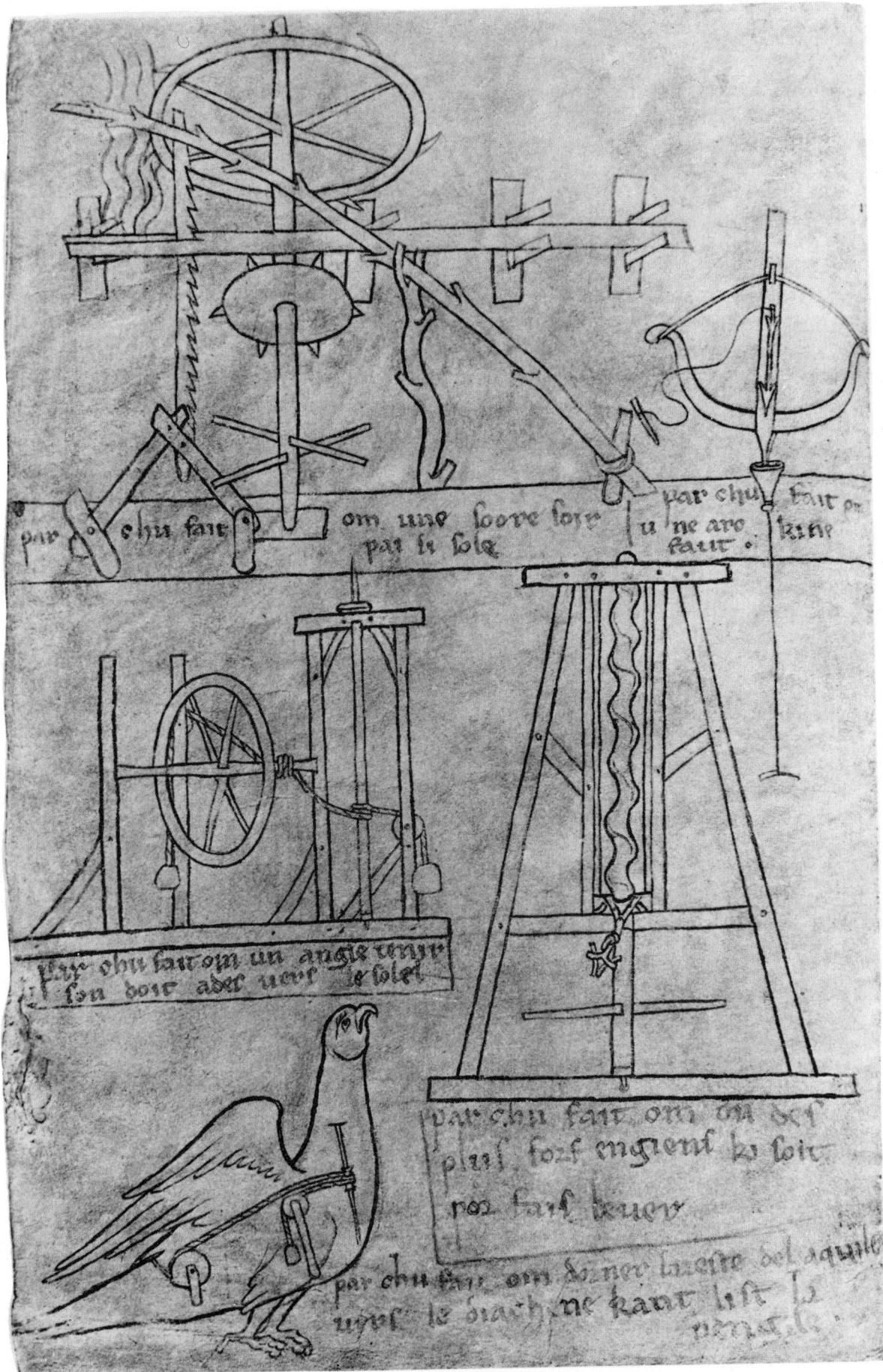

par ø chu fait · om une soore sore u ne aro par chu fait on
par li sole fait · kine

par chu fait om un augle uenir fen dois ader uenr le solel

par chu fait om on der plus fors engiens ki soit por fair leuer

par chu fait om ſonner l'aide del aquile uers le diach ne kant lift le euagile

V45   Underwater Saw

"With this engine one cuts piles in the water, so that one may lay a floor on them." The saw must have rested on a raft which was tied to a pier and which could be adjusted to changing water levels. At the same time it must have been stabilized by means of a heavy weight running over a wheel. Two men would sit on the upper beam and slide the handles secured by a sled, back and forth. The moving members pivoted around dowels affixed to the lower beam and set the horizontally cutting saw in motion. The added level at the right points to the necessity of keeping the frame vertical so that one could achieve a straight horizontal cut.

V45ʰ   Hoisting Wheel

"In this manner one braces (the spokes of) a wheel without damaging the axle." This excellent quadruple bracing system leaves only four of the twelve spokes or levers unstrengthened which makes it an efficient hoisting wheel.

V45   Bracing Apparatus

"In this manner you can build a house from timbers which are too short." One should add: to cover the required spans. The sketch which has been and still is used for mathematical games, shows what seems to be wall encased timbers joined and pegged at the corners of an open shaft. This type of construction was frequently used for a series of narrow platforms in fortification and belltowers.

V45   Tower Floor

"With a bracing device of this type you can straighten up a house sagging to one side, it will no longer lean." This eminently practical device which can also be used to dislocate walls is a simple leverage device. Figure 34 shows the movable horizontal beam in a fixed position about to be moved forward and upward with four long levers. These could be pulled by oxen. Villard typically shows the wall in cross section and switches to a view from above for the straightening device. He clearly displays four stones which served as fulcra for the vertical raising of the beam, and the way the levers are to be weighted with large stones. Similar devices could be used at other points of the wall, and finally dismantled and reused on other occasions.

H 138-140 Nn. 70, 113.

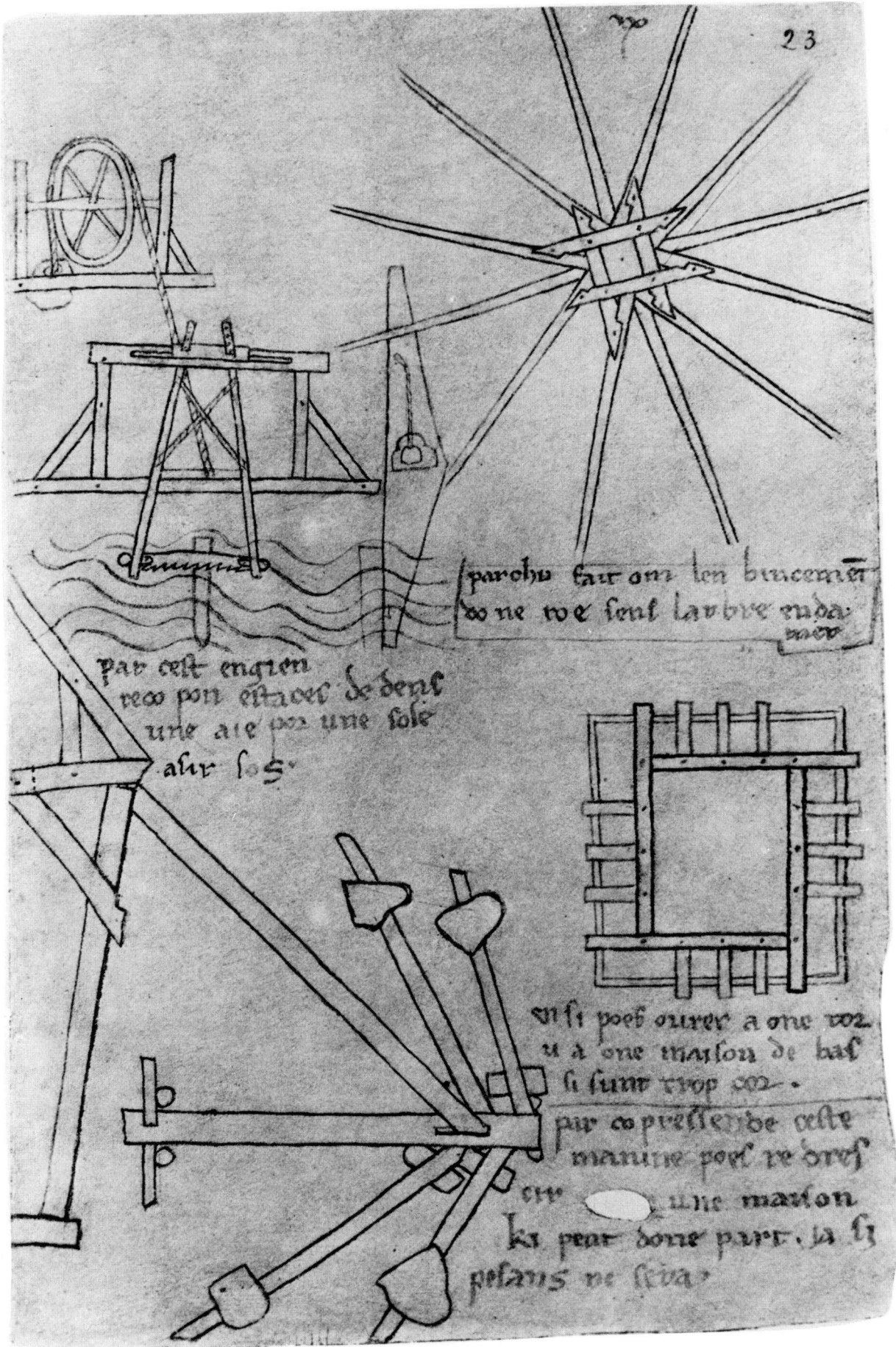

parolu fait om len bracemier
co ne woe fent laubre enda:

par cest engien
reco pon estaces de dent
une are por une sole
atir so§

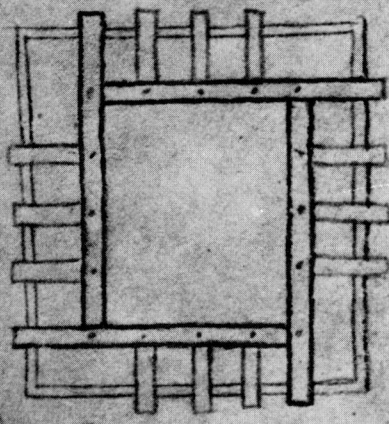

et si poes ourer a one vor
u a one maison de bas
si sunt trop vor.

par co prestende ceste
manine poes re bref
err   une maison
ki peut done part. la si
pesans ne seva

V46a Crouching Apostle

The extraordinarily powerful drawing of a crouching male, doubtlessly a sleeping apostle from the Mount of Olives scene might be derived from a Byzantine manuscript such as the late twelfth century *Hortus Deliciarum.* In his second edition H began to stress that Villard's acute interest in classical figure style did not depend exclusively on the Reims sculptures of the 1220s. The proximity of Liège, Douai, Arras, Tournai and the works emerging from the Mosan region generally were at least as influential (see fig. 16). The masterpieces of Nicolas de Verdun made around 1200, which include two-dimensional as well as exquisite three-dimensional works, the earlier classical baptismal font of Reiner of Huy of 1107-18 or the bronze figure of circa 1240 in the Peter Wilson Collection, London are echoed in Villard.s interest in small and exquisite metal objects with complex surfaces.

V46b Knight Mounting His Horse

H noted the great precision in the representation of the armour and the horse trappings. The figure demonstrates a singular lack of optical space in the handling of the legs both of the knight and of the frontally viewed horse. The lack of back legs was repeated in the lion on V48. The early thirteenth century was a time of hectic expansion and we found the same forced attempt at spatial reality in the touching adoration of the Magi in the German Berthold Missal (Morgan Library, New York, M 710) which is dated before 1232. There another blue (sic!) two legged horse seen from the back trots into a gate, while below a frontally viewed horse gallops out of a gate. In terms of the horse's size, it must be remembered that most horses of the period were smaller than today's mounts. For the erased Félibien inscription see our introduction.

H 140-43 Nn. 71-72 illus. 11, 12, 18-20, 49, 169-74. Swarzenski 1967 illus-253-58, 519-22, 547-48. F. Bucher Medieval Landscape Painting, Medieval and Renaissance Studies, 1968, p. 158, ill. 41.

V47   Lion Tamer

Large inscription: "Lion." Top: "I want to tell you of the training of the lion. He who indoctrinates a lion, he has 2 dogs. When he wants the lion to do anything, he commands him. If the lion growls, he beats his dogs; of this the lion harbours great doubt when he sees the dogs beaten, his courage wanes (refraint), he will do that which he is commanded. I won't talk about his ire, since then he will do neither right nor wrong for anyone. Note well that the lion was drawn from life." This close translation with Villard's punctuation indicates a semiconversational and semidoctrinal stance. It probably stems from one of the many bestiaries or possibly from the *Liber de naturis rerum* by Thomas of Cantimpré, canon of the neighboring Cambrai from 1217-30, whose story on lion taming reappears in Vincent de Beauvais' *Speculum Naturale,* chapter 68. They in turn were based on tales by Ambrosius of Milan (Caeditur canis ut pavescat leo), and of Egbert of Liège who died circa 1023. The story furthermore surfaces in Thomasin of Zaerclaere's *Wälsche Gast,* who, as a canon in Aquileia put it down 1215-16. This long tradition, and the other lions appearing on V48, V52-53 makes it unlikely that Villard drew the scene "al vif." The isolated lion's head with human teeth at the bottom right confirms this. However the tamer appears realistic enough, and lions as well as bears who were taught obedience in the same manner did appear on market days and at Kermesses, or were kept in zoos.

H 143-47, Nn. 73-74, 119-20. See also ills. 47, 161-66. I. Ragusa, An illustrated Psalter from Lyre Abbey, Speculum, 46, 1971.

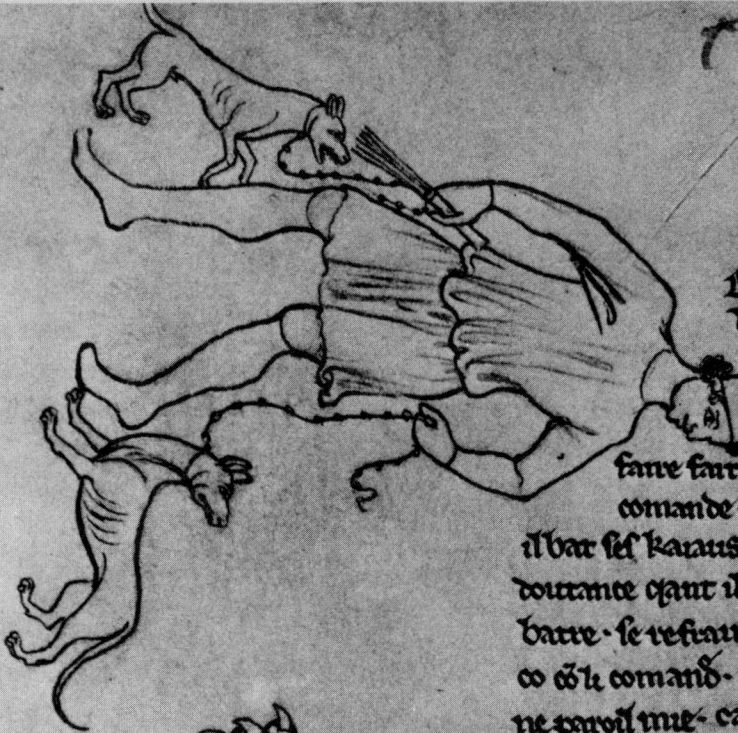

24

Deu faignement del
lion iu uel ge pleir.
Cil q̃ le lið doctrine
il a · ij · chaxaus
q̃aut il uelt lelion
faire faire aucūne coxe se li
comande · se li hons groigne
il bar ses karaus · dont a libons g̃t
dourance q̃aut il uoxt les karaus
batre · se refraint sð coxage z fait
co cõ li comand · z fil est coxecies foxco
ne paroil true · car il ne ferort por
ne lui ne toxt ne droit · z bien sacies
q̃ cis hons fu contrefais al uif.

V48a Lion

"This is a lion as one sees it from the front. Note well that it was drawn from life." This charming, somewhat fat lion possesses human eyes and teeth (see fig. 35 with permission from the Dreyfus Fund Inc.). In addition to Gothic curls it is also geometrically composed through the use of two circles in a 1:2 proportion. The upper center is indicated by a dot between the eyes. We are convinced that the lion was drawn from an aquamanile, a wine or water container in the shape of a lion. This would also explain the slightly spread, firmly implanted legs and the three digit feet resembling those found in a thirteenth century aquamanile at the Cloisters, New York.

V48b Hedgehog

"See here a hedgehog. It is a little beast that shoots its quills when it is aroused." Already Aristotle Pliny and Jerome talked about the *porcus spinosus* using its quills *sicut arma*. Others followed suit including Thomas of Cantimpré, Villard's contemporary and neighbor. Once more we must stress that the presence of animal lore is due to the great interest in zoos, bestiaries and in the analogous Christian symbolism expressed by animals. The hedgehog became, for instance, a symbol of the inviolate virginity of Mary, etc. Many of these animals in their mixed functions appear in stalls or on cathedral reliefs and in secular art. Again we doubt if the "biestelete" was drawn from nature.

H 147-50, illus. 163-66 Nn. 75. S. Ferber *Islam and the Medieval West,* Binghamton 1975 illus. 56.

V49   Seated King

Compared with the figures on V25 and V27 the king is a stately, presumably biblical figure such as Solomon judging the mothers (see V23), Herod, Joseph or an Emperor ordering a martyrdom. The face was redrawn by Villard and the right foot was enlarged.

H 150.

V50a Bearded Saint

The bearded figure is doubtlessly St. John pointing to the lamb of Christ on a sunken dish. Similar figures are found in the north portal of Chartres of circa 1205-10 and in the right door of the west portal at Reims of circa 1220. Reddish outlines of the bistre drawing were reinforced with black ink. This is one of the few figures in which the usual inept handling of the classical contrapposto is resolved. The drawing also displays Villard's orderly sketching technique and schematic face which hardened when the picture was worked over.

V50b Lancer and Archer

These are probably executioners from a martyrdom scene. The legs of the archer are turned unnaturally outward. There is overlapping and a rising horizon, but still no palpable optical space.

H 150-51. Sauerländer 1972, ills. 83, 219-20.

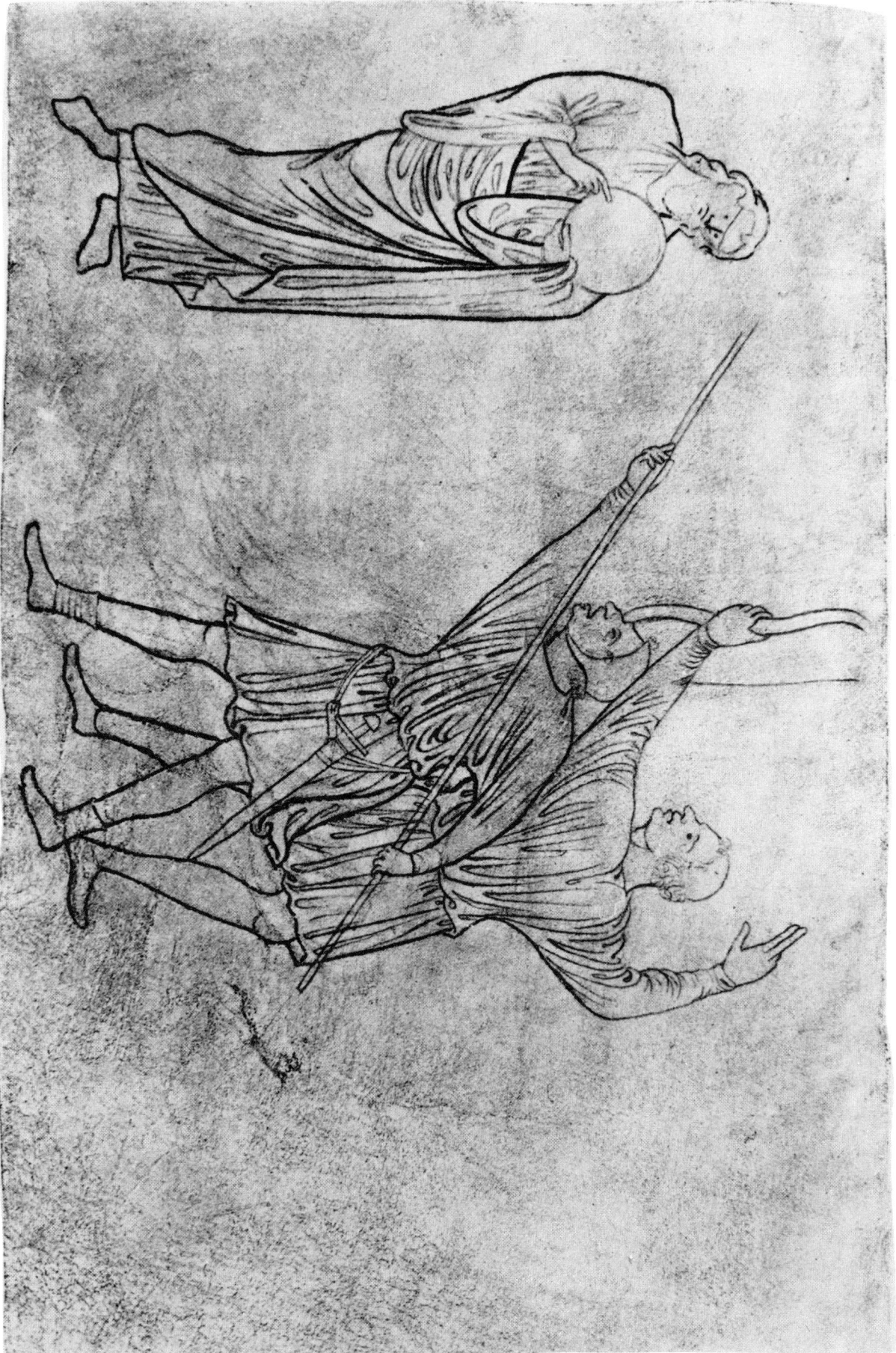

V51a Two Falcons on a Perch

Bowie sees them as parrots. The rounded, somewhat lengthened tails, the "double" wing and their set off necks characterize them as either peregrine falcons or much less likely, hawks. Many falcons are illustrated in Frederick II's *De arte venandi cum avibus* which was composed 1244-50 and is one of the foremost Western studies of birds. There they are shown frontally, dorsally and in profile on fol. 54 and 92 v of the Vatican codex.

V51b Nude Minstrel with Viol, Dancing Dogs, Lady with Falcon

The naked man plays the viol. The woman holding her right glove poses in an elegant hipshot and turns blandly towards him. The dogs are arranged symmetrically, the one at the right jumps or is a spatial mishap. The obscure iconography probably deals with a literary theme. Minstrels were usually accompanied by acrobats, animals and entertainers of all sorts. Once more we deal with a visual note useful for one of the many secular commissions, which an architect of Villard's ilk might well have courted.

H 151-52. C. E. Wood, M. Fyfe, *The Art of Falconry of Frederick II of Hohenstaufen,* Stanford, 1961, pp. 101, 113, 185, 359.

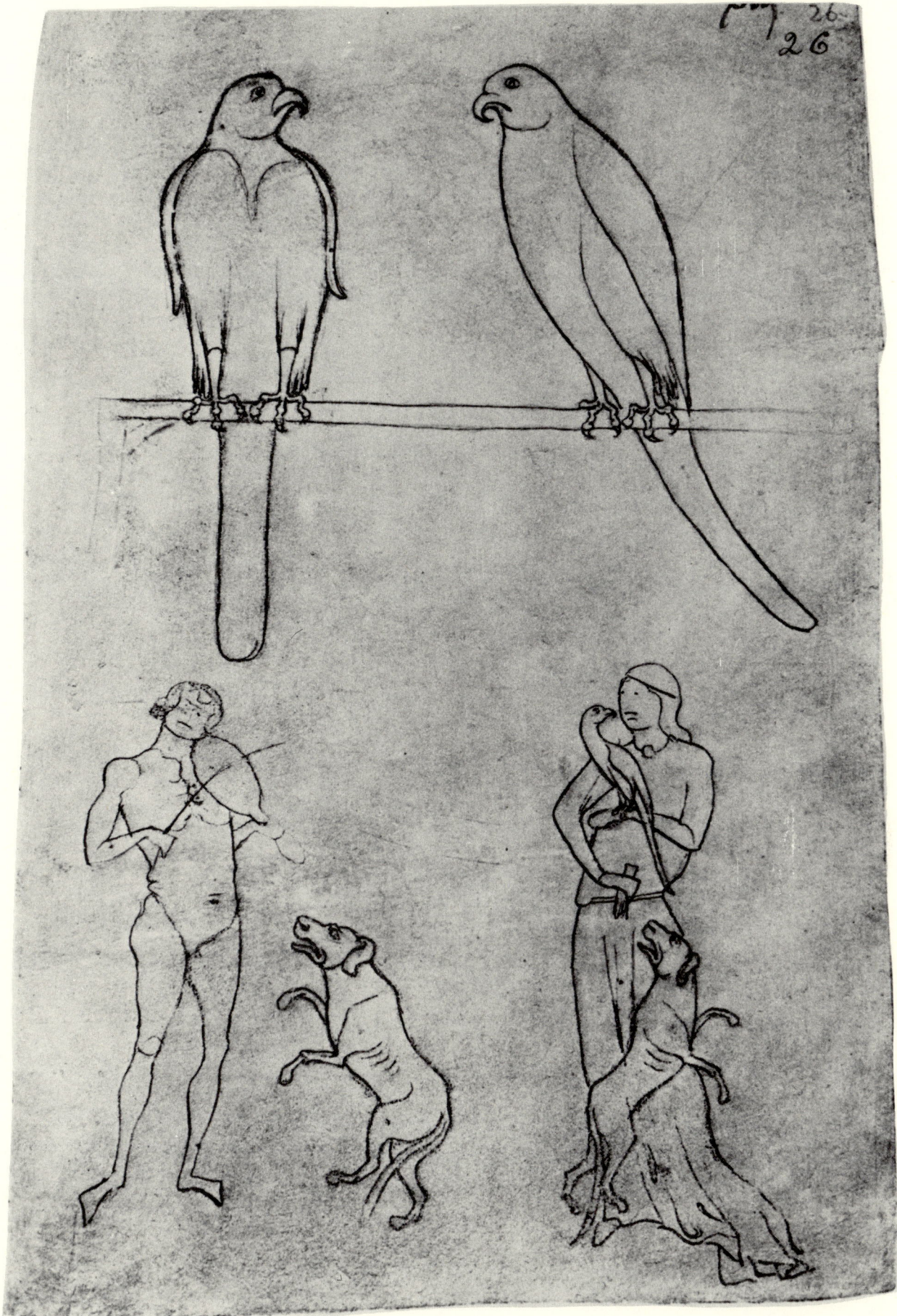

V52   Three Circus Scenes

With the top scene on V54 we are shown four extremely lively classical circus scenes of men fighting lions. Except for the medieval leather caps, the dress of the *bestiarii,* the round shield and the veiled hand are based on late Roman sources. The power of the scenes excludes marginalia and we must search for reliefs or ivories. H. illus. 157 mentions the Basilewsky Diptych in Leningrad, the Borghese mosaic and one of the Cyprus Plates dated around 600 A.D. in the Metropolitan Museum, New York. Ragusa and Swarzensky have thought of Psalter illustrations, specifically two scenes from the Psalter from Lyre Abbey of circa 1230 in the Municipal Library of Evreux (Ms. 4, fol. 132 v) which are close to Villard's sketching style but lack classical dress. An amazingly dynamic relief on the tower of Strasbourg Cathedral showing a seminude man approaching a rearing lion with a club demonstrates the continued interest in the topic. We have already pointed out Villard's archeological and historical interests which he shared with all major architects. Therefore we need not connect these scenes with Christian iconography.

H 152-53, Nn. 76, 120, illus. 155, 157-50, p. 376. Ragusa 1971.

VILLARD DE HONNECOURT

V53a   Lancer Egging on Lion

The leaf was cut at the bottom. The *bestiarius* has disregarded the veiled hand mentioned in a tale of Lysimachus and Alexander in Vincent of Beauvais' *Speculum Historiale,* who based his text on an account by the third century writer Justin. The rearing lion may presuppose a relief, possibly from a sarcophagus or in chased silver. Here we refer back to the examples listed for V52, specifically the Borghese mosaic and the Lenigrad ivory which also shows a lancer.

V53b   Martyrdom of Saints Cosmas and Damian

"See here the martyrdom of Saint(s) Cosmas and Damian." The outlines were carefully reworked by Villard in a vain attempt to improve the clumsy scene. Cosmas and Damian were revered in Paris, and more importantly, were given a chapel in Cambrai. The two Arabic doctors appear together in manuscripts and also in stained glass programs such as in Châlons-sur-Marne.

H 154-155 Nn. 76, 120, illus. 159, 22 on p. 376.

V54a Poppets for Stalls

A humble partition for a stall attached to an inclined wall. The dot indicates a peg around which the seat could be rotated upward. A 1:3 proportion was used.

V54b Christ (See V55)

"See here a light poppet for a stall with 1 partition, completely enclosed by a moulding." Verbatim translation: "surrounded by a whole key." The term "light" must be understood in contrast to the sophisticated, heavier cheek on V57 from which this more modern design was derived. Both drawings show Villard to have been a master of 'micro-architecture' which led to increasingly complex stalls such as the turreted city set in Barcelona Cathedral.

V54c Blessing Christ

The figure is upside down indicating the original loose leafe state of the manuscript. It has to be seen in context with V55. It is derived from the north portal of Reims (fig. 36).

H 155-6 N. 77. For a bibliography on stalls see V57 below.

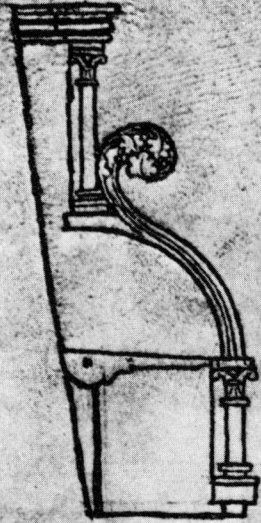

Veſ ki une legiere poupee duiſ
eſtauſ a·i· entreclos atore le clef·

V55   The Blessing Christ, St. John (?), Isaiah (?)

The figure of Christ on V54 and the two male saints on V55 were drawn in sequence before the parchment leaves were bound. They were inspired by Reims sculptures, possibly just before their placement. Christ stands prominently before the trumeau of the judgment portal of the north transept and is dated circa 1230 (fig. 36). The figure with a scroll is probably Isaiah from the right portal in the west facade of circa 1220. Instead of the head looking left, Villard turned it to the right. The figure at the left is more difficult to identify. The contraposto and details such as the veiled hand are reminiscent of the famous Visitation Virgin which Sauerländer dates 1230-33 (fig. 37). But we cannot extend Villard's humor to include a sex change. John of the judgment portal seems the closest prototype though Villard may have made him share the loose collar of St. James and the veiled hand of St. Bartholomew, both housed in the same portal and dated by Sauerländer around 1230. We assume the figures on V55 to be pastiches influenced by the Visitation Master whose group was probably close to completion when Villard sketched the figures. The Lausanne window, the Laon elevation and other examples demonstrate that he tended to combine and/or improve what he saw.

H 156-7, illus. 34-35. Sauerländer 1972, illus. 219, 236-7, 240-41, 246.

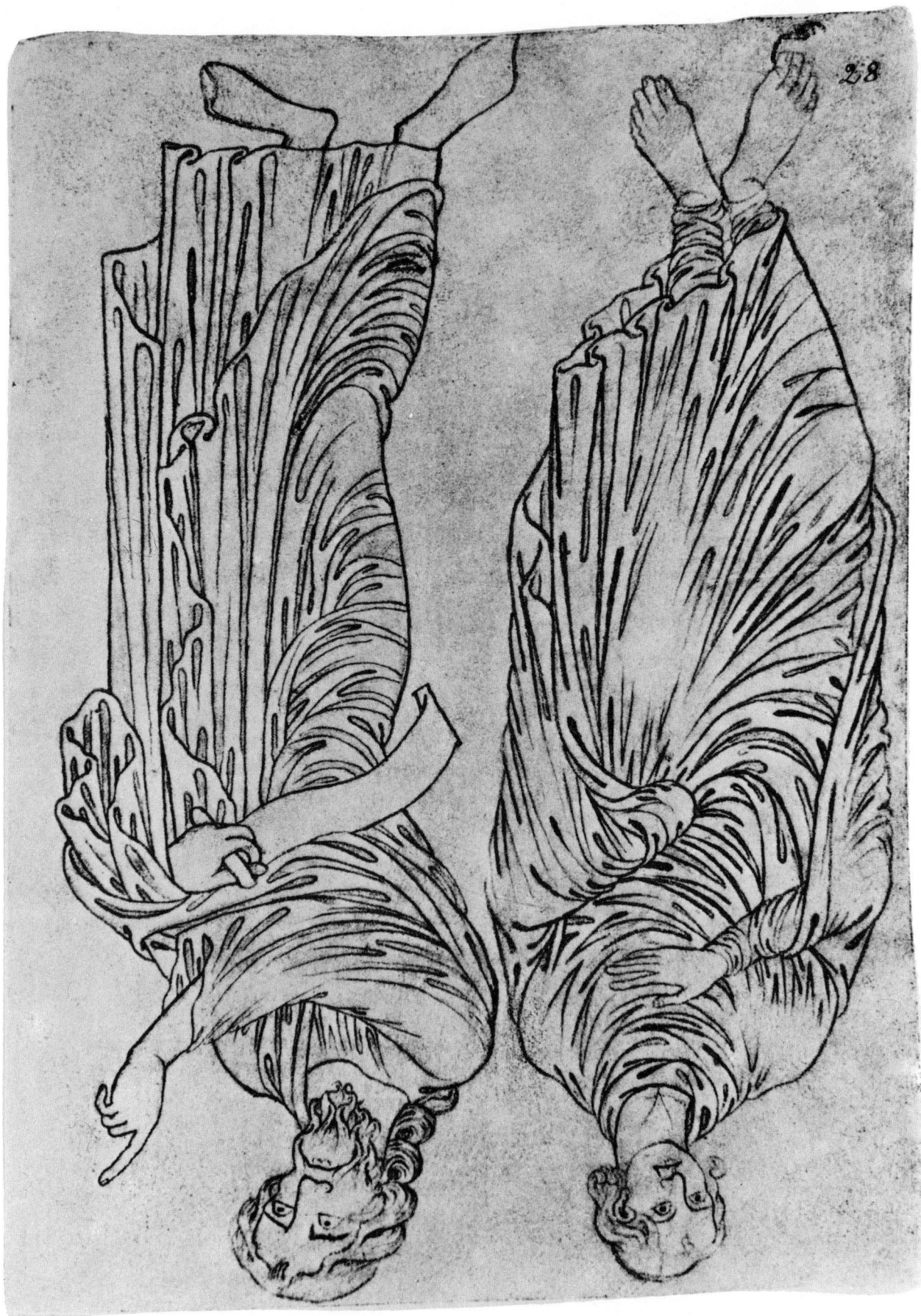

V56   The Flagellation of Christ, Christ being returned to Pilate

An incomplete silverpoint drawing, later crudely inked by Villard. Taking into account that fresh parchment is semi transparent and that the rigid figural groups are lacking life, one might stipulate a direct tracing, or a rapid sketch based on sequential scenes of a Northern French passion cycle.

H 157.

V57   Rich Poppet for a Stall

"If you wish to make a rich poppet for a stall, hold yourself to this one." It is indeed a magnificent, richly worked cheek for expensive stalls. Compared with the simpler scrolls of the poppet on **V54b** the open leaf-volutes rank among the most successful and sensitive ornamental designs of the Middle Ages. The great precision implies a planned and perhaps executed commission which might have included the late drawing of a dragon on V21. We have stressed the importance of furniture such as tabernacles, altars and stalls which were often designed by architects in our earlier work. H illus. 31 shows the cheek of stalls designed for Reims Cathedral. There the volutes were stretched and topped by an angel. Similar stalls are found in St. Gereon in Cologne, in Xanten and in Lausanne, where the stalls dated after 1232 contain a triple volute and a relief of wrestlers which are closely related to Villard's sketch on V28. Except for the outermost, irregularly adjusted half-circle, the lower spiral is constructed according to the method shown in fig. 30. The upper spiral is based on three centers which lie on the curve formed by the innermost half-circle. Here also the outer large curve at the left is designed from two centers which were chosen arbitrarily. The combination of rigid rules with occasional arbitrary design decisions became one of the hallmarks of the best architects. The lively excellence of the drawing is based on this refreshing flexibility in design, a rare and unusually unsuccessful event in Villard's work.

H 158, 251-52, Nn. 77, illus. 24-31. J.C. Biaudet, *Lausanne,* 208-10. R. Busch, *Deutsches Chorgestühl in sechs Jahrhnderten,* Hildesheim 1928. H. Sachs, *Mittelaterliches Chorgestuhl von Erfurt bis Stralsund,* Heidelberg 1964. W. Loose, *Die Chorgestühle des Mittelalters* was unavailable to me.

VILLARD DE HONNECOURT

V58   Man in Chlamys and Skullcap

Compared with the stilted nude on V22 and the heavily articulated figures on V43, this figure shows the considerable freedom Villard acquired in his figural representations. Because the figure strikes a true contrapposto, it does not conform to Villard's standard double triangle schema. H assumes the prototype to have represented Mercury, possibly from an astronomical manuscript. Ivories such as the Eucherius diptych of circa 396, mosaics or a Carolingian manuscript must also be considered. Since this is definitely not an awkward figure, one might consider a neoclassical model from the school of Reiner of Huy. This early twelfth century work would have been closer to Villard's taste than Roman works which fascinated him, but which he could not easily handle.

H 159, 375-76. Swarzenski 1967, *Monuments,* illus. 256-58, 372, 504, 510.

V59   The Catapult or Trebuchet

"If you wish to make a strong engine one calls catapult, pay attention to this. See herein the base as it sits on the ground. See there in front the 2 windlasses (and) the slack rope by which the pole (verge) is hauled down. You can see this on that other page. A great weight must be hauled up, for the counterpoise is very heavy. For it is a hopper full of earth, which is fully 2 fathoms long 9 feet wide, 12 feet deep. Before releasing the missile think, (and) if you pay attention, for it must rest on this front stanchion." This long inscription which accompanies the only precise thirteenth century construction drawing of a catapult is extraordinary in that it includes measurements. These are also shown on the sketch and presumably accompanied the lost side view to which Villard refers. Villard rightfully cautions the future handlers of the "Trepucheta. . . the most powerful machine against walls" as Jean de Garlande called it in 1245, against the dangers involved with its use. Our drawing (fig. 38) gives an idea of the size of these behemoths. In 1378 the catapult of Cherbourg required eight "tendeurs", forty assistants, one master, five carpenters, ten masons and thirty one carts! Our calculations show that the counterpoise alone weighed at least twenty tons. Released and with the leverage of the 30 to 36 foot verge a considerable missile, or a group of barrels with lethally burning pitch could be propelled over a considerable trajectory. The problem was the basket. It had to be stopped short of smashing the machine. The basket was therefore allowed to drop only until the verge had reached a vertical position. The double rope now freed from the second windlass would spring up to the hook above the pulley, and the tremendous forward force was partially absorbed by the two 20' springs protruding beyond the main beams. If not heavily loaded down, the engine would at that moment, still have reared its end and come to a shuddering stop. H (ills. 190-91) illustrates two catapults from the Tickhill Psalter of Circa 1315 (New York, Public Library, Spencer Ms. 26, 99 v) and from Walter de Milimite's *De nobilitate regum* of circa 1326 (Oxford, Bodleian Libr. Ms Christ Church 92, 67 r). The counterweight of one of the catapults is supported by a rod which is about to be dislocated by a reckless swordsman by means of a heavy hammer. The other drawing shows the release of the hook holding the verge again by means of a hammer and a rope flailing the air. Neither the cold, mnemonic drawing by Villard nor the drolerie in a British Museum manuscript (Stowe Ms. 17, fol. 243 v) reproduced in our illustration 39 can give us any inkling of the violence inherent in these machines. Two precise illustrations fol. 30, 31 and 39 of Codex Pal. Germ. 126 in the University Library of Heidelberg largely confirm the author's reconstruction of fig. 38 (fig. 39b, 39c). The *Buch der Stryt* (Book of War) was begun by the Palatine gunsmith Philip Moench in 1476 and completed in 1478. The main difference between our reconstruction (fig. 38) and medieval illustrations lies in the position of the missile closer to the main vertical posts. Perhaps the missile lay on the front stanchion with the number VIII in Villard's drawing. This produces a violent upward thrust and abbreviates the actual launching curve. Moench's catapults allow for a backward motion of the heavy basket, a possibility excluded from our reconstruction and also probably from Villard's machine.

See H. 159-62, N. 78, illus. 80, 190-91. Viollet-le-Duc, *Dictionnaire*, vol. 5, 224-26, fig. 9.

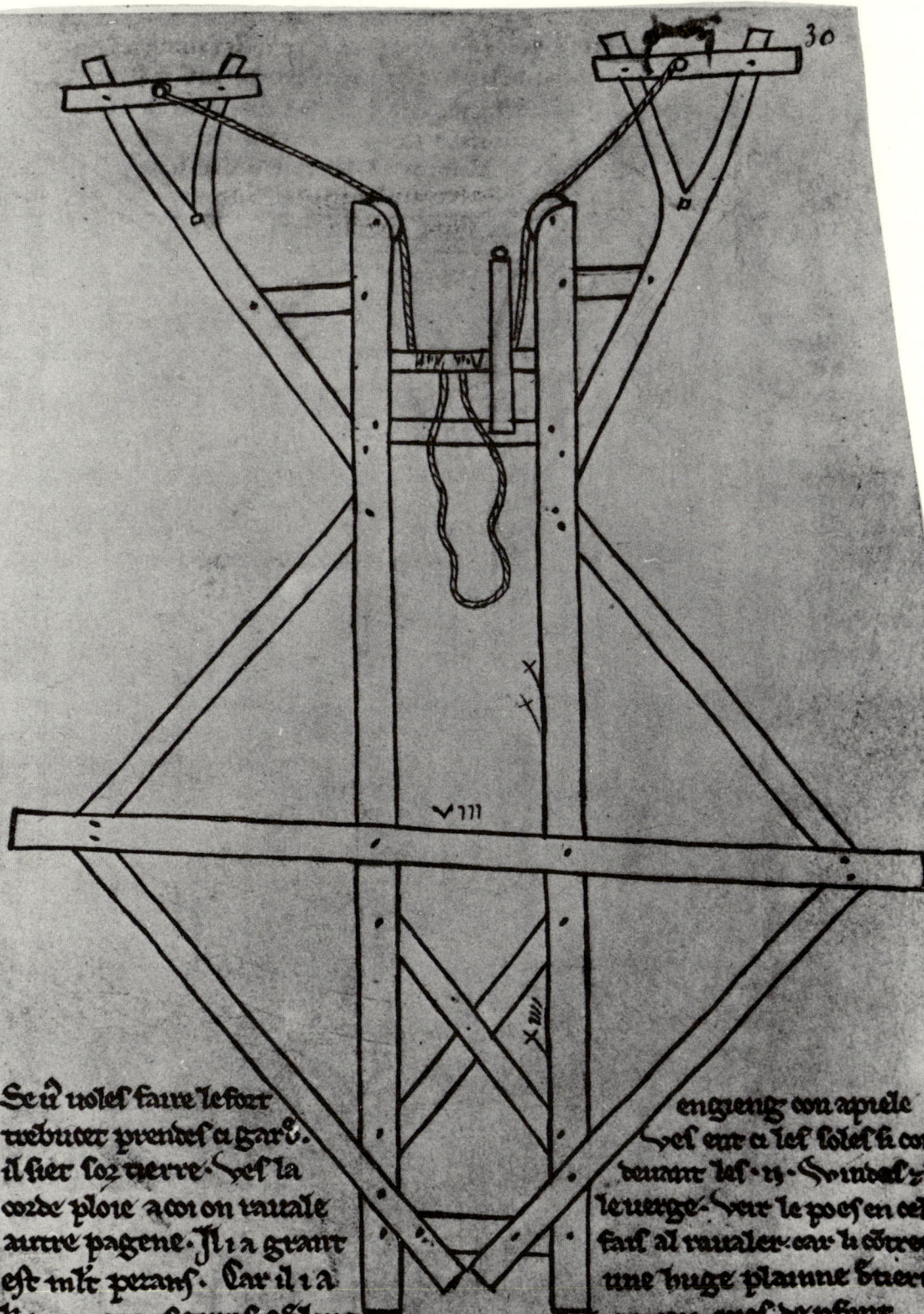

Se ti uoles faire le fort
trebucer prendes i gard.
il siet sor tierre. Ves la
corde ploie acoi on rautale
autre pagene. Il i a grant
est int perans. Car il i a
ka · ij · grans torces ablont
ff al desco cier dele fleke pensef · z
acel estancon la deuant.

engieng con apiele
ves ent ci les soles ti com
deuant les · ij · v uidels z le
leuerge · veir le poes en cele
fait al rautaler car li c ontrepois
une huge plainne dtierre
z · viij · pies dele · xij · piel de pfont.
si ti en vones gard. car il le von estre arenve

VILLARD DE HONNECOURT

V60   Interior of the Choir at Reims Cathedral

Text at the left: "See here the correct elevation of the chapels of the church of Reims (and) the whole manner, how they are inside, straight (correct?) in (each of) their storey." Text at the left below: "See here the inner passages, and the hidden arches (vaults)." Top center text which refers to p. 61: "And on this other (next) page you can see the elevation of the chapels of the church of Reims from the outside, from the base to the top as they exist. In such a manner those of Cambrai must be (made), if done correctly. The upper entablature must form crennelations." Instead of *portraiture* Villard adopted the term *montee,* literally meaning rising masonry, to designate the interior elevation of the two upper stories of Reims Cathedral. Essentially the elevation is accurate (fig. 40). Information we believe was essential to Villard, such as a heavy stress of the base and upper cornices of the triforium, emphasis on the wall thickness through steeply diagonal lines flanking the lancets of the windows which are themselves considerably heightened, all reappear in the St. Quentin elevation which he may have designed. Only the proportions of the triforium are approximately correct. Its openings were narrowed in St. Quentin through the introduction of a third arch. Six masons' or placement marks appear, beginning with a circle crossed by a diagonal diameter in the base between the second and third triforium openings. Several of these marks reappear on V62-63. They indicate that major work on the completion of the upper parts of the choir was in progress. As we pointed out in the introduction, we interpret the presence of the masons' marks on V60-61 as a record of work projects assigned by Villard to masons whom he supervised as one of the subcontractors of the Reims fabric from circa 1228-1233. The vaults are indicated by heavy lines which does not necessarily mean that they were not completed. However the strong emphasis on the interior entablature along the crown of the outside wall strongly indicates that the the construction had proceeded only to the springers of the vault. Branner assumes that the chevet was near completion in the late 1220s. A burgher's insurrection largely interrupted work between 1233 and 1236. Taking into account Villard's fascination with the probably not yet placed nude choir angels (V61), we must place one of Villard's visits to Reims around 1228. Sauerländer dates the choir angels, V61, circa 1230. This is corroborated by Villard's mature, almost offhand but deeply secure perception of the structure, and his automatic handling of changes which reappear in the choir of St. Quentin whose upper structure was begun in 1228.

H 162-168, Nn. 36, 79-82, 95, 105, illus. 55, 57-59, 141-143. R. Branner 1961, Historical Aspects of the Reconstruction of Reims Cathedral 1210-41, *Speculum,* 36. R. Branner's review of H. Reinhardt, La Cathédrale de Reims, *Art Bulletin,* 45, 375-77 offers no viable alternative.

z en cele autre pagene poes tu ueir les montrees des
capieles de le glire de rains par dehors tref le
comencement desci enle fin ensi com eles st.
dautrefel maniere doiuent estre celes
de canbrai so lor fait droit li
derrains entaulemes dour
faire crenaus z.

desci le
droite mote
des capeles
de le glise
de rains z
tout le man
iere ensi com
eles suut p
dedens droite
enlor estage

es et les uoie
dedens z les
orbes arkes.

VILLARD DE HONNECOURT

V61   Elevation of a Choir Chapel of Reims Cathedral

The text on V60 stresses the crennelation and the usefulness of the drawing for the construction of the chapels in Cambrai which must be built just as correctly. Villard as usual changed several aspects of the model (see fig. 41). The base cornice is overemphasized, the proportion of the wall panes is changed from the existing 1:4 to a steep 1:6 proportion. The vegetal ornaments in the arches of the windows and the consoles below the crown cornice are omitted. The angels which were possibly not yet placed are shown nude with extended wings. The detail most revealing about Villard's interests as a builder is his emphasis on the joints of the tracery in the window at the right, especially the stepped or shiplap joints used for the frame of the rose into which six lobes were separately set. By the mid-thirteenth century this method was considered impractical and fell into disuse. We pointed out that this emphasis on precise details indicates Villard's actual cooperation in the construction of parts of the cathedral. He presumably also took part in the discussions of the overall design. For instance, the outer buttresses of Reims are double stepped while Villard keeps the more symmetrical triple step arrangement. The reference to Cambrai, barely 18 kilometers from Honnecourt, seems unlikely had Villard not had a say in its design. Cambrai had been started in 1227; a chapel to St. Nicolas—if it was indeed part of the cathedral—was dedicated in 1230, and another one to St. Elizabeth of Hungary in 1235. As we pointed out in our comments on V28 the choir, which was completed in 1246, followed the Reims model. We assumed earlier one of Villard's visits to Reims to have taken place circa 1226. Once more we must conclude that Villard played at least a consultant's, if not a contractor's, role in the planning of the immense structure after 1228.

H 162-65, Nn. 22, 36, 79-83, 95, 105, ills. 57-59, 60-63 68-69, 211-13. F. Salet La Chronologie de la Cathedrale de Reims, *Bull. Mon.* 1967, vol. 125 347-94, Sauerländer 1972, 250-253.

VILLARD DE HONNECOURT

V62   Reims, Interior and Exterior Nave Elevations

Text by M3: "Consider well these elevations. Before the roof of the side aisles, there must be a passage-way on the entablature and over the roof of the sideaisles there must again be a low crennelation, you can see it in the design before you. And on the tops of your pillars (buttresses) there must be angels, and in front of flying buttresses. In front of the large roof on top there again must be a passage and crennelations on the entablature, so that one can go there for danger of fire. (And) on this entablature (entavlement) there must be gargoyles to throw the water (off). As to the chapels I told you." This clumsy text by the third owner is written in a strongly accented French and is a paraphrase of Villard's text at the bottom of V63 which for reasons of comparison follows here:

"See here the elevation of the church of Reims (and) of the wall pane inside and outside. The first entablature of the sideaisles must have (doit faire) a crennelation so that there may be a passageway before the roof. Opposite this roof there are interior passageways (meaning: triforia), and when these passageways are vaulted and plastered, the corridors lead outward (meaning: curve toward the nave), so that one can pass in front of the window sills. And the last (meaning: highest) entablature must have crennelations so that one can pass before the roof. See here the manner of all storeys (meaning total elevation)."

Villard is intent on the traffic of the fire brigades, he is not interested in the angels, but he gives us directional changes in the triforium passages. This is the practical builder speaking and not an eclectic pedant who finds that items as obvious as gargoyles, which were essential in throwing water clear of the structure, are missing. H feels that the obvious, such as the need for passageways for the use as fire lanes was being confirmed in writing. It was at this point that the verbal tradition became textually codified.

The elevation of the exterior is accurate and unthinkable without lodge drawings such as those still preserved in the Reims palimpsests. Villard consciously compressed and slenderized the interior elevation. The Reims arches, proportioned 1:3 turned into narrow 1:4,7 openings. Once more we see changes probably directed at St. Quentin, where the triforium is less labored than in the Villard drawing. The clerestory is narrowed even more (see fig. 42). Taking the elevation at face value we miss the extraordinary aediculae housing angels on top of the outer buttresses. We reserved their study for V64 where they look massive and where their spirelets lack crockets. If we assume the outside elevation with its truncated buttressing towers and two wall consoles for two flying buttresses abutting the clerestory level to be a copy of a construction drawing, we must stipulate a design of the early 1220s which was later modified in details, probably during the restless years of 1233-36 when major lodge activities came to a halt. This does not exclude the completion of the sideaisles in which Villard notes joints and masons' or placement marks, and the likelihood that the clerestory walls of the nave were well advanced.

H 165-169, Nn. 81-87, 105, illus. 72-74, 141-43, 209-10. See also F. Salet *Chronologie* 1967.

62 VILLARD DE HONNECOURT

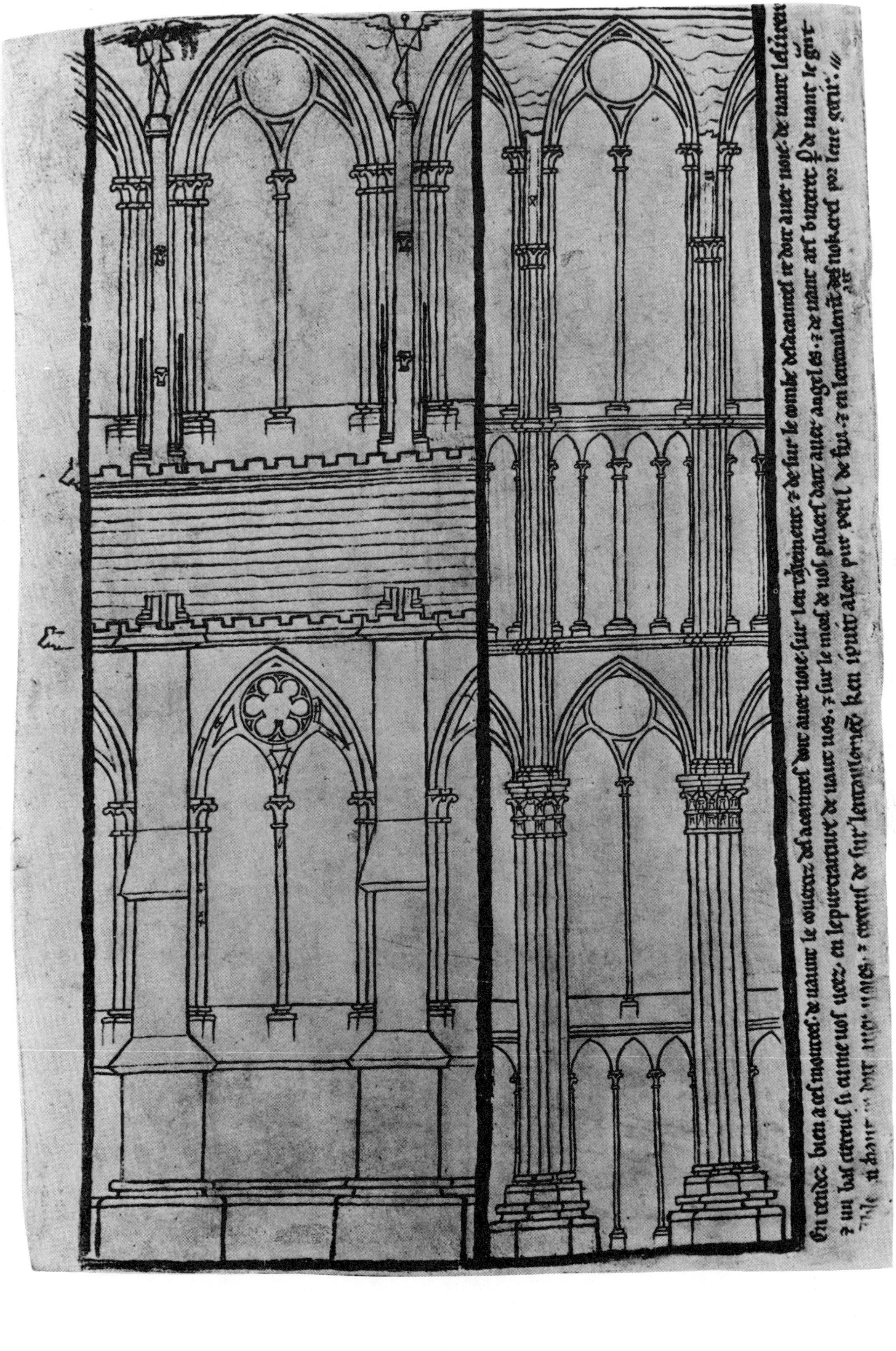

V63 Piers, Jambs, Mullions, and a Plumb Line for the Construction of Reims Cathedral

V63 Piers

"Here you can see one of the tower pillars of the church of Reims, and of those (which stand) between 2 chapels and there is 1 of those of the straight wall and 1 of the nave of the minster. For all these pillars the joints are as they should be." At the left, M3: "Regarding the chapels I have told you." The crossing pier is bilaterally and not quadrilaterally symmetrical and quite accurately shown (see fig. 43).

V63 A compound pier of the sideaisle

V63 A pier of the nave

V63 A compound three quarter pier between two ambulatory chapels.

A string hanging from a nail reminds the user of the absolute necessity to keep the work in precise vertical plumb and may be a symbol of Villard's active cooperation in parts of the construction. Obviously it is difficult to check the joining of these essential structural members accurately. Thier tremendous size made the joining of smaller more easily carved and more lightly handled parts necessary. In the crossing pier one would expect the long crosspiece to serve as an uninterrupted binder to which four quarter segments would be anchored with clamps. The binder then would be turned 90° for the next course. The nave pier was given special consideration through the introduction of a costly tongue and groove joint for two shafts. The core would also have been rotated 90° for the next course. H p. 170 states that the upper drums of the nave piers were indeed constructed as we have suggested. The three front shafts of the ambulatory pier are built of staggered pieces of stone which must have been attached to the body of the pier with iron clamps.

The lower two strips are lumped together in one text: "See here the profiles (molles) of the chapels of the preceeding (page), of the templates (formes = traceries?) of the windows, of the ribs and the transverse arches (doubilaus) and the blind arcades (survols) on high." There is a mine of medieval architectural terminology on this page. *Formes,* which we also define as traceries may usually be templates. Gervasius of Canterbury reports that William of Sens gave the masons "formas quoque ad lapides formandos" which must mean templates. Since these counted among the most precious inventory of a lodge, it would have been easy for Villard to "leaf" through the profiled boards of seasoned wood, which judging from two thirteenth (?) century templates in the York lodge could have been as thick as 1¼ inches. Masons' and placement marks were current since the inception of the twelfth century but appears very rarely in drawings. Their inclusion usually indicates a master's direct involvement in specific parts of the construction. A correlation of these marks between V60-63 shows that the pieces relate to the side aisles and possibly the triforium of the transept. The items **i-m** refer to a side aisle window and consist of the following: **e-g**: ambs and a mullion; **h**: a lobe of the rose on V62 bottom left; **i**: profile of the outer circle of the rose; **k**: arches below the rose; **l**: center mullion; **m**: inner large arch above the rose; **n**: according to Lassus triforium base of south transept, indicating the loss of a plan and possibly an elevation design; **o**: profile for a blind arch based on a lost drawing; **p**: Lassus calls it a cornice below the side aisle window(?); **q**: transverse rib, possibly from the top part of the interior elevation V62; **r**: cross section through a sophisticated diagonal rib; **s**: a member with three shafts on a base with crockets; **t**: the base and colonnettes for the triforium zone on V60. For the bottom text on the elevation see V62.

H 169-73, Nn. 87-90, illus. 70-74. L. Shelby *Templates.* C. Brunel L'origine du mot ogive *Romania*, vol. 81, 1960

32

Ci poes iu veir l'un des pilers totaus de le
glize de rains. z .i. de ceus dentre .ii. capeles.
z sen i a .z. del plain pen.
z .i. de ceus de le nef del
moustier. par tos ces
pilers sunt les
loizons teles com
eles i doivent estre.

pur les capeles los di.

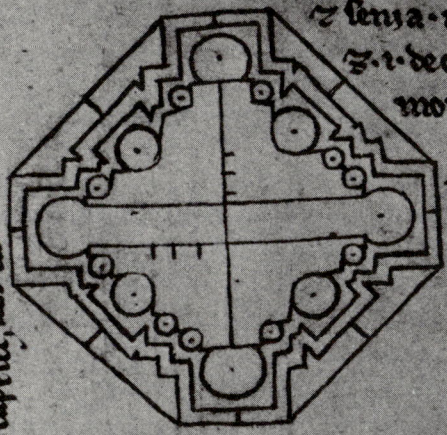

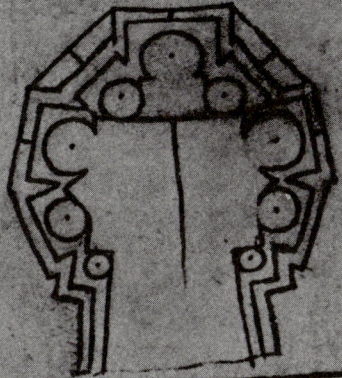

Veci le molle des chapeles de cele pagne la devant. des formes z des
verieres. des ogives z des doublaus. z des formols p de seure.

Veci les montees de leglize de rains z del plain pen. dedens z de hors.
Li premiers estauilemens des acantes doit faire cretaus si ql puist
avoir voie devant le covertic. encontre ce metent sunt les voies dedens.
z qant ces voies sunt volses z entailees. dont revenent les voies dehors
q puet aler devant les suels des verieres. en lentauilement deerai doit aver
...traus con puist aler devant le covertic. ves aluec les maisnes honnes l...

VILLARD DE HONNECOURT

V64   The Choir Buttresses at Reims Cathedral

This is the most forceful architectural design of the thirteenth century, and among Villard's last. It shows the straightforward and clear vision of a mature master who not only understood a complex combination of parts but also their structural dynamics. He minimized the precious vertical staggering of the flying buttresses, which in the extreme would have led to a rotation within the intermediate buttressing tower and an eventual collapse (see fig. 44).

Within Villard's work the drawing ranks with those of the apostle V46, the stall V57 and the catapult V59. Together they show Villard's combined interests in architecture, sculpture, furniture, machine and structural dynamics. Except for a correction of the vertical dislocation, we believe that this is a rendering of the original lodge design for choir buttressing probably preceding the year 1225, and not a simplification of the present scheme. The proportions are narrowed as usual. More significantly the lower buttress meets the tas de charge precisely, while the upper one is placed higher so as to effectively contain the windloads transmitted from the roof. A hidden buttress is attached to the outer buttressing tower and the finials are very heavy. Through this Villard presents us with the classical Gothic load distribution system. On V18 he squeezed in an aedicula with a placement or mason's mark which may indicate his participation in the design of the finials and his already expressed interest in the uppermost levels. These finials with niches for angels were completed after Villard's death which we assume to have occured before 1236.

H 172-73, Nn. 88-90, 104-105, illus. 77-79. E. Panofsky, Ueber die Reihenfolge der vier Meister von Reims, Jahrb. f. Kunstwissenschaft, 1927, 55 stipulates a change of plan in 1225.

VILLARD DE HONNECOURT

V65a   Potion for any Injury

"Remember what I shall tell you. Take leaves of red cabbage and gilly flower, that is a plant which one calls galion filate, take an herb called wood's fern (tanesie) and hemp (canvre), that is seed of hemp. Crush these four plants so that of one there is not one bit more than of the other. Then take madder (warance) twice the amount as (that used) for one of the 4 herbs, and then crush them. Then put these 5 herbs into 1 pot, add white wine for the infusion, the best you can obtain in a mixture measured in such a way that the beverage is not too thick, so that one may drink it. Don't drink too much of it (sic!), in an egg shell you will have enough of it, assuming it is full. Whichever wound you might have, you will be healed of it. Rub your wound with a little oakum (also tow, coarse and broken part of hemp) cover it with a leaf of red cabbage, then drink of the beverage in the morning and at Vespers, 2 in a day. Mixed with sweet cider it is more helpful than with other wine, but it must be good! The cider will mix with the plants. But if you mix it with old wine, let it stand for 2 days before drinking of it."

Medical advice is frequent in medieval work manuals, which in a large sense were recipe books. Because of their work masons were exposed to abrasions, and worst of all to falls from great heights. One such accident took place on 13 September 1178 around 5 p.m. when William of Sens, architect of Canterbury fell and was so badly hurt, he eventually resigned his commission. A similar accident is depicted in Alfonso el Sabio's *Las Cantigas* where a painter is seen falling from a scaffolding, only to be saved by the Virgin. As a rule injuries seem to have been as frequent as they are today. Authors hitherto have missed the medical importance of *cannabis sativa*, especially in medieval medicine. The commanding literary flair and authoritative tone used by Villard and his warning "n'en beviez mie trop" indicates experience with the surely pleasant effects of a drink made up of 1/6th of hashish mixed with the best of white wines or cider. More unusual seems the external treatment of a wound with cannabis which was available in broken ropes and covered with the leaf of red cabbage, which as late as 1629 was still considered a means to ease "gripin paines, shorteness of breath and every disease." Here again the treatment was combined with a twice daily internal consumption. As attractive as it might seem to explain some of Villard's inaccuracies such as his drawing of the Lausanne rose, as an expression of being intoxicated, we must remember that Villard's recipe is coupled with his overall advice to architects. On V18 he says that an architect only does what is "wise and prudent."

V65b   Recipe for the Preservation of Flowers

"Pluck your flowers of various colors in the morning, so that one doesn't touch the other. Take a specific stone which one carves with a chisel. It should be white, (and) ground finely. And if you put your flowers into this powder, each separately, you will preserve the colors of your flowers."
Lassus assumes the stone to be talc. The statement is related to a passage in Heraclius' *De coloribus et artibus Romanorum* in which fresh flowers mixed with gypsum are to be used for the preparation of colors.

H 173-75, J.E. Keller, Daily Living as Presented in the Canticles of Alfonso the Learned, *Speculum*, 33, 1958, 484-489.
J. Parkinson, *Paradisi in sole: Paradisus terrestris*, London, 1629, 503-506.

V66   Fifteenth Century Inscriptions

"In this book there are forty and 1 leaves, J. Mancel." Below in an almost effaced Gothic *scriptä Jehanne Martian.*" Neither has been identified. At present the manuscript has 33 leaves which means that since the fifteenth century 8 leaves or 16 pages were lost. For an analysis of the manuscript and its possible losses see Introduction, pp. 28-30.

33

Reteneis co que io u' dirai · prendes fuelles de col roges ·
⁊ sauemonde cest une erbe con clanme galio filare
prendes une erbe con clamne tanesie ⁊ ameuurze
cest semence deuature · estampes ces · iiij · erbes si
quil mait ment pl° de lune q̃ de lautre · apres
si prendeis Waraince · ii · tans q̃ de lune des · iiij ·
erbes · ⁊ puis si lestampes puis si meteis ces S·
erbes en · i· por ⁊ si meteis blanc uin al destemprer
le meiller q̃ u' poes auoir · auƞs teupreement q̃ les
puizonz ne soient trop espessez sicõ les puist boire ·
nen beueiz une trop en une escargne · duef en ares
u' aseiz por q̃le soit plaunne · quel plaie q̃ u' aies u²
en garies · tergies uo plaie dun por destoupes
meres sus une fuelle de col roge · puis si beueis
des puizonz al matin ⁊ aluespre · ij · fois le ior ·
eles ualent iumx destemprees de moust douc
q̃ dautre Win · mais q̃l soit bons si paerra li
moust auec les erbes · ⁊ se u' les destempres de
uies Win laissies les · ii · iors ancois cõ en boiue ·

¶Cueillies uos flors au mati de diuerses colors lie
lune ne touce alautre · prendes une maniere d
piere cõtaille acirrel q̃ le soit blance molue ⁊ deliue ·
puis si meteis uos flors en ceste ioure · cascune
maniere pli si dueront uos flors en lor colors ·

175

Illustrations for Villard de Honnecourt

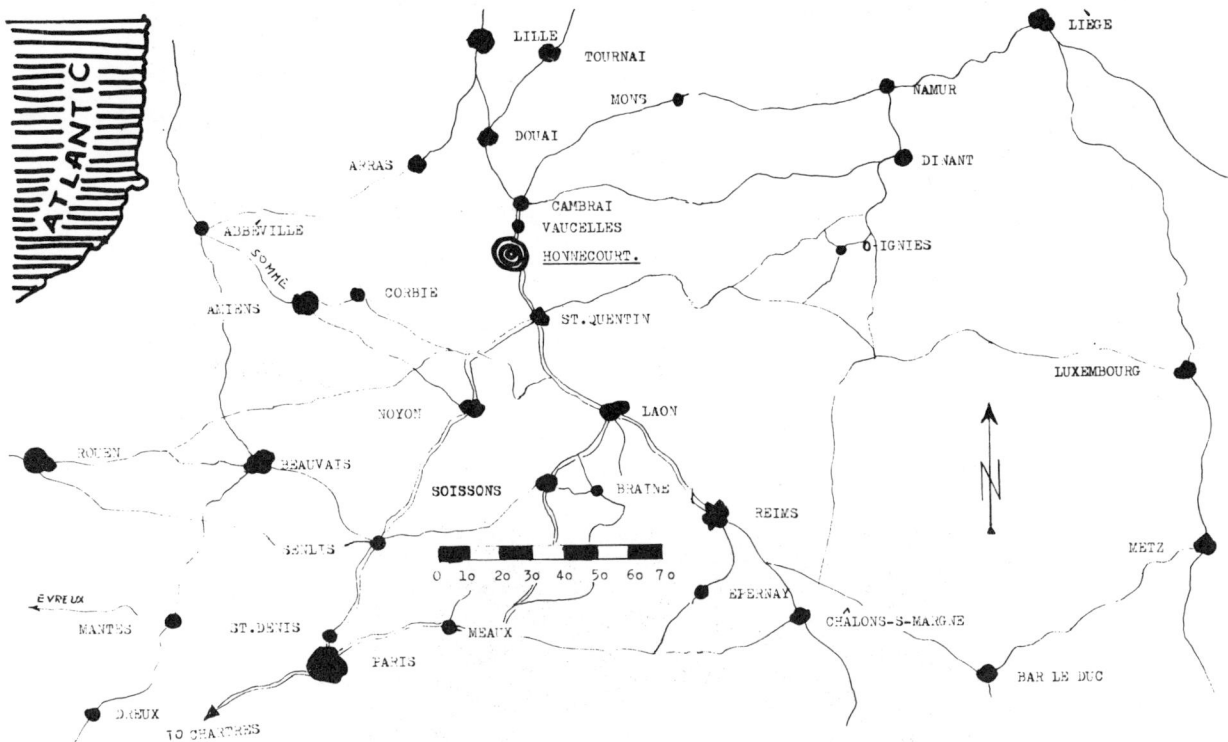

fig. 1 Northwestern France, artistically active centers 1180-1240

fig. 2 Salome, Rouen Cathedral, West portal, c. 1240 V2

fig. 3 Gerardus cross, San Marco,
Venice, c. 1206 V2, 15

177

fig. 4 Pride Falls, Chartres Cathedral, South porch, c. 1220 V6

fig. 5 Swan, Oxford, Bodleian Libr. Ms. Ashmole 1511
f.71 V7

fig. 6a Leaf head corbel. Reims Cathedral, choir,
c.1230   Vl0,43

fig. 6b Leaf head capital. Istanbul, Ottoman Museum

fig. 7 Housing for clock V12

fig. 8 Lectern, from V13

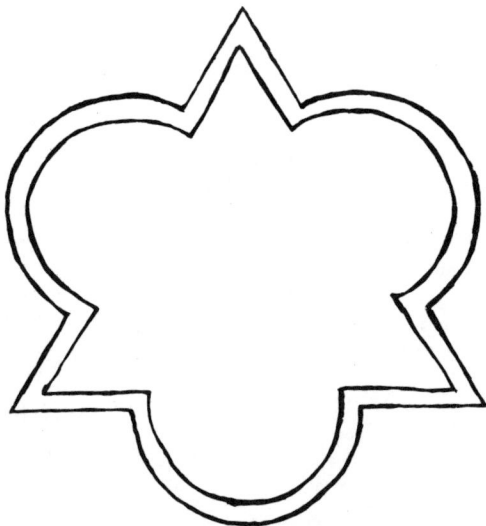

fig. 9 Geometry underlying the foot of the lectern V13

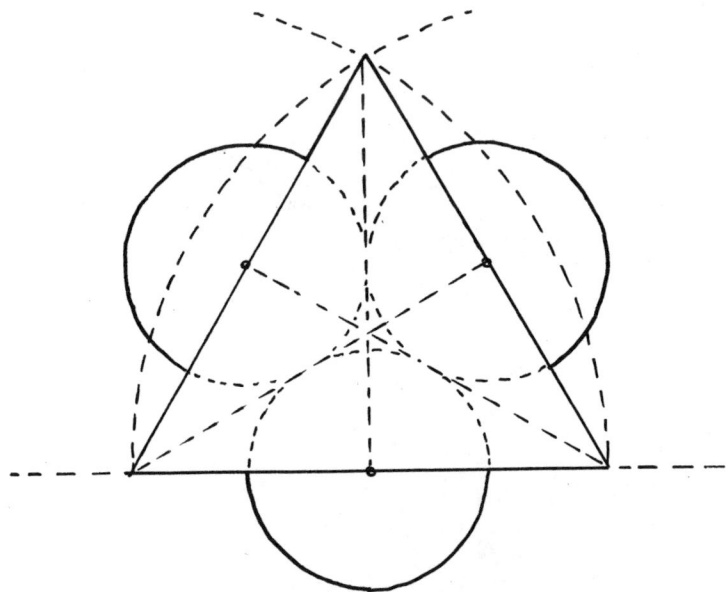

fig. 9 *a* Lectern, plan of foot

fig. 10 Cat, Cambridge, Magdalene College Libr. Ms. 1916, c. 1380 V14

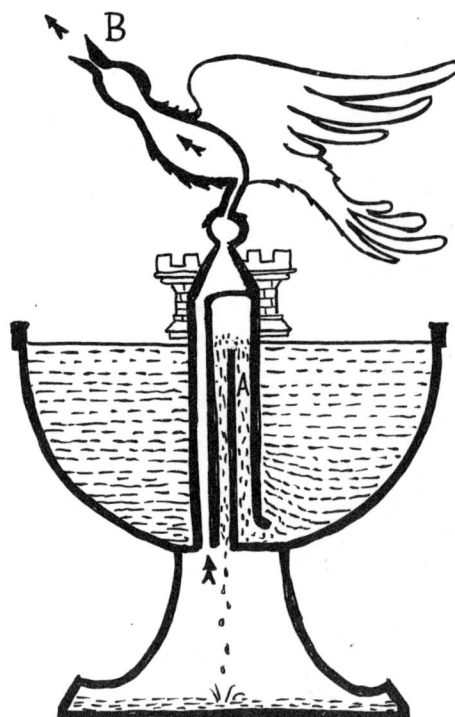

fig. 13 *a* Cantepleure, stationary bird

fig. 11 Le Lieu Jérusalem, Saint Quentin, 1493-95 V14

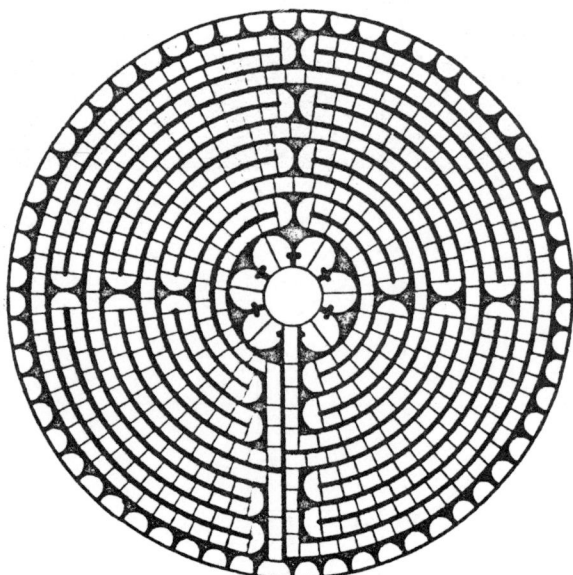

fig. 12 Labyrinth, Chartes Cathedral, nave, c. 1220

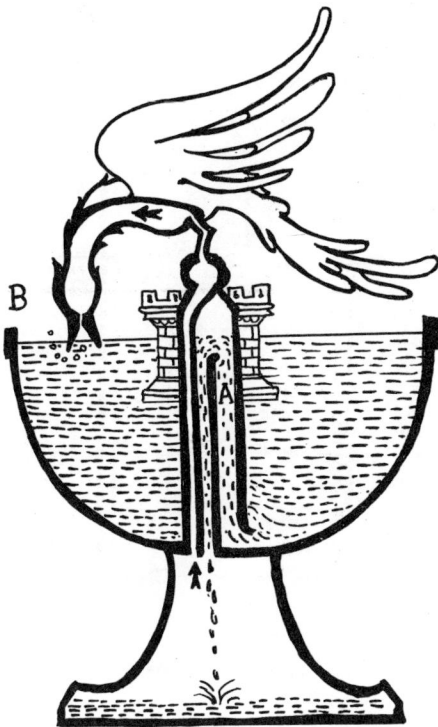

fig. 13 *b* Stationary drinking bird

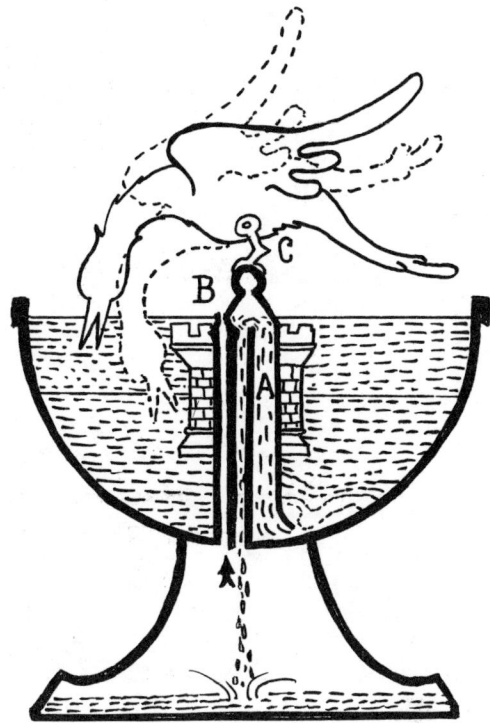

fig. 13 *c* Hinged bird in floating and arrested positions V17

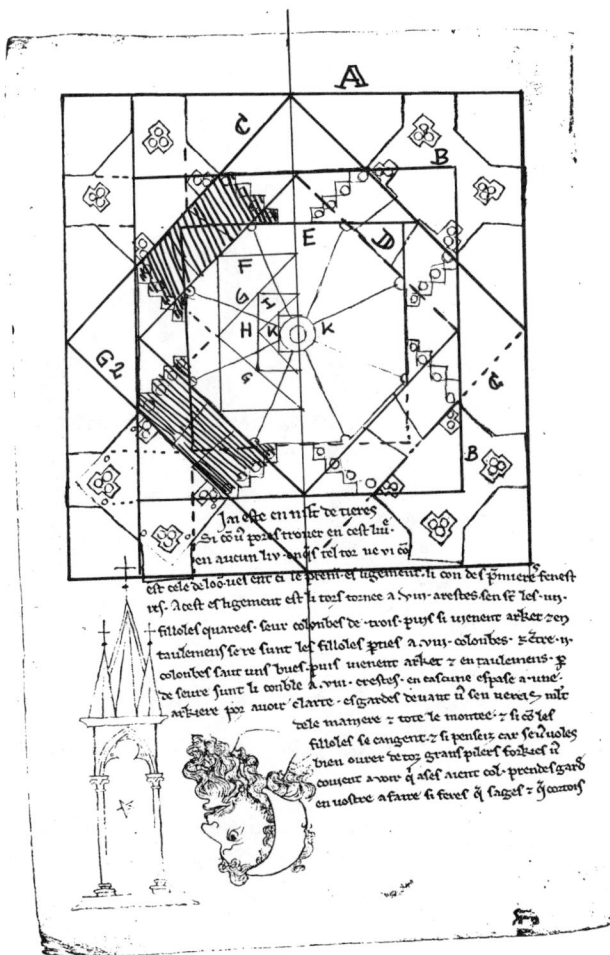

fig. 14 Schema of tower plan, Laon Cathedral V18

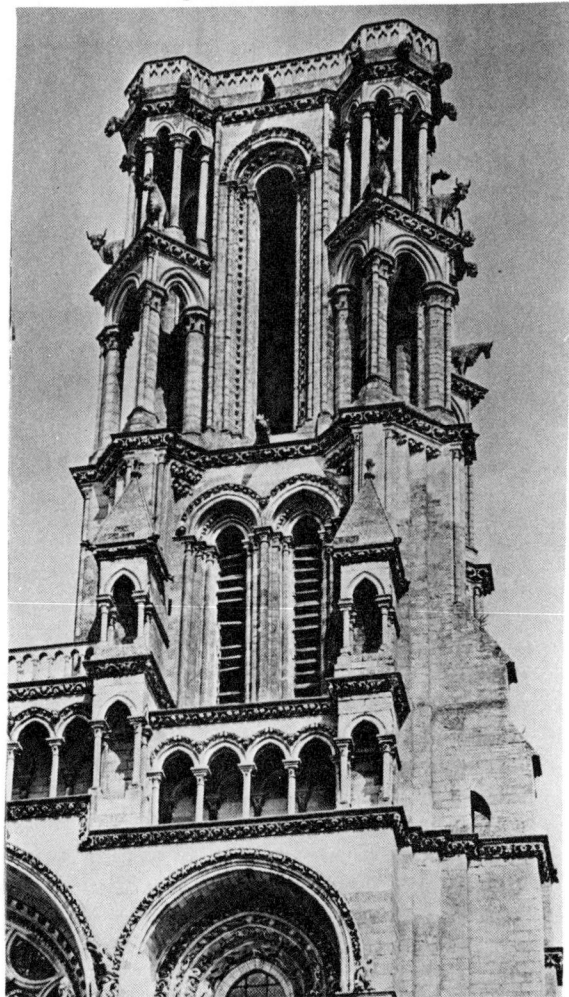

fig. 15 View of South tower, Laon Cathedral V19

181

fig. 16 Phylactery of Hugo of Oignies, Namur, Saint Andrew, c. 123Ò
V21, 32

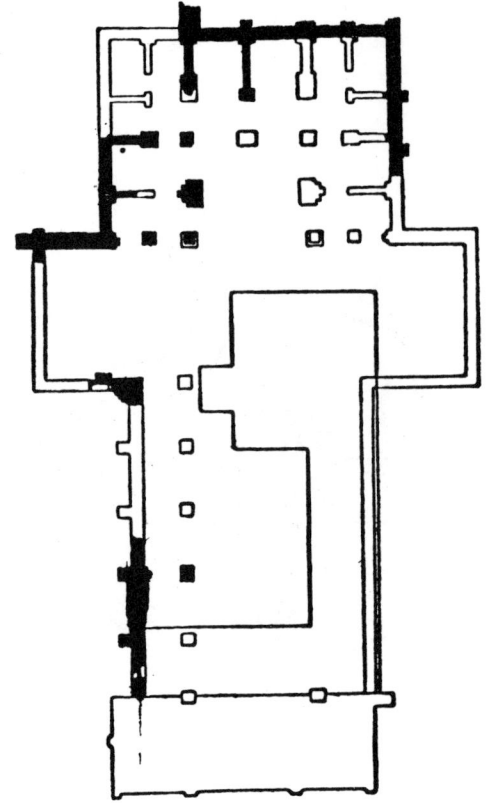

fig. 17 *a* Morimond Abbey, 1155-70, excavation
plan (D)

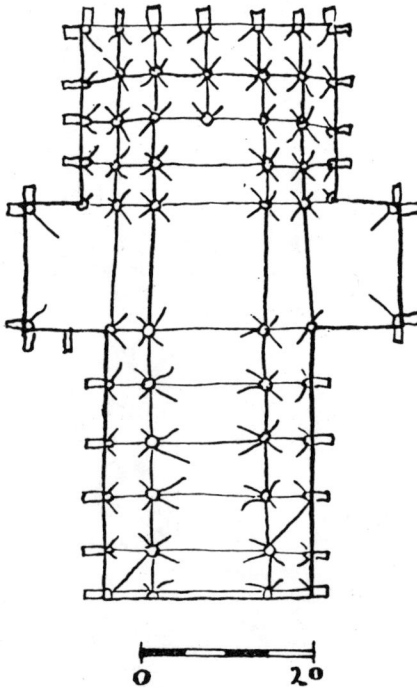

fig. 17 *b* Reconstruction of Morimund,
V28.

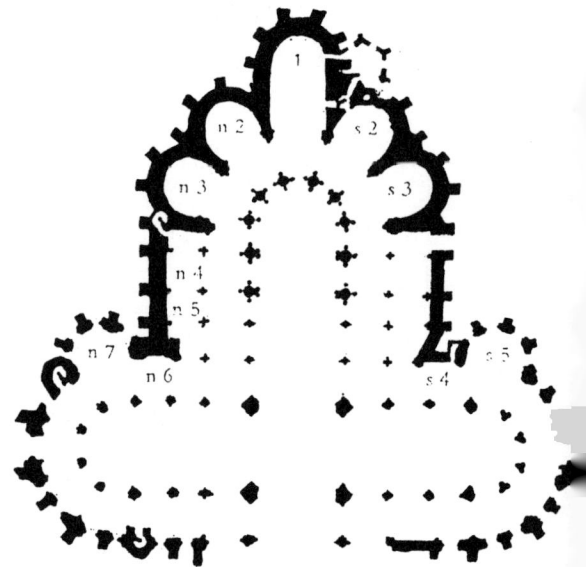

fig. 18 Cambrai Cathedral V28 and plan of Le Gl.
Nr. 3 chapel of Saint Nicolas, 1230-21, Nr
chapel of Saint Elizabeth of Hungary 1239

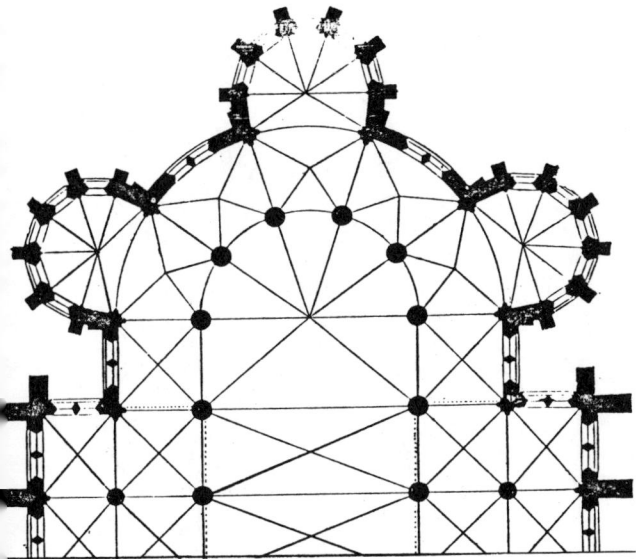

fig. 19 Original plan, Meaux, Saint Stephen, 1198-1213 V29

fig. 20 Tiles from the tower chapel, Saint Quentin Collegiate Church (B) V30

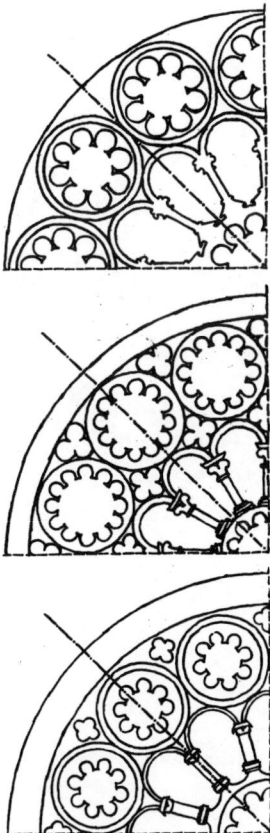

fig. 21 Rose window, Chartres Cathedral, V30, graffito Saint Quentin (top)

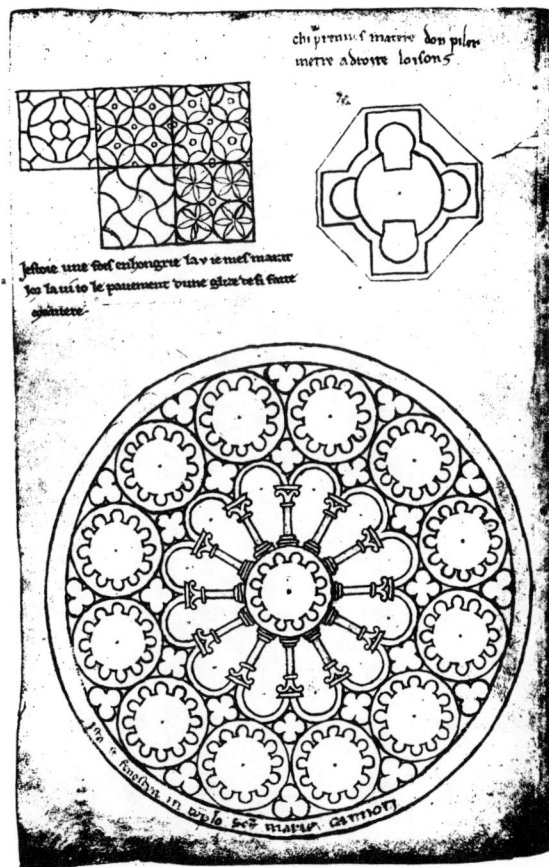

fig. 22 a V30 "Chartres" rose, pavement pier.

fig. 22 *b* Graffito Saint Quentin

fig. 22 *c* Reconstruction graffito Saint Quentin

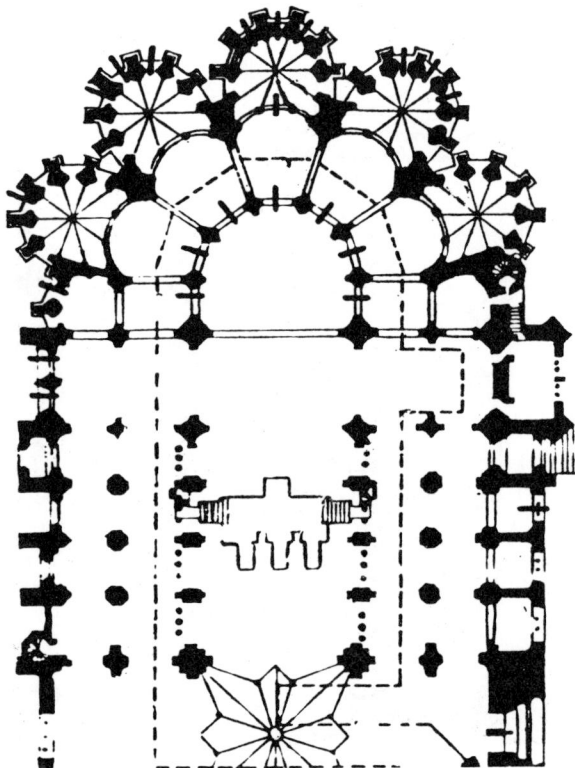

fig. 22 *d* Choir, St. Quentin

fig. 22 *e* Longitudinal section, Choir, St. Quentin

184

fig. 23 *a* Rose window as it exists, Lausanne
Cathedral, c. 1220 V31

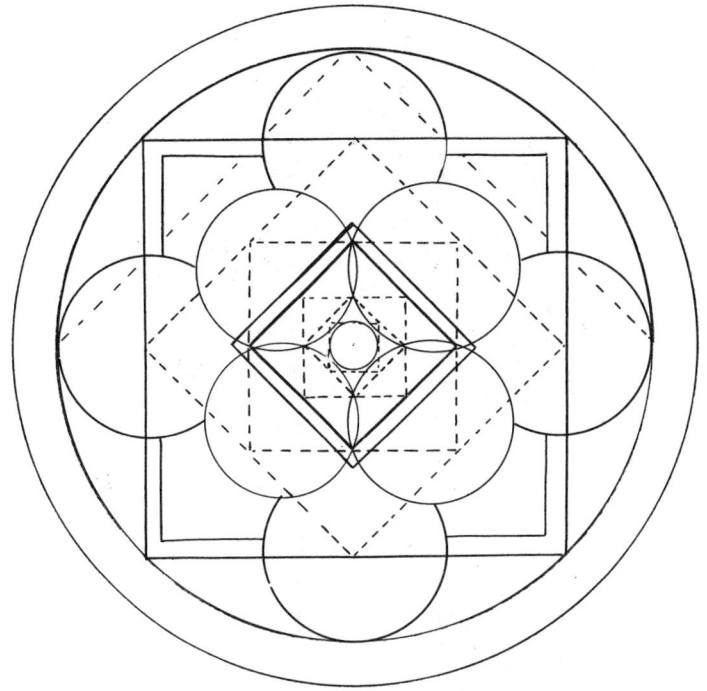

fig. 23 *b* Schematic analysis

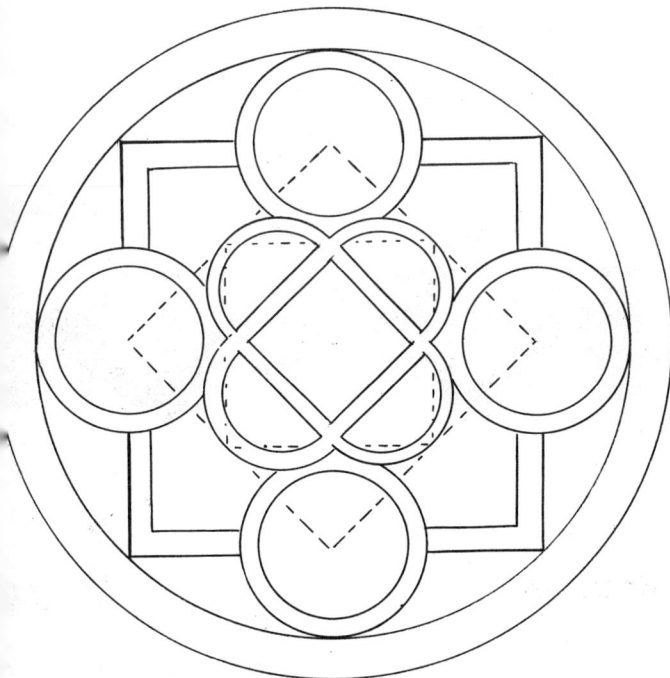

fig. 23 *c* Presumed original concept

fig. 23 *d* In juxtaposition with Villard's sketch

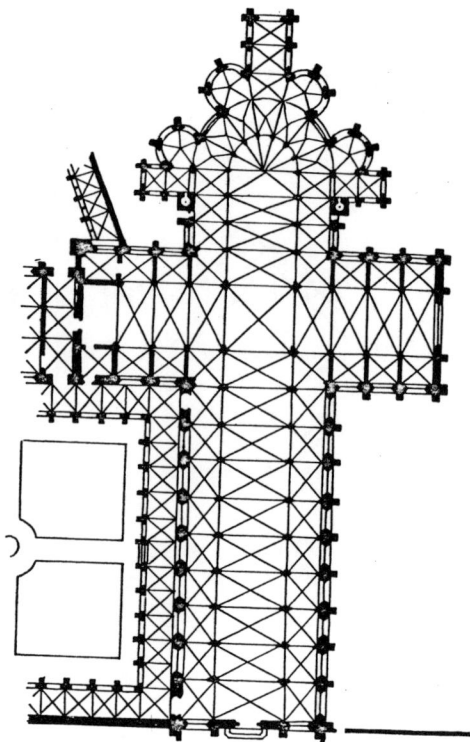

fig. 24 Cistercian Abbey, Vaucelles, 1190-1235
V33

fig. 25 *a* Geometric schema underlying overlap of masons
V38

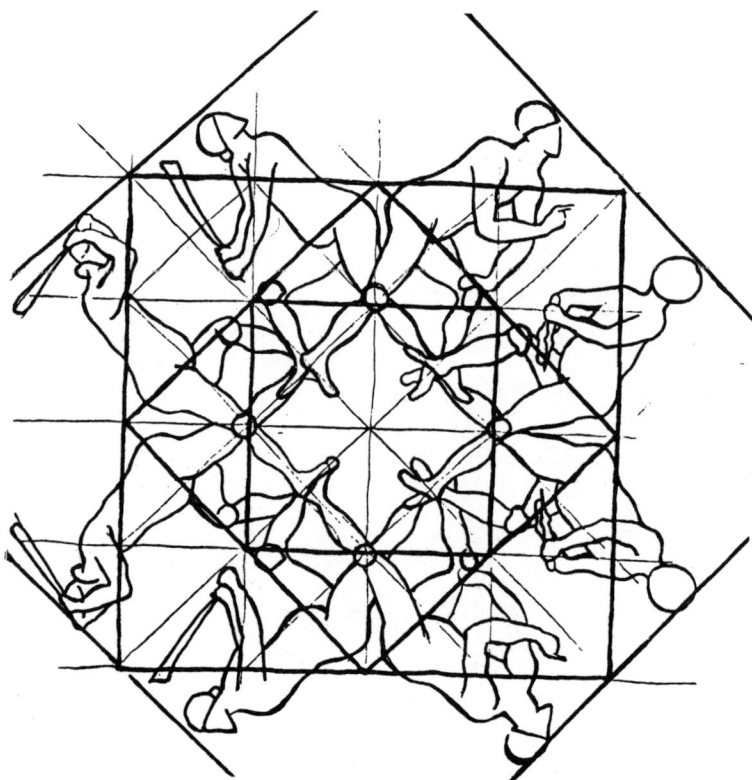

fig. 25 *b* Geometric schema underlying group of fighters (H) V38

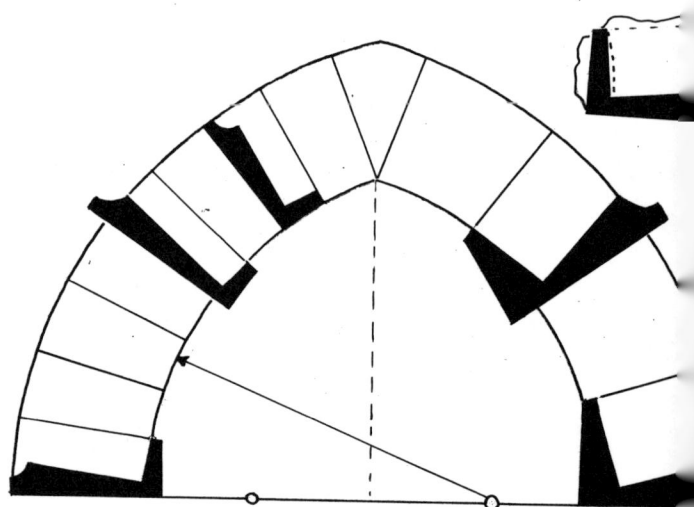

fig. 26 Possible use of a voussoir square for a tiers-point arc
four or eight voussoirs

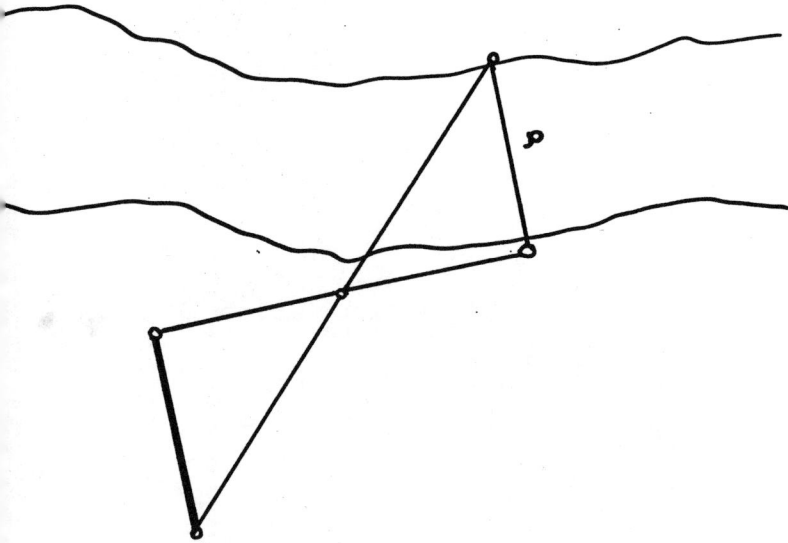

7 Determination of an unbridgeable distance according to Nipsus and
   Africanus V39

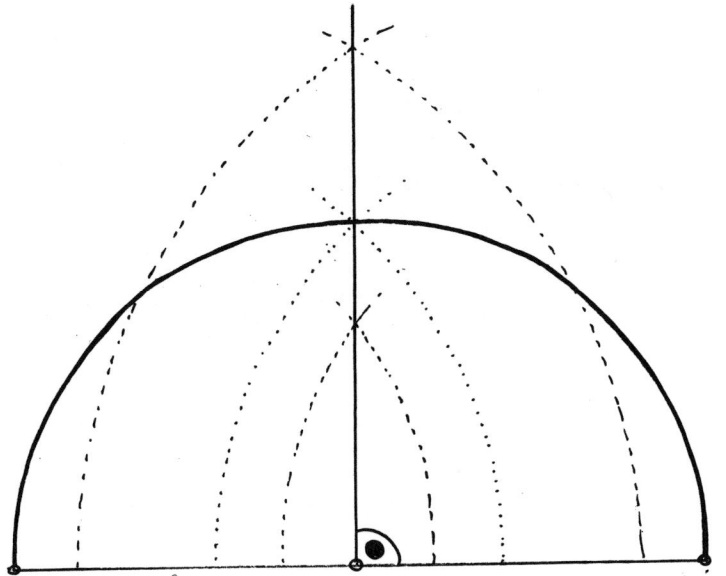

fig. 28 Determination of a right angle through the use of arcs
   V39

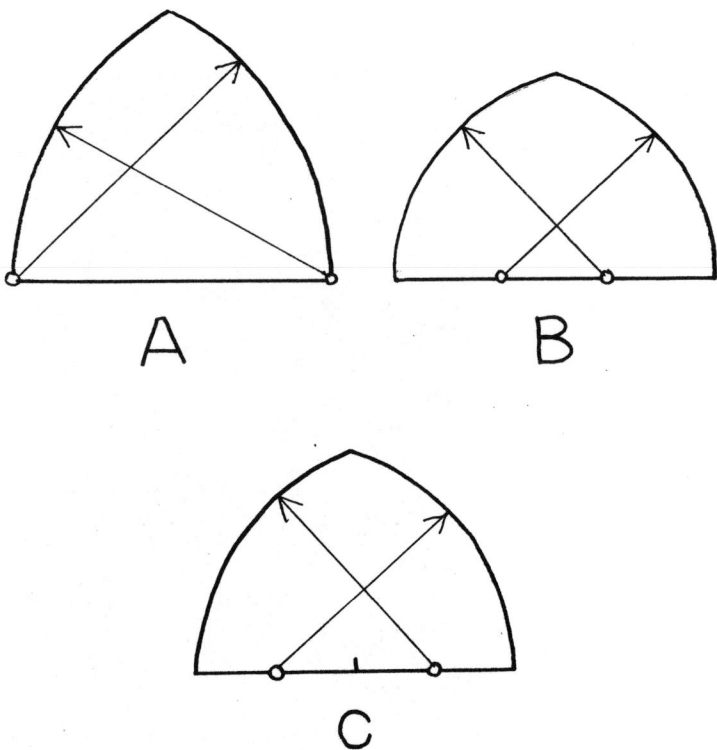

fig. 29 Construction of two point, tiers points and quint point
   arches V41

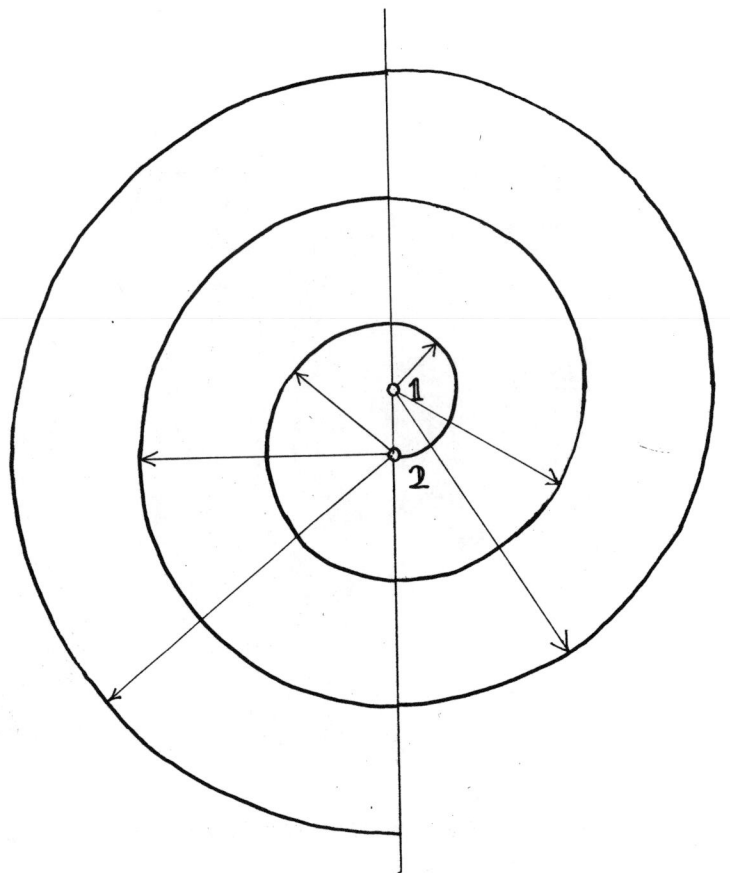

fig. 30 Construction of an Archimedes spiral V40

fig. 31 Reconstruction of the automatic saw V44

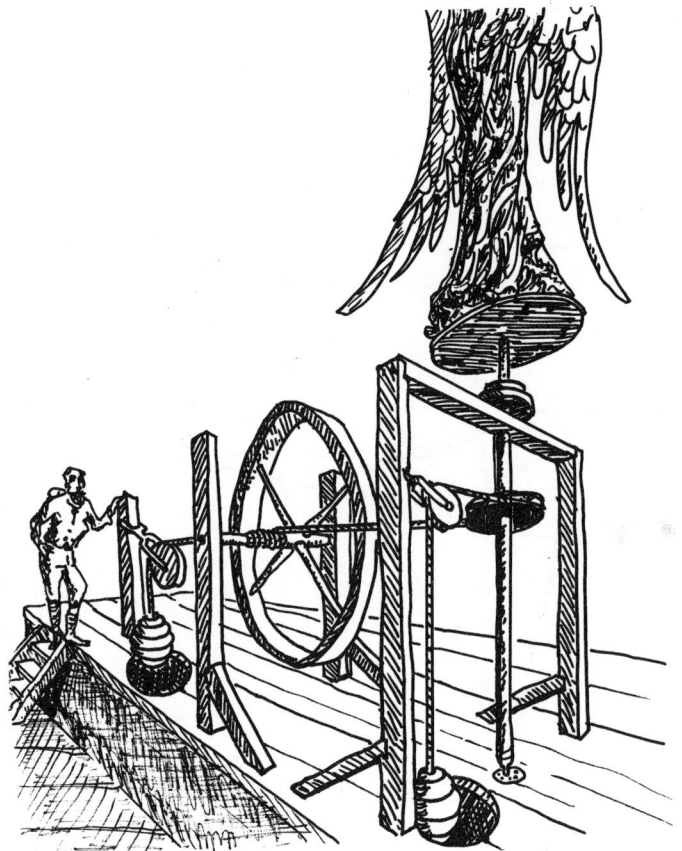

fig. 32 *a* "Clockwork" for an angel pointing toward the sun, with friction plates V45

fig. 32 *b* "Clockwork" for angel pointing at the sun, simplified system V45

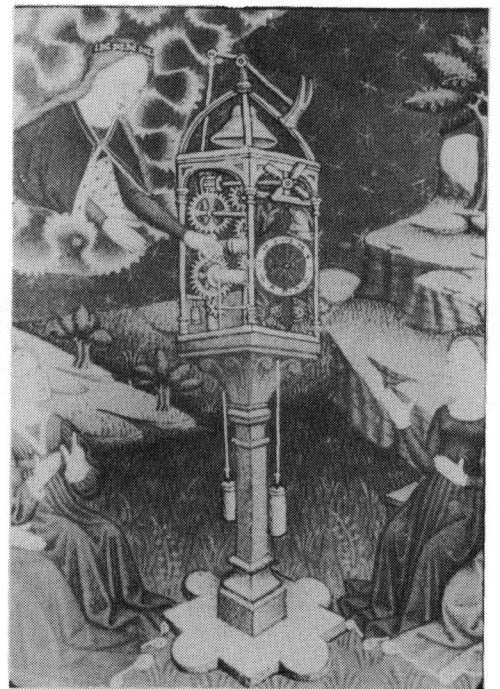

fig. 33 Temperance with clockwork showing possible pendulum, Oxford, Bodleian Libr. Ms. Laud. Misc. 570 f. 28

fig. 34 Bracing jack for sagging house V45

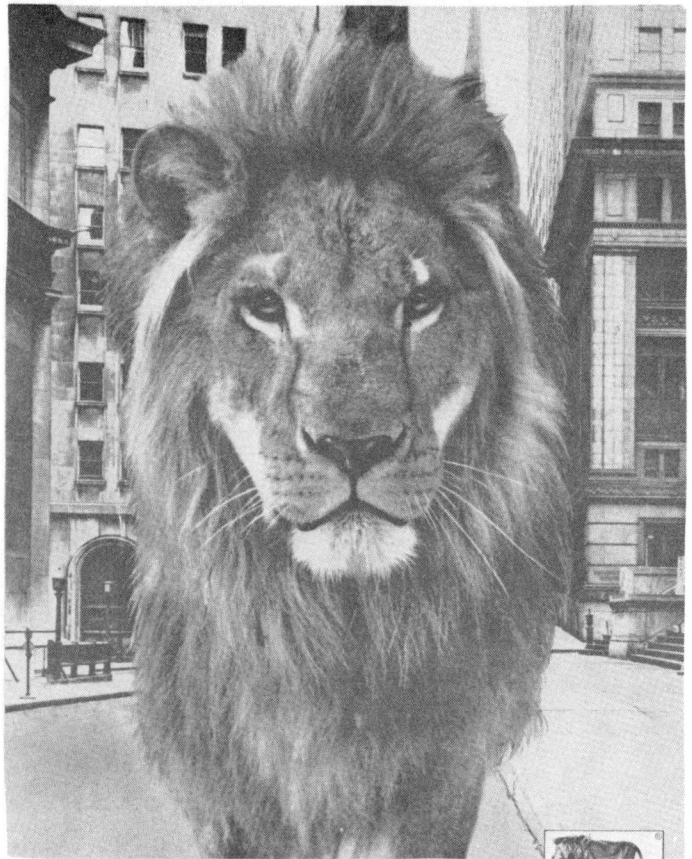

fig. 35 Lion V48, with permission of the Dreyfus Fund

fig. 36 Blessing Christ, Reims
Cathedral, North
portal, c. 1220 V54

fig. 36 *b* Blessing Christ, Reims Cathedral, North
portal, c. 1220, V54 (present state)

189

fig. 37 *a* Visitation group, Reims Cathedral, West portal, c. 1220 V55

fig. 37 *b* Paul, James, John, Reims Cathedral, North transept, c. 1230 V55

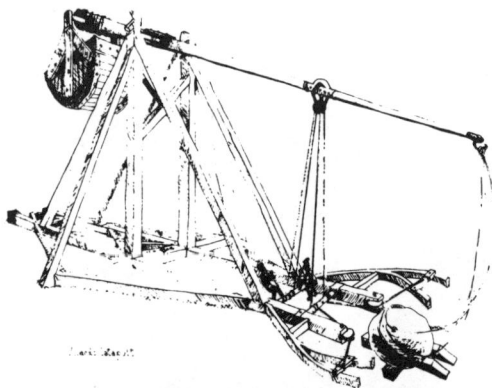

fig. 38 Catapult V59

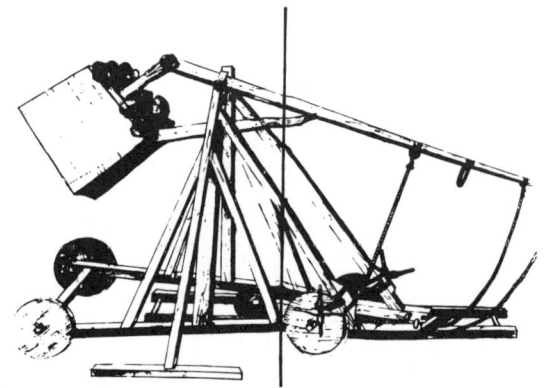

fig. 39b Philip Mönch, *Book of War*. Catapult. Heidelberg University Library.

fig. 39a Catapult, London, British Museum, Stowe Ms. 17 fol. 243 v, V59

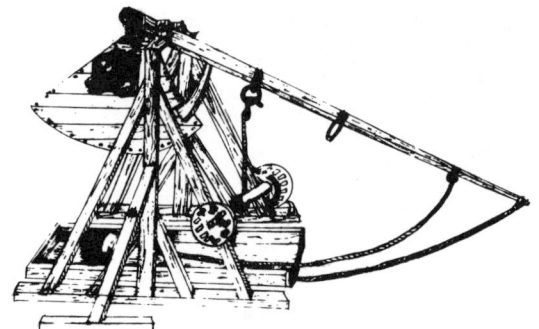

fig. 39c Philip Mönch, *Book of War*. Catapult. Heidelberg University Library.

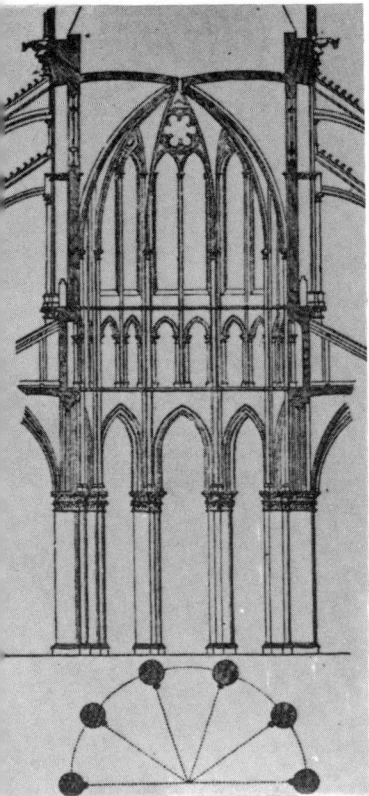

fig. 40 Choirs of Reims

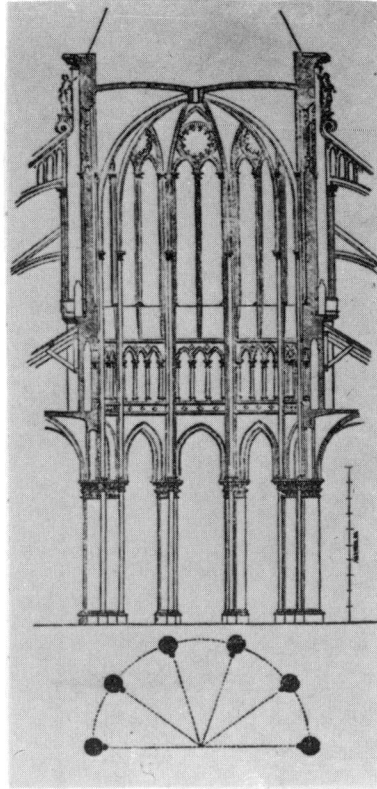

fig. 40 *a* Choirs of Reims, St. Quentin V60

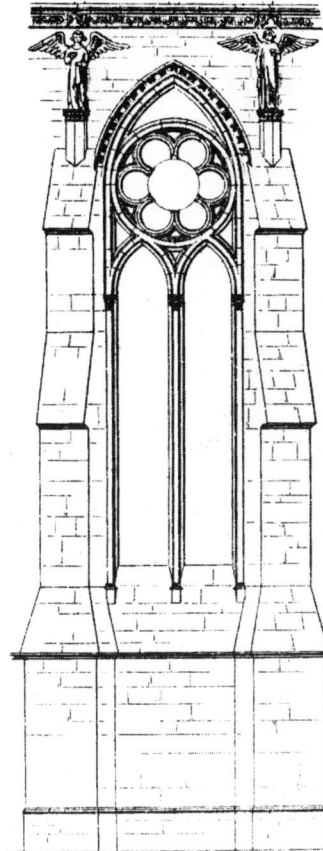

fig. 41 *a* Choir chapel, Reims

fig. 41 *b* Choir chapel, Reims, V61

fig. 41 *c* Choir chapel, Reims

191

fig. 42 Exterior elevation, Reims

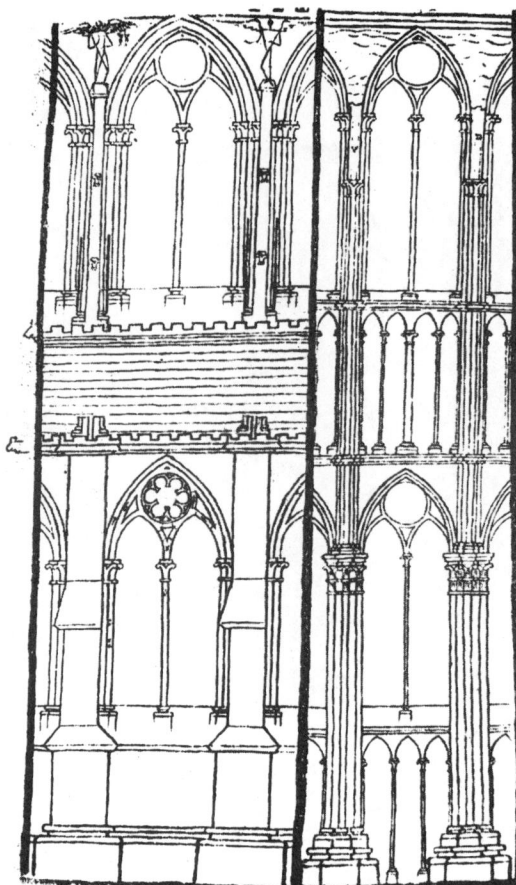

fig. 42 *a*. V62

fig. 42 *c* Interior elevation, Reims

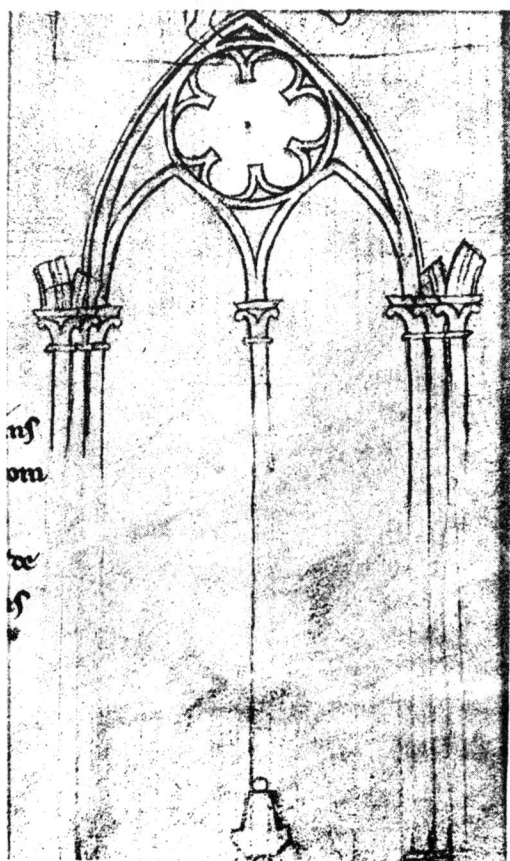

fig. 42 *d*. V20

fig. 42 *e* Side aisle window, Reims

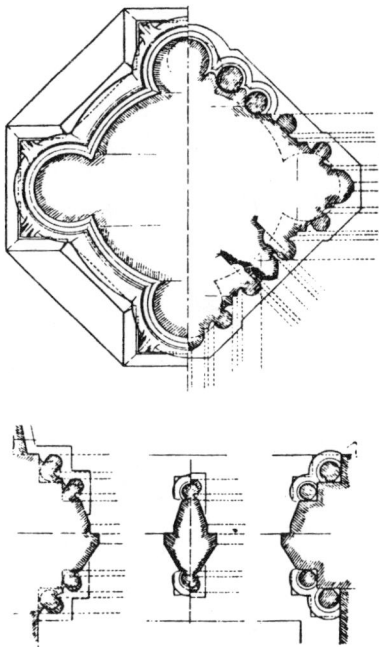

fig. 43 Reims Cathedral, Cross section through a nave window and piers (H) V63

fig. 44a Choir, present buttressing system, Reims Cathedral (H) V64

fig. 44b Choir, present buttressing system, Reims Cathedral (H) V64

fig. 45 Exterior view of buttressing system, Reims Cathedral

Master WG

The Sketchbook and Pattern Book of Master WG (active 1560-72)

Designation: WG

This excellently preserved manuscript is now in the library of the Städelsches Kunstinstitut in Frankfurt-am-Main. It has the number 8-494 and the old inventory number 2026, and retains its original leather binding with two engraved clasps. It measures 220 x 168 x 45 mm. The cover is stamped with rinceaux patterns, and the frame contains repeated figures of Christ, St. Peter, and St. John in half-length, as well as several blank escutcheons. In the upper right we find the date of the binding, 1560. There is also a small rectangle on the cover containing the stamped initials of the author, WG, and the date 1572 with the number two reversed. Two flyleaves are glued to the covers.

The manuscript contains 316 pages each measuring about 200 x 150 mm., with the exception of page forty-six which is only 149 mm. wide. Most gatherings consist of three bifolia or twelve pages. Some consist of four bifolia, and a very few, such as pages forty-nine through fifty-two are only bifolia. The gatherings seem to be in their original sequence with several watermarks through the gutter. There have been some repairs. Water damage is noticeable, though slight. The leaf that should be between pages 188 and 189 is lost, page twenty is blank, and the last gathering which contains eighteen bifolia includes 31 blank pages (281-312). There are also several cutout patterns such as those on pages 133, 233, and 313 which were probably removed and glued back. The pagination is sequential through page 100.

The watermarks mentioned above occur repeatedly in the volume. The first is a saltcellar which Briquet (2169-79) located in Munich (1541-61) and the neighboring towns of Augsburg (1544) and Freising (1536-61). The second is a coat of arms with the appended initials WF which Briquet (1111-15) found in Bavaria (1527-42), Salzburg (1580) and Hungary (1581). The watermarks appear to localize the papermill in Bavaria, most likely Munich, where the emblems are frequently found.

The author's initials WG and his mason's mark or a combination of both appear nine times in the manuscript. The mason's mark even becomes a cutout pattern on page 202. The same mason's mark appears in Stuttgart in the church of St. Leonhard (c.1491) where it accompanies the coat of arms of Abelin (or Aberlin) Jörg. In the staircase tower of the Convent Church of the Holy Cross (1495), it is carved opposite Jörg's coat of arms which contains a square and three stars. Peter Parler had introduced coats of arms for architects in 1380. These were sometimes different from their mason's marks. Gerstenberg points out that Jörg, the son of the sculptor-architect Hänslin also used the more formal name of Georg.[1] It is tempting to connect WG's sketchbook with the Aberlin Jörg family, especially since one of the last identifiable examples of a vault on page 201 refers to the Frauenkirche in Munich which was completed by Jörg van Halsbach in 1492. The presence of the manuscript in Höchst, southeast of Frankfurt, and the rich, varied material in the book makes it equally tempting to connect WG with the Gerthener family, whose most famous member, Madern Gerthener, was active in the first half of the fifteenth century. His reputation as an architect-draftsman rivalled those of Hans von Burghausen (alias Stethaimer) and Michael Knab (Chnab), and has been described by Ringhausen.[2] The testamentary nature of the sketchbooks makes it very likely that this one was descended through one of these families. It is more than probable that the author was a member of a family of builders and thus felt duty-bound to systematically organize, copy, and "complete" a group of fifteenth century architectural drawings which was close at hand. Like Lechler and, later, Simon Garcia, the author must have been fully conscious that Gothic architecture had come to an end, but that its principles and richness were worth preserving for future generations. In addition, the manuscript may have been undertaken as a gesture of filial piety.

The book itself was made in 1560. The drawings were clearly based on a collection of pre-existing sketches. These were loosely organized into topics such as windows, vault projection schemata, single vault designs, and projects for vaulting entire spaces and were copied in quick succession. Many drawings served as examples for the cut-out patterns which probably did not form part of the originally purchased volume but were bound into it in a haphazard manner. The book was then paginated, copiously signed, and dated no less than five times in 1572, thus certifying the time of its completion. Finally, the monogram of the master and the completion date were stamped on the leather cover. Beyond its probable origin in or around Munich, nothing is known about the provenance of the volume until Peter Seitz of Höchst-am-Main declared himself its owner in 1835. On page 317 he mentions the birth of his son Valentin on 27 May 1826. From there, it entered the possession of the Frankfurt museum director, J.D. Passavant who gave the "Steinmetzenbuch" to the Städelsches Kunstinstitut in 1861.

Contents and Style

Two hundred and twenty-two projects are illustrated in the volume. They fall into the following categories:

Windows: 9 drawings and 14 patterns, or a total of 23
Single vaults of one or two bays: 12 drawings and 61 patterns, or a total of 73
Vaults for complete spaces: 7 drawings, 5 advanced drawings, 62 patterns, or a total of 74
Theoretical, geometric and decorative drawings: 6
Mullions: 3 drawings
Sundials: 4 drawings
Vault projection schemata: 28 drawings
Stairs: 4 drawings
Gables: 1 drawing, 6 cut-out patterns

A standard technique was used in these designs. With the help of a straight edge the designs were incised with an iron or bronze stylus of which one example still exists in Regensburg. Circles were incised with a divider. The lines are visible in most photographs. Some drawings, such as those on pages 3, 4, 9, 10, and the cut-out on page 228 were completed with a bistre pencil, but most were finished with brown ink. In most vault projection schemata, a reddish-brown wash was added presumably to indicate the height of the diagonal rib and that of the subsidiary ribs or of the cross arch. The cut-out patterns of pages 49-200 were simply incised and then cut out with a straight-edge and a knife. Brown leaves were inserted behind some of the patterns to highlight the design.

The most fascinating aspect of the manuscript is its late date. It is nearly inconceivable that a volume so steeped in Gothic nostalgia should have been painstakingly assembled at a time when Filarete and Alberti were passé, Philibert de l'Orme had already published his *Premier tome de l'Architecture* (1568), and Palladio had released his *Four Books of Architecture* (1570). It is even more ironic that Sebastiano Serlio, who had edited his *Regole Generali di Architettura* between 1537-47 sold a *Settimo Libro d'Architettura* to Jacopo della Strada who was to publish it in Frankfurt (*sic*) in 1575, three years after the completion of Master

WG's labors.

By 1572, the Gothic style had ended. Its last great burst at the end of the fifteenth century which added numerous and often incongruously elegant net vault choirs and star vault choirs to earlier buildings, had ebbed by the end of the first quarter of the sixteenth century. The fireworks of the last great medieval architects, who resisted the planar and arithmetic approach of the Renaissance, died in the glory of some of the most complex statements of Western architectural history. Benedikt Ried whose Rider Staircase in the Hradcani in Prague (1503-05) was a miracle of upward flowing, doubly curved and "breaking" ribs, Erhard Heydenreich's double plane floral vaults in the Frauenkirche in Ingolstadt (1509-24), or Anton Pilgram's pulpit in St. Stephen in Vienna (1505) were all a matter of the past. These and other supremely sophisticated works with doubly curved arches, hanging keystones, or bent finials had exhausted the style. Gothic structures continued to be erected only in the most provincial locations. In the centers, however, we begin to see the first manifestations of the Gothic revival described by Paul Frankl.[3] He calls the resurgence from the past "survival." One wonders if the nostalgic custodians of the dead style, whose pupils were still subjected to examinations involving spiral staircases and the vaulting of irregular spaces as late as 1723, did not foresee and foster the continued thrust of the Gothic.[4] Master WG would not have composed his book, had he not been aware of the sophistication, disciplined flexibility and romantic appeal of the Gothic, in contrast to the often pseudo-rational architecture of the Renaissance. In spite of this, WG's formal vocabulary was influenced by sixteenth-century designs. The strong emphasis on interlocking circles in window tracery, the often heavy arithmetic use of 2:3 or 3:5 divisions instead of geometric grids heralded the new trend. The planar "marquetterie" vault on page 267 or the fascinating combination of central plan elements and Renaissance clarity with Gothic longitudinal thrusts in the plan on page 269 are unthinkable earlier, and are part of an underground survival. Accompanying this new emphasis on arithmetic and the number is the rare representation of a measuring rod on page 46. Subdivided into twelve units of 14 mm. it measures 154 mm. If it is related to the theoretical sketch of a rectangular vault and the rotational schema of a square, the diagonal of the vault would measure eight units and the vault would be circa seven units wide, or possibly seven feet, barely enough to span a corridor.

Despite the marriage between absolute measurements and geometric procedures to which any numerical figure might be assigned, Master WG was uneasy with this union. He was no longer comfortable with the solid geometric concepts established in thirteenth century France which were transferred to the lodges of Prague, Strasbourg, and Cologne.

The genesis and development of the vault systems illustrated by WG will be analyzed later. As we have seen a simple star vault already appeared on page 41 of Villard de Honnecourt's notebook. His drawing may have been influenced by major, contemporary vault designs created in England. The ridge-rib for instance was used from the early thirteenth century onward and complex configurations which display a consummate knowledge of the decorative possibilities of the rib were introduced in the nave of Lincoln Cathedral. They include the so-called "crazy vaults" which stress forward thrusting diagonal elements which disturb the standard bilateral vault symmetry. This vault, presumably dated after 1239 is faintly echoed in WG's patterns on pages 227 and 271. These experiments were followed by multifacetted vaults. Some of them, such as the elaborate star vaults and net vaults of Tewkesbury and Gloucester are dated by Geoffrey Webb to the second quarter of the fourteenth century.[5]

Compared with the English designs, Peter Parler's large star vault over the Wenceslas Chapel (1367) adjoining St. Vitus in Prague seems overrated. The influence of the decorative use of the rib in England on the Parler family and leading German architects has yet to be explored. They must have been familiar with these architectural designs which they at first simplified, and later elaborated. We know that complex English patterns appeared in Northern Germany and helped to shape the organization of the crystal vaults of Danzig (Gdansk). This subject was recently analyzed in context with the theoretical vaulting treatise of Bartel Ranisch by Helene C. Kaplan.[6] It is only through the use of doubly curved rib systems (*Schlingenrippengewölbe*) in the orbit of Benedikt Ried, Anton Pilgram and others around 1500, that Northern Europe developed a uniquely sophisticated vaulting statement.[7] Many of the vaults illustrated by WG were destined for parish churches of little consequence such as Schorndorf (fig. 1) or the church of St. Peter in Gerlingen (fig. 2) of 1463 (cf. pages 17, 100, 233, 249). Only nine, awkward doubly curved rib elements appear, such as the example on page 263. The only successful experiment in this direction on pages 13, and 195 shows an early and tentative doubly curved star similar to that found in the Collegiate Church of Aschaffenburg (fig. 3). Only a few trans-penetrating rib systems are shown (pages 101, 133). Since these designs came into wider use at the end of the century, a cutoff date before 1500 must be postulated for the original material used by WG. This is corroborated by a typically precise star vault in the choir of the recently restored Protestant townhouse of Bad Cannstatt (fig. 4) whose vaults (1465-71) contain bosses showing Aberlin Jörg's coat-of-arms, once more, in connection with a mason's mark which is nearly identical with that found in our manuscript on pages 44, 95, 98, 111, 280.

The many star-vaults shown by WG have early German antecedents in the substructure of the choir in Alt Breisach, the Maulbronn chapterhouse, the roughly contemporary summer refectory at Bebenhausen of c. 1335 and the great refectory at Marienburg of c. 1320.[8] More complex net vault patterns such as those on pages 231, 233, and 259 echo those found in Braunsburg, Kellermarkt and especially St. Jakon in Burghausen.[9] The possible variations in combinations of net and star vaults, including the use of "compressed" or "stretched" stars, and rhomboids adding up to a "super-rhomboid" appear in dozens of southern German churches. The illustrations below show Bernhard Engelberg's airy vault over the northern side aisles of Ulm Cathedral (fig. 5) built 1502-07 and Hans Felber's charming net vault in the minute upper Nun's Chapel in Waiblingen (fig. 6) which is seen in its original painted state. These vaults can be compared with pages 23, 101, 197, 201, 255, and 273 in WG's sketchbook. The grandiose and powerful designs for longitudinal vaults centered around a rhomb on pages 93, 109, and 159 echo the northern side aisle of the church of Our Lady in Ingolstadt (fig. 7) which precede Heydenreich's early sixteenth century double vaults by several decades. The most amazing correspondence between a design and its execution is found in William Joy's mesh vault at Wells (1329). This "marquetterie" design precisely replicates WG's page 162.[10] Further examples will be listed in the note at the end of this introduction.

The last great triumphs of Gothic are small works with complex vault baldachins. WG treats most vaults as academic experiments and adds complexities which are often unconvincing when they depart from the theoretical rigour exemplified by the sketches in the *Dresden Sketch Book of Vault Projection* treated later in this series. The usual, systematic approach is apparent in WG's progression from single line designs to ink sketches and, finally, cutout patterns. This procedure is exemplified in the tilted cross vaults on pages 10, 14, and 201 which already had been executed in the side aisle of the Frauenkirche in Munich (fig. 8) (1468-92). WG's exercises in the vaulting of large spaces are of increasing complexity. In addition, he must have had a strong awareness of the optics of vault geometry. Drawings and cut-out patterns alike often stress patterns which can be read alternatively as multiplying rhomboids expanding into six-point stars or multifaceted hexagons (see page 17, 253 and figs. 1, 6). WG understood that striving for minimal size changes in the ribs of a plan facilitated the projection process, was less expensive and increased its graphic rationality. It must be remembered that a model or a plan would often suffice to secure a commission in the highly competitive building business. For these reasons WG included 147 vault projects in his book, and gave lavish attention to the cutout patterns. They also appear in the Rixner Lodge Book of the 1480s and were not, as some have assumed, the amusing embellishments of later owners. Aside from their decorative appeal which helped to sell vault and tracery elements, they served another purpose. By bending the sheet into a tunnel shape, lowering one's head to look at the pattern from below, one could gain a rough idea of the eventual appearance of the vault. The view was, of course, badly distorted since the short springing ribs in the plans are in reality very long. Despite distortions the little paper models offered the lay client a more convincing view of the interaction between the rib elements.

Many unsatisfactory designs show WG'S hesitancy of choice between a geometric and an arithmetical design procedure. This led to a loss of control in tracery patterns and is also present in vault projects. For instance on page 19 the radii of a hexagon defining a star vault do not touch square two of the quadrature. This not only breaks with tradition, but also makes the nine ribs which spring from the corners too powerful and destroys the balance of opposites. The pattern demonstrates the flexibility of Gothic planning and at the same time emphasizes the dangers of discarding the Vitruvian adage to the effect that every element must relate to the whole "in accordance with a certain part selected as standard." [11] Even when the prevailing Renaissance methods of arithmetic progression were employed, such as in the star vault on page 125 where one-sixth of the center line is used, the result seems more rigid. The Gothic design concept thrived on the arithmetic irrationality of geometrically staggered proportions which are instinctively pleasant to the eye, but, at the same time a puzzle to the measuring mind.

Most of the vault cut-outs were based on arithmetic sequences. Most often the designs are variations upon traditional patterns. The cut-out pattern on page 178 for instance uses the repetition of equal rhombs (figs. 1, 2, 6, 9). A more sophisticated use of the same element appers on page 249. It contains rhombs in rows that first turn into a four-part rhomb, then into horizontally stretched stars, wide hexagons, and extremely stretched hexagons. To the Gothic architect, this kind of vault, resembling the nave of the church of the Holy Cross in Schwäbisch-Gmünd (figs. 9 and 10) must have seemed an uninspired design (WG 91, 98, 111, 114, 219). But it appealed and still appeals to the layman. It is this boring predictability which led Master WG to design vaults such as those on pages 154, 262, 263, and 277. They are unsuccessful. We seem to perceive the conflict that existed in WG's mind. He was torn between two styles and two methods of design. Some drawings still use the quadrature aseptically, such as in the scheme on page 21. There is still the instinctive, but misunderstood sense of the importance and personal ownership of profiles. But the signed, dated and marked mullion on page 9 is not the personal statement WG may have intended. Instead it shows the standardized rotation of the square in search of a mullion in which square two determines its initial length, and square three its width. In its clearer counterpart, on page 28, square six provides the lower width and square seven the upper width of the mullion, while square eight defines the triangular recesses and the length of the dowel hole. The corners of square one determine the curve of the upper circular segments of the face piece whereas the centers of the lower circles were traditionally chosen arbitrarily. The pentagon on page 18 is present as a shape but its construction which is demonstrated in Roriczer's *Geometry*, is not given. The circle inscirbed in an octagon on the same page is too large for the quadrature which it usually would have followed. The arbitrary centers for tracery on pages 68 and 69 produced ungainly results. Even the proportions of the window panes, which are often larger in the upper parts of the frame to correct the effects of foreshortening, are subject to whims. The aesthetic results of these random choices become most obvious in the erratic vault patterns on pages 154, 261, 262, 237, 277, and the disastrous page 263. At its height the whimsy of Gothic architecture was controlled by the frame of geometric discipline. By 1572 these limitations were no longer functioning.

Master WG had heard of the renowned Parler Staircase of 1372 attached to the south transept of St. Vitus in Prague, and its amazing offshoot, the receding spire stairs of Strasbourg Cathedral, which one broadsheet went so far as to proclaim the eighth wonder of the world. He dutifully, and quite ineptly, included it on page 9. Like the authors of some sketchbooks discussed in this volume, Master WG was no longer working on design inventions within the style he recorded. As such, his patterns lack the decorative dynamics of the International Style, the flamboyant vigor of the tracery of a Guy de Dammartin, or even the madness of a Heydenreich design. WG carefully preserved for us the treasure of designs he found in southern Germany, perhaps in Munich. Clearly he no longer stood *in medias res.*

Note

Elke Weber, *Das Steinmetzebuch "W.G. 1572" im Städelschen Kunstinstitut zu Frankfurt-am-Main,* Master's Thesis, University of Cologne, 1977, became available to me after the above text was completed. Among several items not considered by me, the following are discussed by E. Weber: she had traced the paper to the Potschner mill in Munich. She states that the leaf 115-16 was added. She does not reach any firm conclusions as to the identity of WG but states the Peter Seitz, the nineteenth century owner, may have been connected with fifteenth century glass makers from Hessen. Weber correctly relates the designs of the sundials by WG to the activities of the architects and mentions the portraits of mason Konrad Syfer in Strasbourg and of Nikolaus Eseler the Elder in Dinkelsbühl, both of which are portrayed above sundials (see Gerstenberg, *Baumeisterbildnisse,* pp. 198-201). She discusses the late Gothic interest in choirs in connection with Wolf Jakob Stromer's collection of plans and elevations. In the case of the Nürnberg patrician Stromer (1561-1614) we deal with a non-specific collection of views and architectural information which we shall compare with the even later Nicolai volumes of architectural designs in Stuttgart. See also Werner Müller, Die Zeichnungsvorlagen für Friedrich Hoffstadt's "Gothisches A.B.C.-Buch" und der Nach-lass des Nürnberger Ratsbaumeisters Wolf Jacob Stromer, 1561-1614, *Wiener Jarhbuch für Kunstgeschichte,* 28, 1975, pp. 39-54. Above all Weber compares vaults in the WG manuscript with the following churches: WG pages 28, 187, 203, 231, 255, and 273, compared with Grossachsenheim (1484), Wildberg (1467), Unterjesingen (1477-84), and WG's page 268 with St. Vinzenz in Heiligenblut of c. 1450. In addition, E. Weber connects drawings 16896 and 16924 in the Akademie der Bildenden Künste, Vienna, with WG pages 201, and 208. One could add many more sketches of the Vienna collection which correspond to patterns by WG (see Hans Koepf, *Die gotischen Planrisse der Wiener Sammlungen*, Vienna, 1969, illustrations 139, 140-149, 254, 256-57, 294, etc.). She furthermore compares the 185 x 881 mm. drawing of the Parler Staircase in Ulm which was drawn in 1482 with WG's plan of the same staircase on page 19 (see Hans Koepf, *Die gotischen Planrisse der Ulmer Sammlungen*, Ulm, 1977, pp. 123-30). It seems likely to me that WG or his source copied the Ulm drawing which is difficult to read, and which itself might be based on plans from the Parler lodge in Prague.

E. Weber's competent text, although lacking firm conclusions, reinforces my interpretation of WG's manuscript as a highly conscientious and thoroughly eclectic compendium assembled by a mason who gathered material dealing with the architecture of the years 1400-1485.

My thanks go to Peter Pause, Dr. Gerhard Ringhausen, and the exceptionally hospitable staff of the Städelsches Kunstinstitut, especially Dr. M. Stuffman, Dr. Lutz, S. Malke and the photographer Mr. Anton. The *Reproduktion des Ms. für den 65 Geburtstag von Prof. H.R. Rosenau.* Frankfurt, 1965 was not available to me.

The captions are as explicit as possible and include the steps necessary for the completion of the designs. Many of them can be fully designed with fewer elements and are added as a guide to the reader.

1   Gerstenberg, Kurt. 1966. *Die Deutschen Meisterbildnisse des Mittelalters,*Berlin, p. 175.
2   Ringhausen, G.J. 1968. "Madern Gerthener, Leben und Werk nach den Urkunden," Dissertation, Göttingen.
3   Frankl, P. 1962. *Gothic Architecture,* Baltimore, p. 215.
4   Müller, Werner. 1972. "Die Lehrbogenkonstruktion in den Proberissen der Augsburger Maurermeister aus den Jahren 1553-1723 und die gleichzeitige französische Theorie," *Zeitschrift für Geschichte der Architektur,* pp. 17-33.
5   Webb, Geoffrey. 1965. *Architecture in Britain, the Middle Ages,*Baltimore, pp. 77, 78, 141.
6   Kaplan, H.C. 1974. "The Danzig Churches: A Study in Late Vault Development," Dissertation, Binghamton, New York.
7   Clasen, Karl Heinz. 1958. *Deutsche Gewölbe der Spätgotik,* Berlin.
    Schulze, Konrad. 1939. *Die Gewölbe im spätgotischen Kirchenbau in Schwaben von 1450-1520.* Reutlingen.
8   Clasen, pp. 41, 54-57.
9   Clasen, pp. 37-75.
10 Acland, James. 1972. *The Gothic Vault,* Toronto, p. 145 and W.G. 162, 217, 267.
11 Vitruvius, *The Ten Books of Architecture,* Book 1, Chapt. II/4.

The Frankfurt Lodge Book of Master WG

Binding: 218 x 168 x 45 mm. Stamped leather with repeated busts of Christ, Moses, Paul and John, escutcheons. Dated 1560 in the upper right frame. Original brass clasps. The monogram W · G and the date 1572 are later additions.

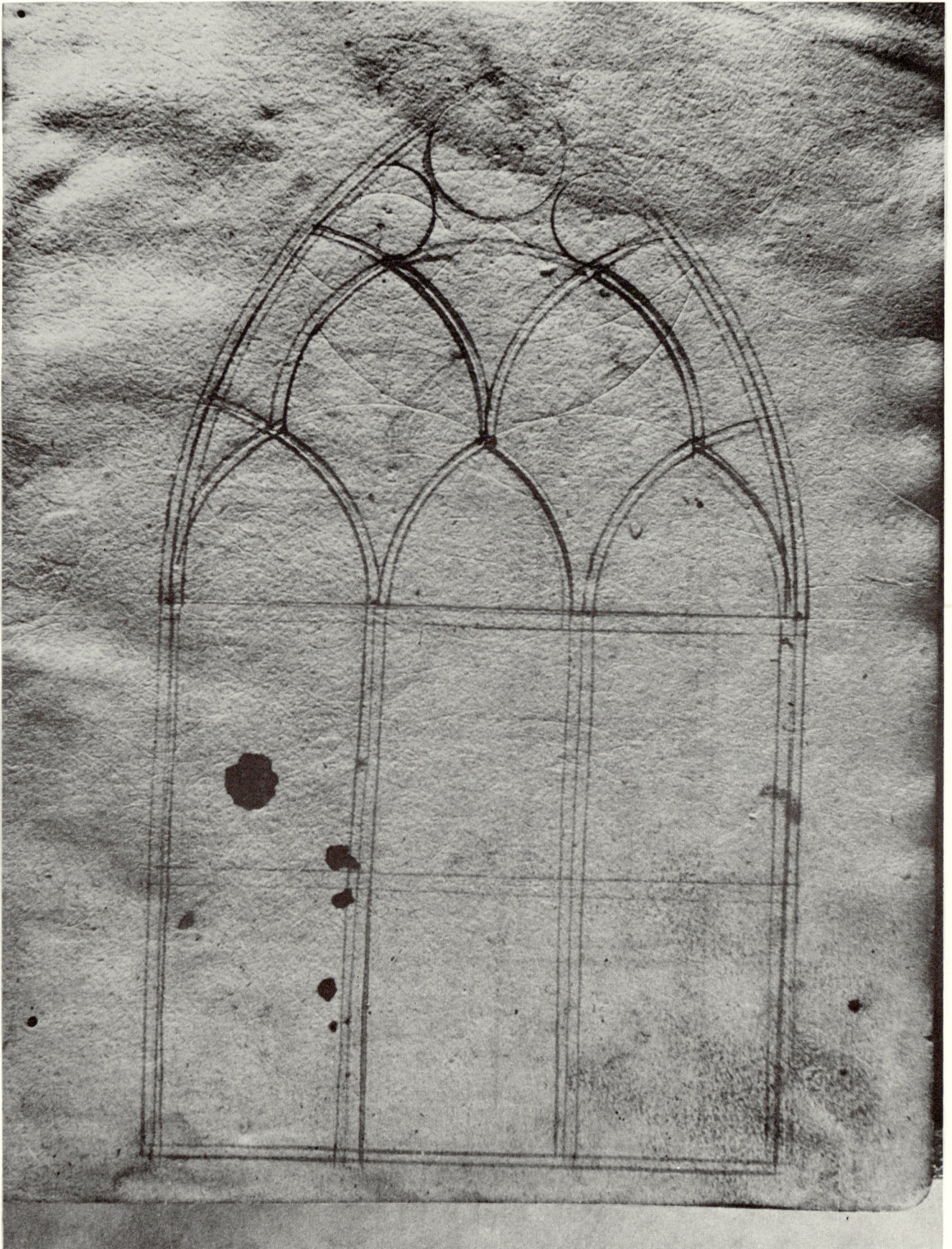

WG 1   Triple lancet window based on six diagons and interlocked half circles for the tracery design.

WG 2   Triple lancet window with tracery based on interlocked half- and quarter circles,
and thence to the center of the vault. See Dresden Sketchbook of Vault Projection

203

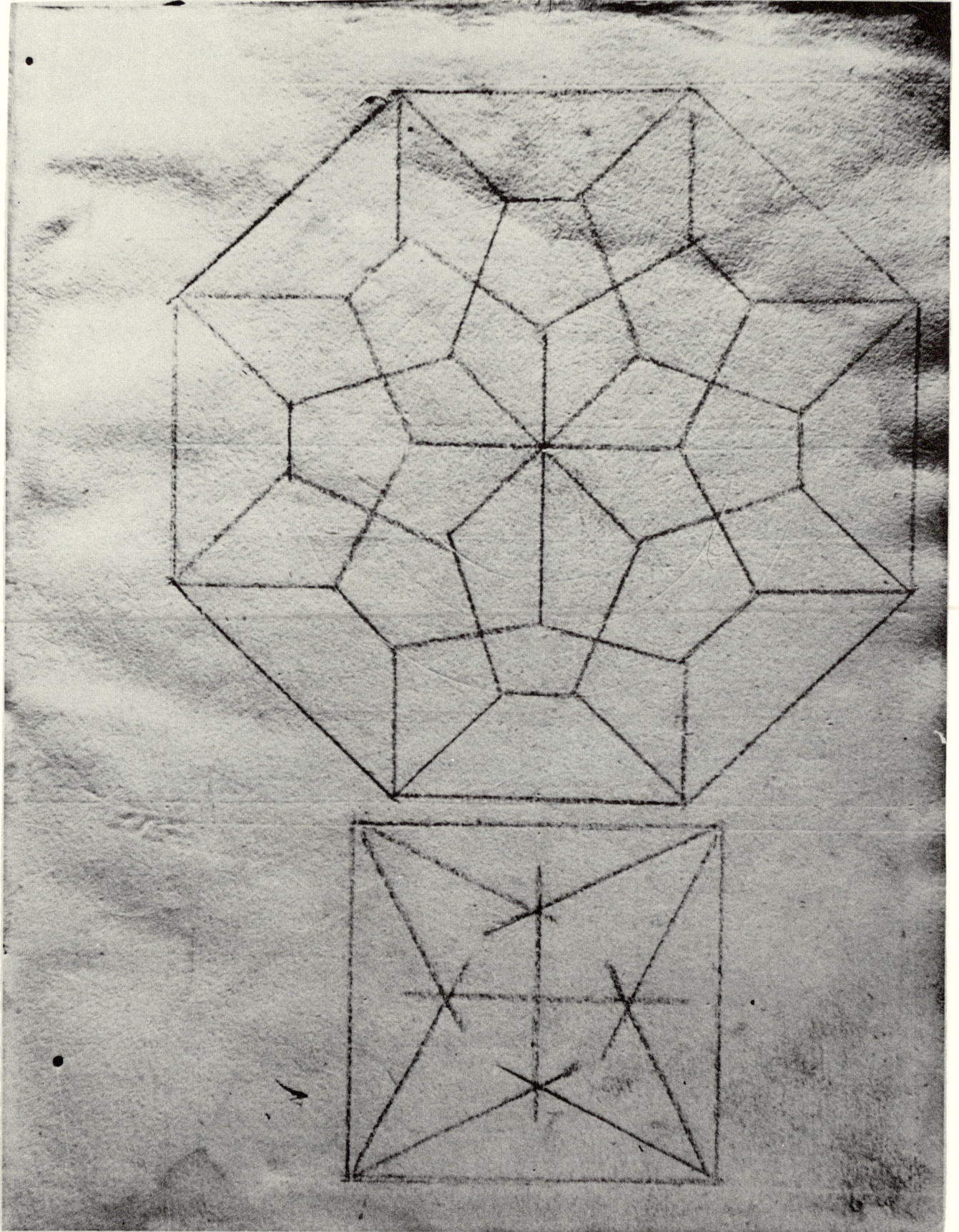

WG 3 Square bay with lengthened, slide-through ribs leading to an octagonal, ribbed structure. Its geometry is based on four circles. The doubling of the radius of Circle Two determines the outer perimeter. Compare with cut-out pattern WG 85.

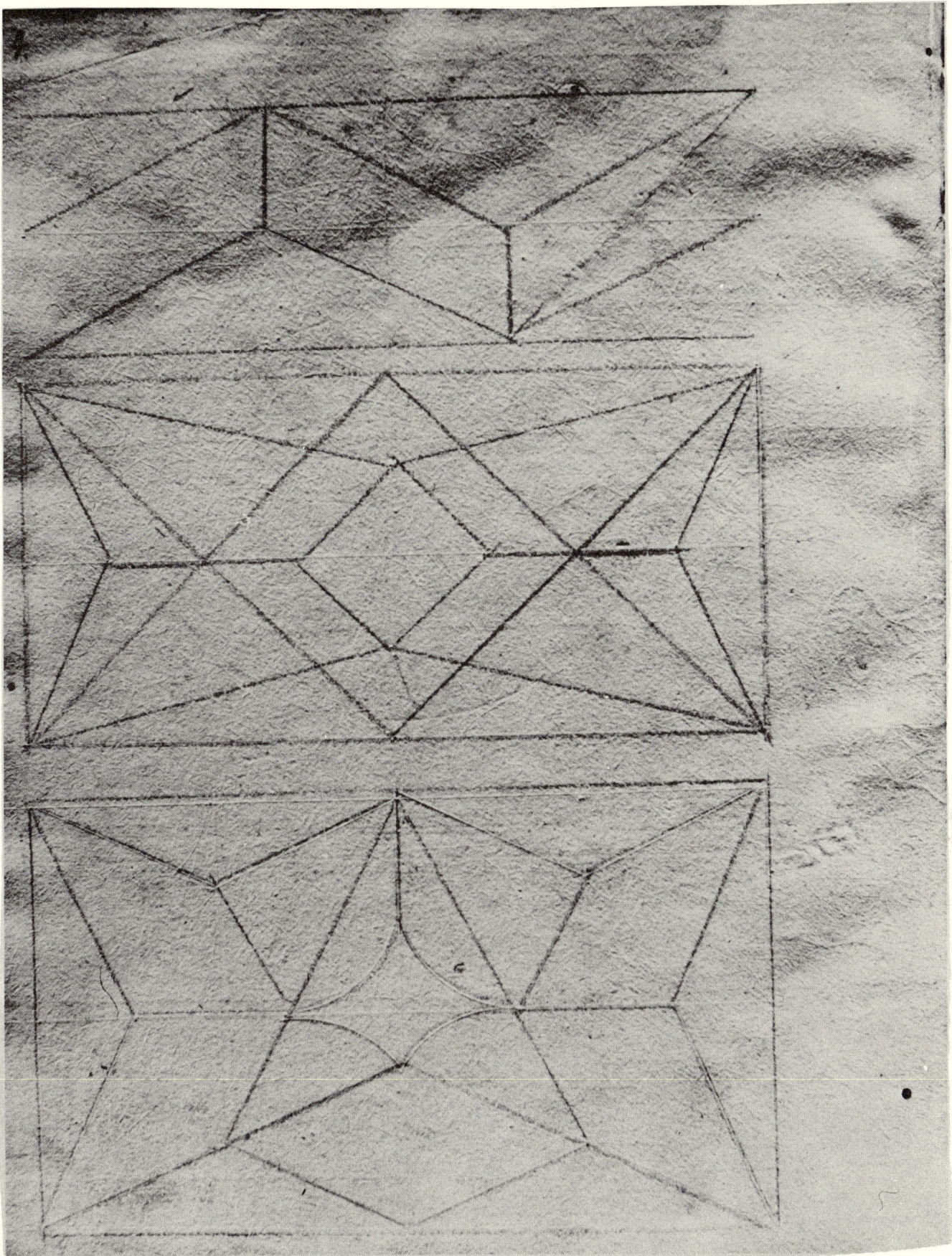

WG 4   Sideaisle or corridor vault. Rectangular vault based on a double square, the rotation of a square through the center line whereby squares one and three determine the rib system. Double square vault with ribs determined by vertical quarters, a circle drawn from the center and a haphazard central lozenge with doubly curved ribs.

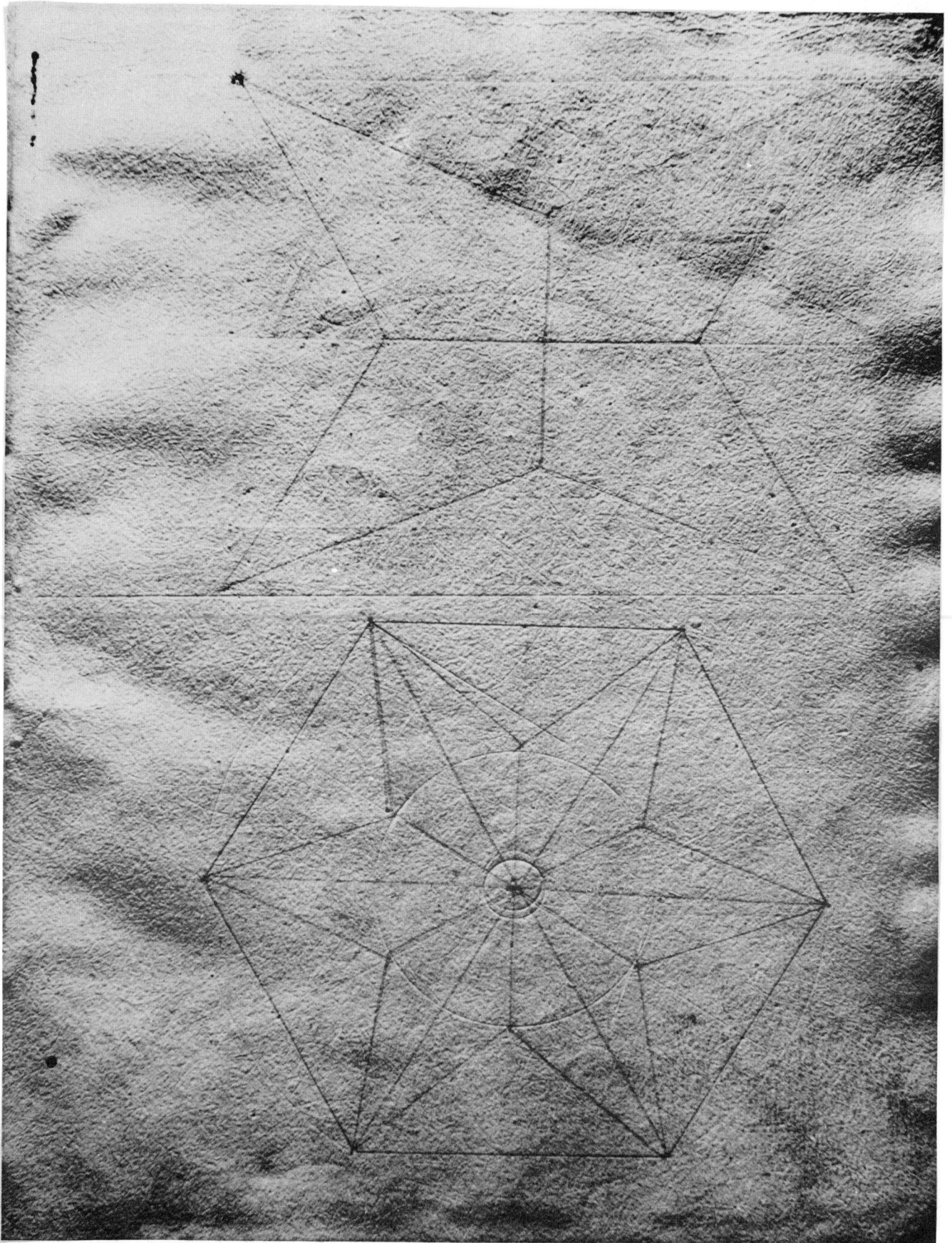

WG 5   Quadripartite star vault determined by halving the center lines. Hexagon with inscribed star vault based on a division of the second circle into twelve equal parts.

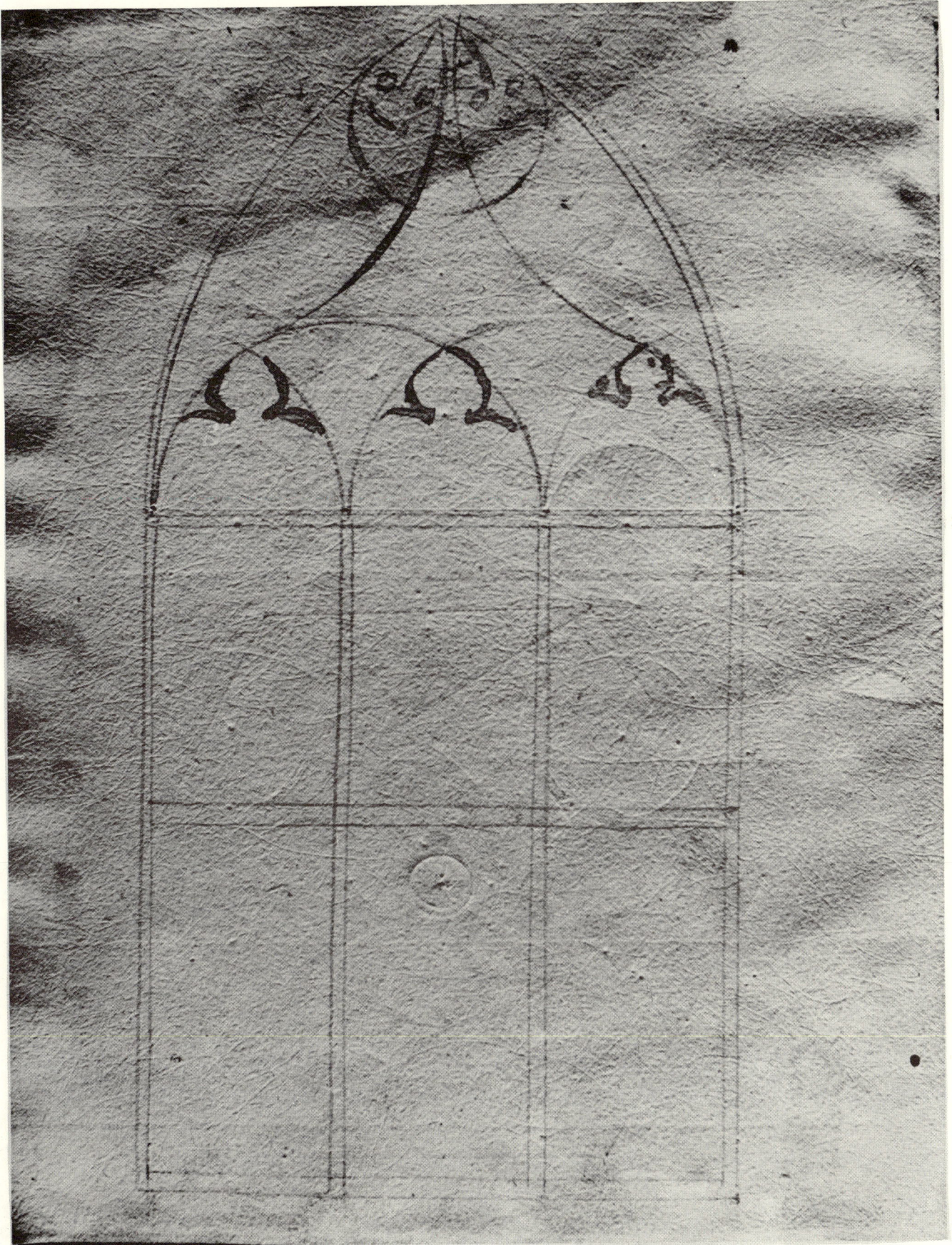

WG 6   Triple lancet window with tracery based on interlocking half circles and two segments, arbitrarily centered on a line prolonging the jambs.

WG 7   Four lancet window with two point arch containing tracery based on interlocking half circles and four mouchettes. The monogram of the master appears in two segmental triangles, above his mason's mark.

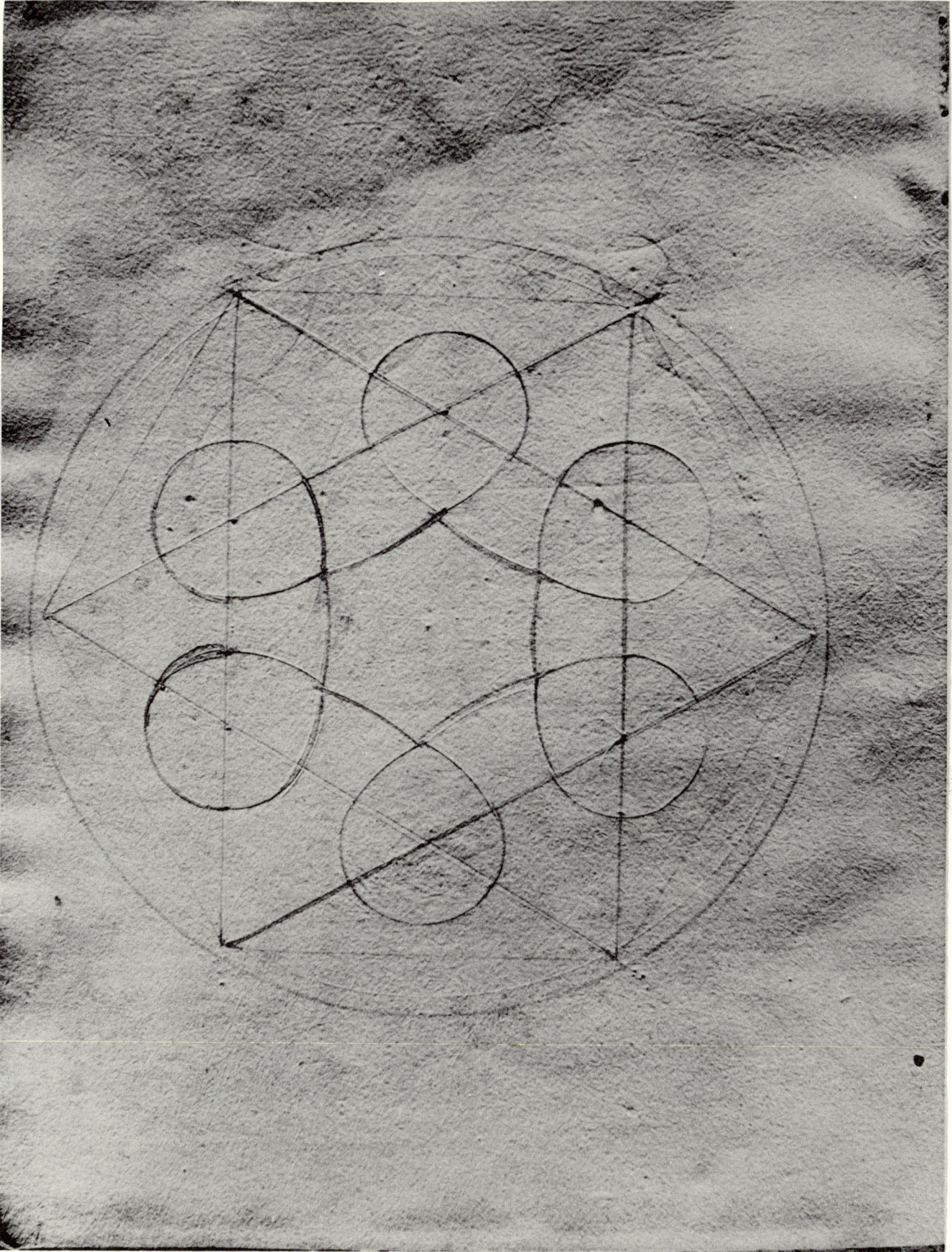

WG 8   Rough sketch of a hexagon with two inscribed equilateral triangles which determine the centers of three quarter circles merging in a curved hexagon. Compare with WG 22.

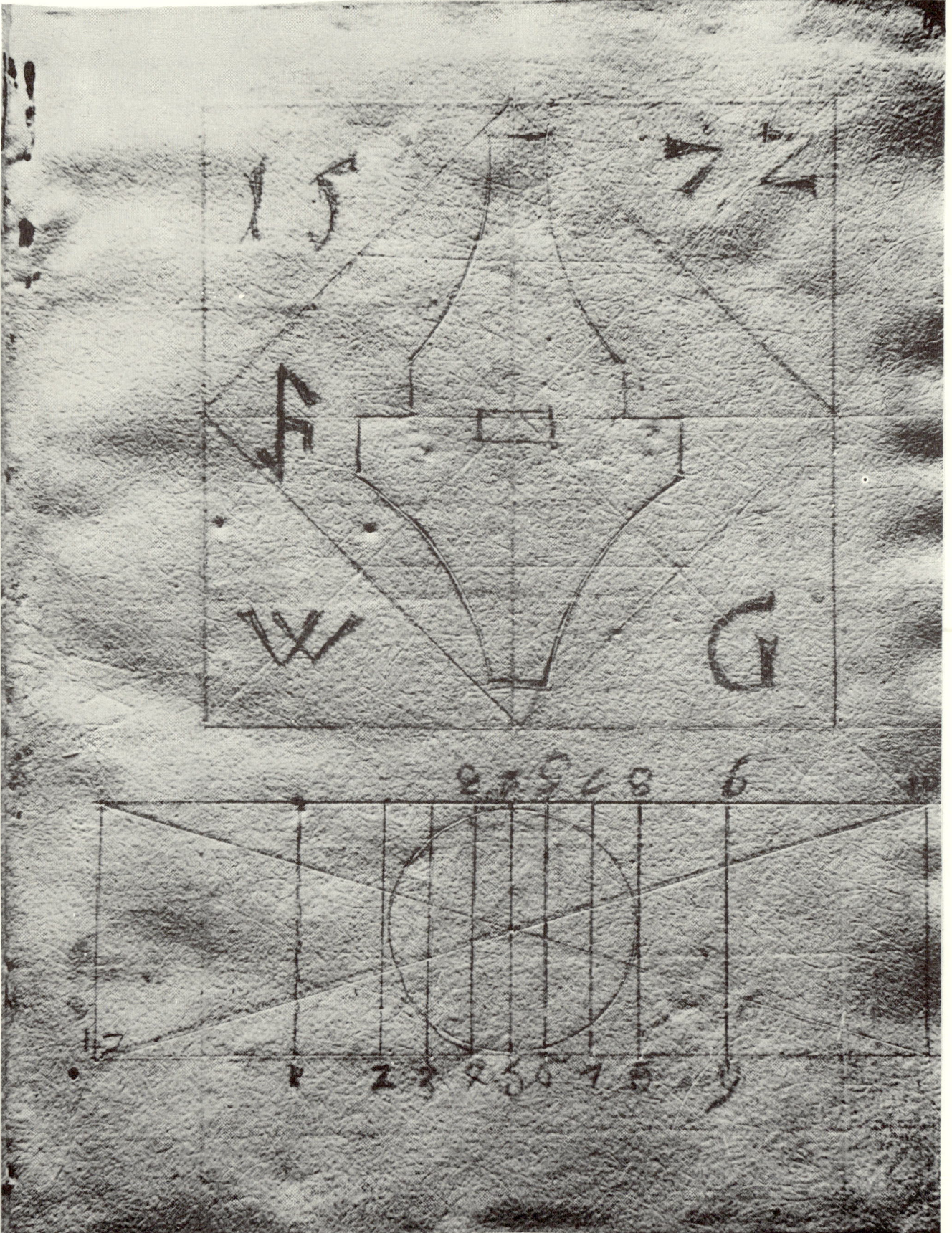

WG 9 Fundamental, signed and dated mullion design based on the rotation of the square. Square Two limits the length, Square Three the width, Square Four the two upper curves, Square Seven, the width of the dowel hold and Square Seven, the straight edges. Compare with WG 28. Design for a sundial based on the partitioning of a circle into twenty parts. Compare with WG 25, 36.

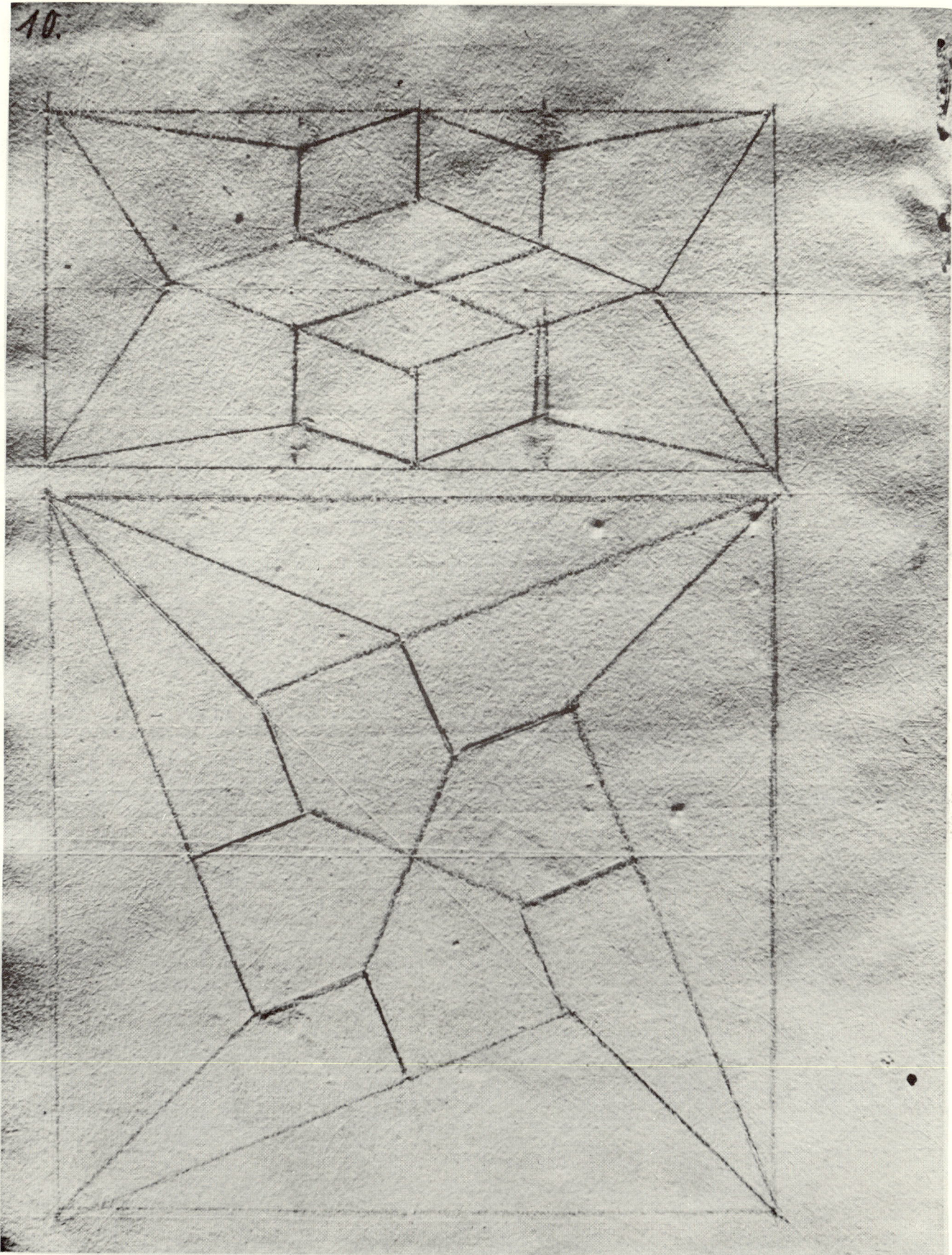

WG 10 Double square vault with ribs determined by two center lines comprising a third of each square. Popular "rotating cross" vault based on thirds of the center line giving the size of an octagon. Connect corners of the cross.

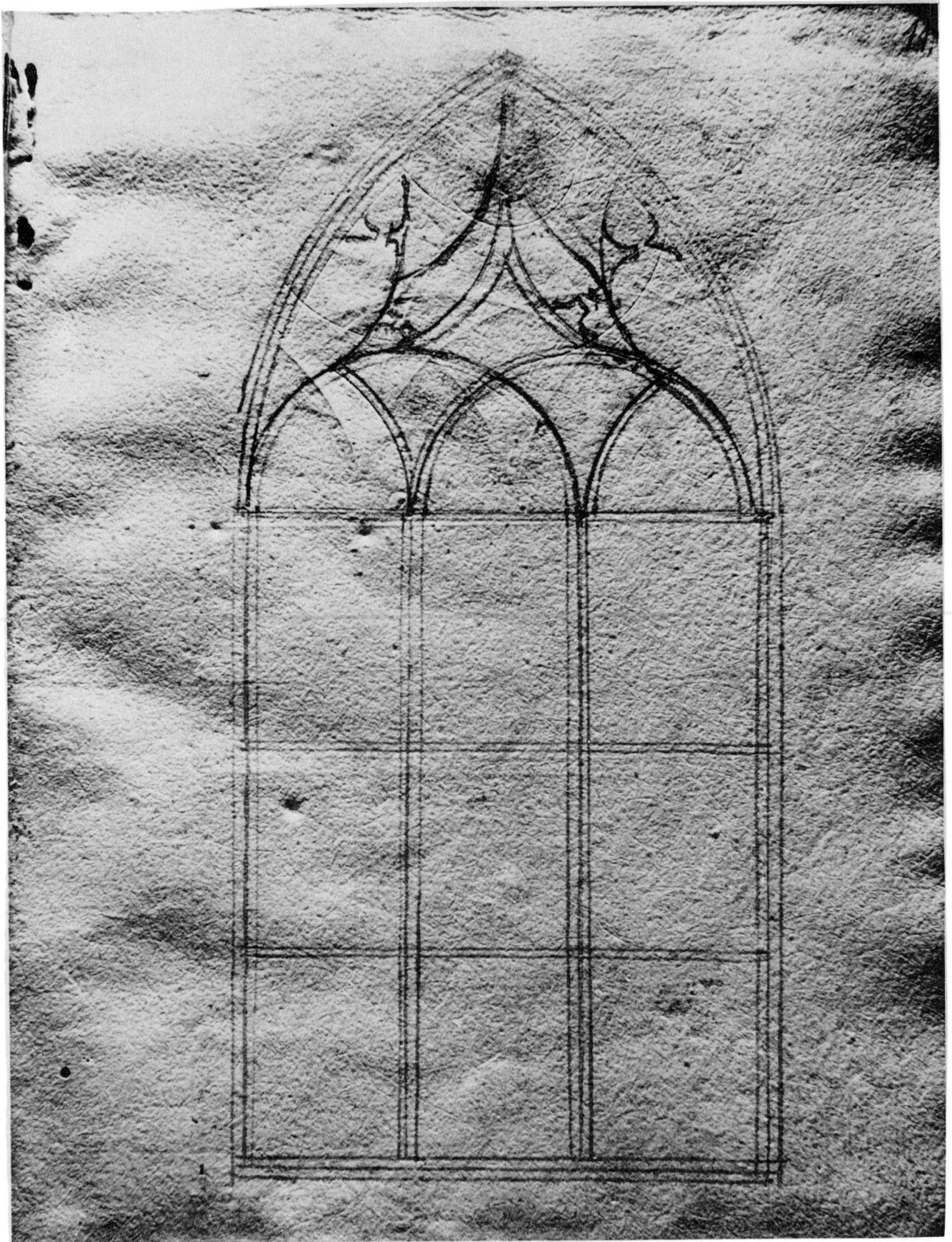

WG 11 Triple lancet window with some diagons, interlocking half circles for the tracery and four mouchettes.

WG 12 Quadruple lancet window with exceptional tiers point arch, some diagons, tracery based on interlocking
circles and two large mouchettes.

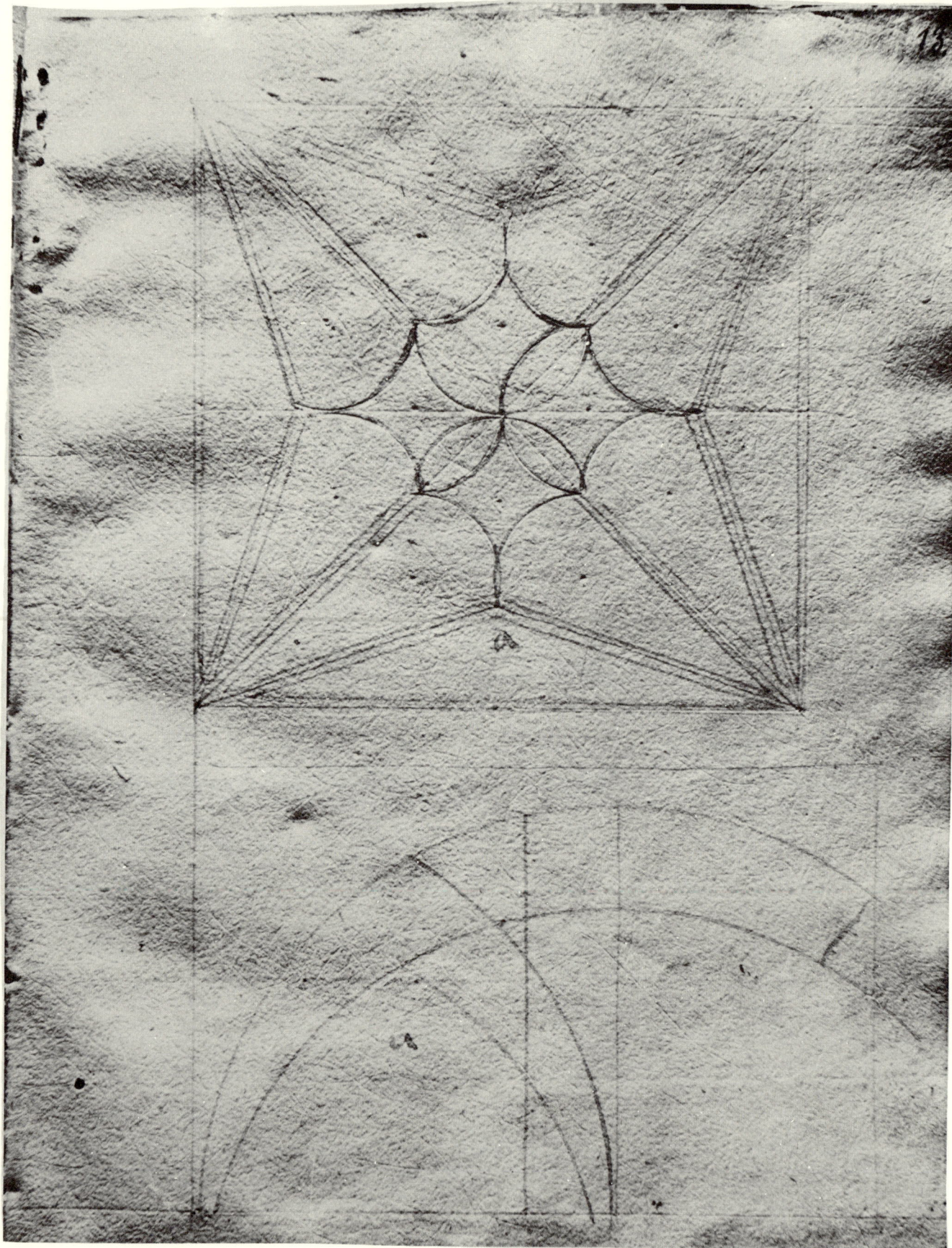

WG 13 Quadripartite vault with clover leaf center inscribed in the scalloped square three. First of many theoretical sketches establishing the circular curvature and length of the ribs from the corner to the first line "a" and thence to the center of the vault. See Dresden Sketch-Book of Vault Projection.

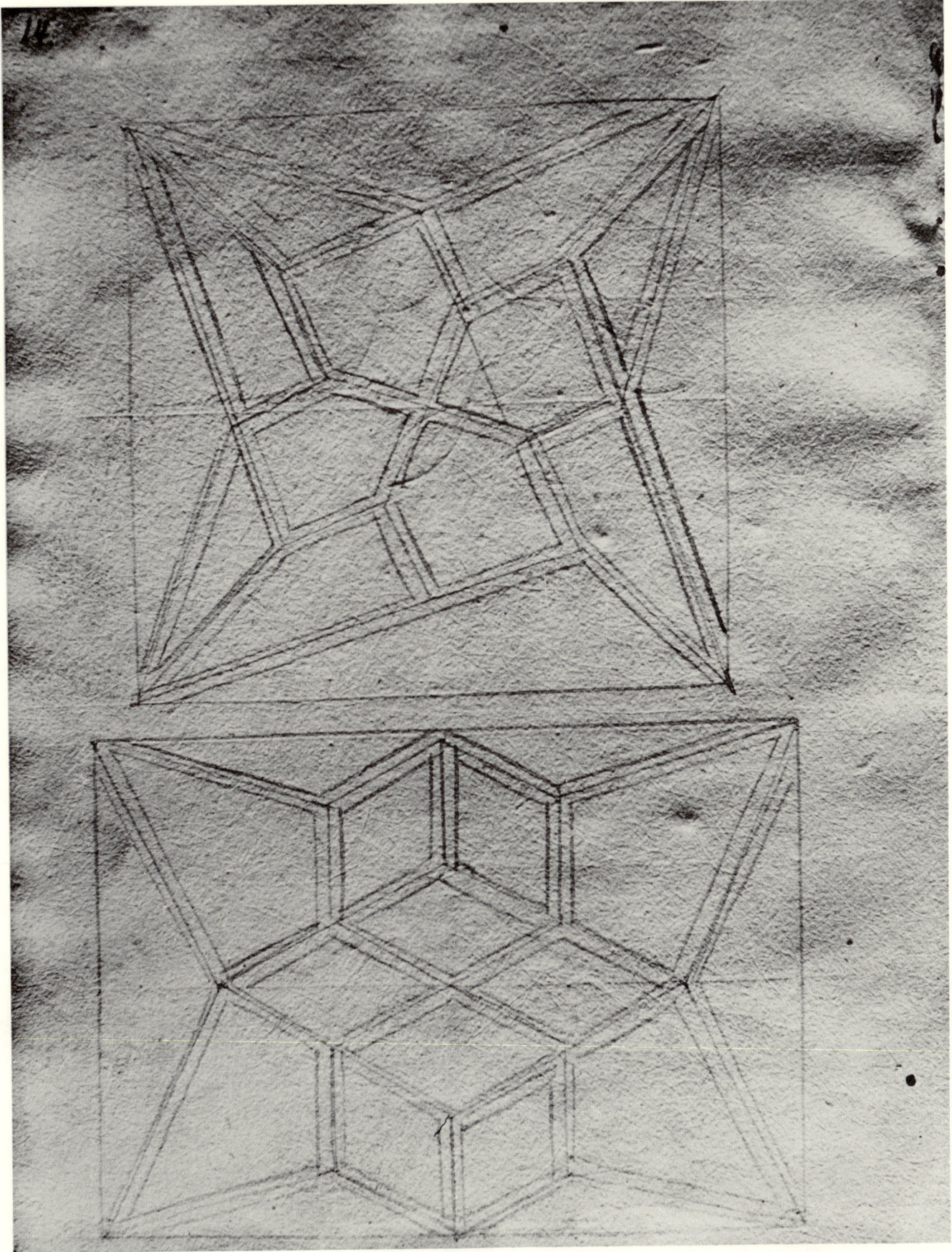

WG 14 More explicit repetition of the vaults on p. 10 using the same proportions for the vault with the rotating cross. The lower vault is inscribed in a diagon and folds out vertically in halves, horizontally in thirds.

215

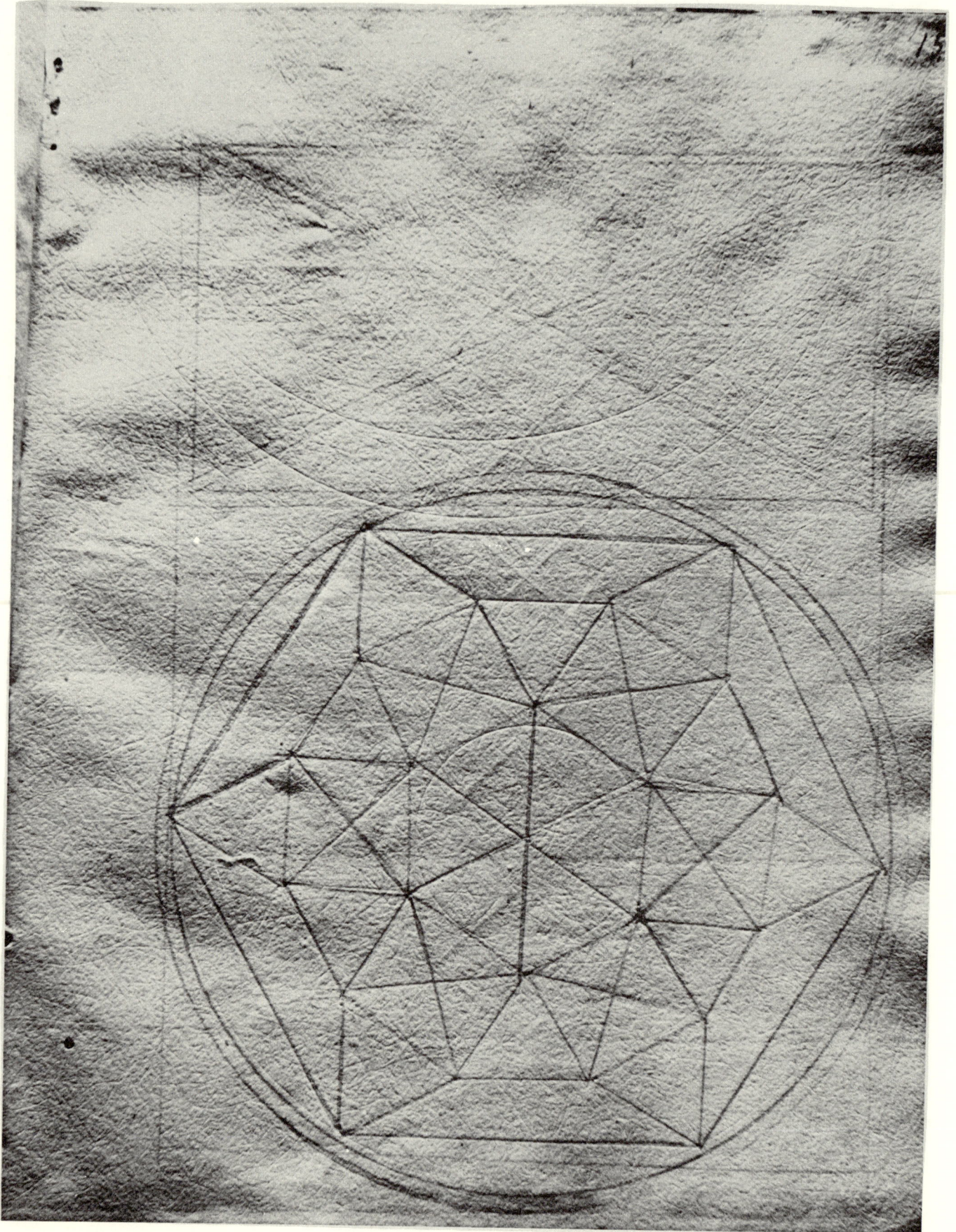

WG 15 Quadripartite vault with projection of diagonal ribs. Circular structure with two hexagonal and some dodecagonal parts. The radii of the governing circles are determined by four squares, three of them in rotation.

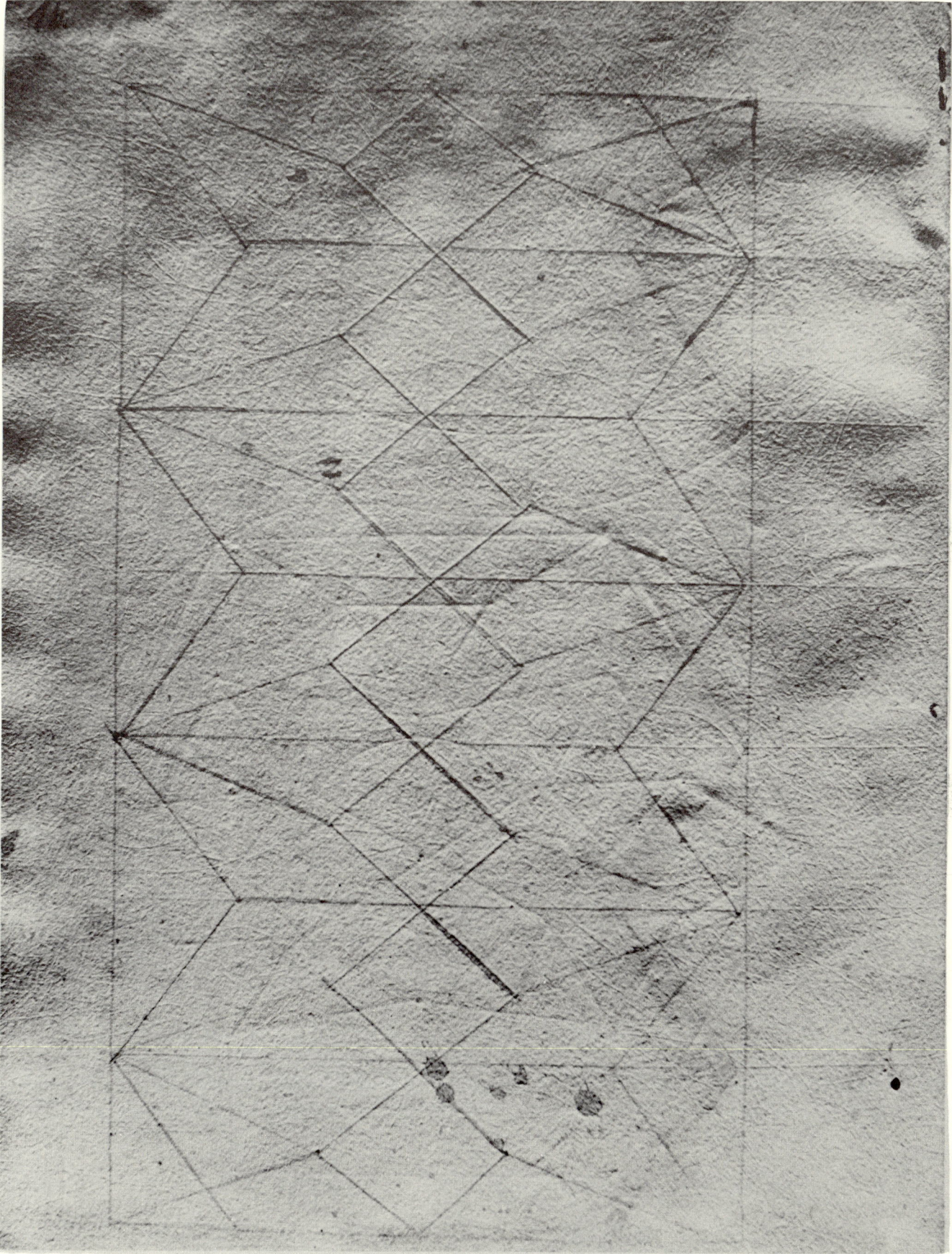

WG 16 Longitudinal vault intended to produce a diagonal effect. Compare with WG 23. Modular regularity is preserved through the squares whose diagonals are repeated in the ribs flanking the walls.

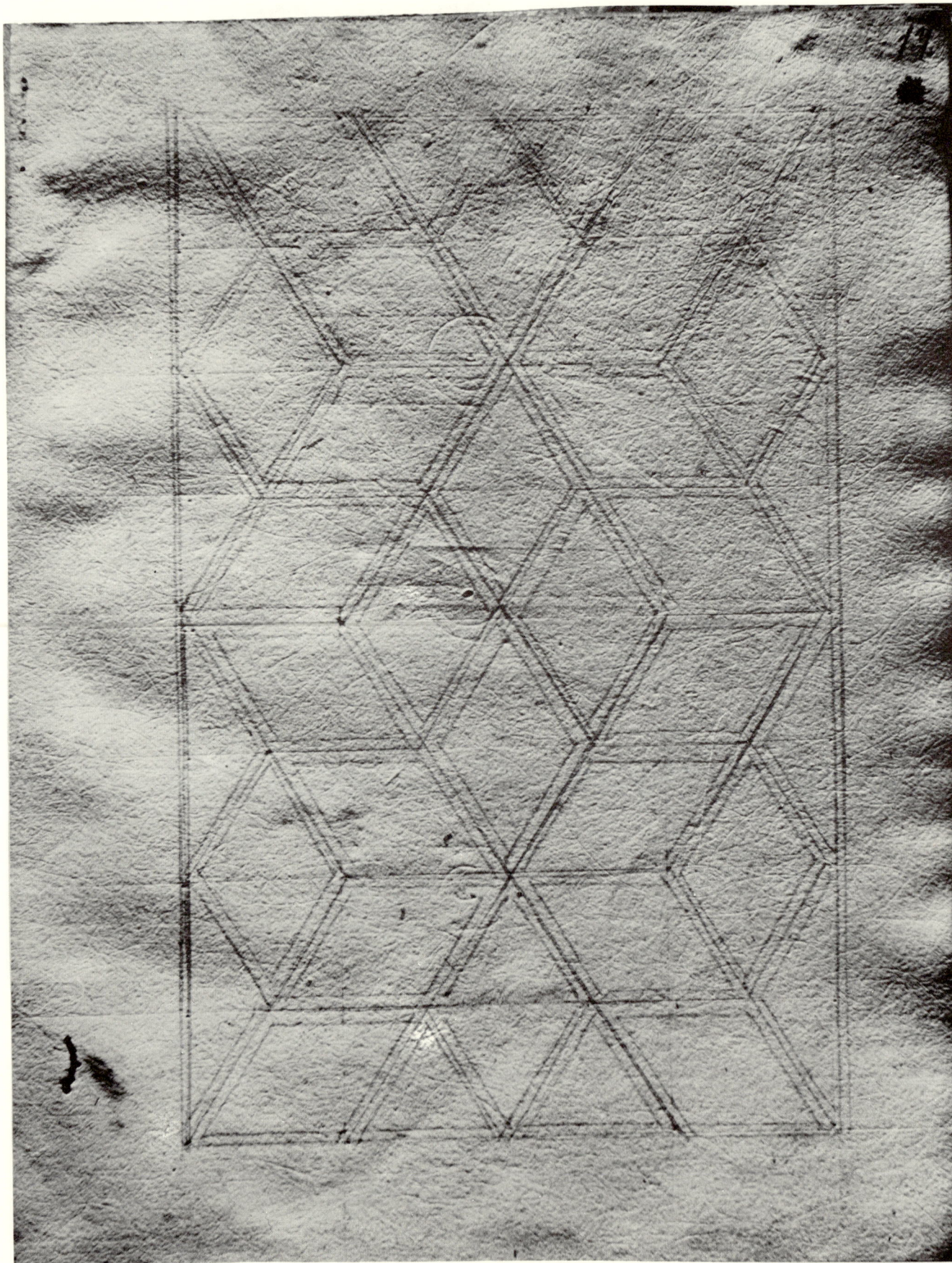

WG 17 Longitudinal, ca 1:3 vault with equal rhombs which can also be read as four part rhomboid shapes, three part hexagons or a twelve part central super hexagon.

WG 18 Circle with inscribed pentagon. For the construction process—not shown here— see Roriczer, *Geometria Deutsch*, p. 3.

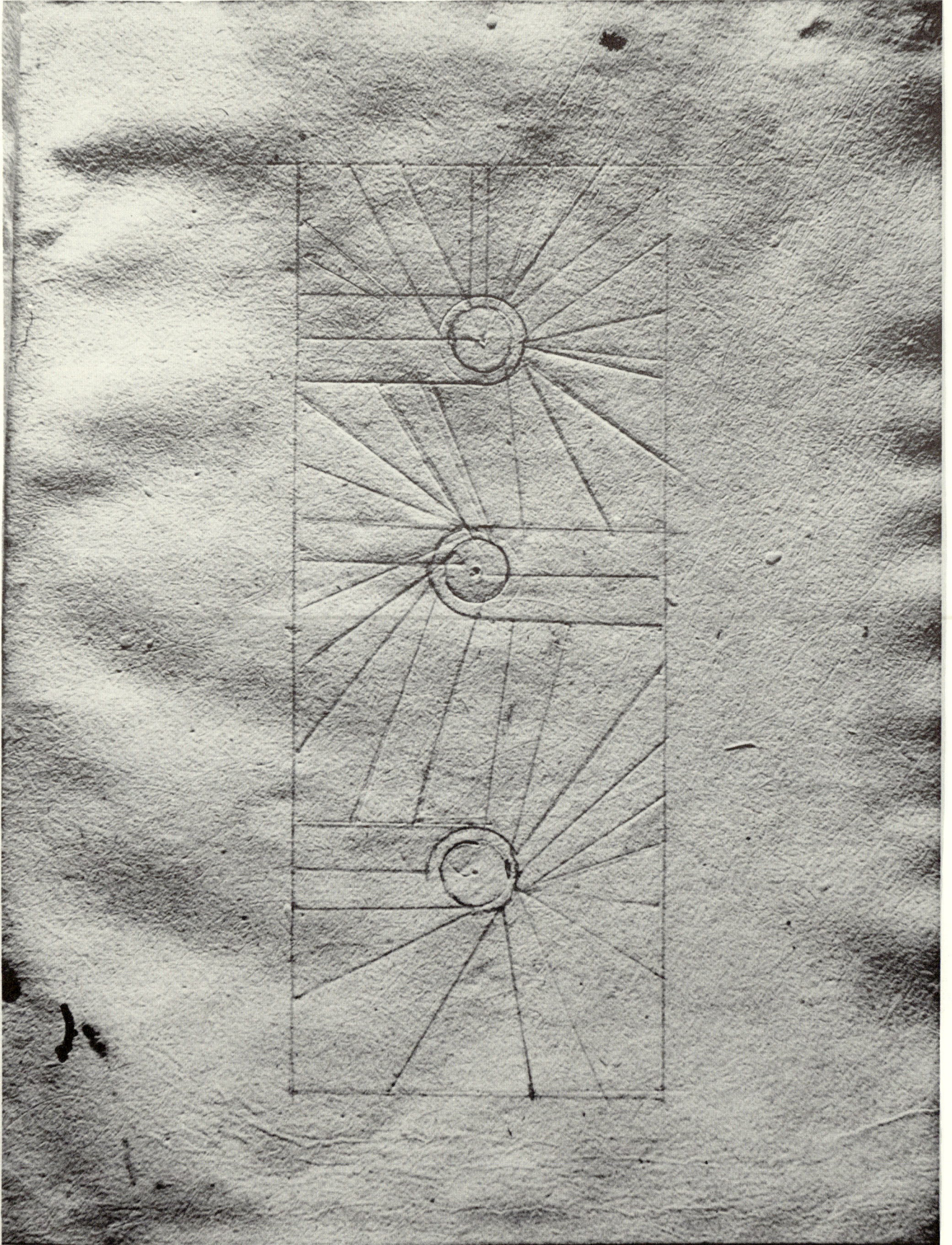

WG 19 Very schematic receding triple spiralling stair derived from Ulrich von Ensingen's and Johannes Hültz's
famous Strasbourg spire. The direction of ascent or descent is reversed in each of the three stories.

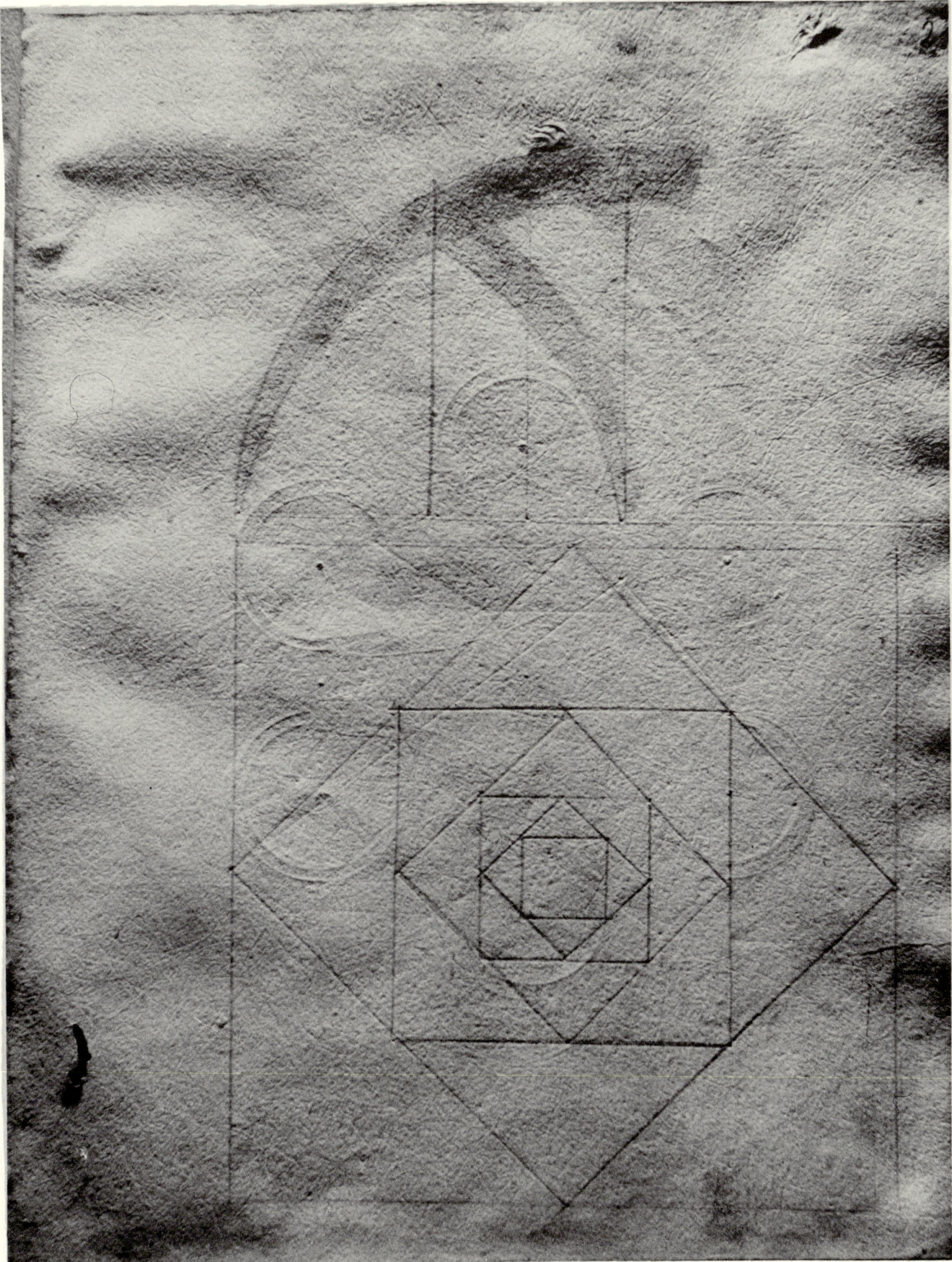

WG 21   Schema of vault with two possible rib systems. Fundamental Gothic schema of the rotation of the square, often called quadrature. Beginning from the largest square we progress to square two by connecting the centers of the sides of the original square. Square Three contains one-quarter of the surface of Square One, Square Five one-sixteenth, etc.

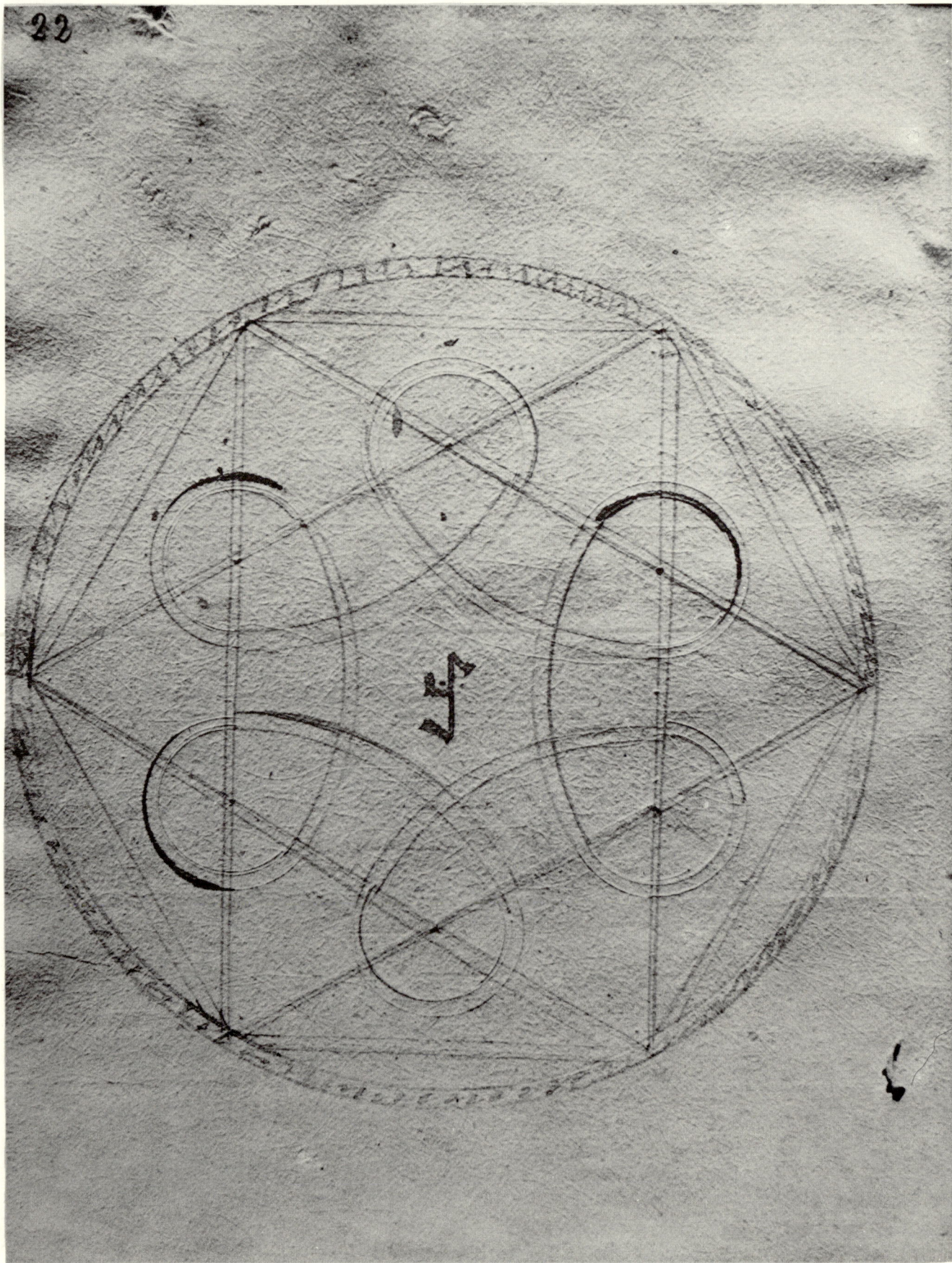

WG 22 Application of the schema on p. 8 expressing the visual ambivalence of a ribbed dome based on a hexagon with inscribed equilateral triangles forming three rectangles tied together by doubly curved and ornamental rib loops. The master's mark is upside down in the center.

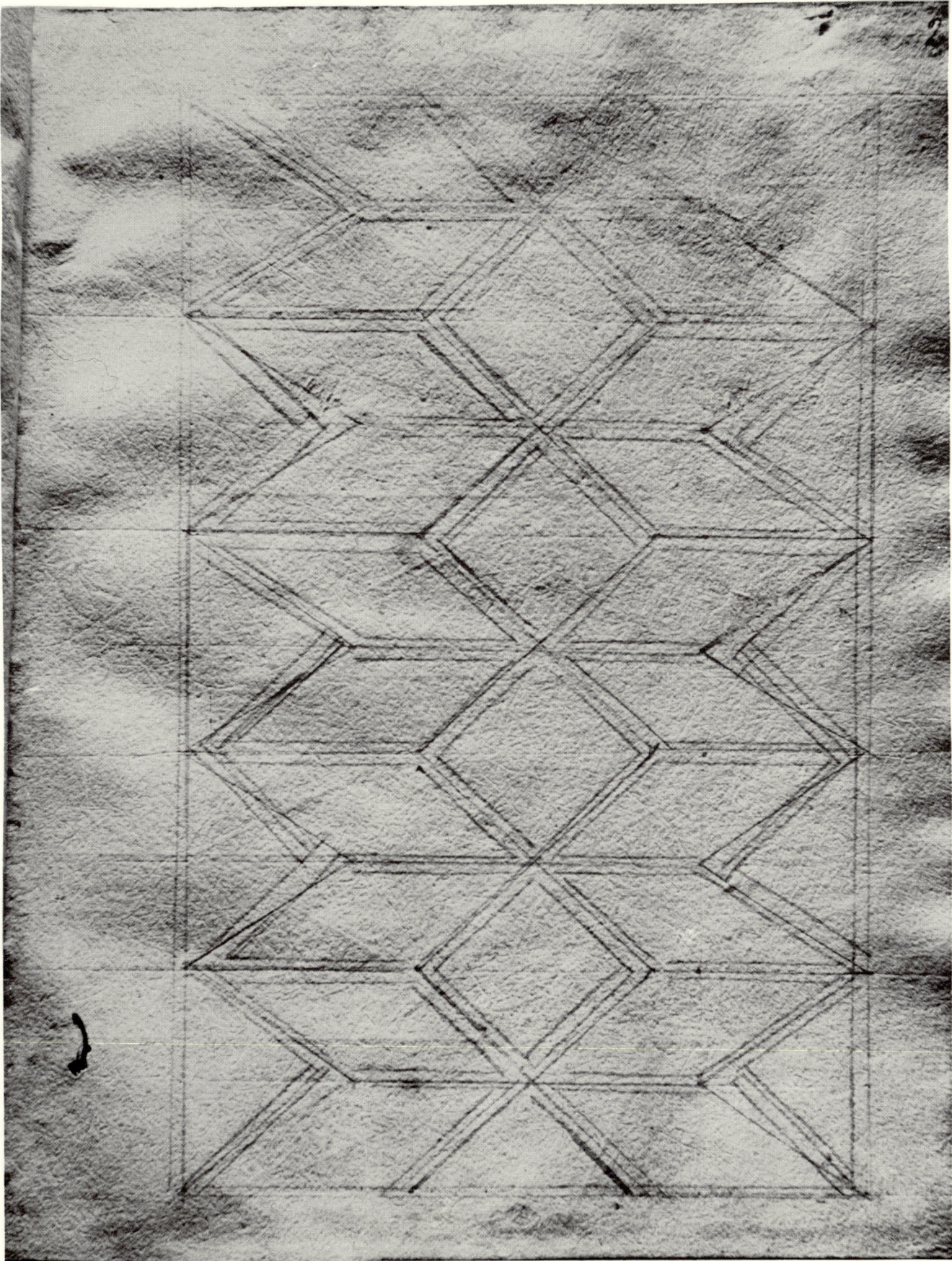

WG 23   Longitudinal vault with squares, triangles and rhombs.

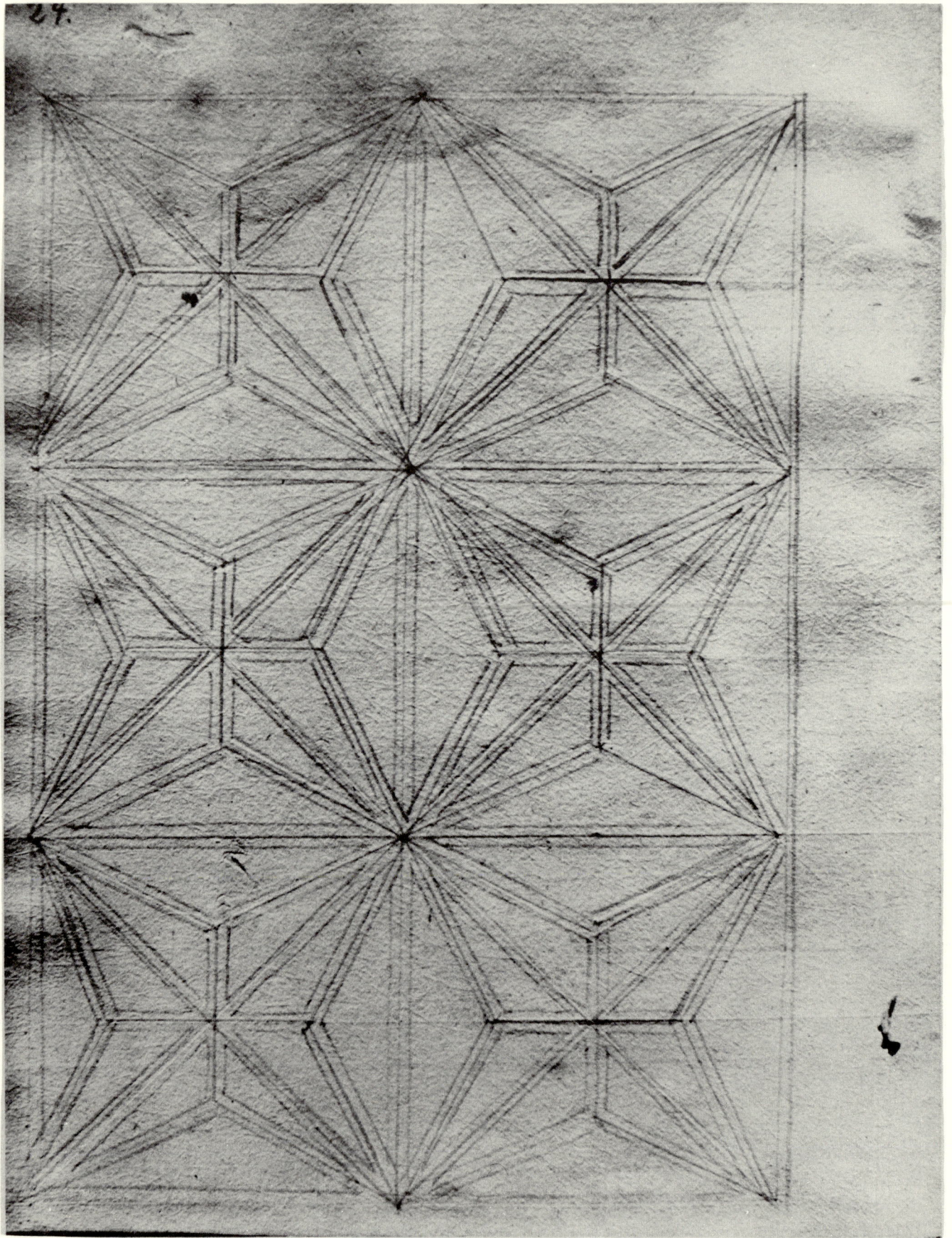

WG 24 Tree bay vault in a 2:3 rectangle based on six squares with star patterns whose main intersections are determined by Square Two. The vault can also be read as two interlocked large stars within two squares.

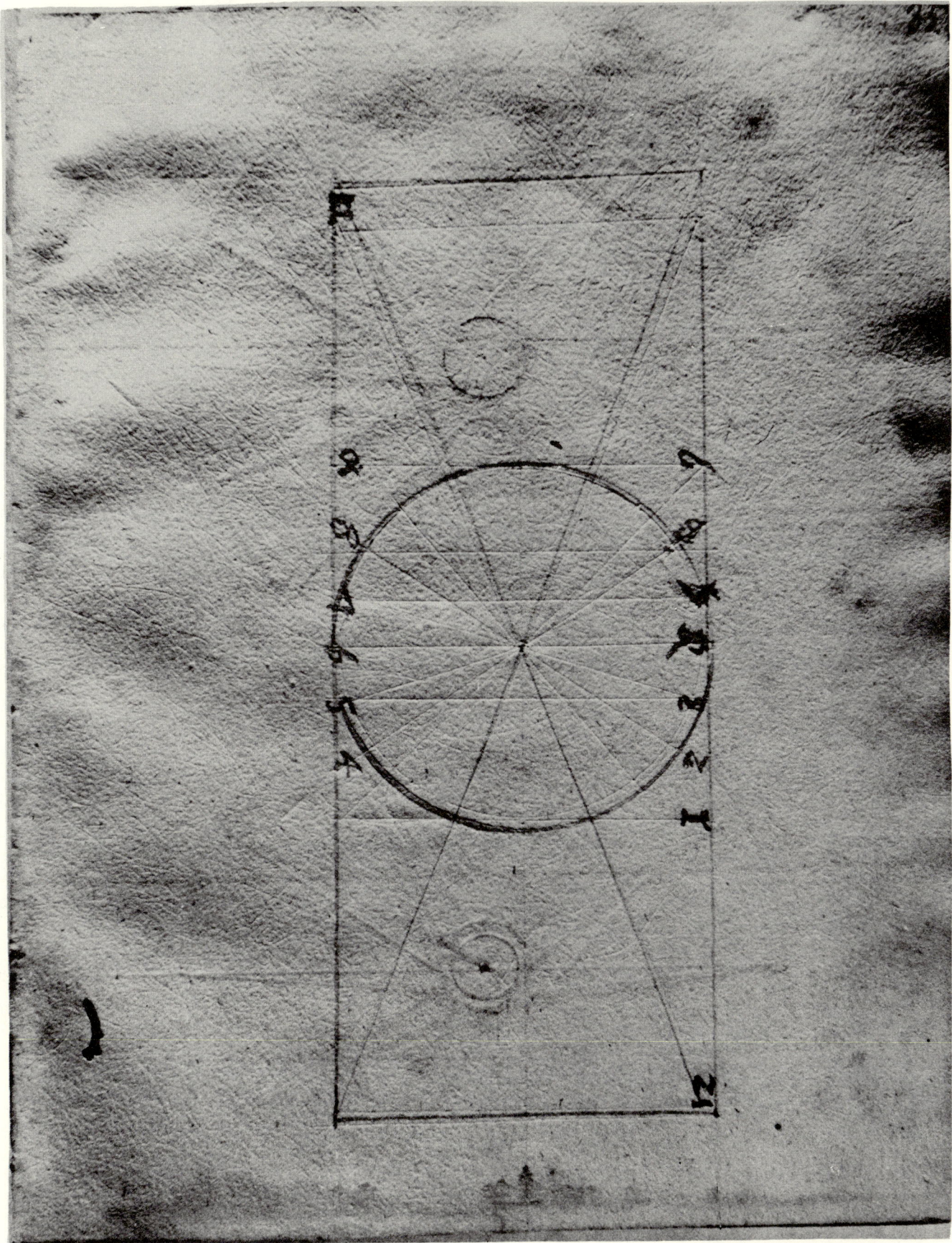

WG 25 Sketch for a sundial based on the division of the circle into twenty parts and a rectangle whose length is determined through the lines closest to the centerline.

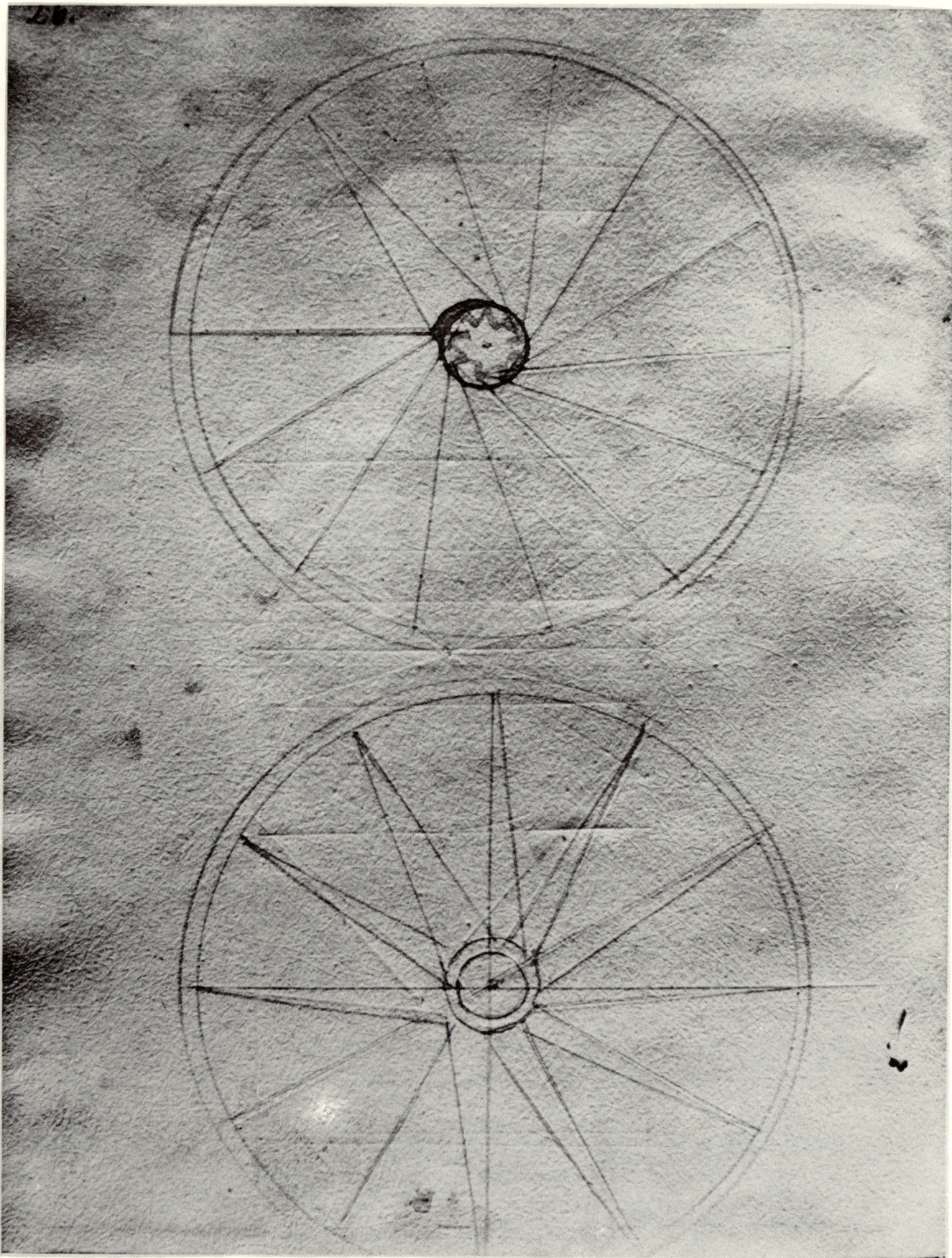

WG 26 Spiralling staircases with solid spindles, the first with fourteen steps per turn, the second on a standard
dodecagon derived from a hexagon whose sides are determined by the sixfold transposition of the radius
upon the circle.

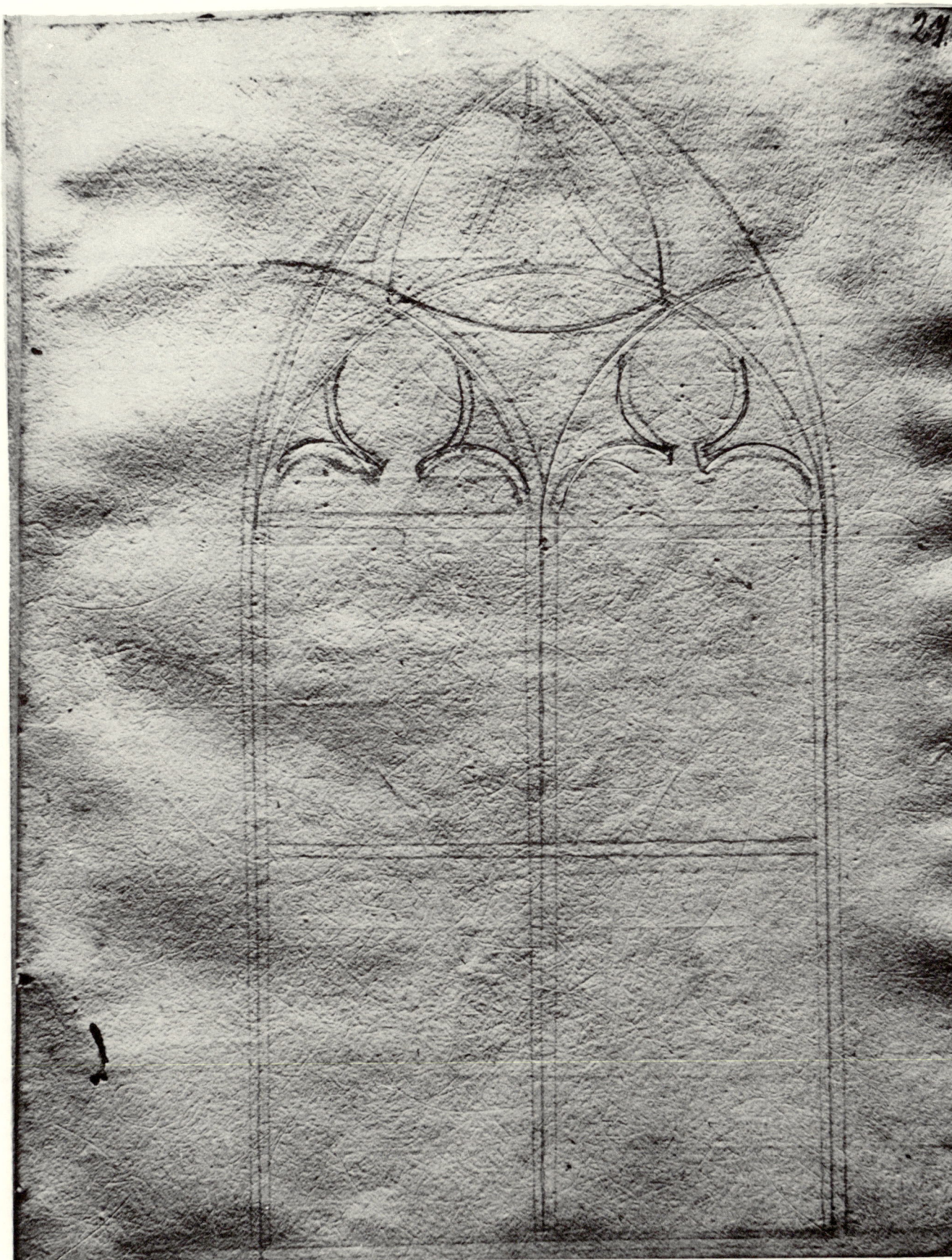

WG 27 Two lancet windows surmounted by a two point arch containing tracery inscribed in a half circle, and segments of circles using the same radius. These determine the dimensions of the segmental triangle.

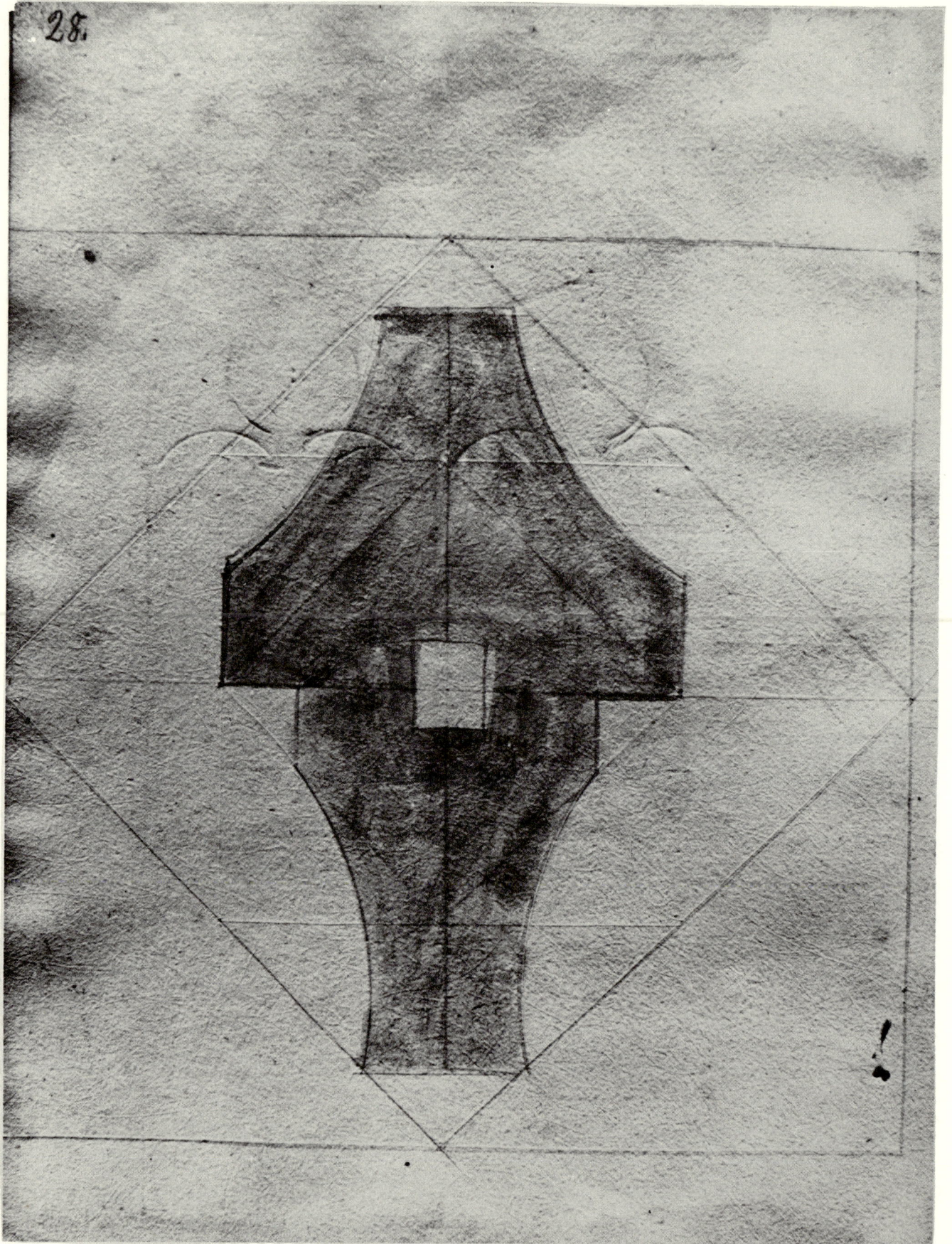

WG 28   Basic mullion design, based on the rotation of the square. See text and compare with WG 9.

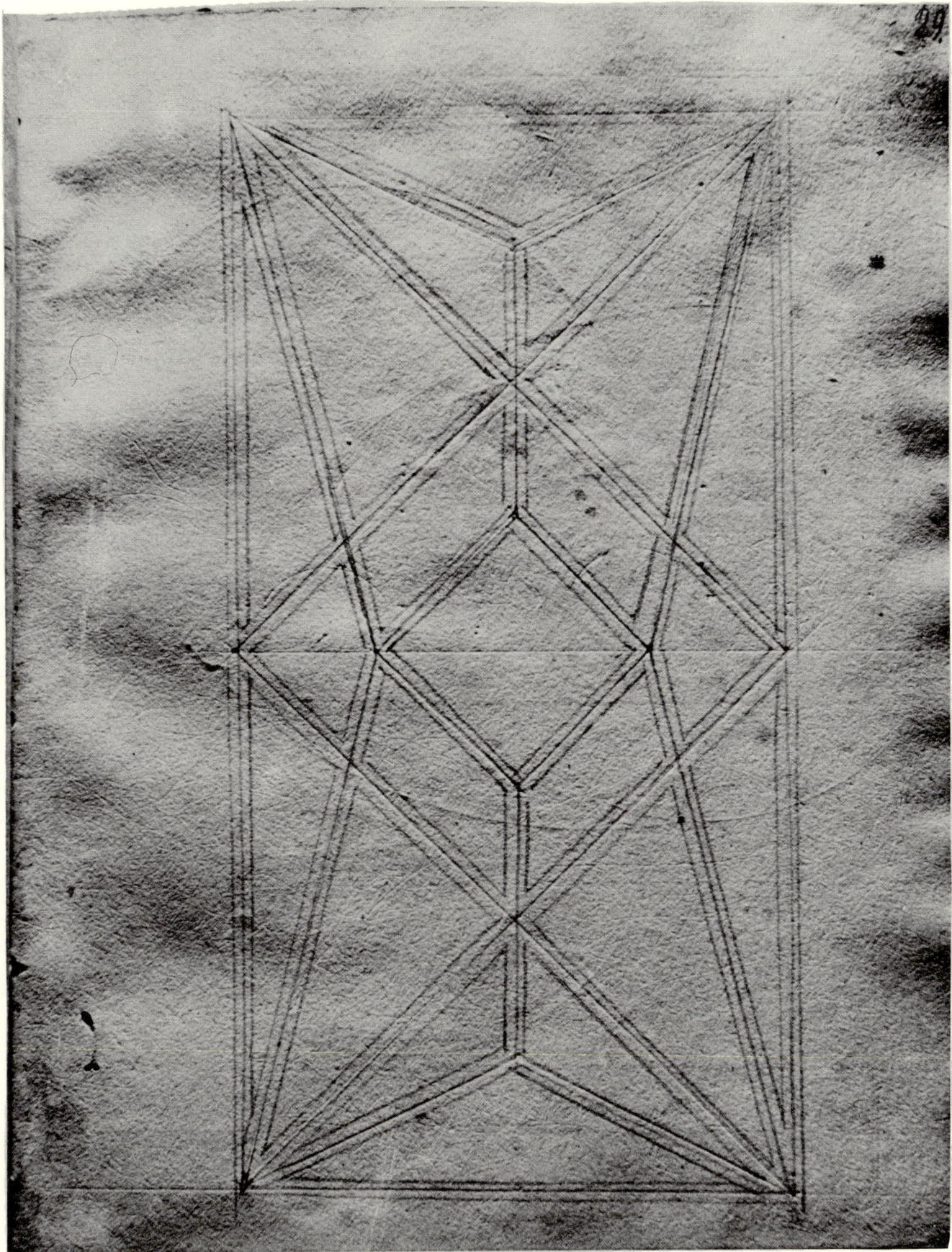

WG 29   Longitudinal 1:2 vault based on three central squares. The innermost square of the rough sketch is
square three of the largest square.

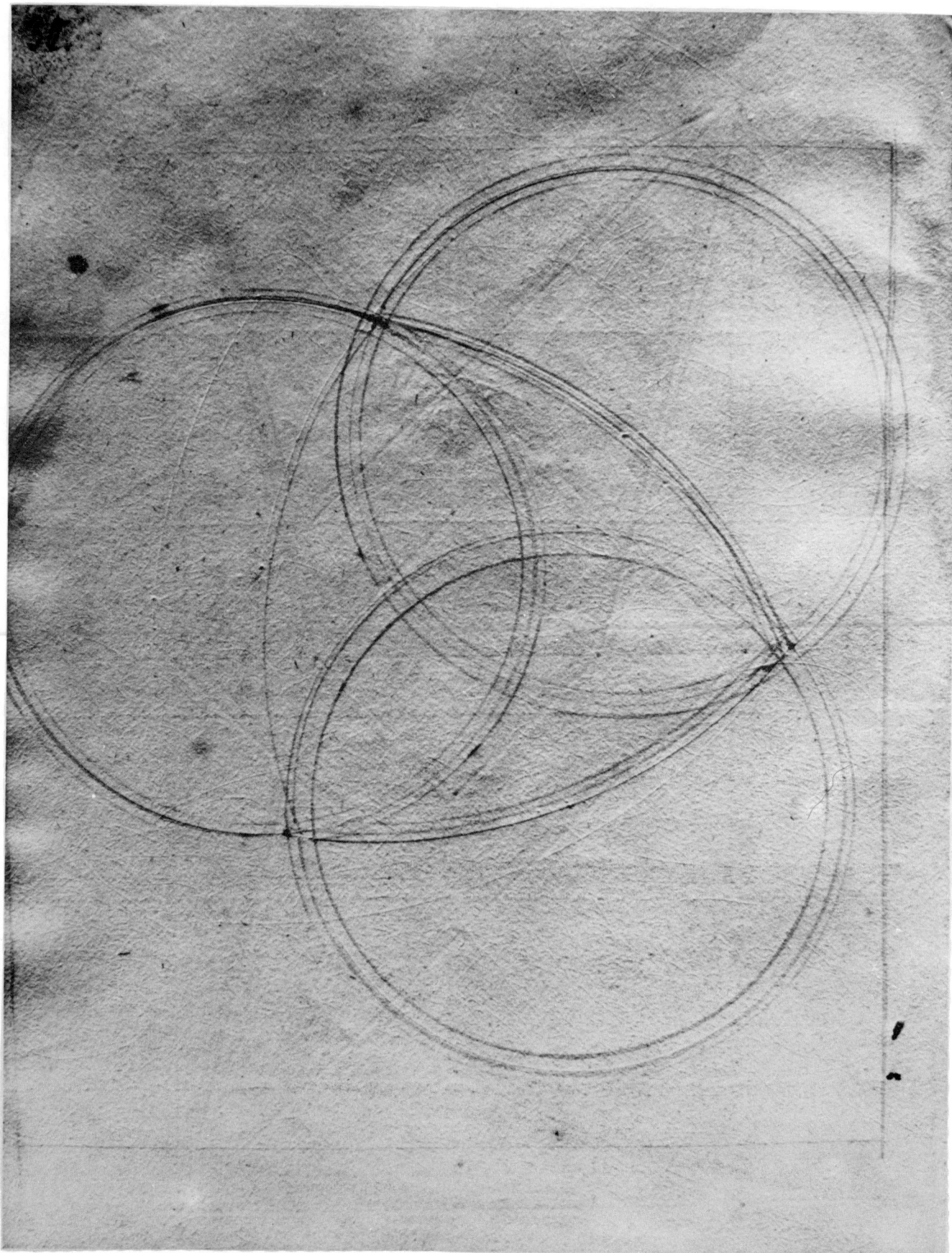

WG 30 Playful vault for a circular space based on a segmental triangle with an inscribed equilateral triangle which establishes the centers for the circles. Constructed exclusively from doubly curved ribs, the drawing reflects many late Gothic experiments such as the rib patterns over the entrance hall of the minster in Constance.

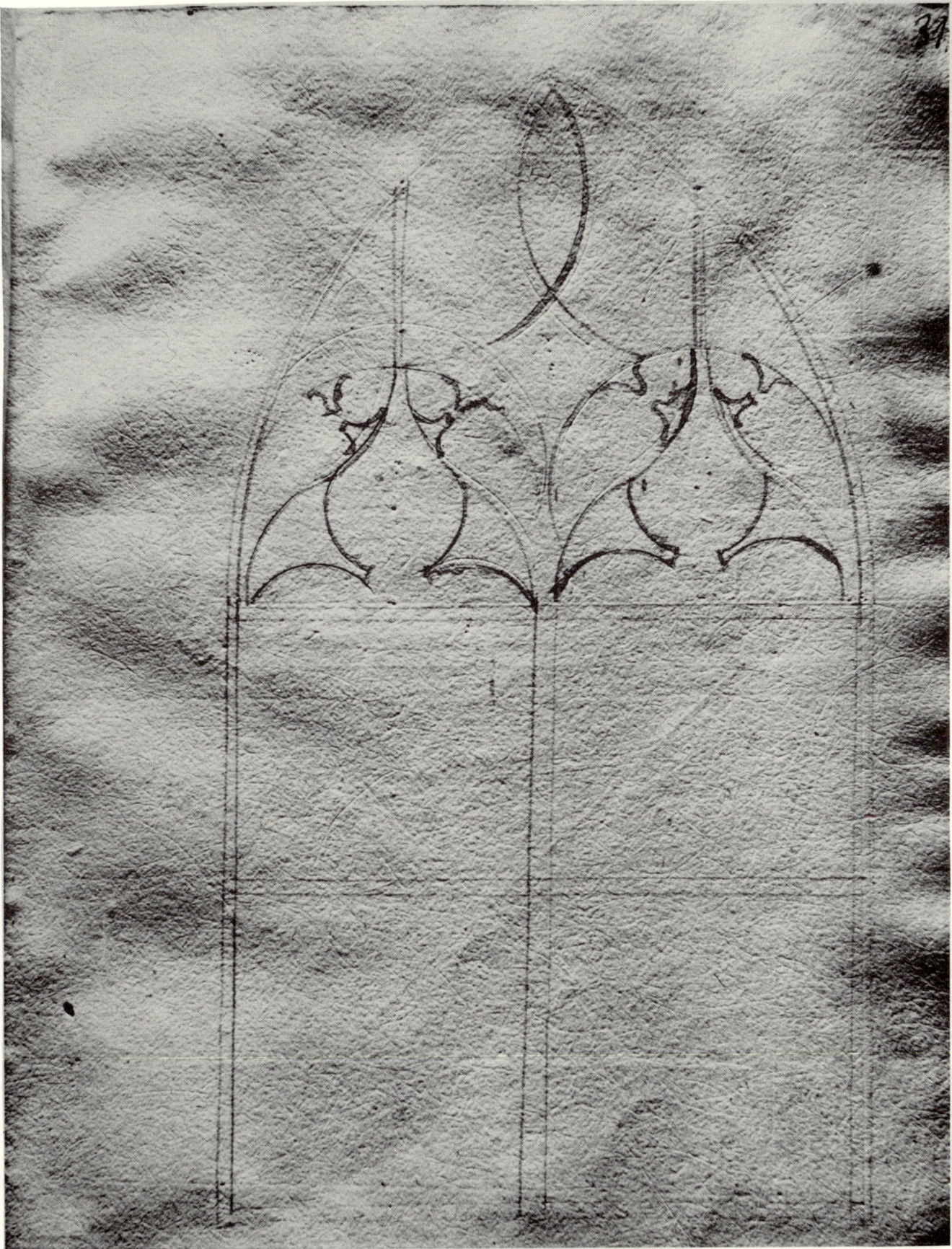

WG 31   Rough sketch for a double lancet with four mouchettes.

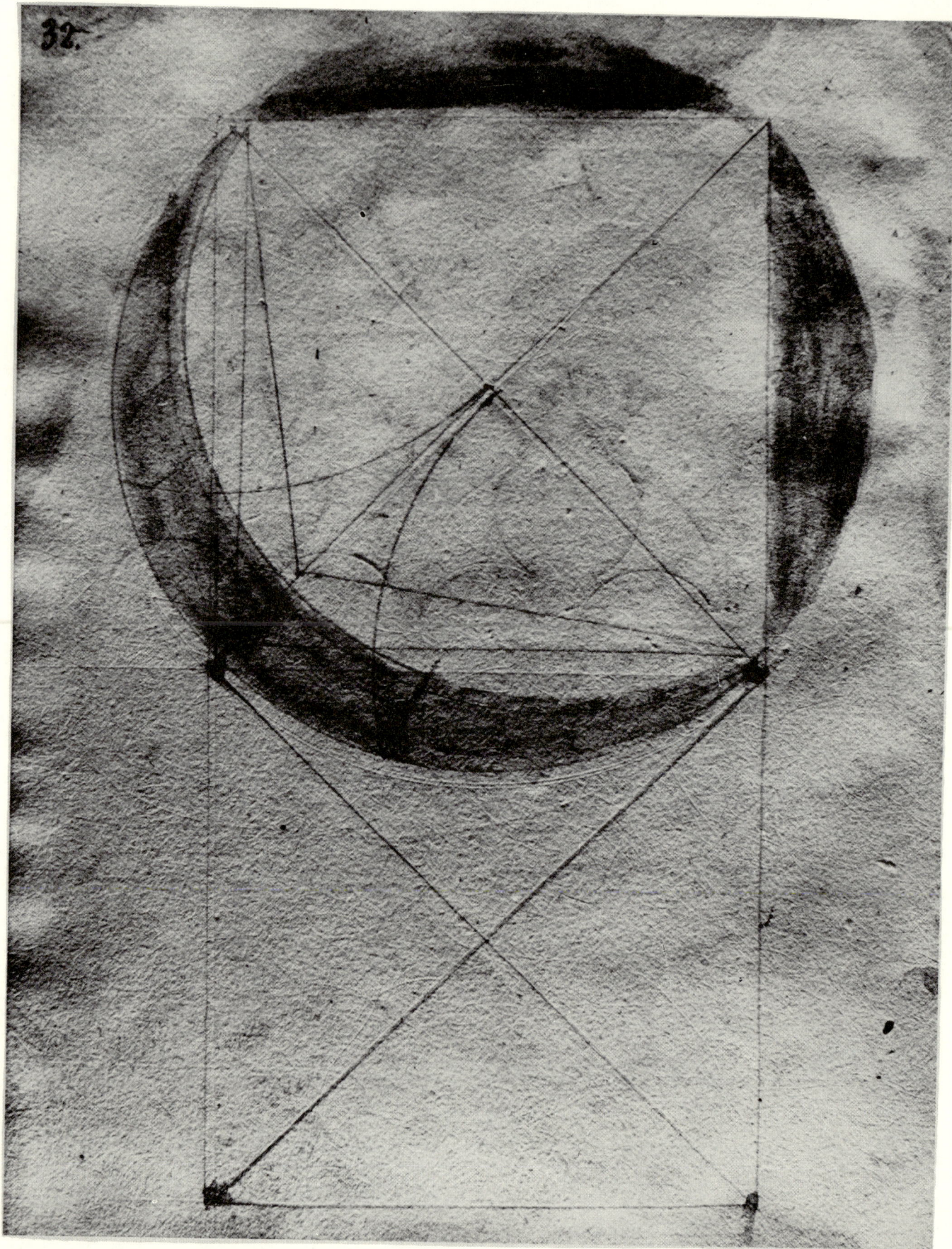

WG 32   Theoretical sketch giving the semi-circular curvature of the ribs, and two two point arches. The lower curve may apply to the height of the arch crossing the nave at right angles.

WG 33 Two double lancet windows, their tracery based on half circles, two point arches mouchettes and a segmental triangle. At the top a cross section through a window mullion.

233

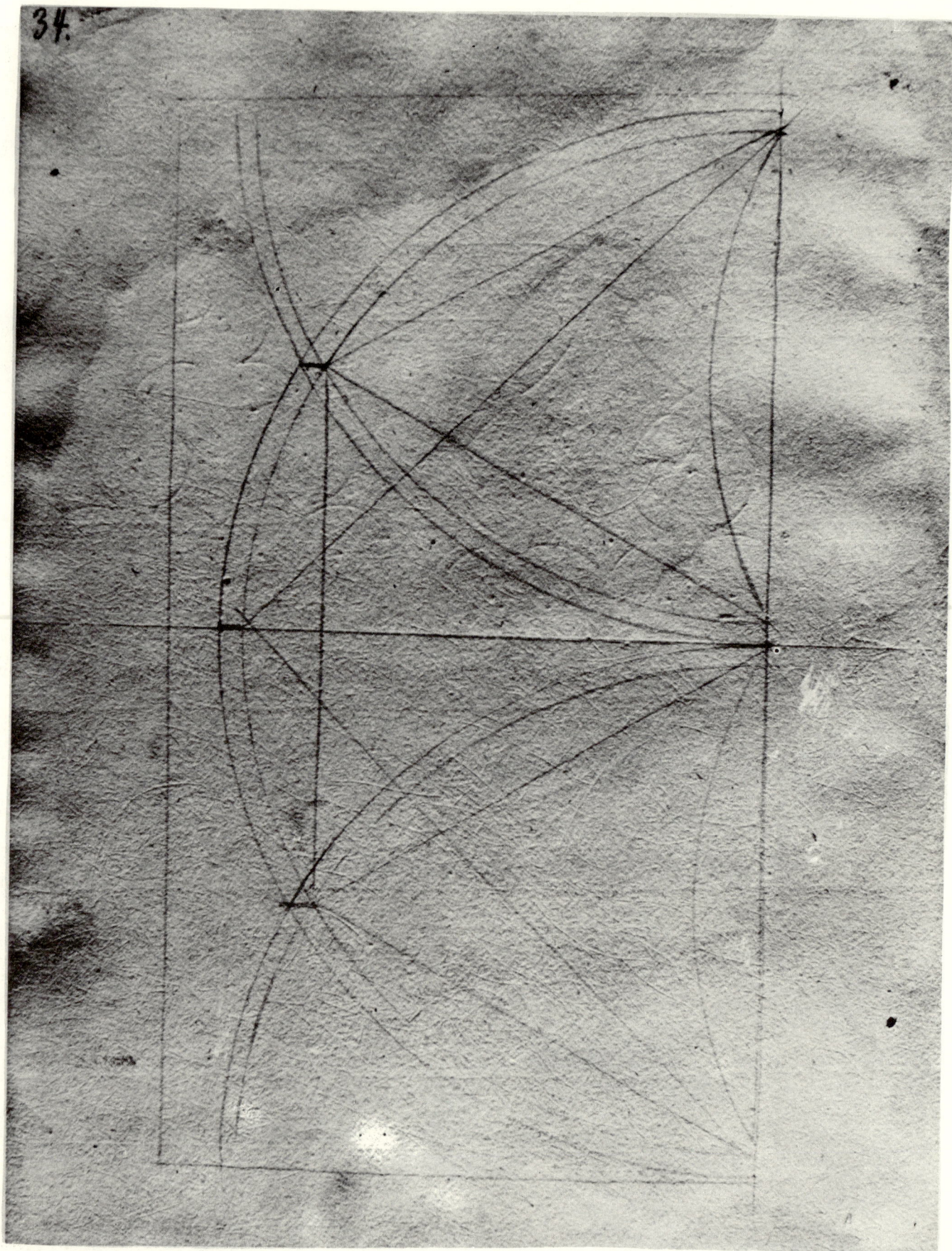

WG 34 Doodle for tracery or a wall decoration based on semi-circles and segments of a circle. The inscribed
lines stand for the Gothic geometric obsession.

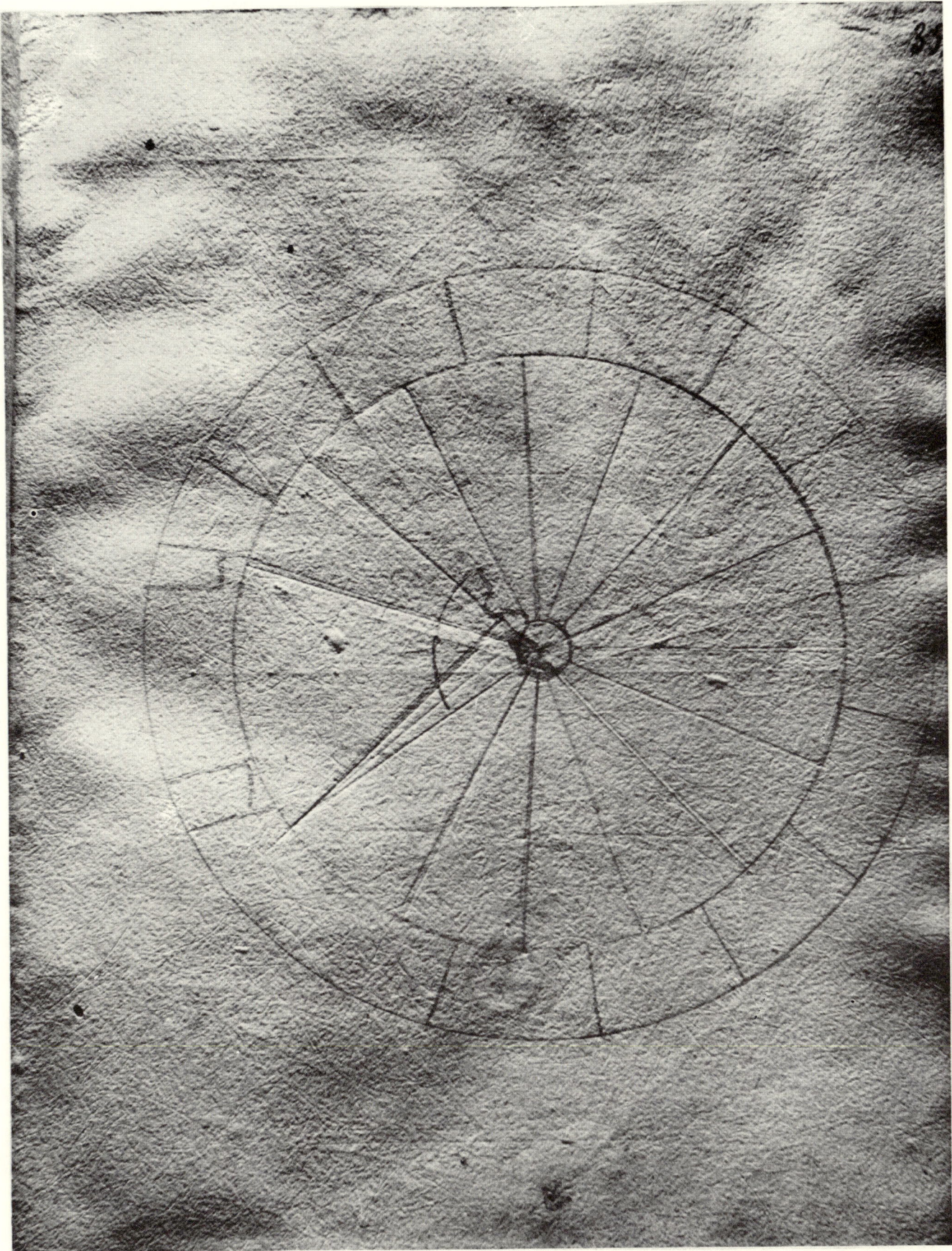

WG 35 Spiralling staircase with an entrance at the left and a heavy bannister attached to the spindle.

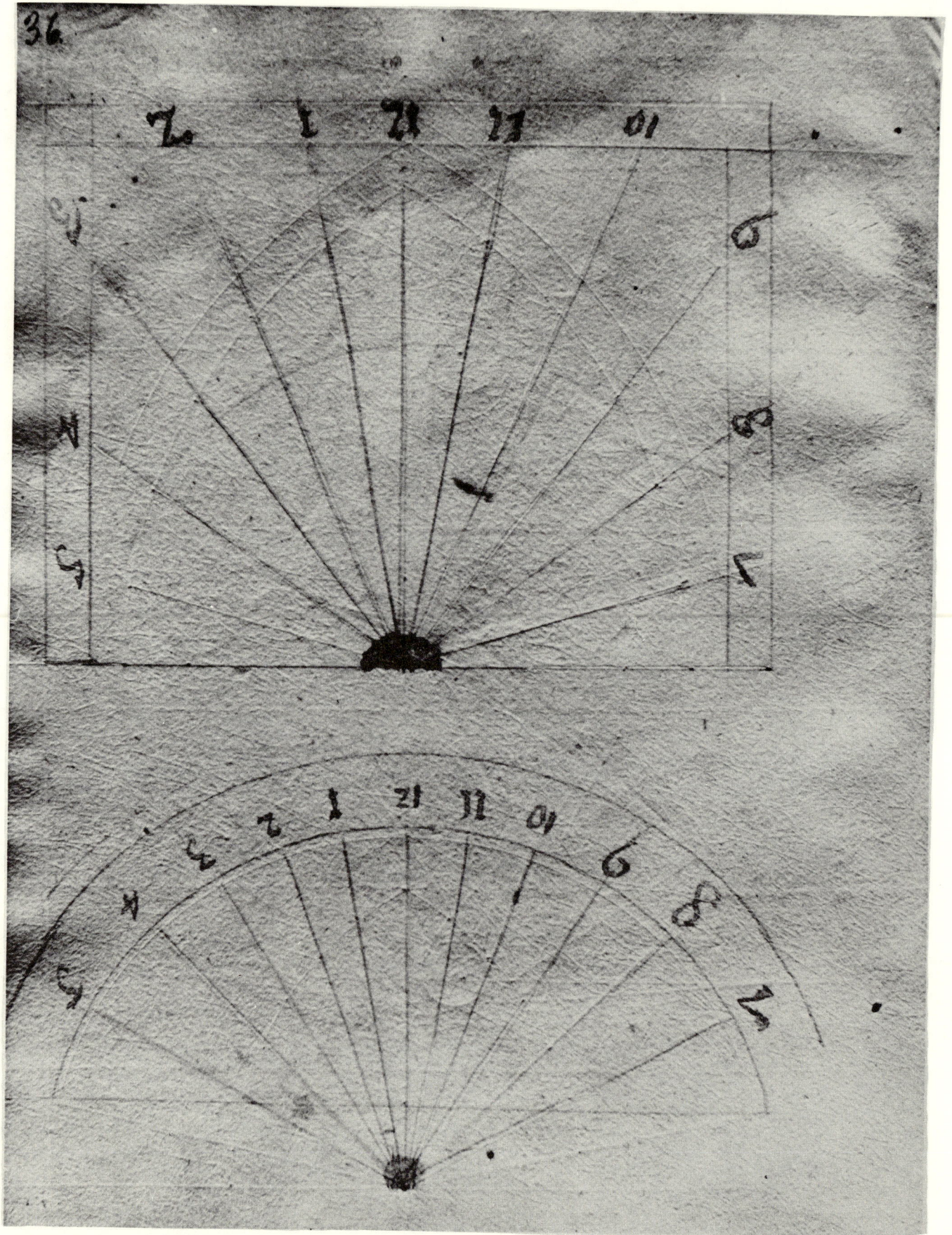

WG 36 Two twelve hour sundials based a) on a semi-circle and a two-point arch taking into account the changing ratios of the shadow's movement on the rectangular frame, and b) on a half-circle and a two-point arch divided into fourteen parts which result in unequal widths of the hour segment on half-circle.

236

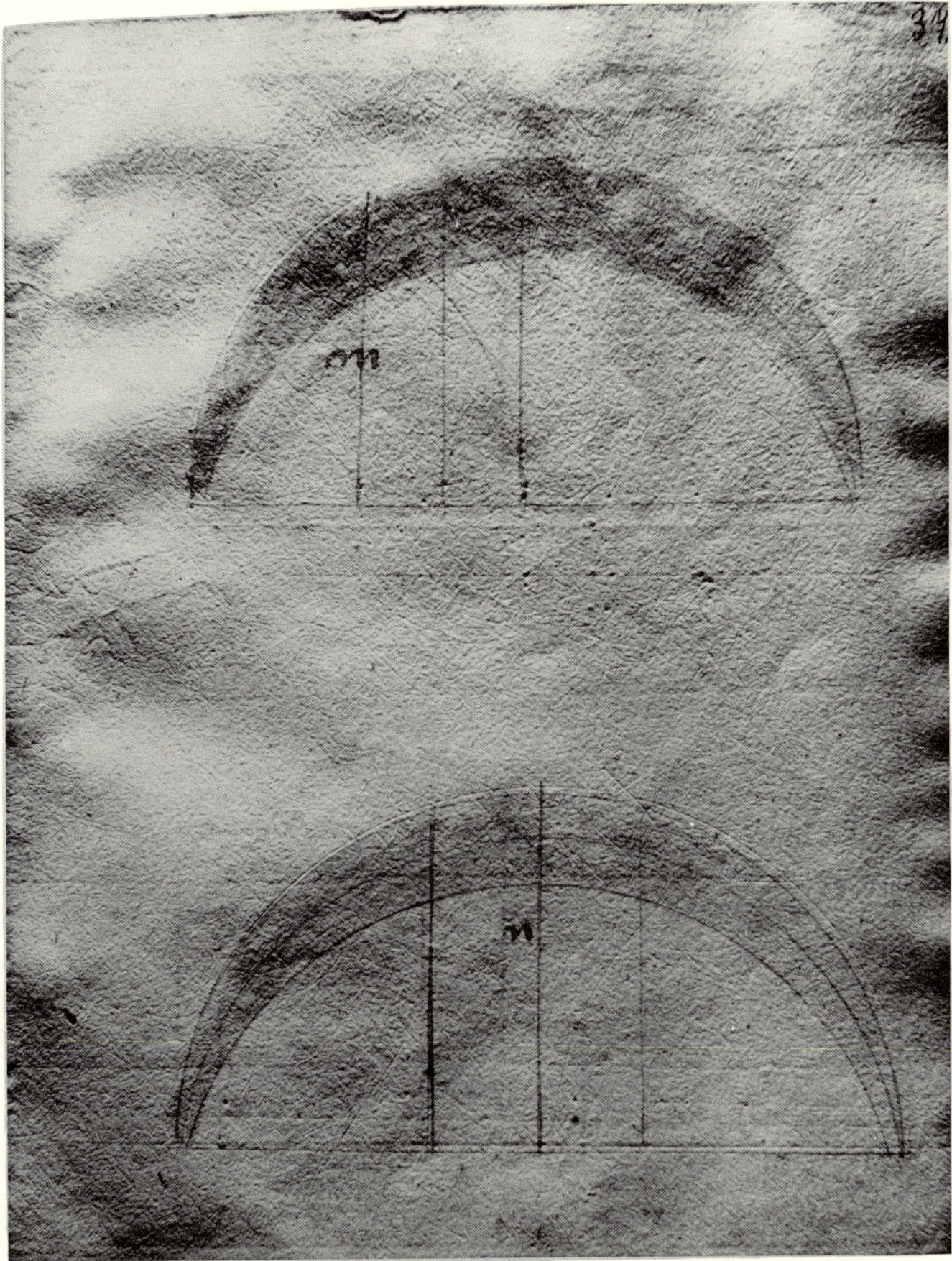

WG 37 Theoretical sketch establishing the half circular curvature and length of the diagonal ribs and the curvature and length of subsidiary ribs. Compare with WG 32 and the Dresden Sketchbook of Vault Projection.

237

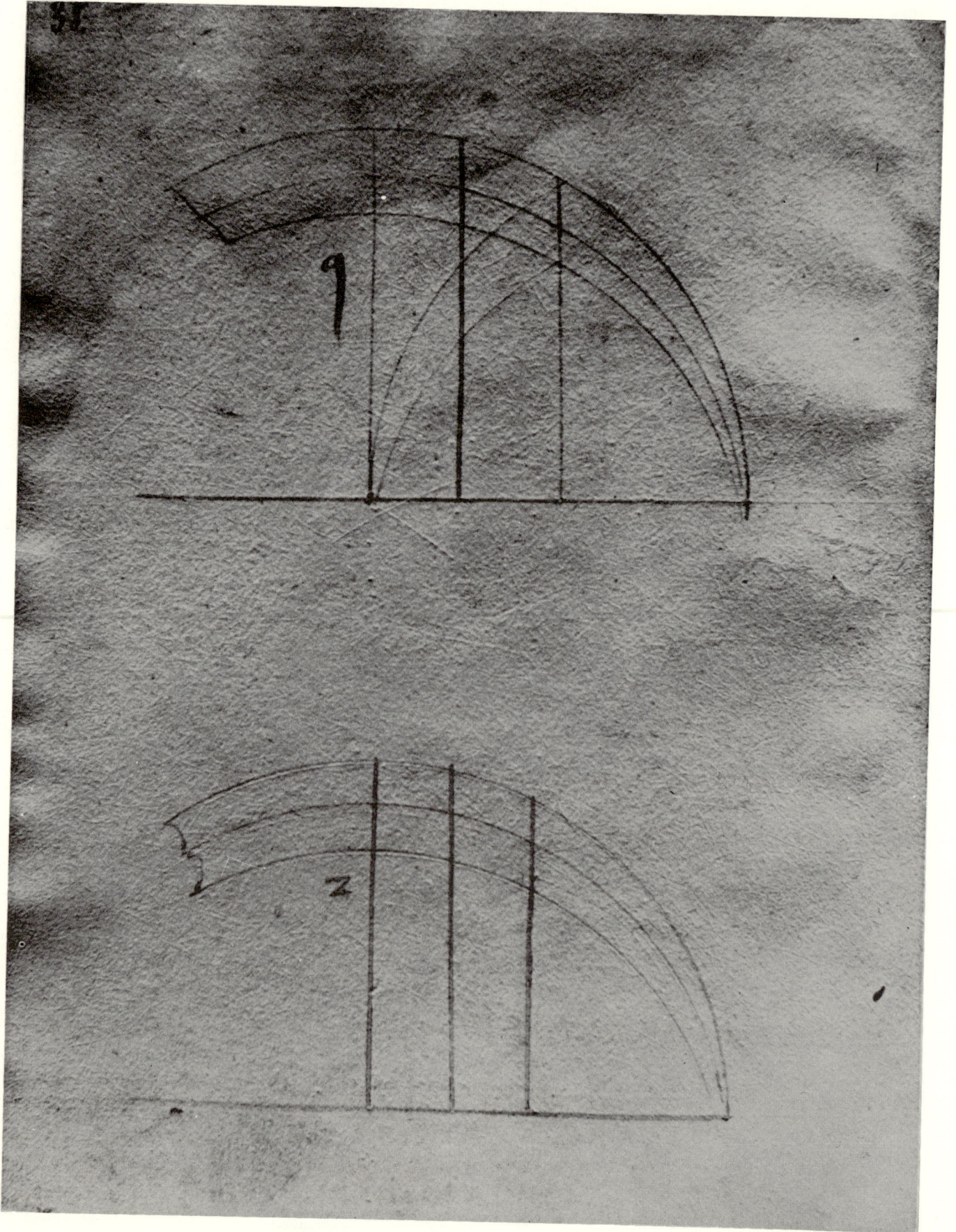

WG 38   Same as WG 37.

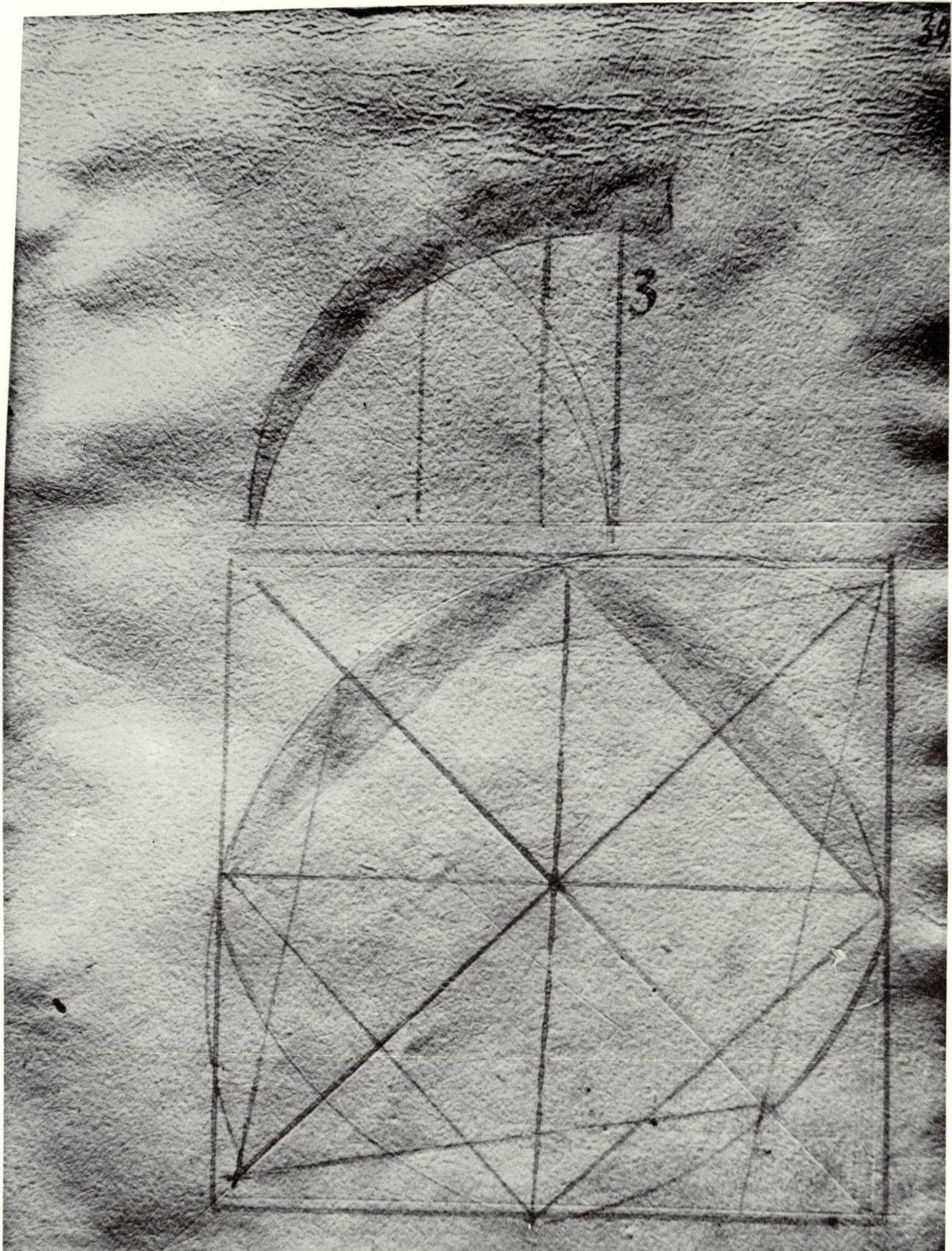

WG 39 Top same as WG 37. Bottom. Experimental sketch related to WG 32. The center of the circle at the right lies on the engraved line left and below the center of the square, while the center of the segment of the circle at the left is determined by the rhomb.

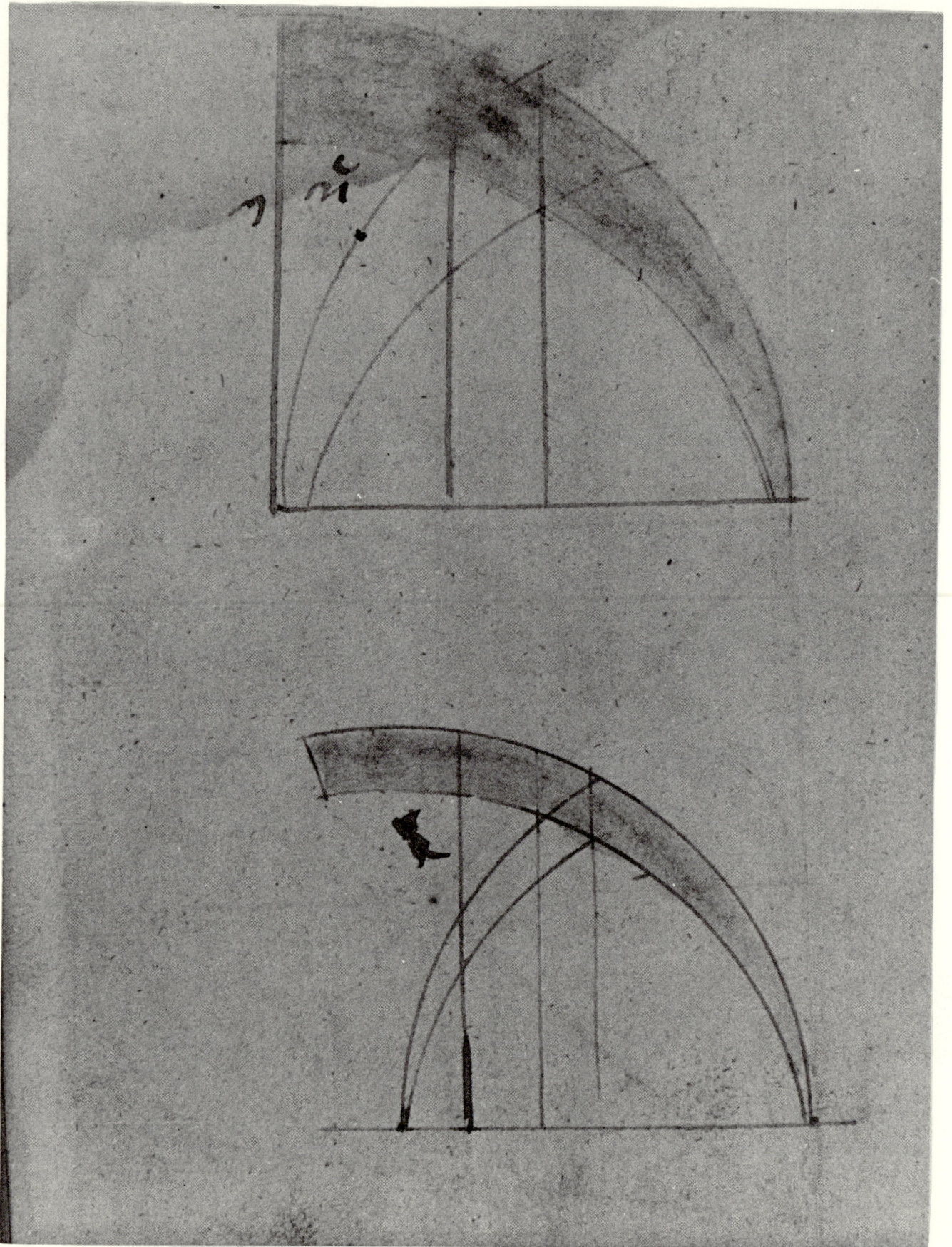

WG 40   Same as WG 37.

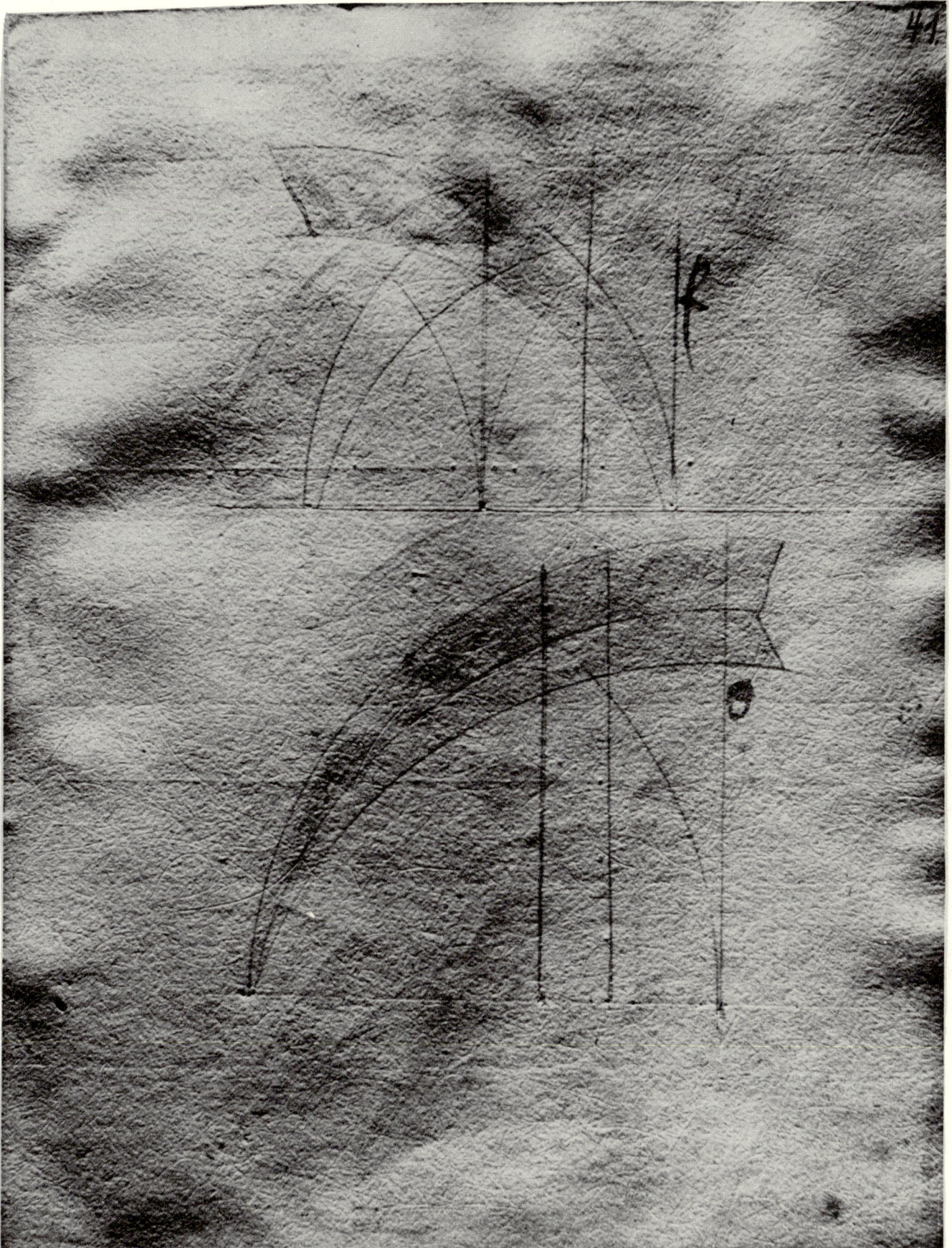

WG 41   Same as WG 37.

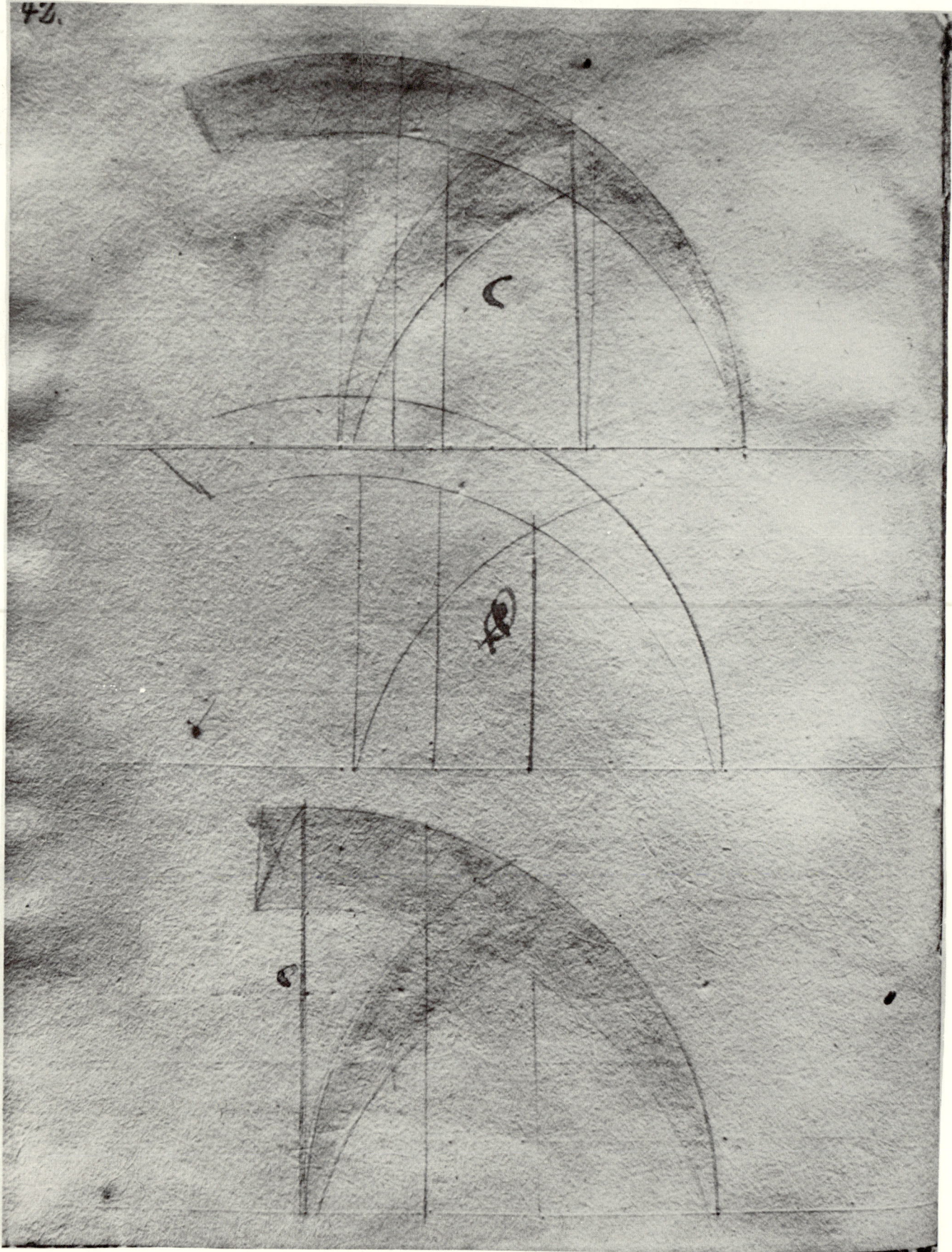

WG 42   Same as WG 37.

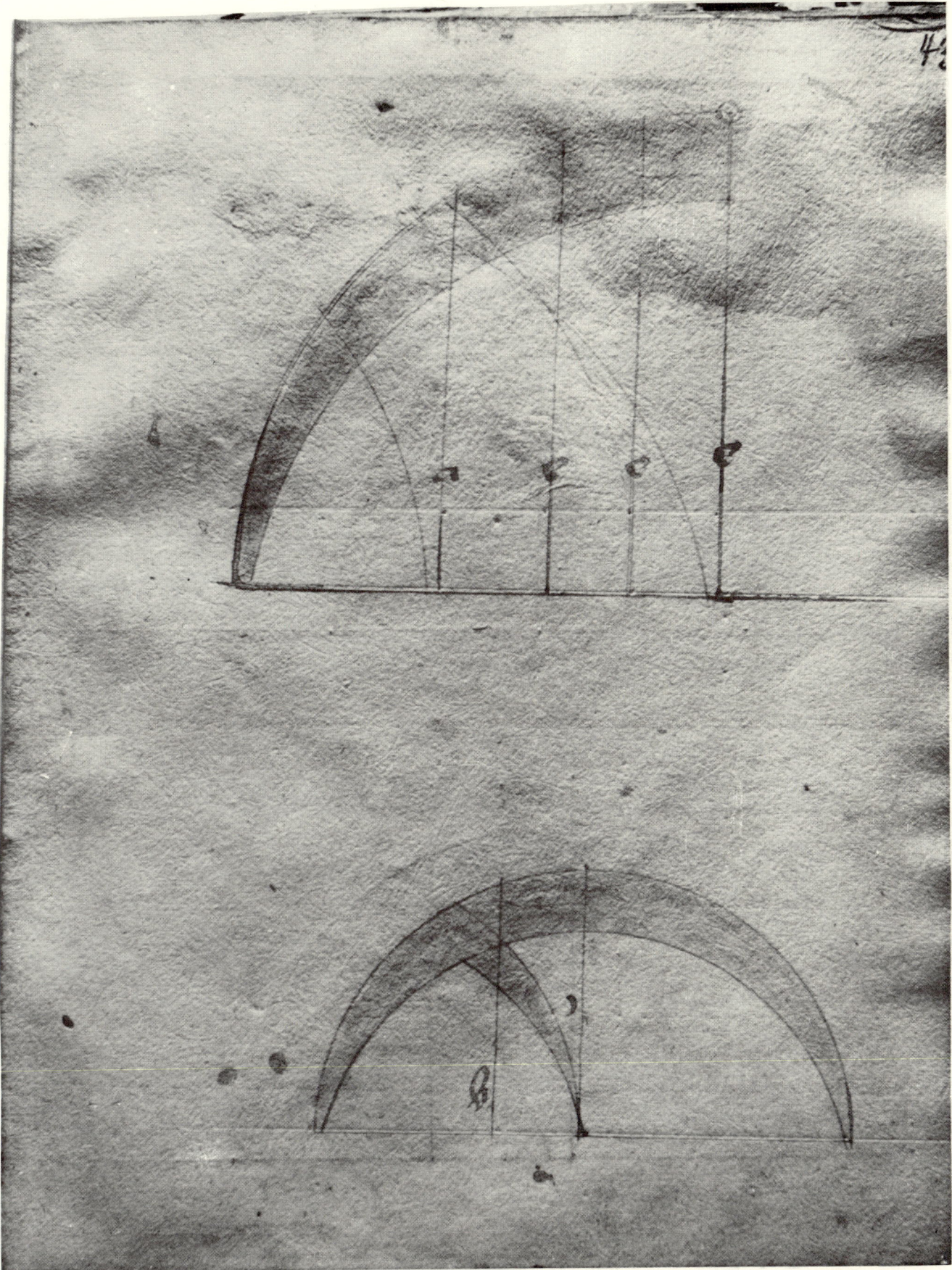

WG 43 Same as WG 37.

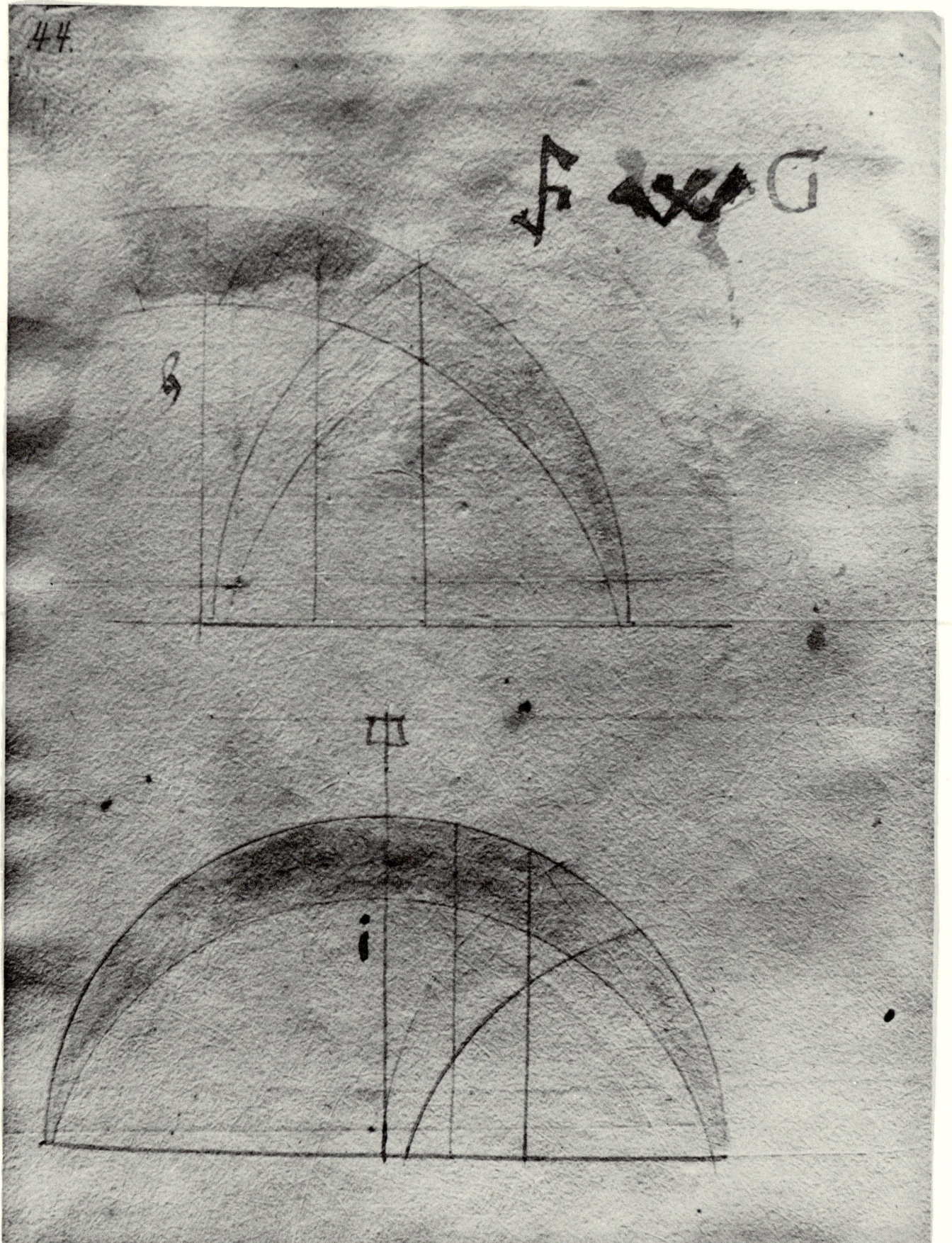

WG 44 Same as WG 37 with the addition of WG's monogram and mason's mark.

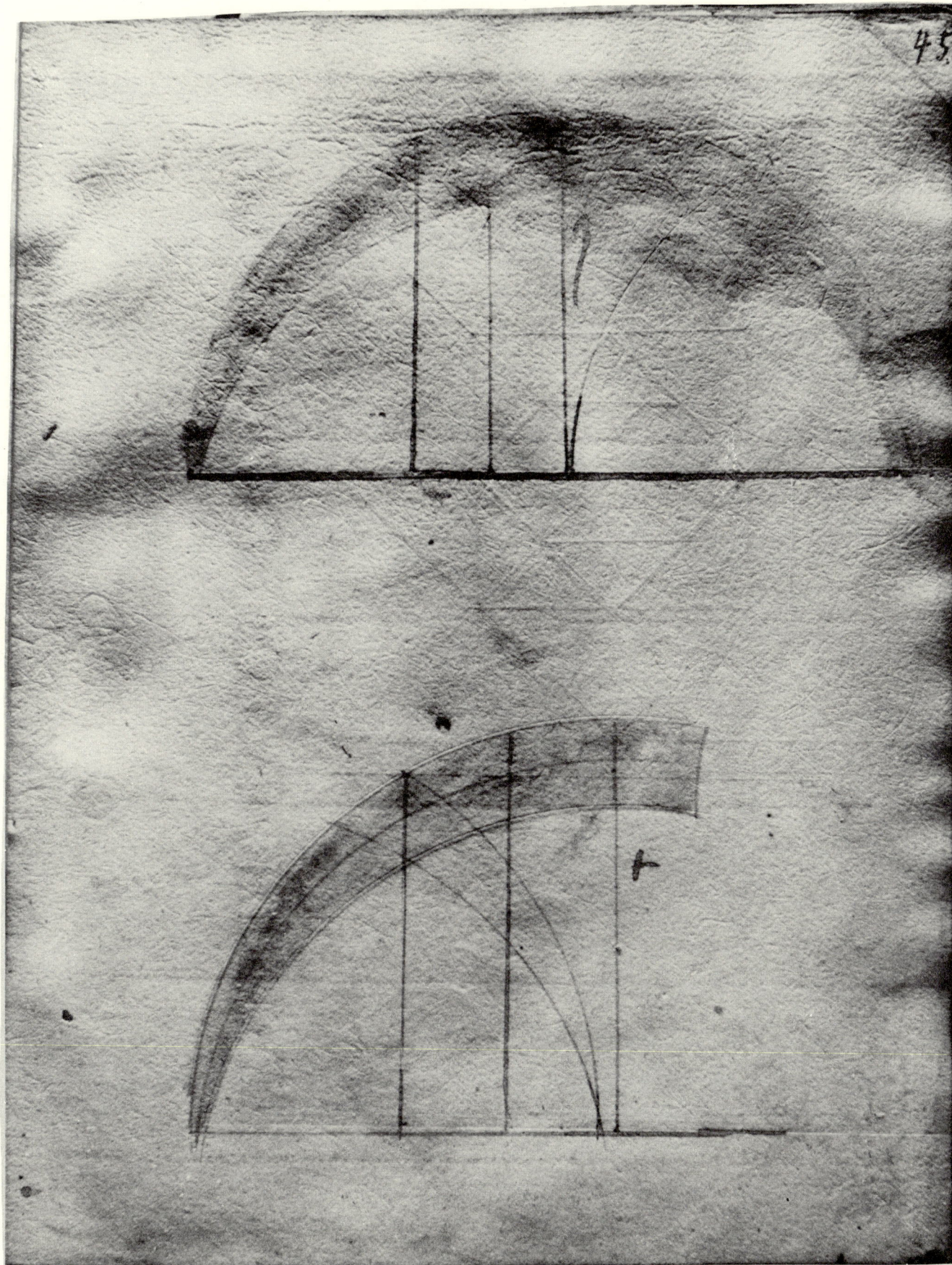

WG 45   Same as WG 37.

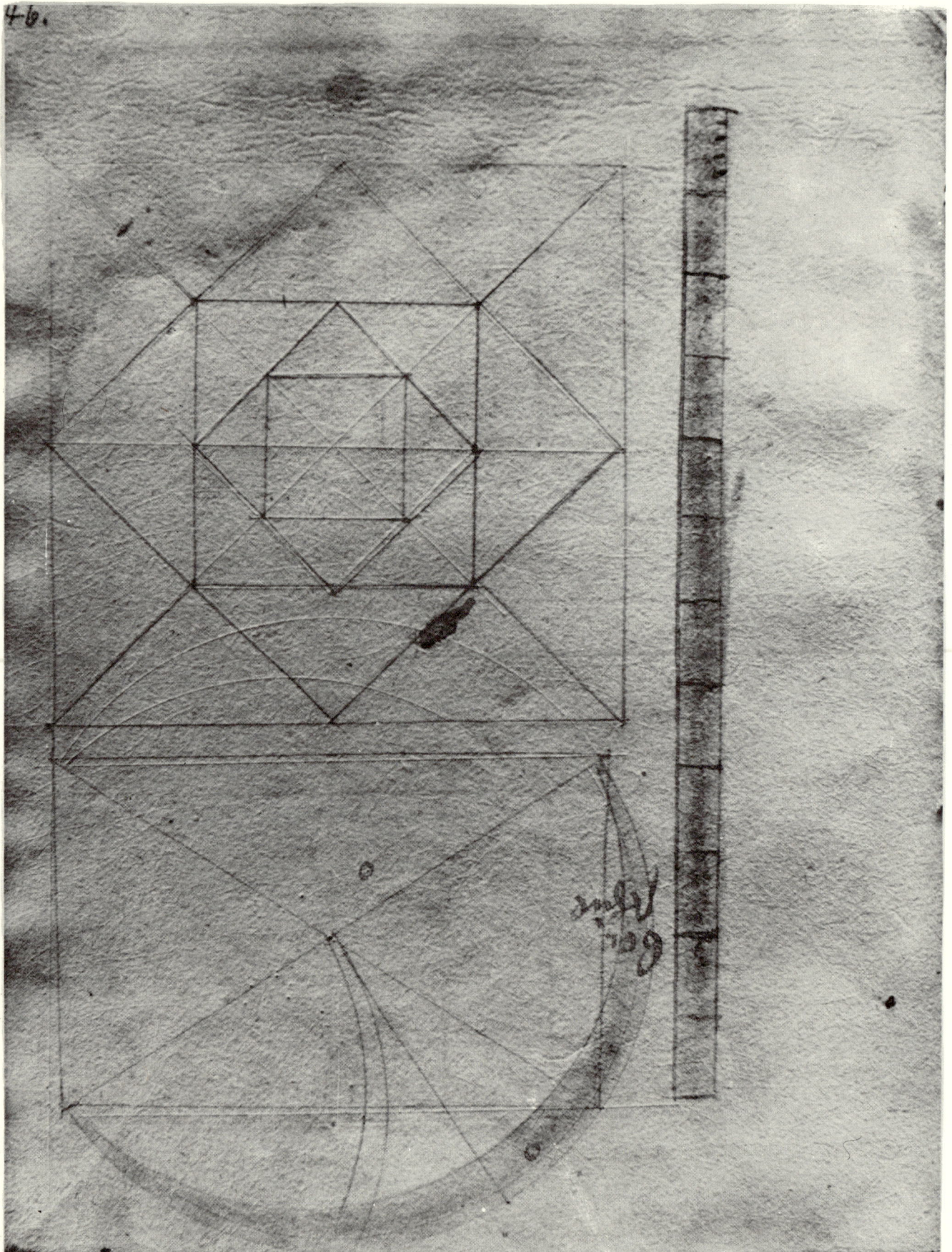

WG 46 Top same as WG 37. Bottom. The rotation of the square which can be called the Gothic canon. The vertical center line through the square which would have facilitated the sketching process was omitted. At left a very rare drawing of a scale or measuring rod. It contains twelve units of 9/16 inches adding up to 6-5/8 inches. The scale seems unrelated to the drawings even though Square One and Two measure seven and four units respectively, and the diagonal of the upper rectangle contains eight units.

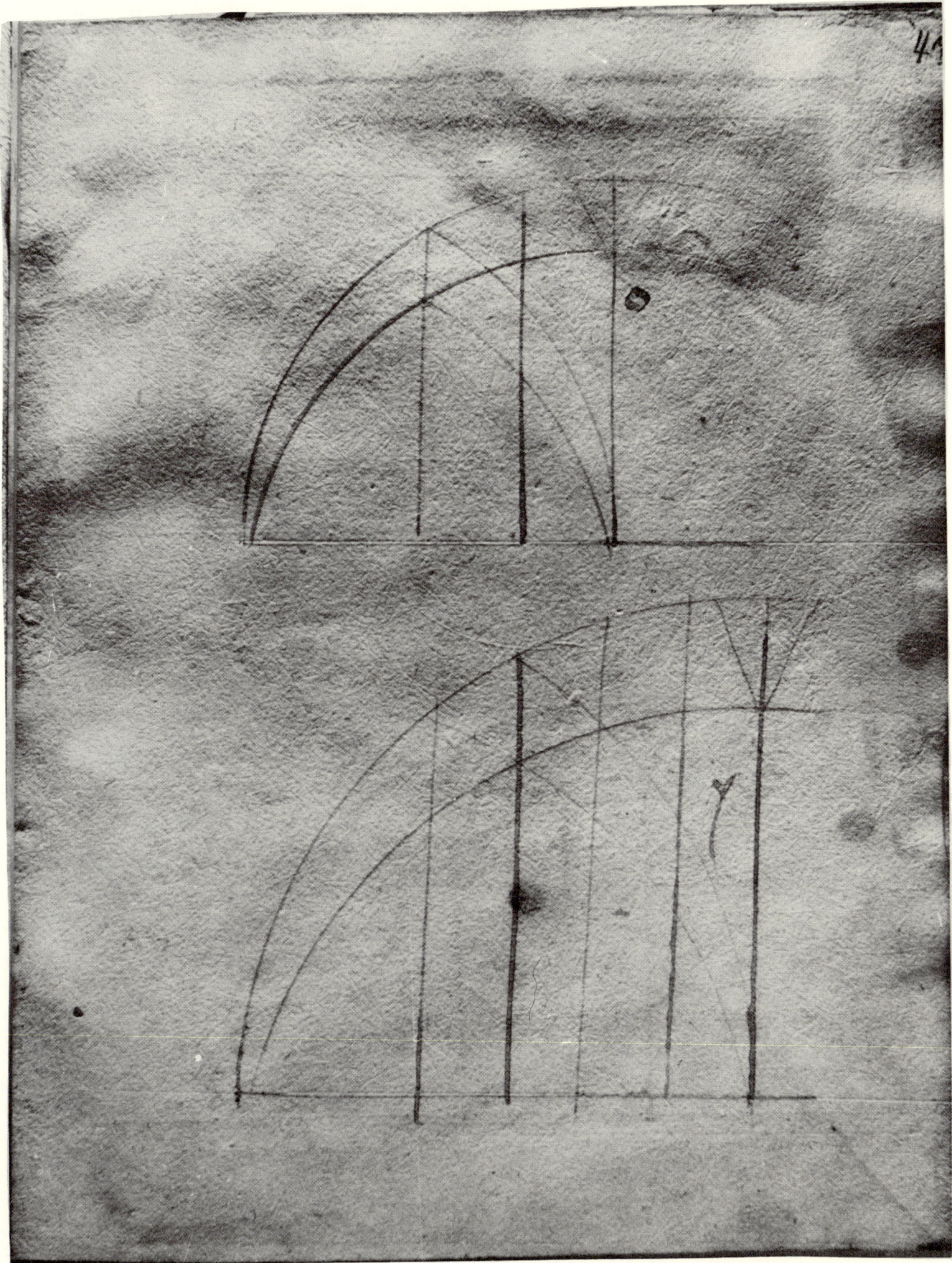

WG 47 Same as WG 37. The lower sketch gives the rib length and curvatures for five elements of a complex net or star vault.

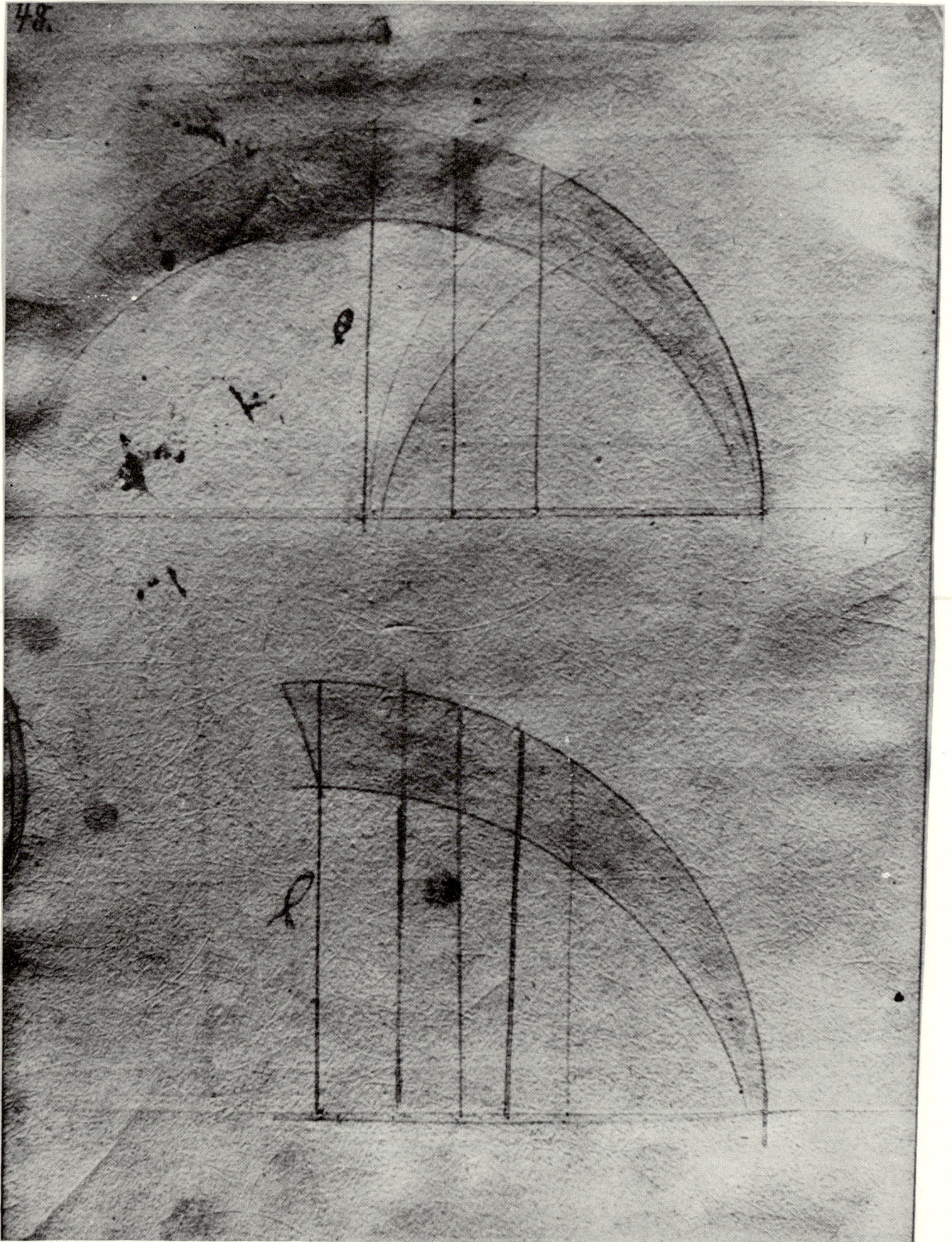

WG 48 Same as WG 37.

WG 50 Gable with four windows and decorative fortification elements.

WG 51   Tongued gable with large attic opening surmounted by rectangular hole for a crane.

WG 54   Scalloped gable with finial.

WG 56 Two vault patterns, the lower one widened by one third.

58.

WG 57 Double square vault with stars based on a division of the main square into 16 equal squares.

WG 59 Gable with crenellation, a ventilation hole and, perhaps, a plan for a rectangular porch .

WG 62   Triple lancet window with nine square panes, a two point arch and tracery, based
on interlocked half circles, and two mouchettes.

WG 63 Quadruple lancet window with a lower row of diagon panes, a two point arch and tracery based on three interlocked half circles with two stretched mouchettes.

66.

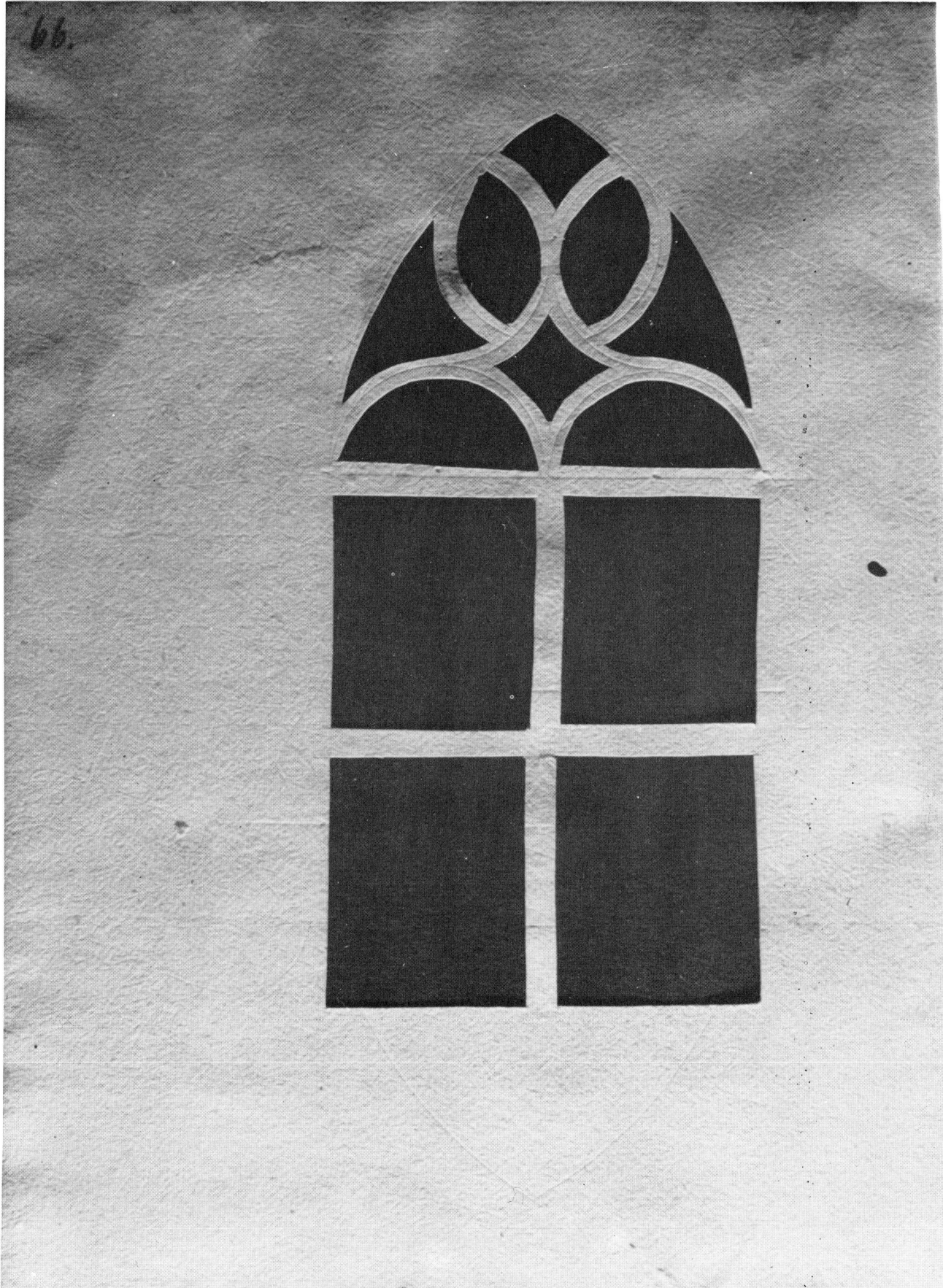

WG 67 Two lancet windows with four panes, two-point arches and tracery based on two half-circles, a curved rhomb and two divergent mandorla-shaped openings.

257

WG 68   Unusual window with two lower and four upper diagon panes, a strong horizontal bar and a two
point arch whose base lies above the bar. The steep lower arch has its centers at the outer edges
of the bar, the uppermost tracery arch is arbitrary and fails visually.

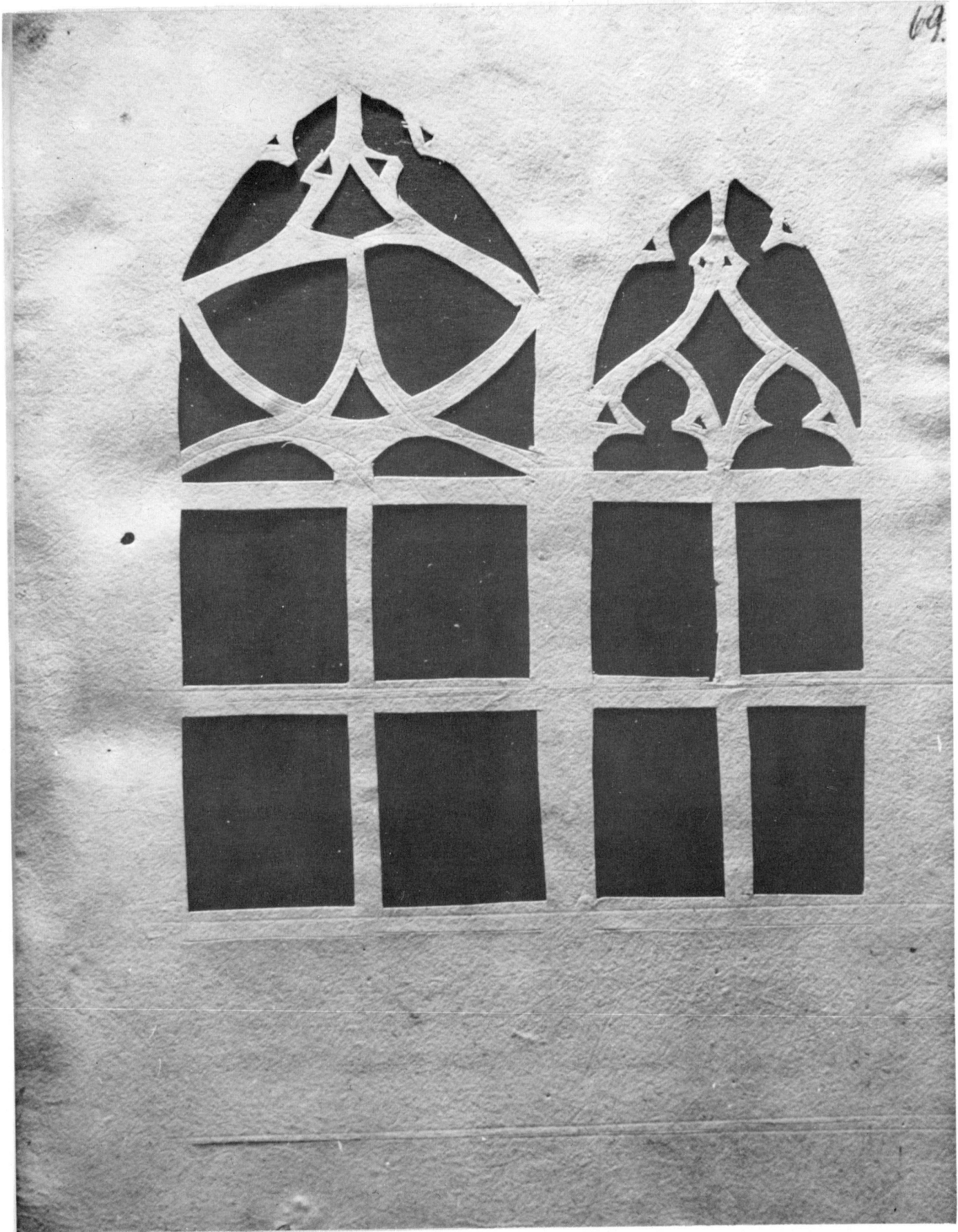

WG 69 Two double lancet windows whose tracery with segmental triangles, mouchettes, etc., is based on arbitrary centers.

WG 71 Triple lancet with approximately square panes, two heavy cross bars and a tiers point arch whose
centers lie in the vertical mullions below the cross bar. The same arbitrary choice of centers
underlies the trilobed tracery.

74.

WG 74 Double lancet with heavy cross bars and a two point arch. The tracery is determined by a half
circle, two point arches with trilobes, surmounted by other arches whose centers lie at the
intersections of the lower tracery arches.

WG 76 Two double lancet windows, the left example topped by a two point arch with mouchettes, the example at the right topped by an arch with three inscribed circles whose right center is indicated by the black dot.

WG 77 Four lancet windows topped by a fourth point arch, two-point lancent tops, segmental triangles and large inverted mouchettes.

WG 79   Quadruple lancet window whose tracery is governed by two flat arches whose centers lie on the upper cross bar. They are topped by two monumental mouchettes.

WG 82 Interesting double lancet window with a quadruple lower organization. The two two point arches with trilobes are topped by two sagging segmental triangles.

WG 84   Wide double lancet window with a quadruple lower organization. Variation of WG 79 with
         arbitrary centers for the low arches and the main arch, while the upper mullions of the large
         mouchettes are determined by a semicircle based on the upper cross bar.

266

WG 85 Pattern execution of WG 3. Identical size of the square bay and octagonal space. The pattern is not very precise and seems to be based on the rotation of the two equal squares defining the octagon. This is also indicated by the engraved lines.

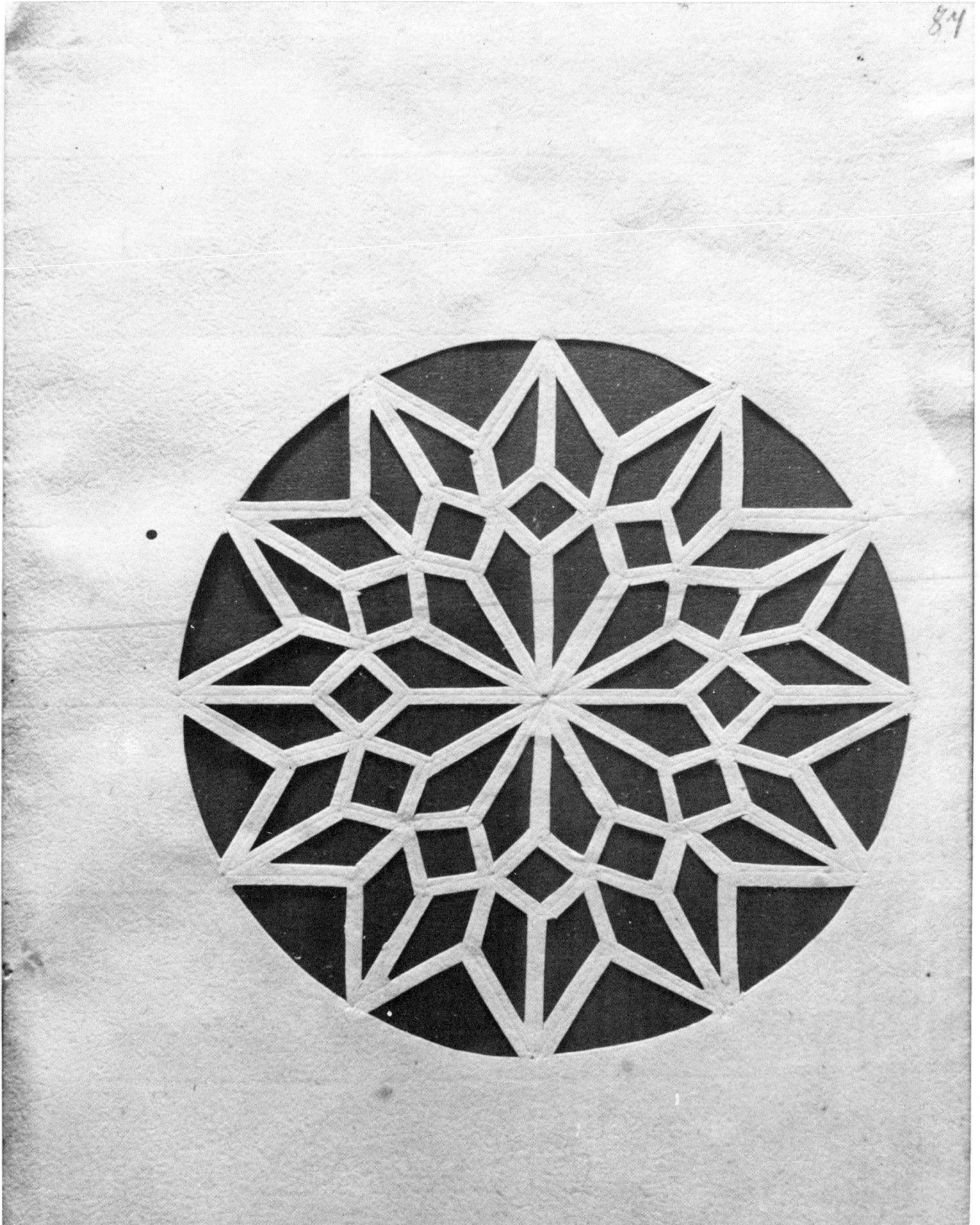

WG 87 Circular space with dodecagonal star vault, easily laid out through the doubling of a hexagon.
The proportion of the straight radial ribs interrupted by the 45° squares is 1:1, which is
sufficient for the determination of all main points of the design. The pattern is too heavy for
use in a rose window at that time.

90.

WG 90 Hexagonal space redefined by an internal ribbed hexagon containing a star. The tangential ribs
connecting the hexagon with the wall give the design a clockwise rotational force. Repaired
lower right.

WG 92 Heavy, overorganized net vault with its main intersections determined by the rotation of the square, including square one. Another possibility, not used, would have been the application of three circles whose radii would have been increased by one third.

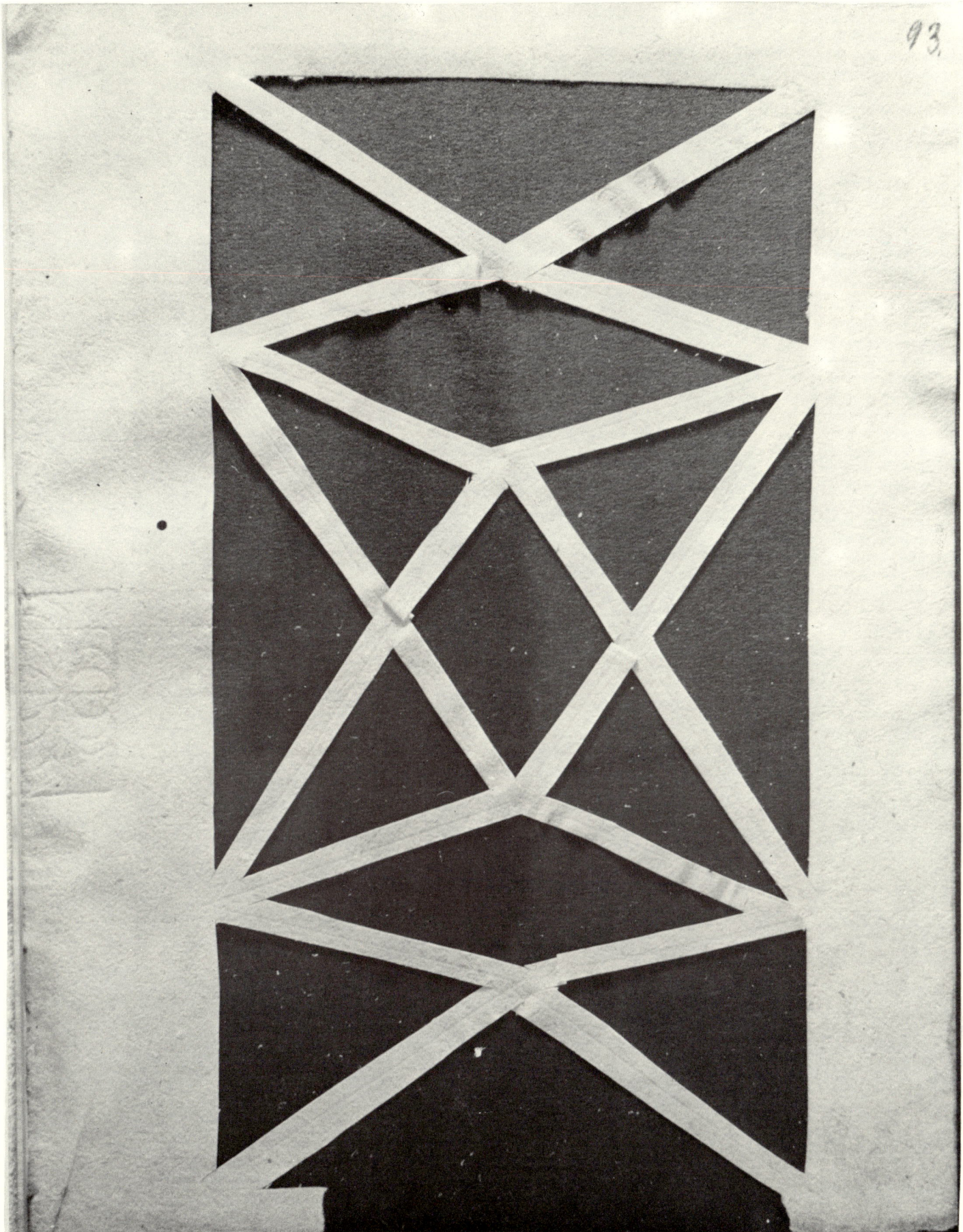

WG 93 Roughly double squared longitudinal vault with central element defined by a square, whose corners are diagonally connected with the corners of the rectangle thereby defining all elements by derivation.

271

95.

WG 95 Octagonal star vault whose elements are rapidly defined by the diameter of a circle measuring
half the diagonal of the square.

98.

WG 98 Double square star vault using the same principle described in WG 95.

WG 100 Two square net vaults. The upper one is constructed by using two-thirds of half of the diagonal of the square as a radius for the circle circumscribing the hexagon. The lower vault is based on a division of half a center line into four equal parts, the first two resulting in the radius of the circle.

WG 101   Square and rectangular net vaults. The upper vault is determined by square three or a circle
whose radius measures one half of the center line.

WG 103   Pentagon with inscribed pentagonal star defined by two triangles connecting the sides of the
pentagon.   Hexagonal vault defined by two circles, the inner one based on half a radius,
therefore resulting in ribs of equal lengths.

106.

WG 106   Rectangular net vault based on a rhomb connecting with the half points of the shorter sides and
a vertical division of the square into three equal parts.

108

WG 108 Interesting "asymmetrical" double square net vault with doubly curved central element. Horizontal
subdivision of the rectangle into four equal parts is followed by alignment of the diagonals from the
corners with the centers of the first, respectively the third lines cutting across the rectangle, thus defining
the longest ribs at the right and the first angled ribs at the left. The bisecting lines, now crossed by the
ribs give us the four intersections for the ribs headed toward the dividing line between the two squares.
The two circular segments of the center shape at the right have their centers on the frame where the
bisecting lines one and three are located. The centers of the circular segments at the left are chosen
arbitrarily.

109

WG 109 Net vaults. The upper example is based on a division of the square into three equal vertical
parts and connecting the thirds with diagonal lines drawn from the corners. The lower vault
is defined by the large rhomb and its nine parallel subdivisions.

111.

WG 111 Star and net vaults. The star vault consists of a star constructed from a circle whose radius measures one quarter of the center line and square one which is touched by all the outer points of the star. The lower vault is based on four vertical section lines.

WG 114 Design for one of many seemingly complex late Gothic net vaults. The two to three rectangle
is divided into three equal horizontal and four vertical bands. The two central vertical bands
are filled with hexagons containing six pointed stars. The outer horizontal ribs measure one
half of the width between the hexagons and the outer edges.

281

116.

WG 116 Two net vaults. The upper vault is based on four equal horizontal and vertical partitions. The lower vault is based on four horizontal and four vertical segments or sixteen squares.

WG 117 The consciously lopsided, interesting net vault is constructed on the basis of three equal vertical and six equal horizontal lines connecting the edges of the rectangle. Some additional jiggling of angles reinforces the playfulness triggered by the unusual design.

WG 119 The radius of the hexagon of the upper star vault breaks with tradition since it does not measure one quarter of the diagonal, or touch square one. The lower rectangular vault is constructed on the basis of two equal horizontal and four equal vertical segments.

WG 122 Ornamental rectangular pattern based on interlocked half circles. Square net vault with eight pointed star determined by square two, and/or its circle. An arbitrary widening of the outer triangles formed by the star leads to an extremely sophisticated, but in the end heavy irregular cross pattern.

WG 124 Stretched, eight pointed star vault based on four equal horizontal and vertical segments and
points on the frame distributed in equal thirds on the top and bottom edges and equal thirds
along the right and left edge which gives all the dimensions.

125.

WG 125   The upper net vault is based on the partitioning of the centerlines into equal sixths, and amazingly not on the rotation of the square. The lower, corridor vault consists of three squares.

WG 127 Longitudinal star vault with stretched cloverleaf center. All major points lie on a grid determined by six equidistant vertical and horizontal lines except for the arbitrary angle given to the four ribs at the right and the left of the center.

WG 130 Double square net vault with doubly curved ribs. Two interlocked half circles are divided into six equal parts each giving four additional section points. The centers for the segments of circles of the inscribed figure seem—as in many other cases—to have been defined arbitrarily.

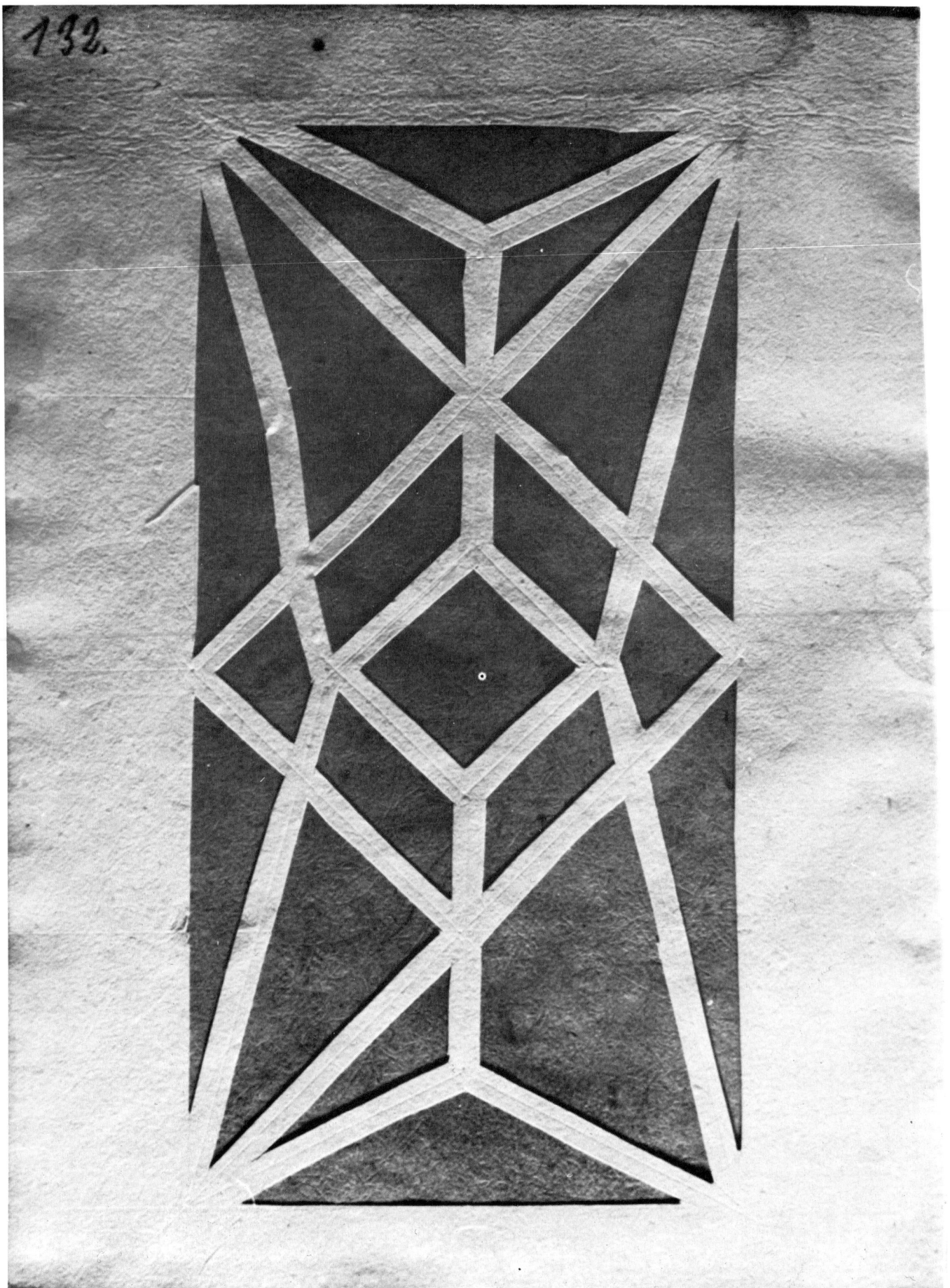

WG 132 Stretched, double square net vault designed through the use of four equal vertical and eight horizontal divisions beginning with the two central squares.

133.

WG 133   Square star vault with trans-penetrating ribs. The cutout is not precise, but the major points of
construction seem determined by the rotation of the square. Below: Double square longitudinal
vault based on three equidistant horizontal segments and six equal vertical strips.

WG 135 Two square net vaults. The upper example is an arbitrary construction, and the lower more dynamic vault shows a mathematically identical arbitrariness which indicates that both vaults were conceived as a longitudinal sequence.

738.

WG 138 Bold net vault uniting a square with star patterns. Developed from three equidistant horizontal
compartments with three horizontal guidelines at the half points. The design is easily developed
from the central square.

WG 140   Two square net vaults, the upper one made interesting through an interloping rectangle which gives the vault a clockwise tilt. The reason is the absence of a short rib segment in the upper right quadrant. The main points are based on the rotation of the square. The large lower vault radiates from a central octagon. The construction seems arbitrary which explains the fortunate lack of parallels in the outer trapezoids.

WG 141 Stretched star vault based on a central octagonal star which determines all further rib activity.

143

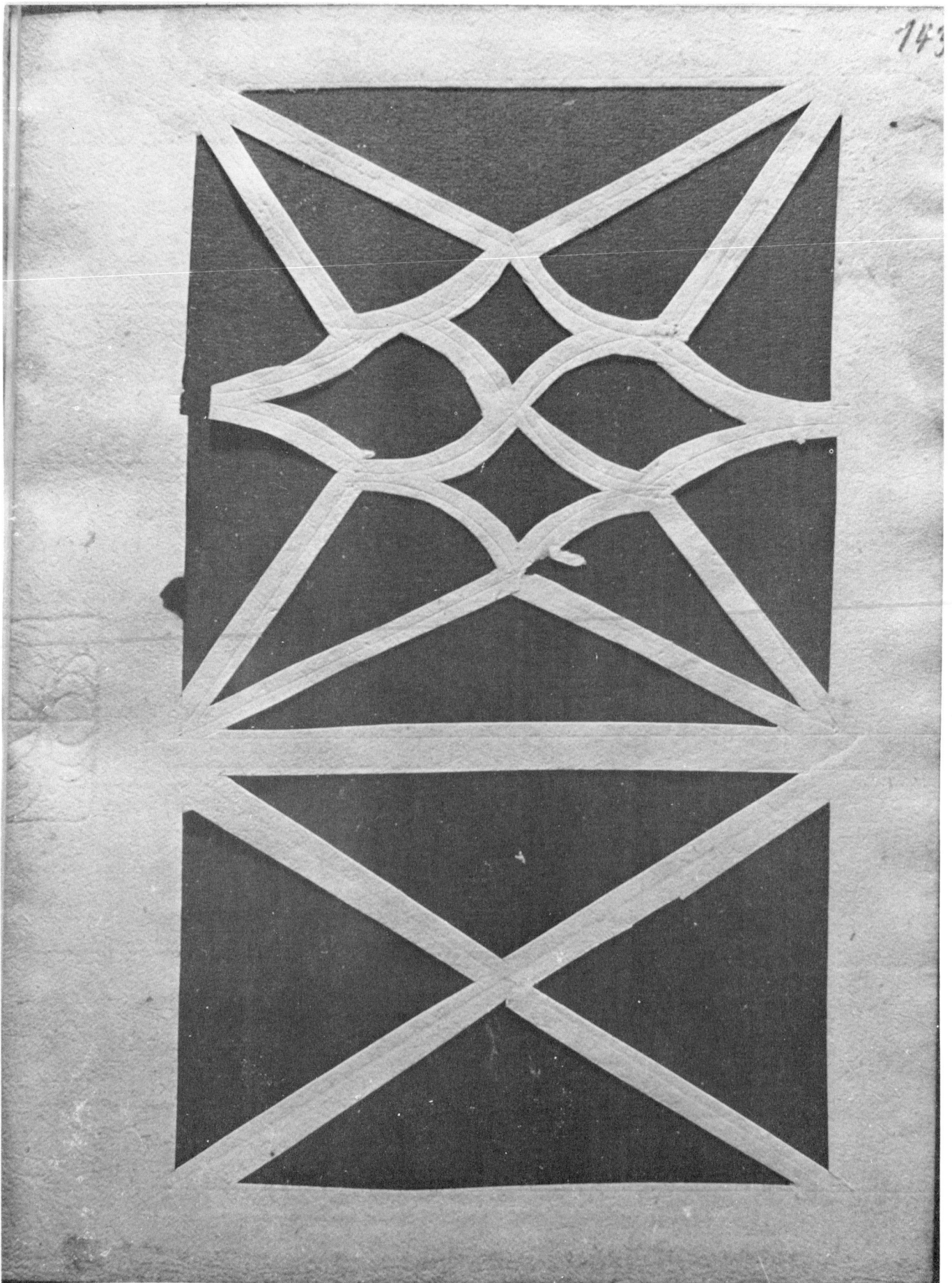

WG 143 Scalloped rhomb vault whose construction depends on four horizontal and vertical segments which determine the main intersections and radii. Below: Dutiful filler containing a quadripartite vault.

146.

WG 146 Net vault in 3 : 4 rectangle whose main points are given by a tripartite horizontal and a
quadripartite vertical division. Lower octagon dominated vault. The size of the octagon was
determined by the wish to have its prolonged sides connect with the corners.

WG 148 Double square standard net vault based on eight equal horizontal and four equal vertical
strips. Optically the blurred star patterns expand into strong hexagons.

WG 149 Longitudinal net vault based on two interlocked squares.

WG 151   3:2 net vault based on six vertical and four horizontal divisions which determine all points of intersection.

154.

WG 154   Erratic net vault in a double square rectangle.   One of the few Gothic free form designs.

WG 156   Net vault with a complex, dense frame of ribs abutting against a diagon frame. This seems to be
an arbitrary design whose basic conception allows for a great deal of freedom.

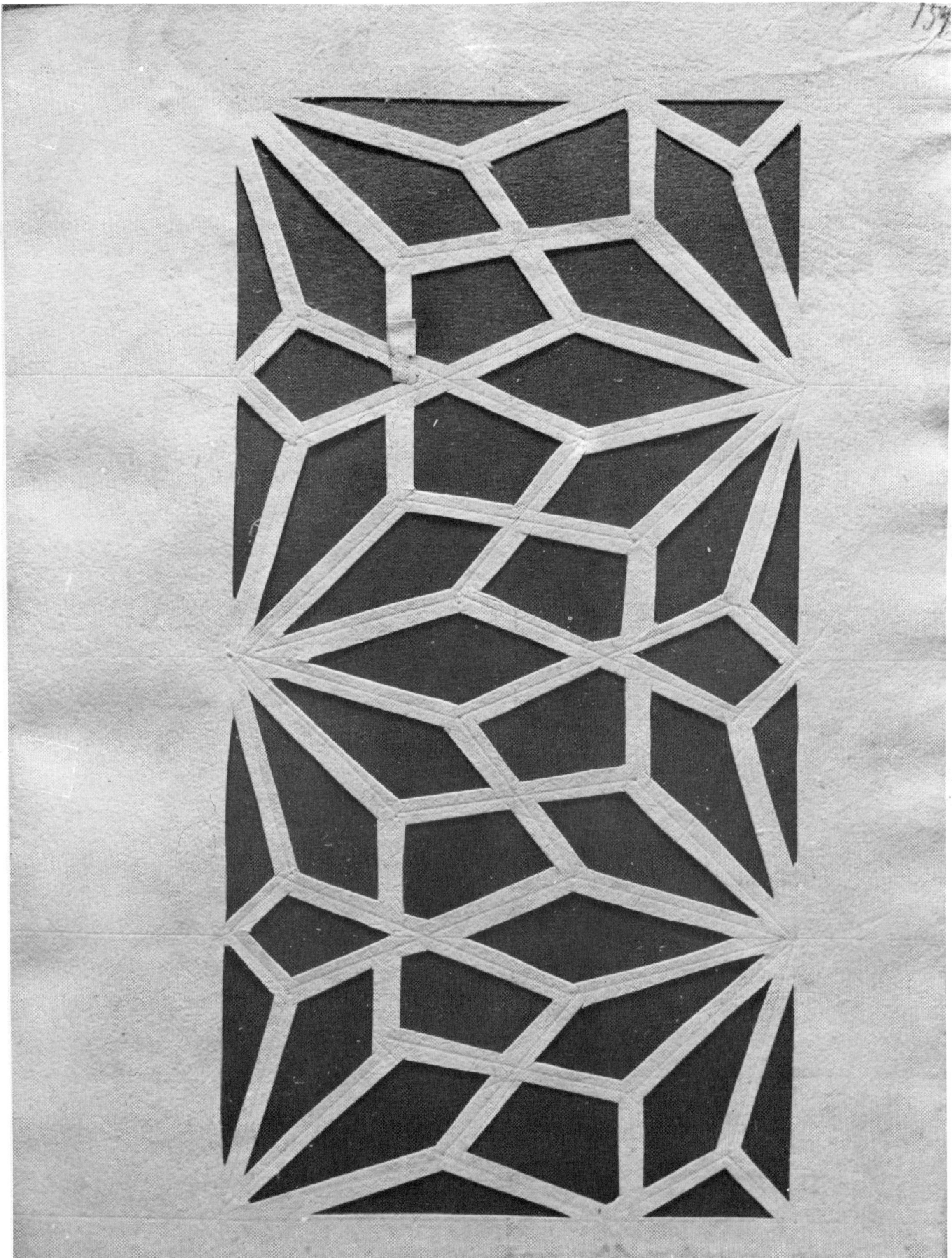

WG 157   Complex and stimulating net vault which is the left half of a square star vault with dodecagonal stars.
These ebb into two irregular pentagons facing to the right and one in the middle facing left. The design
is based on a highly complex geometric grid which, however, produces only four types of ribs in plan.

WG 159   Double square net vault based on four vertical sections and a central octagon from which the whole system is derived.

162.

WG 162 Neat, strongly "two dimensional" vault based on four equal vertical and six horizontal sections which produce only two types of ribs.

164.

WG 164 Double square vault with quadripartite stars determined by crosses measuring one half of a center line.
Heavy handed octagon star with inscribed cross. The star is constructed from four isosceles triangles, the
size of the cross is based on the desire to obtain as many ribs of equal length as possible.

WG 165 One half of a courtyard or cloister with two star vaults constructed as WG 164, the left bay derived from a division of the rectangle into two and three equal segments, and the bottom vault based on rhombs which are unrelated to the total concept of an ambulatory space.

WG 167   Interesting anti-longitudinal net vault based on a series of rhombs from which ribs emerge which are at a right angle to the direction of the walls, therefore visually slowing a forward progress. The choice of equilateral triangles along the wall prevents the usual parallelism of ribs and enhances the power of the transverse stretched hexagons.

WG 170 Another cloister or courtyard exercise with a double square vault based on a horizontal and vertical division
into three equal parts, a quadripartite vault, and a visually interesting bottom vault based on a horizontal
and vertical triple grid. The omission or rearrangement of ribs transforms a predictable and structurally solid
pattern into a surprisingly playful statement.

309

172.

WG 172   A highly standardized cloister or courtyard design with quadripartite stars determined by crosses measuring one half of the center line, and a quadripartite vault at the right.

WG 173 Fascinating "optical effect" vault constructed from three double square vaults with irregular six pointed stars whose "vertical" ribs measure one half of the center line, while the two "horizontal" rhombs span the center line of the square. The result is of a high visual complexity forcing the viewer to see three hexagons, a horizontally flaring star with ten compartments, six six-pointed stars and other shapes in constant transformation.

WG 175 Uninteresting longitudinal vault based on a quadripartite vertical and sexpartite horizontal grid and using three types of ribs.

178.

WG 178 Highly standard, structurally over engineered longitudinal vault based on a quadripartite vertical and a five-partite horizontal grid. An architectural bore, this type of vault amused the public.

180.

WG 180   Two vaults with crosses. The upper is based on four quarter circles with their centers in the corners. The cut off points are determined by connecting the corners with the centers of the opposite sides. Because of the doubly curved ribs, buttressed only in part by the webbing, the vault could develop tension. The cross of the lower vault is developed from four bars measuring one half of the center lines, the rest follows.

314

WG 181 Unimaginative vault based on a quadripartite vertical and horizontal grid. Cheaper to construct because all ribs are of equal length in plan.

315

183

WG 183 Stretched star vault based on a quadripartite vertical grid and two triangles connecting the short sides of the rectangle with the opposite centers. The need for six types of ribs of differing lengths raises the cost considerably.

186.

WG 186 Extremely strange double corridor vault with a dynamic forward movement. This is most likely the left
half of a design which — completed — shows a stretched four pointed star inscribed in an interesting
stretched and irregular octagon. The direction of the rhombs and parallelograms at the left would
presumably be reversed in a side aisle at the right. The construction at the left can be achieved with a
tripartite vertical and horizontal grid while one unit of the vaults at the right requires four horizontal and
two vertical segments.

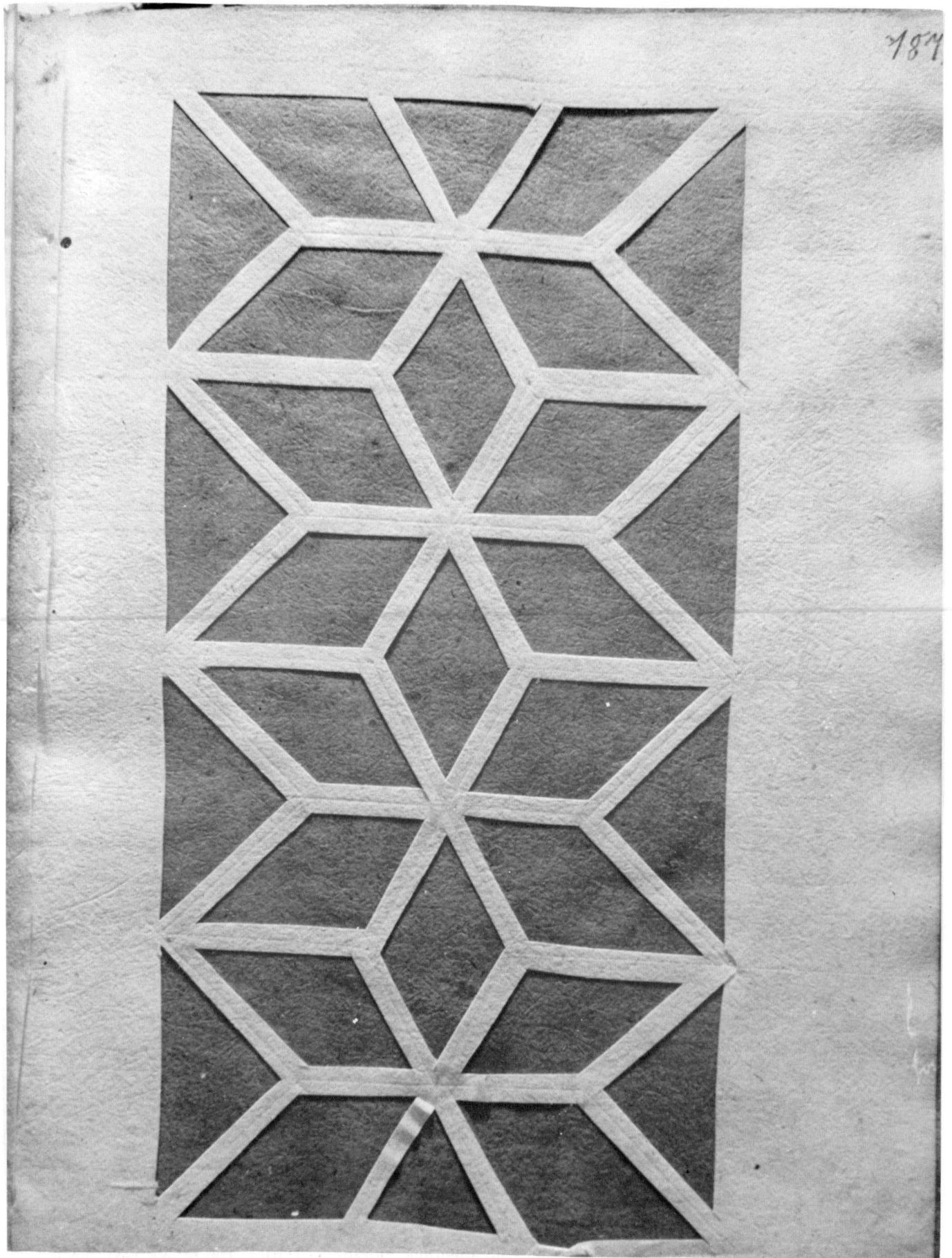

WG 187 Net vault based on rhomboids. Even less complex than WG 181 this boring vault is based on ribs of two
      varying lengths, a tripartite vertical partition with a more narrow center strip and an eight partite
      horizontal division.

318

WG 189   This slow moving vault is based on a quadripartite grid both horizontally and vertically. It is
conceived as four quadripartite bays, but not perceived as such.

192.

WG 192 This mannered vault was conceived as a hexagon from which all parts, including the inscribed rhomb can easily be derived. The very simplicity of the seemingly complex design may have inspired Master WG to the variation in the upper part. It failed.

194.

WG 194 Two variations on the four pointed star. A vertically quadripartite and horizontally tripartite grid results in the central rhomb. The lower, very clean design was conceived on the rotating square principle or on the basis of three concentric circles with radii of one-quarter, one-half and of the full use of one-half of a diagonal of the square. As usual there is a lack of absolute precision.

WG 195 The top shows the execution of drawing WG 13 but is not based on the rotation of the square which only changes the angles of the ribs closest to the edge. The lower vault uses quadripartite vertical and horizontal divisions.

WG 197 Longitudinal vault—approximating a golden section—with stretch star and hexagon patterns
to be read interchangeably. Five vertical segments and three equal horizontal parts make the
construction of the design possible.

200.

WG 200 Probably the left half of a star-and-net vault with complex star patterns containing eight
compartments of varying size. The vertical quadripartite and horizontal seven part grid provides
all major points.

WG 201-02   Exactly the same patterns as those found on WG 10 and WG 15. Their construction is the same.

WG 203-04   Standard longitudinal vault with squares and rhomboids with only two types of ribs. Constructed from four vertical and five horizontal lines.

WG 205-06   Four square star vaults forming a four pointed large star with ridge ribs. Constructed according to the rotation of the square, square three being the inscribed square. Longitudinal vault based on four equal horizontal and three equal vertical divisions.

WG 207-208 A series of five net vaults, all except for the second one based on a double square. The four longitudinal vaults share in their construction four vertical divisions and horizontal bisection. The vault at the bottom right is an interesting variation of the vault seen on WG 125. At the top left is the mason's mark of W.G.

WG 209-10   Complex rectangular net vault to be compared with WG 156. Basically constructed from four
equal horizontal and vertical divisions the design relies on the repeated minimum and maximum
use of only three types of ribs, thus providing for an apparently expensive, but in fact relatively
reasonable vault.

329

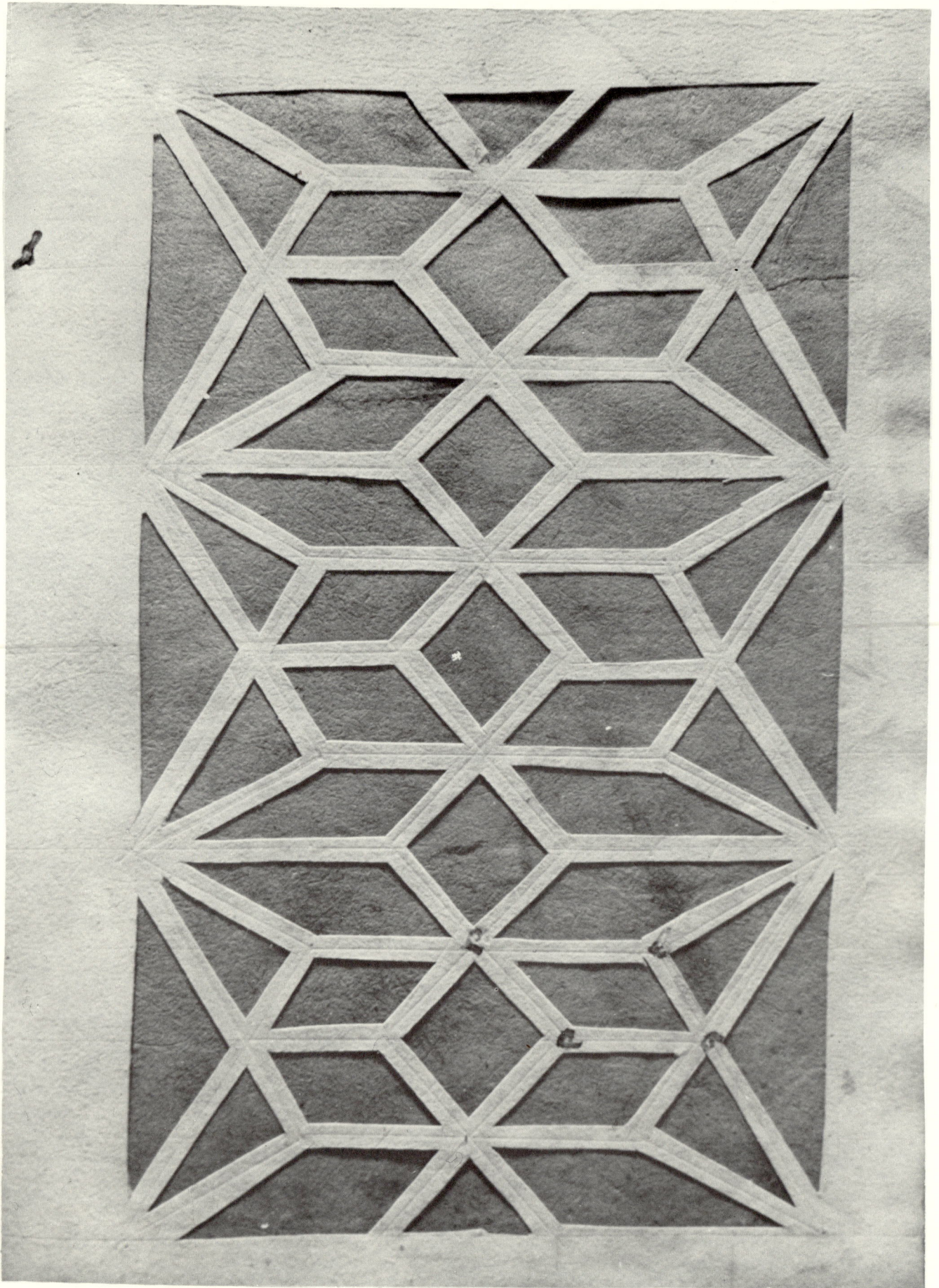

WG 211-212 Compared with WG 203-204, this more interesting vault alternates between more and less stretched hexagons inscribed in a larger hexagon which gives three horizontal units a starlike appearance. Each unit requires three vertical and minimally three horizontal divisions not including one half unit at the top and the bottom.

WG 213-14   Familiar stretched and regular star patterns to be compared with WG 58. The upper example is
based on an arbitrarily chosen circle used for a hexagon whose sides are connected with the centers
of the frame and the corners. The lower more classical pattern on a circle and hexagon is centered
in a rectangle.

WG 215-16   A clean longitudinal net vault with a central rhomb whose diagonal measures half of the width of the rectangle. From it all parts are automatically developed.

WG 217-18   A precise, strongly two dimensional design for a net vault governed by a stretched hexagon interlocked with rhombs and triangles, using only three types of ribs in plan.   Four vertical divisions.
The need for only one vertical center line and three horizontal cross lines coupled with the introduction of isosceles triangles proves the cerebral clarity of this somewhat ungothic design.

WG 219-20   Net vault for a choir with a variation of the rhomb and star motif.   Four equal vertical divisions and six horizontal cross lines will provide the grid.

WG 221-22   Repeated stretched star pattern based on four vertical and three and a half horizontal divisions. Cutting off the pattern above the two lower units would have provided an honest apse solution. Instead the uppermost square was crushed to give the star a pointed reverse thrust.

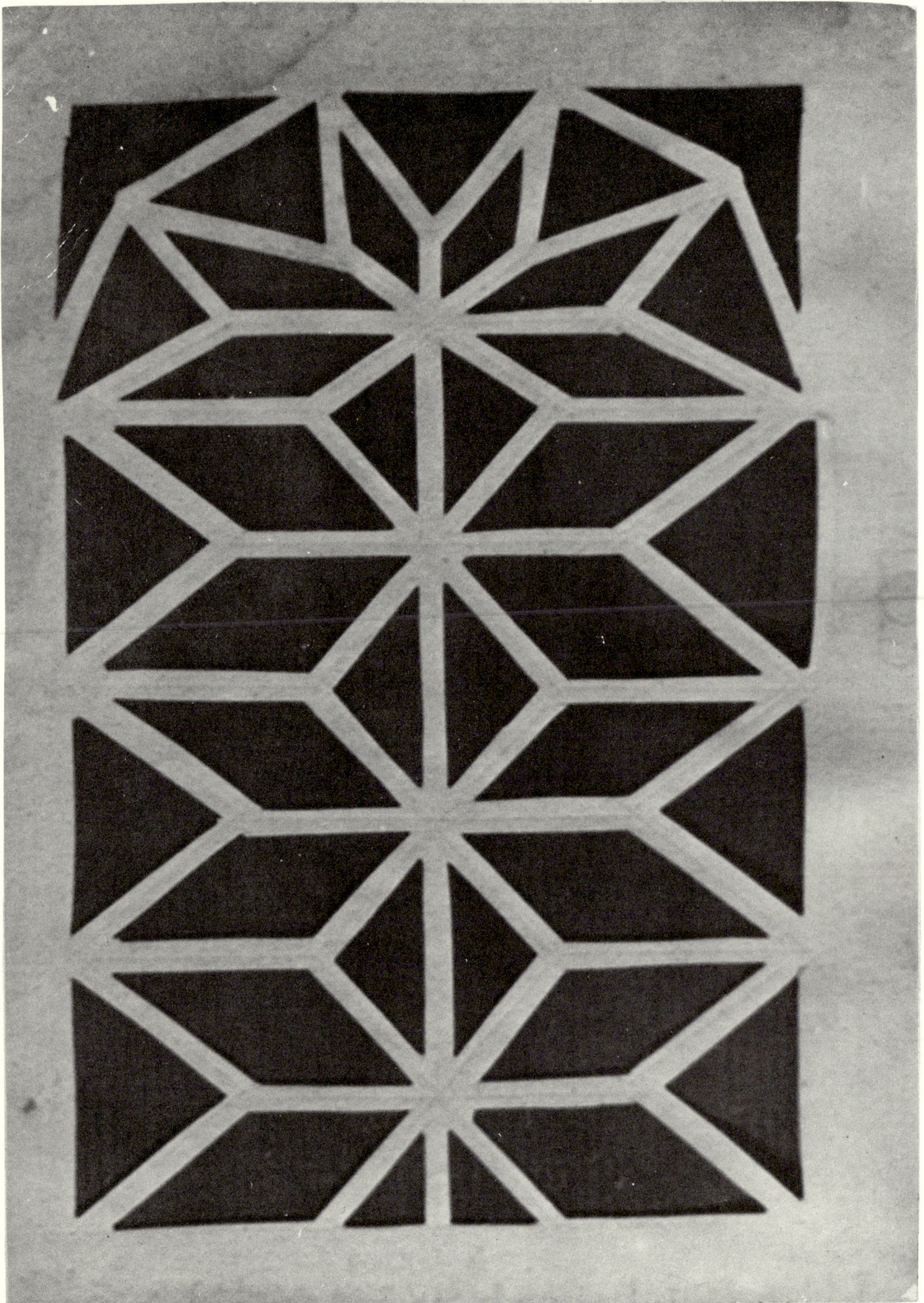

WG 223-24 Net vault for choir based on three and one half rhomboids, four vertical divisions and readjustments performed in the apse including a successful "crushing" of the uppermost rhomboid. The central division by a ridge rib enhances axial movement.

WG 225-26   Vault design for a large, presumably, hall church. A fourfold vertical and a threefold horizontal
division establishes the grid for the square "nave" and aisles, to which are added half a bay and
an archaically unsuccessful design for the ambulatory vaults. A rib in the left pane of the main
apse is missing.

WG 227-28 Original, disciplined net vault for a choir. The reversal of the five unit pattern through the
relocation of the square on alternate sides enhances the strong and cerebral zig-zag approach.

WG 229-30   A very classical execution of the design initiated in WG 24 and WG 29, and turned into a pattern in WG 138. The identical repetition stands for the appreciation it received, last but not least due to its simple quadripartite and horizontal sexpartite organization producing a 2:3 proportion.

WG 231-32   Standard, very clean net vault for a choir, similar to WG 203-04 but more canonical in the use of three equidistant verticals. The horizontals are given by the squares angled at 45⁰, and in the plan, only two types of ribs.

WG 233-34   Net vault based on four rhombs defined by the diagonal wall to wall ribs from which all elements can easily be derived.

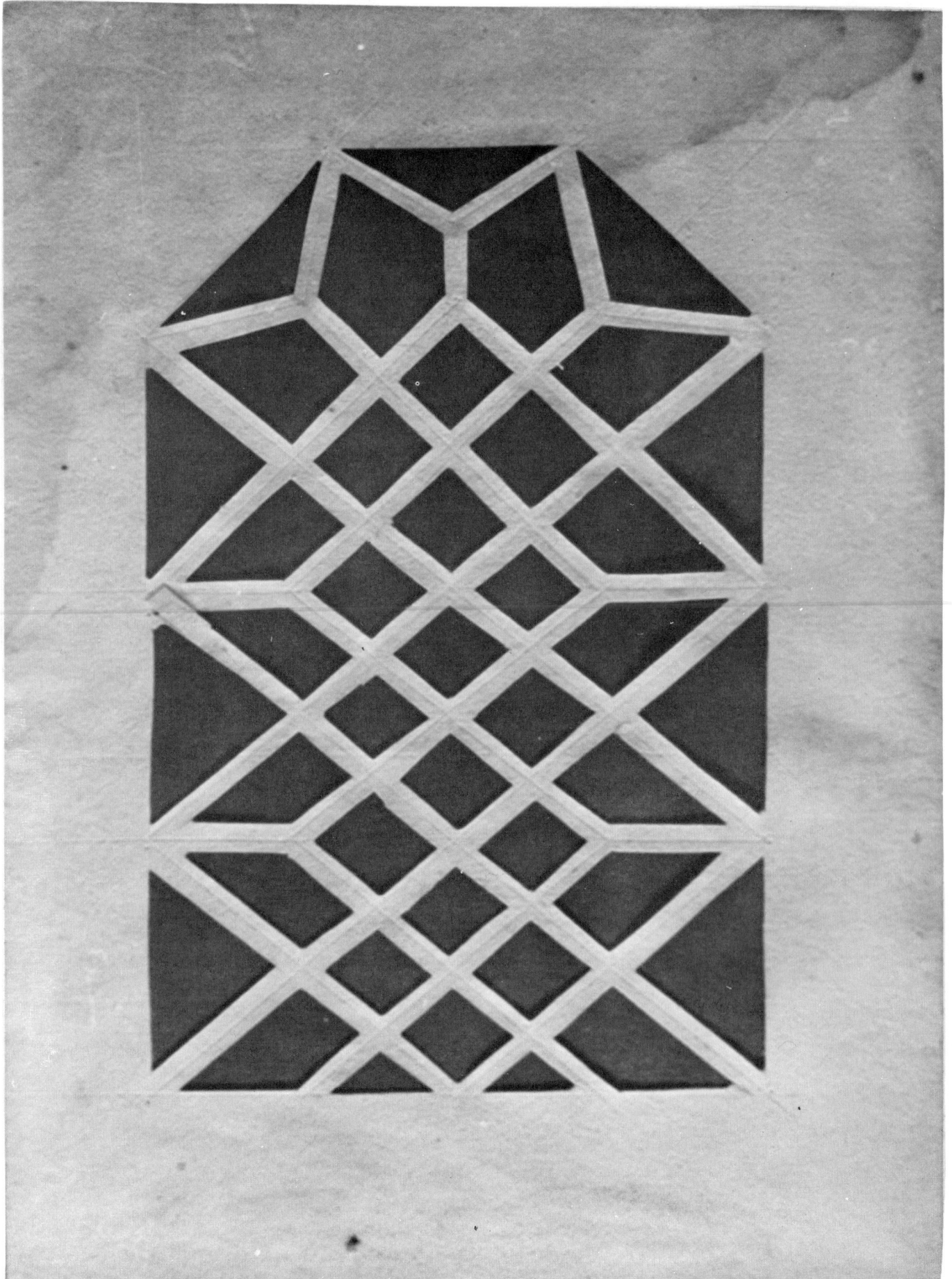

WG 235-36   Very neat net vault based on two rhombs and willful adjustments on top which are due to an
adjustment of the three choir panes downward.

WG 237-38   Two part net-vault based on four irregular vertical axes and three horizontal divisions for the rectangular bay. The upper irregular rhomb arrangement is the result of an incorrect alignment of the long, diagonal ribs.

WG 239-40   Clean construction design for a choir vault based on horizontally stretched stars using a grid
made up of three unequal vertical divisions and one centerline per unit.

WG 241-42   Chapel or choir vault with a complex net pattern based on a vertical division into five parts and two auxiliary lines roughly corresponding to the top choir wall. In addition six, or preferably eleven equidistant horizontal lines are needed to complete the construction grid.

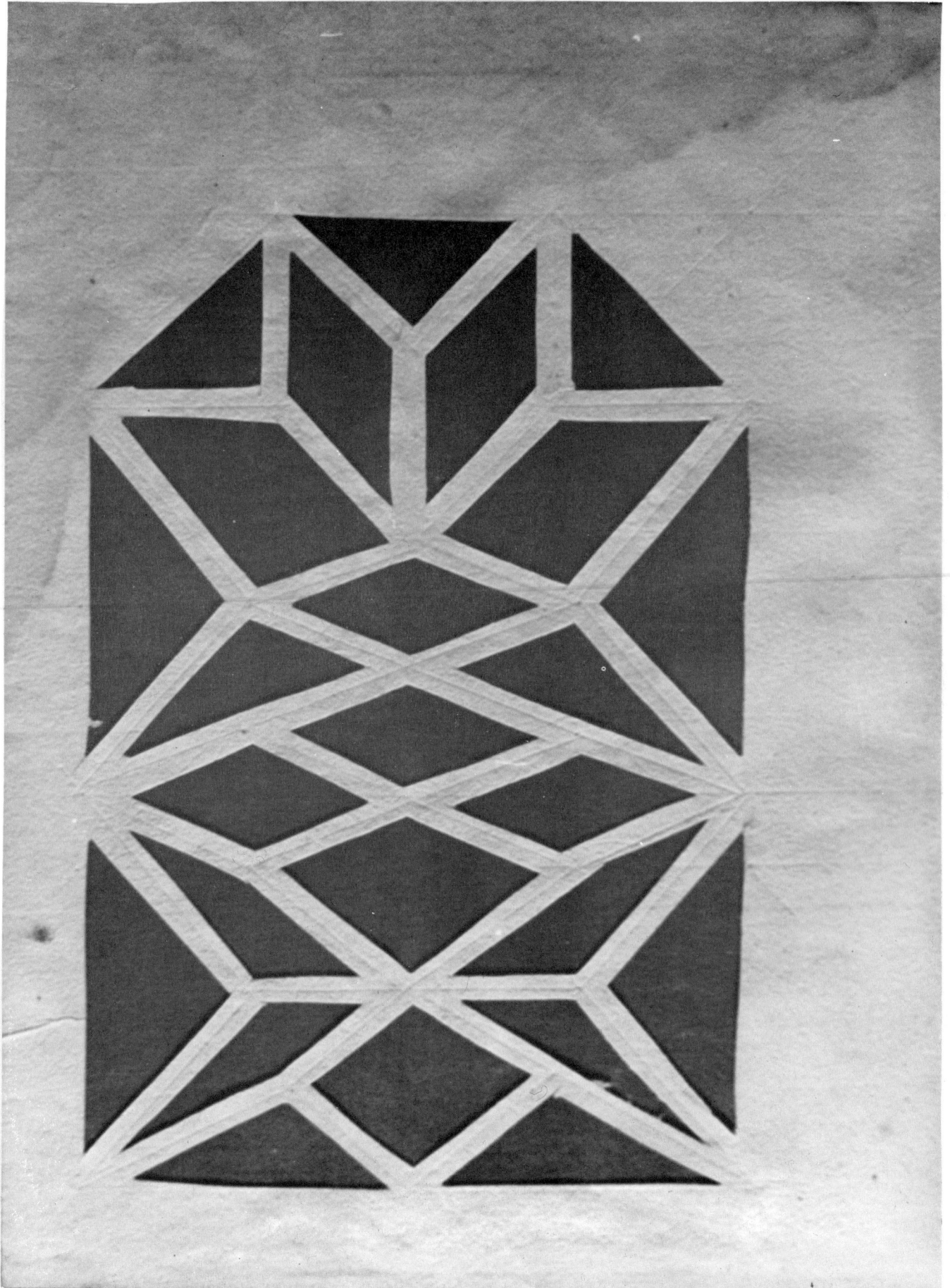

WG 243-44   Net vault for choir vault which is clearly separated from the nave rhombs. Because of the small triangle introduced above the cross rib the design falters, but is saved in its uppermost parts.

WG 245-46   1:2 chapel vault designed from a centerline succession of five and one half rhombs, with an additional open half rhomb at the top, and an arbitrary choir conclusion.

WG 247-48   Chapel or choir vault based on six rhombs and a vertical partition into four equal parts.

WG 249-50   Seemingly complex net vault covering a large choir or church. The vault is based on a tripartite
vertical division but more simply on 26 regularly interspaced diagonals, 16 horizontals, 12
"vertical" ribs and two "horizontal" ribs at the top which are spaced to top squares.

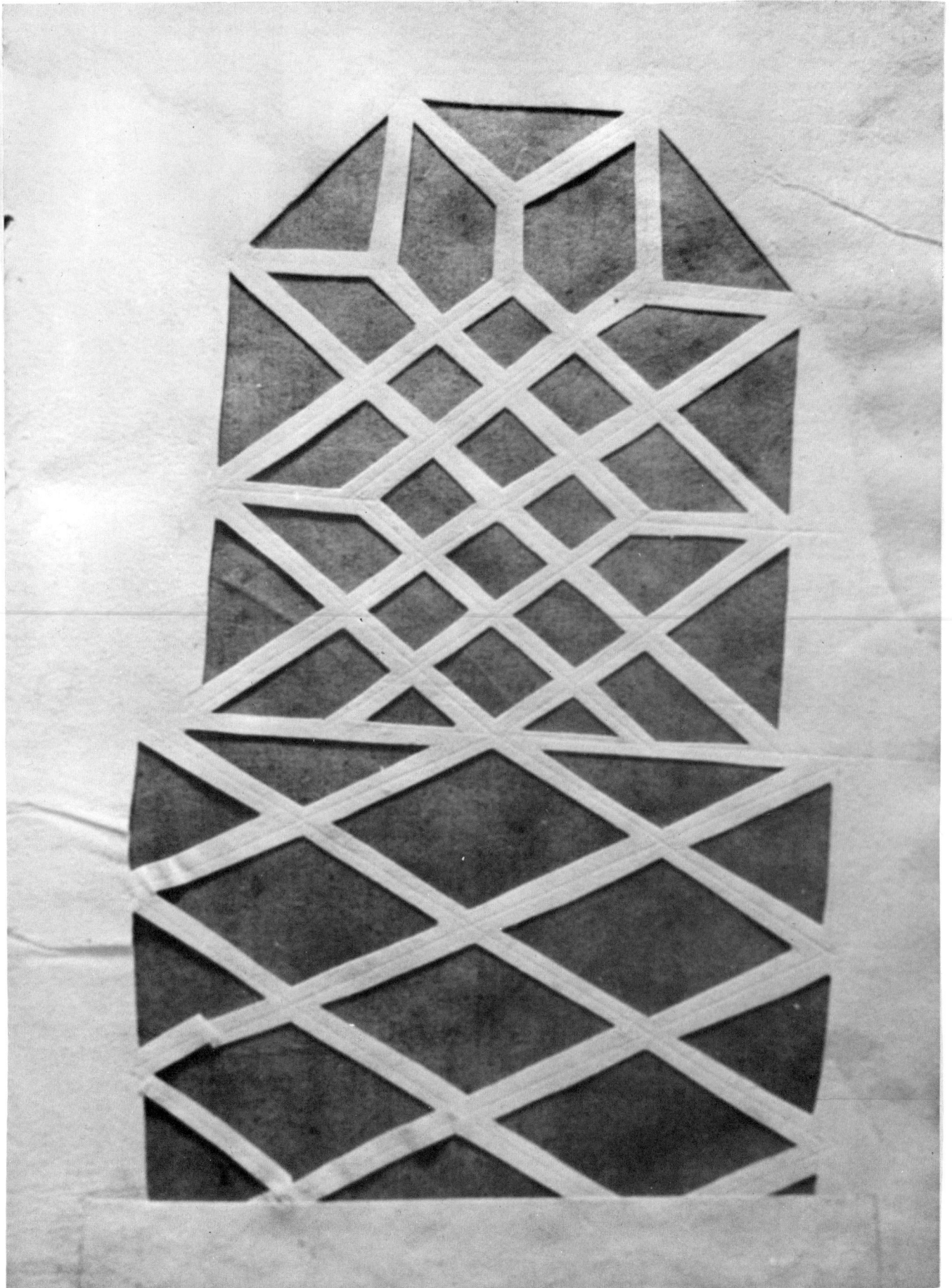

WG 251-52 Completely standard nave bay with attached apse, both based on a rhomb. Most likely the shorter diagonal of the choir rhomb was intended to measure one half of the width.

WG 253-54 Star and hexagon choir vault based on four equal horizontal and vertical divisions. As in
WG 221-22 the uppermost rhomb is crushed and the result is not noteworthy.

WG 255-56   Standard net vault for choir based on rhomboids. The uppermost one is compressed to accommodate the ribs of the apse.

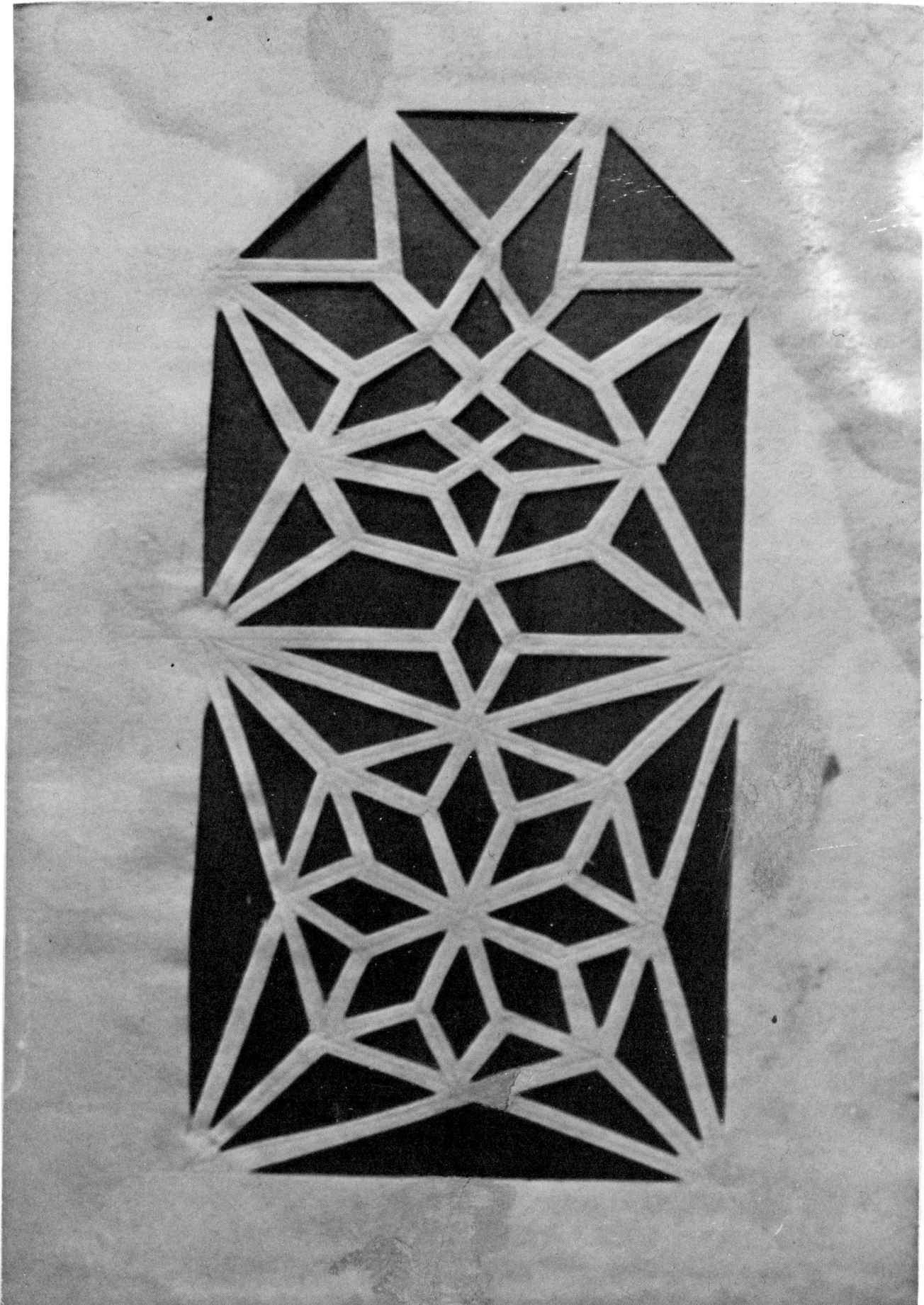

WG 257-58   Interesting two bay choir vault with an octagon whose radius measures one quarter of the diagonals of the lower square, and an inscribed eight pointed star. The construction of the upper octagon, **which** is fractured at the top and contains a four pointed star, is largely experimental.

WG 259-60 Unusual net vault for a choir based on five unequal vertical divisions and four equal horizontal
parts, excluding the segment containing the apse walls. The interchangeable patterns of an eight
pointed star and an irregular horizontally stretched octagon do not emerge clearly.

WG 261-62 Optically disorienting vault for a choir based on seven vertical and minimally three horizontal divisions excluding the panes of the apse. The compression of the upper pattern in relation to the lower design results in a disturbing, converging effect.

WG 263-64   Choir vault with central, doubly curved elements. Vertical division into four roughly equal parts and five horizontal strips establish the grid. The centers of the circles which determine the curved ribs were chosen arbitrarily, which gives the vault a flabby appearance.

WG 265-66   Chapel or choir vault based on a three part horizontal division, eight and two half rhombs and
a quadripartite vertical division.

WG 267-68 A choir vault with Gothic survival overtones reminiscent of mannerist marqueterie. Disregarding the repair at the bottom, the construction grid consists of five and a half horizontal and five vertical divisions, and much experimentation along the way. A flat and not a three dimensional and structural concept.

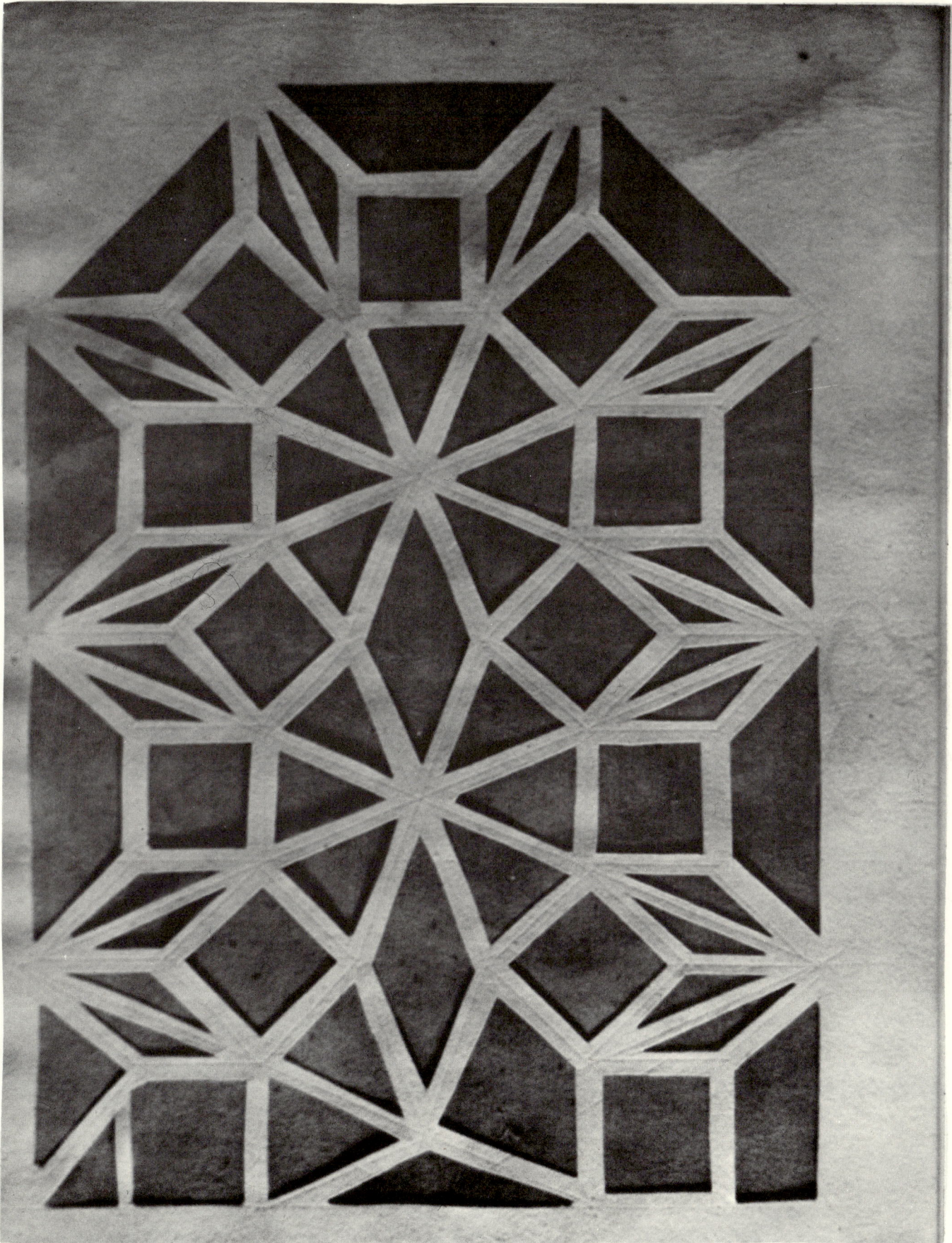

WG 269-70 Perhaps the most original net vault designed or copied by Master WG. It logically combines central plan and longitudinal motifs. Based on seven equal vertical and ten unequal horizontal divisions, it follows the module given by the alternation between horizontal squares and squares shifted to a 45° angle. The possible flip-flop effect was magnificently counterpoised by the strong five rib fan springing from the walls.

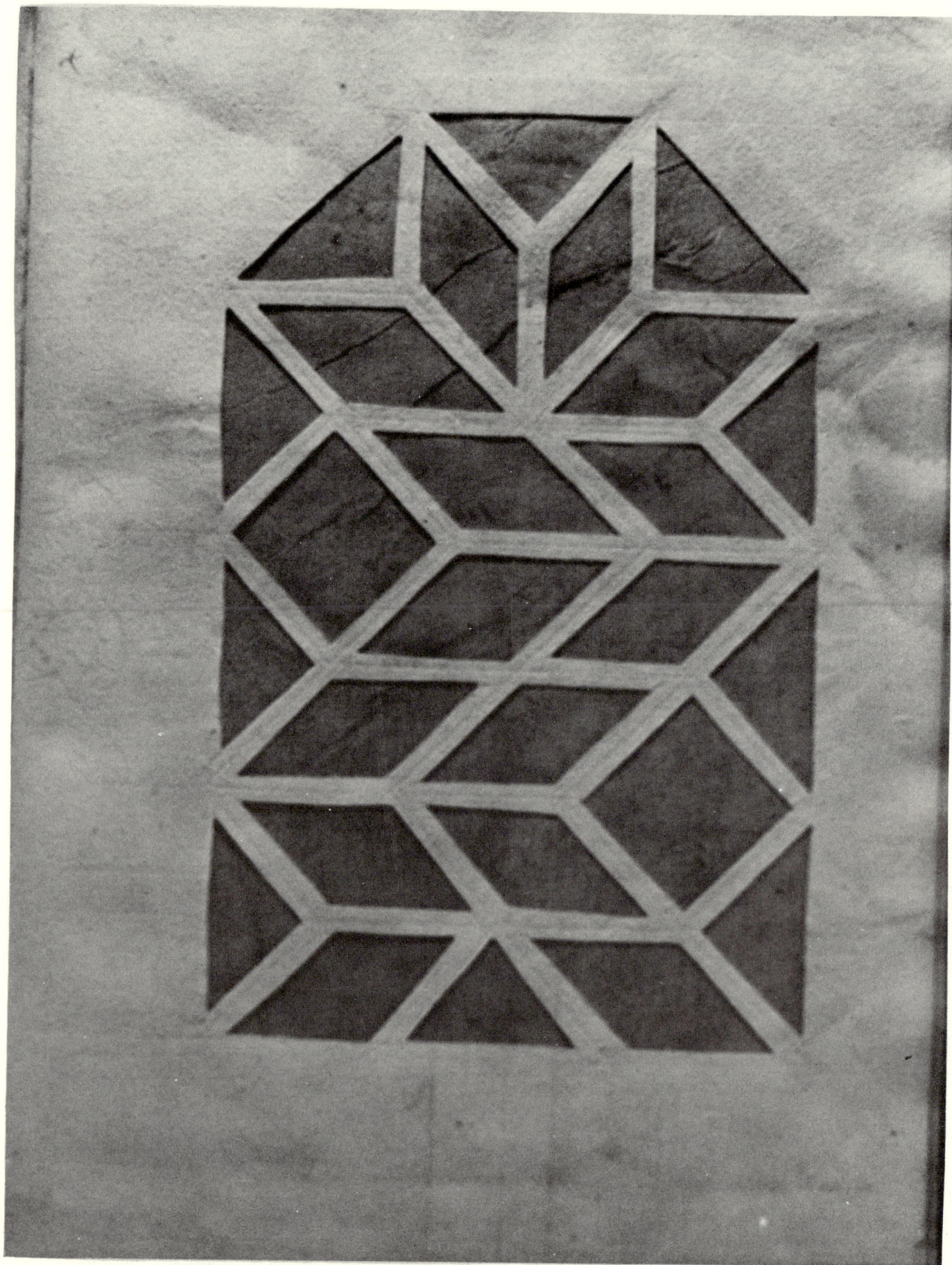

WG 271-72   Disciplined net vault with a reversal of the five unit pattern, producing a cerebral zig-zag effect.
In contrast to the similar vault on WG 227-28, the effect is dampened by the introduction of a
triangular cell over the choir entrance.

WG 273-74   This is the standard, usually medium sized choir vault used by most minor masters. A tripartite vertical and a safe five partite horizontal division—excluding the obvious apse-solution made this unassumingly logical design very popular. In addition it ideally contains only one rib length in plan which made the projection process almost foolproof.

WG 275-76   Very interesting choir solution with a lower bay based on a longitudinally stretched star inscribed in an irregular hexagon or rhomb, whose upper corner established the keystone location for the apse. The connection from the center with the seven equal panes through seven pairs of ribs along the panes, of which five pairs connect with irregular rhombs and two with squares, in spite of the mishap at the right. An increased concentration of dynamic parts thus occurs in the direction of the apse.

WG 277-78   Choir vault based on three equal horizontal and equal vertical divisions. The great variety of crushing, dropping of elements and unexpected directional changes which occur gives the vault nothing short of a mangled appearance.

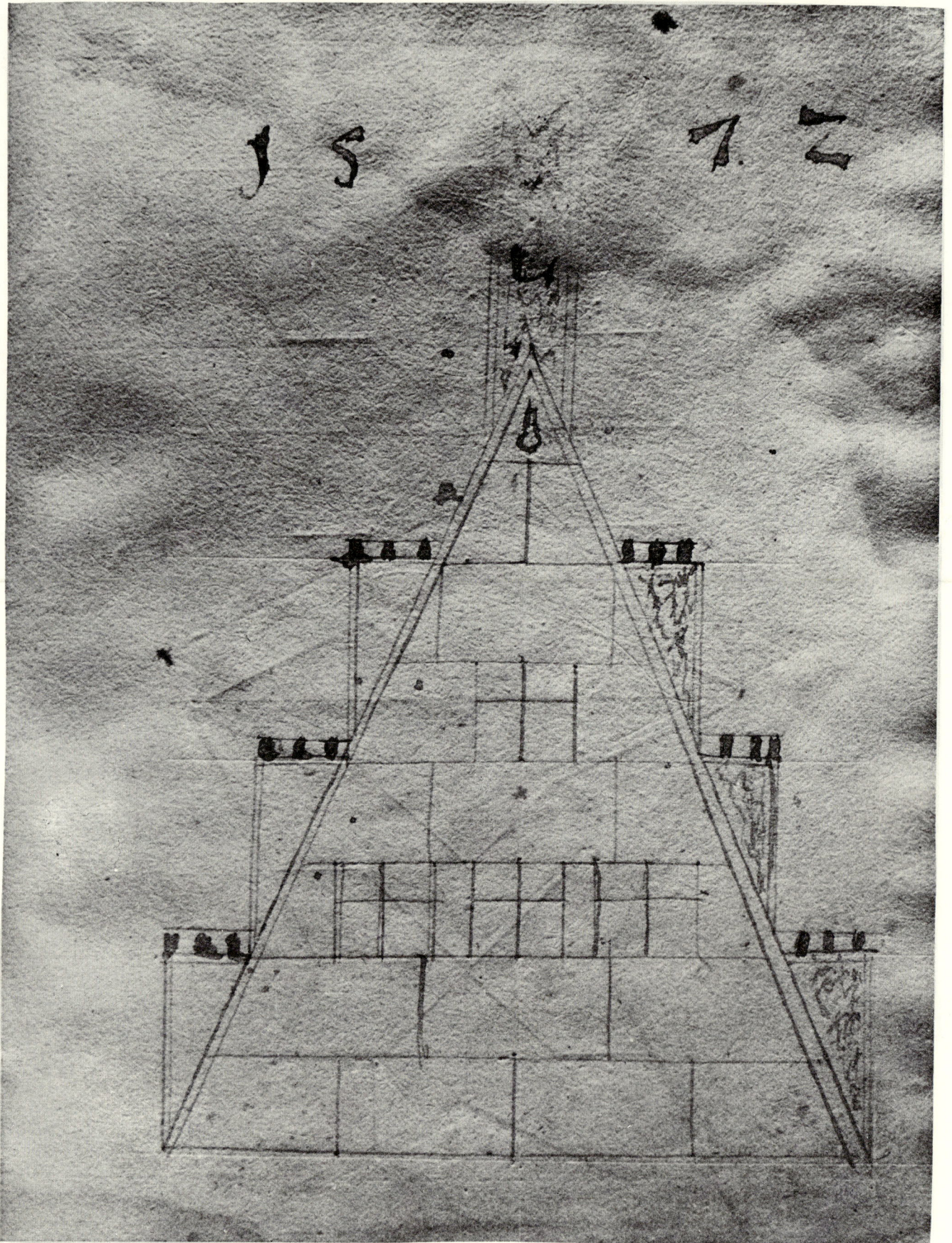

WG 279 Staircase gable with four windows and ornamental fortification elements. The date 1572 signifies the completion of the volume.

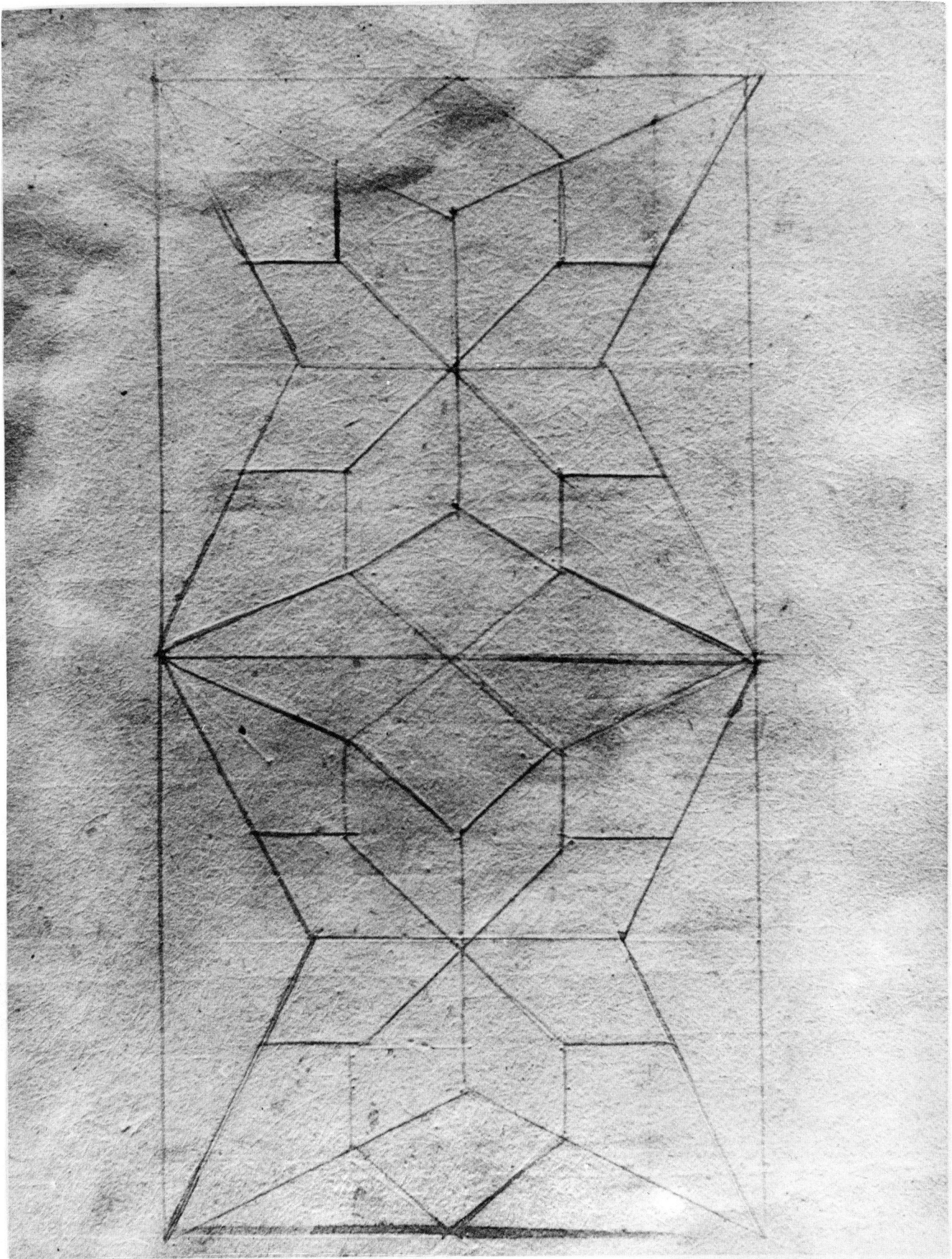

WG 280 Double square star vault based on bisecting the angles formed by the diagonals and arbitrary re-adjustments leading to a "cracked" rhomb in the center.

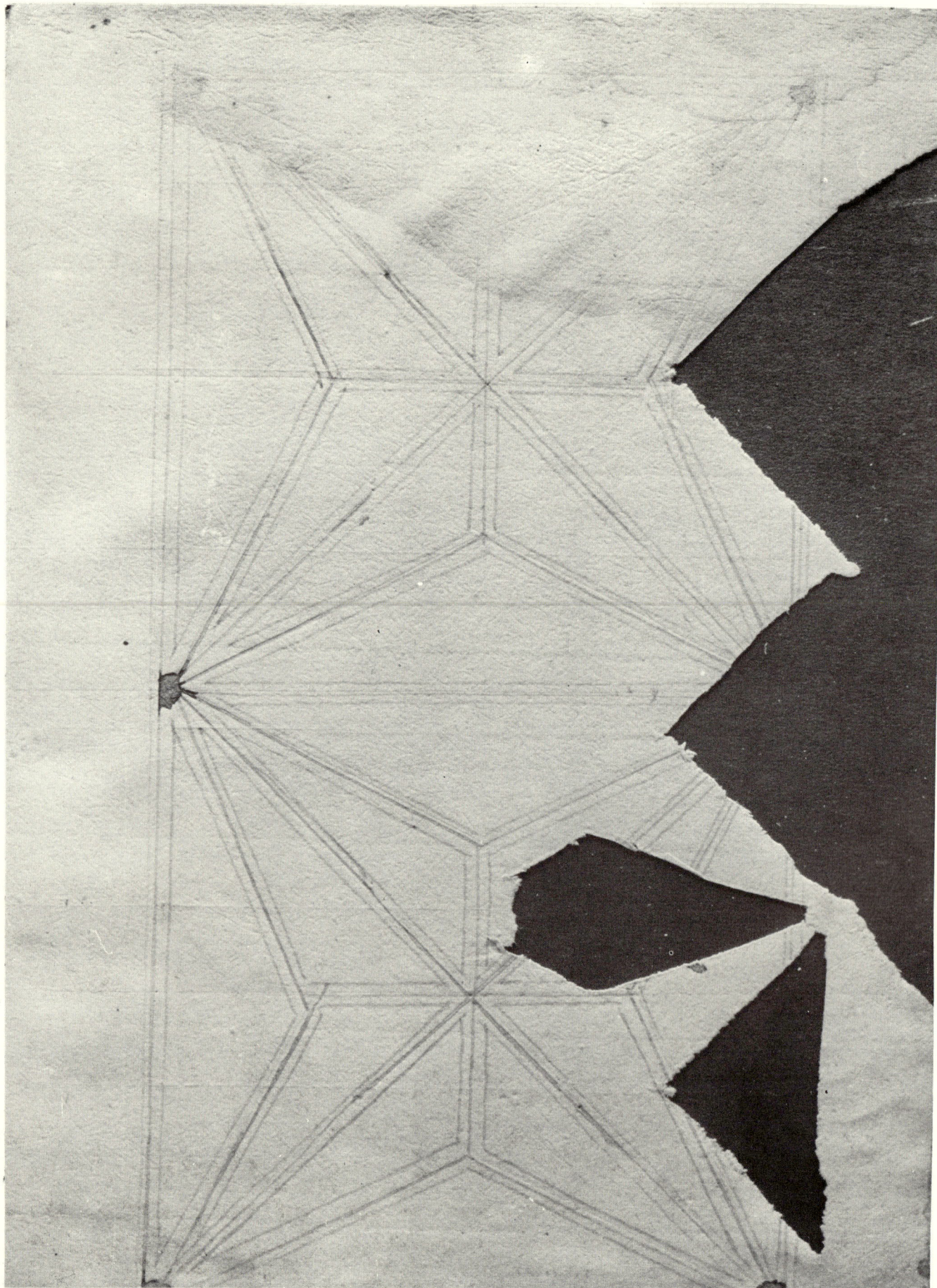

WG 313   Two standard four pointed stars, their widths determined by one quarter of the center lines.

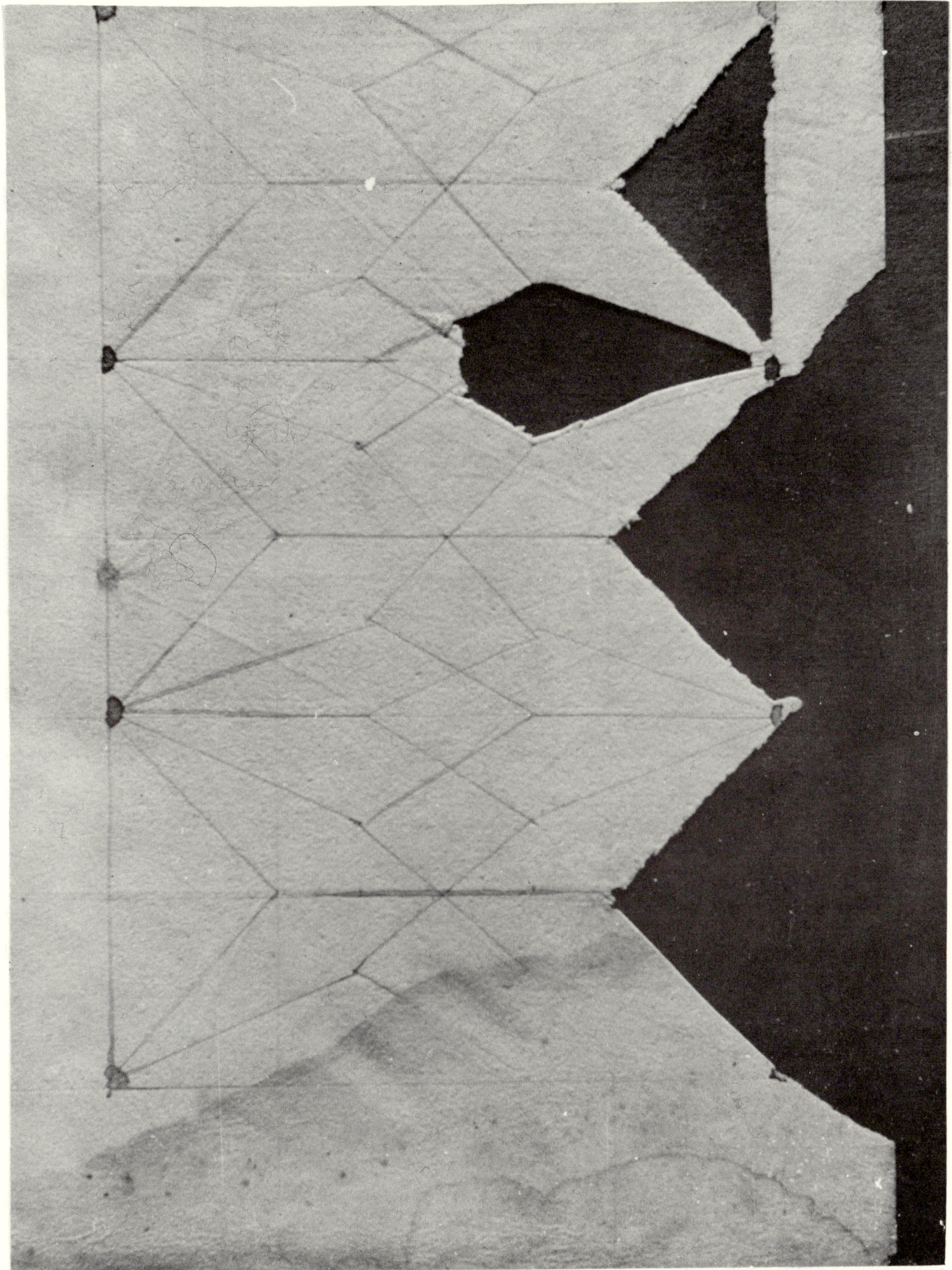

WG 314 Tentative sketch for a net vault related to WG 247-48. The vertical quadripartite and sexpartite
horizontal division and the interconnecting guidelines are clearly visible.

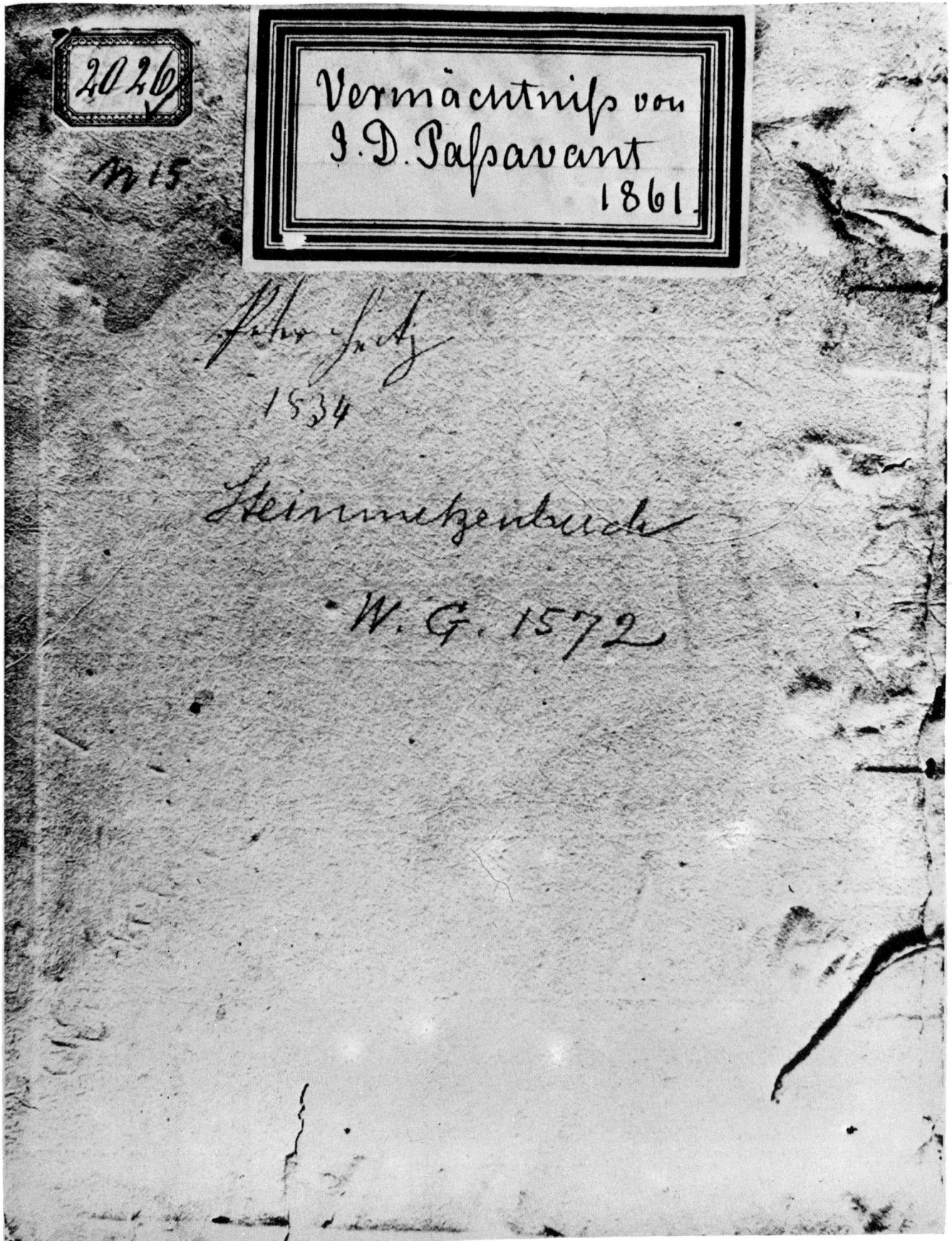

Flyleaf recto: *Steimetzenbuch* [a mason's book]. The names are those of two later owners, Peter Seitz 1834, and J. D. Passavant who donated the manuscript to the Städelsches Kunstinistitut in Frankfurt in 1861. Top left: original library signature.

Flyleaf verso: Dedication of the book by Peter Seitz dated 9 May 1837, to his son Valentin, born
27 May 1826.

Illustrations for Master WG

fig. 1   Schondorf, Parish Church. c.1500

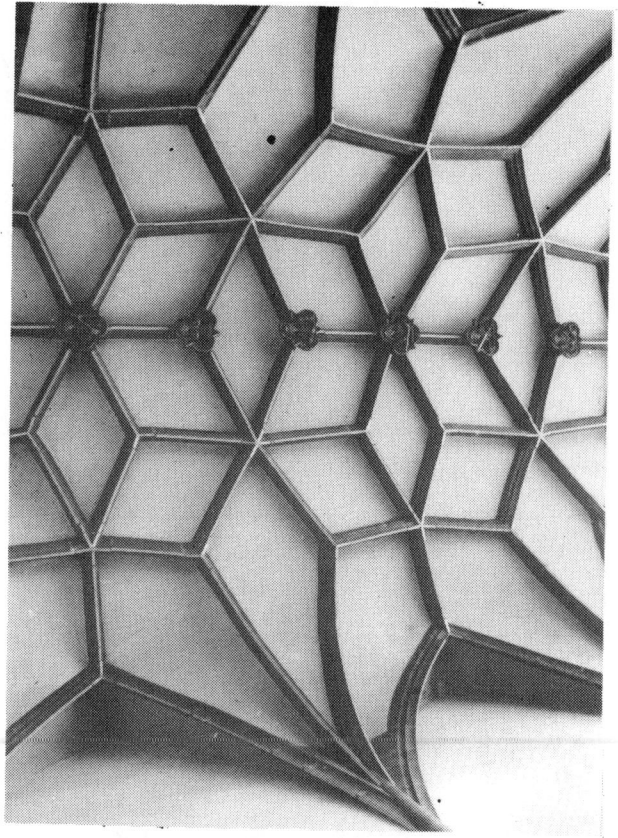

fig. 2   Gerlingen, St. Peter's Church. 1463

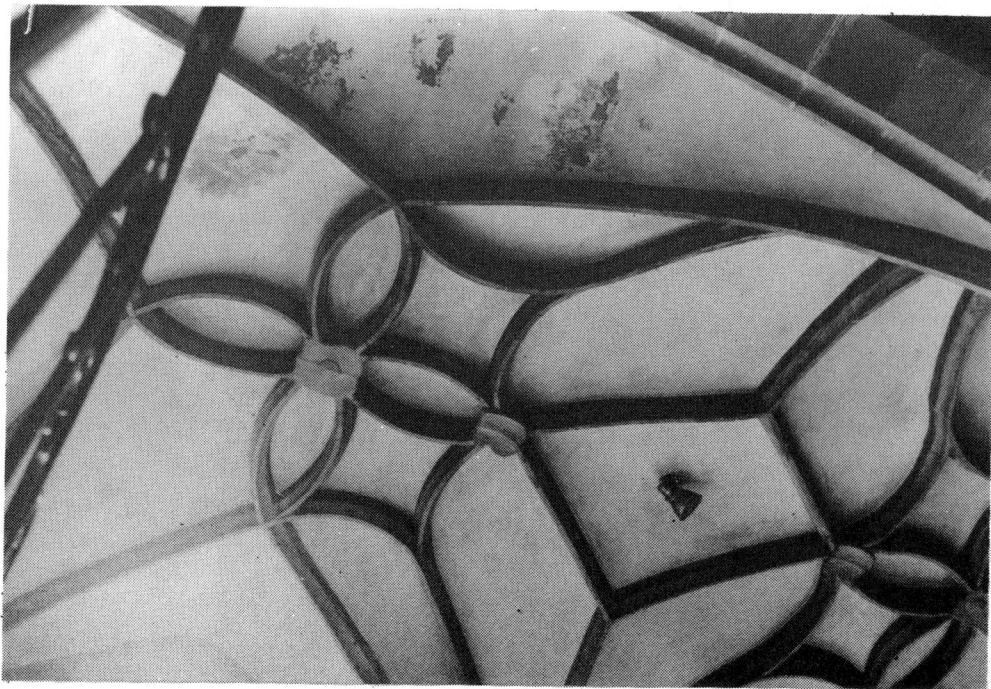

fig. 3   Aschaffenburg, Collegiate Church. Star-vault c.1500

fig. 4   Bad Cannstatt, Town Church. Choir vault, 1465-71

fig. 5   Ulm, Cathedral. Side aisle vaults, 1502-07

fig. 6   Waiblingen, Upper Nun's Chapel. Net vault, 1496-1515

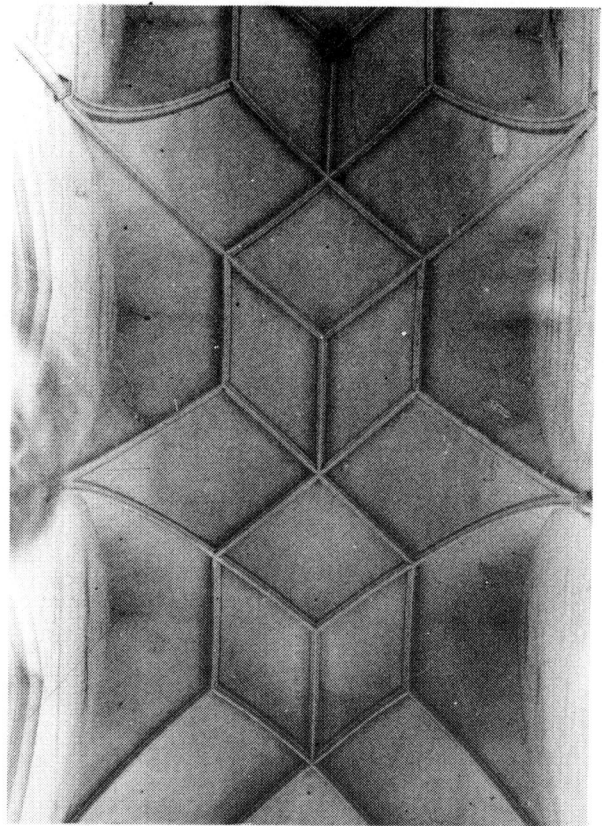

fig. 7   Ingolstadt, Liebfrauen münster. Side aisle vaults

fig. 8   Munich, Frauenkirche. Side aisle vaults, before 1492

fig. 9   Schwäbisch Gmünd, Heilighreuz-
            münster. **Vaults**, 1521

fig. 10   Schwäbisch Gmünd, Heiligkreuzmünster. Side aisle vaults, 1491-1521

373

Hans Boeblinger

Designation: H.B.

The seemingly insignificant twenty-page booklet with leaf patterns shown to me by Edith Chorherr, Librarian of the *Bayerisches Nationalmuseum* in Munich is basic to our understanding of the decisive influence of architecture on the arts of the fifteenth century. Therefore the booklet is of primary importance also for the history of fifteenth century graphics. Prepared by an excellent mason and progenitor of an active and tightly knit clan of builders, its illustrations are evidence of the comprehensive education of architects who were charged not only with building, but also with the design and execution of sculpture, furniture, and other significant decorative elements which assure or impair the success of large structures.

Prepared by an excellent mason and progenitor of an active and tightly knit clan of builders, its illustrations are evidence of the comprehensive education of architects who were charged not only with building, but also with the design and execution of sculpture, furniture, and other significant decorative elements which assure or impair the success of large structures.

Hans Boeblinger's booklet is the logical successor to Villard's leaf.heads, choir stalls and sculptural exercises. It foreshadows the concern with ornamental gables, sculpture and liturgical objects found in sketchbooks which will be discussed subsequently. By the fifteenth century the multiple role of the mason-contractor-architect had been fully codified. Allowing for local variations, it usually consisted of a five-year apprenticeship beginning at age fourteen. This was followed by a year's travel. On returning, he began a two-year assistantship with an established master and was called a *Geselle* (literally "associate"). As a *Kunstdiener* (i.e. servant of art) he was permitted to act as *Parlier* (Ballier or foreman) responsible for schedules and the actual operation of the workshop, including the cleaning of tools. The Strasbourg Ordinance of 1459 prescribed two additional years of specialization as a matter of course. The Querfurt Ordinance of 1574 spelled out a two year "post master" curriculum. The first year was dedicated to the study of staircases and vault construction both in theory and practice. By accepting a second year, the young master mason declared himself ready to be examined about his knowledge of projection methods, ornamental sculpture, *leaf cutting* and portraiture. It stands to reason that the mason who had completed the full seven to nine-year course of study had a better chance of obtaining important commissions than a well-trained mason-contractor with less theoretical and artistic schooling.

Boeblinger's leaf-pattern book is most likely the result of his last year of study at Constance, in southernmost Germany. In a recent essay on "Micro-Architecture" we drew attention to the ability of medieval architects to design on both a monumental and on an intimate scale. But we neglected to point out the impressive and disciplined quality control that was the result of the specialized education of the masters. Boeblinger's leaf-patterns preceded, and perhaps influenced the superbly abstracted Gothic leaf designs of the engravers, Master E.S. and Martin Schongauer. Accordingly, it is possible that the architect, not the goldsmith and painter, created and codified the most painterly and the most pervasively Gothic element, the pseudo-natural, supremely graphic leaf which patterned and enlivened fifteenth and sixteenth century cornices, finials, portals, tabernacles, fonts, and roof lines. We know now that many of these small architectural gems were designed and supervised by the trained architect.

HANS BOEBLINGER

Description

The cover displays the accession number 3604 of the Bayerische Staatsbibliothek in Munich and the inscription *Vierhundert Jahre alte Zeichnung 1435-1836*. The back cover gives the name of a nineteenth-century owner, "Martin Jos(ef) Reider, Bamberg 1836, Apr. 9" and the title, *Monogramm des Boeblinger (Steinmetzzeichen) 9. April 1836*. On p. 12 appears a partly erased notation in a nineteenth-century hand *angehörig dem Johann Michael* (belonging to Johann Michael).

The manuscript consists of twenty pages or five bifolia measuring 216 x 154 mm. Leaves 3/4 and 17/18 show an ox's head watermark. According to Briquet (vol. 4, nos. 14299, 14325, 14329-31 and 14338) this watermark occurs in paper from southwestern France. Closely related examples appear in Toulouse and Montpellier (1441-54), Pignerol (1428), and variants also at Rudolfszell and Wallenstadt (1465-68). The crown motif described by Pause (p. 198) cannot be identified. Most likely the paper was made in the region of Montpellier and exported to Constance, whose international, humanistic and theological activities reached a high point with the Council of 1414/18. Its dramatic meetings which were attended by the clergy, Emperor Sigismund and a large number of intellectuals resulted in the execution of Jan Hus. The bifolia are organized in sequence and seem to be in their original order except for pages 5/6-15/16 which were inverted during rebinding. The drawings are in pen and jet black ink. There are thirty-one leaf patterns including four arrangements destined for consoles. The leaves are sometimes sharply serrated; there are grapes, thistles, berries and clumsy acorns. The first three leaves attest to the quick comprehension of the young Boeblinger. The first leaf and branch are, in part, poorly shaded and the distribution of highlights unconvincing. This still holds true for a console showing extensive cross-hatching on pages 2 and 3. The quality of the drawings becomes progressively better, is masterful beginning on page 8, and superb in the handling of form and modeling on pages 12 to 16. The quality suffers on pages 19 and 20, since Boeblinger worked on the open bifolia before binding.

Hans Boeblinger (von Boeblingen, Böblinger, Beblinger) the Elder ca. 1412-1482.

The owner and draftsman clearly identifies himself with his name and mason's mark on page 1, *Ich, hanns von boeblingen ain stainmetz*. He dates his book 1435. It was probably written in Constance.

After nine years of apprenticeship begun at the customary age of fourteen, the young man would have been about twenty-three years old. Accordingly, his birthdate, usually given as ca. 1420, was probably closer to 1412.

If Honnecourt was a short distance from major building sites of the thirteenth century, Boeblingen, a good two hour's walk southwest of Stuttgart, was equally close to major building projects of Southern Germany in the fifteenth century. Churches were under construction at Stuttgart, Esslingen, Reutlingen, Constance, Nürnberg, Ingolstadt, Munich and Schwäbisch-Gmünd. The spatial megalomania of the thirteenth century was supplanted by an obsession with spires, of which the single-tower facade of Freiburg Cathedral was the first example. The north tower of Strasbourg Cathedral was counted among the wonders of the world. Other huge towers were constructed in Bern, Regensburg, Freiburg (Switzerland), and most importantly in Esslingen and in Ulm, two monuments to which the Boeblinger family would contribute considerably. At that time, there was a large demand for architects in the region.

One may assume that Hans completed his studies at Constance the very year written on his leaf-pattern booklet. In 1435 he also drew an eclectic plan and elevation for a tower that is a unique amalgam of a double portal tower surmounted by a baldachin-like structure crowned by a gigantic finial. This parchment (89 x 13.3 cm) is now no. 11 in the City Archive of Ulm (fig. 1). Hans signed the drawing with the pride of a young genius, *Das berinment han ich zu Kostentz gerissen* (I drew this parchment in Constance), adding his recently acquired master's mark and the date 1435. The academic yet accomplished sketch may have derived from a problem posed during the last year of his studies.

In the same year, 1435, he entered the services of the Counts of Württemberg and on 8 April 1439 the city council of Esslingen confirmed this relationship in its records: *Hans von Boeblingen, der hat aber unser gnädigen Herrschaft von Virtemberg geschworen* (Hans from Boeblingen, he has again sworn allegiance to our gracious lordship of Würtemberg). On December 26, that same year he was recommended to the building committee of the Frauenkirche in Esslingen by Matthaeus Ensinger, son of Ulrich, the renowned architect of Ulm, Strasbourg and Bern and consultant for the construction of Milan Cathedral, who died in 1428. Matthaeus had taken over as master of the works of the Frauenkirche in 1429 and seems to have kept the supervision of the project even from Bern where he was in charge of the cathedral. His foreman and deputy in Esslingen was Huelin, who died in 1436. Ensinger's brother, Matthias took over until he too died in 1438. After his move to Ulm, Matthaeus still retained overall responsibility for the Esslingen project, until his death in 463. This was in part made possible by the relatively modest size of the Frauenkirche. Among the most elegant hall churches of Southern Germany, its relatively small size (nave: 49 m.; width: 18.5 m.; vaults: 15.5 m.) was visually enlarged only by a roof of 32.5 meters in height and the highly ornate spire which was to reach 72 meters (figs. 2, 3). The long time span taken up by construction is indicative of the great sophistication of detail which had replaced the earlier stress on immense size of the High Gothic cathedrals (figs. 4, 5). On 22 April 1440, Hans Boeblinger signed the contract that would tie him and his family to projects in Esslingen and vicinity for a long time to come. Secure in his appointments, he married Ursula Koch. Their five sons, Hans, Matthew, Marx (Marcus), Lux (Lucas), and Nisi (Dionysius) all became masons. A daughter, Ursula, later married the builder Stefan Waid von Waldorf, and, after his death in 1405, Martin von Diessen. As a token of profound respect for his civic and professional activities, the city, in 1456, gave Boeblinger a lifetime contract and relieved him of all future taxes, guild dues and other fees. In 1459 Hans Boeblinger, accompanied by his son Matthew, attended the memorable Meeting of Masons in Regensburg. His is the fifth signature on the declaration issued by that assembly. Among other items it stated that "no worker, nor master, nor foreman, nor journeyman shall instruct anyone who is not a member of the guild and who has never worked as a mason, in the technique of deriving an elevation from a plan." Often misconstrued, this statement could not effectively prevent the leakage of the "trade secret". Yet it demonstrates the profession's possessive pride.

Between 1460 and 1464 Boeblinger erected the church tower in Möhringen near Stuttgart. It includes two cross-vaulted storeys and was to be surmounted by a stone spire instead of the present wooden roof. After the death of Matthaeus Ensinger in 1463, Boeblinger was appointed master of construction of the Frauenkirche in Esslingen. His mason's mark had appeared as early as 1440 on the 132nd step in the southwest corner of the spiral staircase turret located above the first platform of the tower that was fused with the facade. Construction was briefly taken over by his foreman, Hans Gugelin. The mark recurs on the door of the lower octagon platform and in 1449, on the upper door of the circular staircase. In 1465 the work had reached the upper octagonal platform. That same year Boeblinger attended the stone masons' meeting in Speyer where his signature is the second one on the document issued by the assembly. There he may have met Mathes Roriczer, the author of a treatise on finials, of which more below. Roriczer was dismissed from his position as master of the works at St. Lorenz Church in Nuremberg, in September 1466, after a tenure of only three years (see Shelby 1977, pp. 19-20). Roriczer, Ulrich Sercker from Baden, and Hans' son Marx, probably joined Boeblinger in about 1468 as journeymen on the fabric of the Frauenkirche at Esslingen. Roriczer remained there until ca. 1472 and eventually became the *Thumbmaister* or "master of the works" at the cathedral of Regensburg.

In 1468 Boeblinger arbitrated a dispute between Master Hans von Mingolsheim and another mason in Heilbronn. By 1471 the central upper staircase of the tower of the Frauenkirche was under construction, and the pyramid of the spire was begun. The

HANS BOEBLINGER

South German intercity conflicts of the mid-fifteenth century slowed down the construction of the complex spire on several occasions, and gave Hans Boeblinger some time to carve the exquisite capitals in the octagon of the belfry, which are closely akin to those found in the pattern book (figs. 6, 9). Boeblinger's son, Matthew, who had worked under him, and who, as an apprentice, also signed the Regensburg Declaration of 1459 had by now been replaced by his brothers, Marx and Lux (the latter became a foreman in the early 1480s). Dionysius, nicknamed Nisi, was the last of Boeblinger's sons to receive architectural training in his father's lodge. By 1479, the upper octagon and central staircase were well under way and signed by Hans Boeblinger. On 4 January 1482 Boeblinger passed away, aged about seventy. He was buried under the sophisticated *baldachin* in the south transept that he had constructed and adorned with a shield and a keystone boldly carrying his mason's mark on a Gothic escutcheon. It shows the same shield which had already appeared on one of the north piers of the nave (figs. 7, 8).

The Boeblinger Dynasty of Masons

The southern German family of Boeblingen, (Böblinger, Beblinger) was not untypical of clans of masons whose dynamic thinking made architecture a challenging occupation. The leaf-pattern booklet almost certainly remained in the family-operated lodge. Hans the Younger, eldest of the sons, studied in Regensburg as well as in Esslingen with his father. He received his master's diploma in 1475 when he was about twenty-four years old. Perhaps he is identical with Hans Ernst Boeblinger, who is mentioned as a wood carver and sculptor in Stuttgart in 1505 and as a mason in 1509. In 1510 he was appointed *fürstlicher Baumeister* (architect of the prince). He died ca. 1531/32. Matthew, the second and most famous of the sons, studied at Cologne and may have traveled to Milan. As an apprentice, he worked on the tower of the Frauenkirche in Esslingen, and in 1474, designed the well-known "Mount of Olives Monument" for the cathedral square in Ulm (fig. 13). His inscription on the exquisite drawing (now in the Ulm Archive, deposited by the *Evangelische Gesamt Kirchengemeinde*) reads," This Mount of Olives was designed by Mathes Boeblinger of Esslingen near Ulm, who also carved many a stone for it in the years around 1474, three years after I had been engaged by the city councillors of Ulm to build their church." The drawing which I originally attributed to Matthew's son, Hans, was correctly ascribed to Matthew by Hans Koepf (1977, p. 59). Matthew never saw the completed monument. The work is of interest to us for two reasons. It shows the masterly draftsmanship that had become a family tradition of the Boeblingers; and it largely ignores the lively leaf-patterns which could have been taken from the booklet by Hans the Elder. Instead, Matthew used the much more rigidly standardized system of crocket-like leaves that can be observed in most second-rate work during the fifteenth and early sixteenth centuries (figs. 10-12).

On the other hand, on a baptismal font, designed for the church of St. Martin in Langenau, Matthew did use the leaf motifs found on p. 12 of the pattern booklet. The same dynamic, scrolled leaves, though lacking stems may be discerned in the circular segments below the font's rim (fig. 14). The finials of the baldachin above the choir of the Frauenkirche in Esslingen also display the complex and refined leafwork that derives from Hans Boeblinger's patterns on pages 4, 9 (top), 17 and 19 in the booklet. The weathering makes them appear simpler and rougher than the original design figures. In 1477, Matthew transferred the responsibility for construction of a building in Zell to one of his brothers so that he could serve as a consultant in Ulm. He was given a contract to work on the huge tower of the minster, where his master's shield appears on a finial dated 1478. In 1480 he was hired for life. Concurrently with the heavy responsibility of the increasingly complex construction of the Ulm tower, Matthew was engaged in important design and consulting work in Frankfurt and Esslingen. He lightened his obligations by transferring lesser tasks to his brother Lux and his brother-in-law, Stefan Waid. Taking the place of Ulrich von Ensingen, Matthew was in charge of the Ulm colossus until 1492. The detection of cracks in the structure begun by his predecessor led to sharp criticism from a hastily assembled group of twenty-eight experts and resulted in his dismissal and banishment from Ulm. He was replaced by Burkhart Engelberg from Hornberg. The dismissal of medieval architects for structural shortcomings was not unusual, however, in this instance the decree was particularly severe. Exonerated two years later, but still unwelcome in Ulm, Matthew was awarded several commissions in his native Esslingen, became master of the works of the Frauenkirche in 1502 and worked in Reutlingen and in Memmingen. Ironically, in 1496, he was asked for his expert opinion concerning the damaged tower of the Church of the Holy Cross in Schwäbisch-Gmünd. Compared with the construction of the Ulm tower these commissions were simple, almost leisurely pursuits which allowed him time to mediate a dispute involving the mason-contractor and fountain builder, Peter of Koblenz. Later, Matthew undertook secular projects for Margrave Christopher of Baden (Klaiber, p. 372). He died in Esslingen in 1505 leaving a great number of designs, some of which are still extant and was buried beside his father under the baldachin in the Frauenkirche. The continued close family ties of the Boeblingers are evident in a drawing of the Spitalkirche in Esslingen which Hans, the name-sake of his grandfather, dedicated to his father Matthew in 1501 (fig. 15). This precise, almost "engraved" drawing depicts the now-destroyed church with its exquisite south portal. Hans represented himself as a young and elegant dandy looking out a window near the roof, stating with typical Boeblinger assurance: *den baw hat gemachet metheus beblinger mein Vatter zu Esslingenn im spittal dass han ich hans beblinger abgemacht, wie es do statt, in dem iar 1501* (My father Matthew Boeblinger erected this building in the hospital at Esslingen. I, Hans Boeblinger, have copied it as it stands in the year 1501). Hans' grandson appears to have worked only on smaller monuments, among them a tabernacle in Bopfingen from 2 December 1508 through 1510. He died in Strasbourg a year later.

Family dynasties of masons are not infrequent, and since they reflect the cohesive discipline of the profession most cogently, it seems appropriate to follow the progression of the Boeblinger clan to the end of the male line. Lux or Lucas, probably the third son of Hans the Elder, worked in Esslingen, Ulm, Basel and as master in Constance, where he completed the extremely sophisticated vault over the west portal of the cathedral. Its elegant, doubly curved ribs enclosing a circular keystone which could be opened for the raising of bells, precede those of Benedikt Ried and Bernhard Nonnenmacher (fig. 16). Lux died in 1502 and was probably succeeded by his son Michael who worked in Constance and Ulm, and who then returned to the minster in Constance to become a leaf-cutter. If the booklet of Hans the Elder was still in the family, he would have been its most likely recipient and user.

A fourth son, Marx, received his master's diploma in 1472 and worked on the elegant yet simple church of St. Dionysius in Esslingen until ca. 1484. He was close to his brother Matthew who allowed him to build sections of the west gable and south transept of *unserer Frowen Cappell* in Esslingen, including parts of the spire which bear his mason's mark. He died in 1492.

Dionysius, nicknamed Nisi, was the youngest of the brothers. Apprenticed in Esslingen, he became a foreman or *ballier* thanks to a recommendation by his brother-in-law, Stefan Waid, taking over the construction of the church of Köngen near Esslingen. Concurrently, he became master of the works of the choir of the Frauenkirche in Esslingen and applied unsuccessfully for the position of city architect in Gmünd. In 1513 he began the church of St. Ulrich in Stockach and completed its net-vaulted choir before his death in 1515/16.

The picture of a tightly-knit family group teaching each other and exchanging jobs would not be complete without Ursula, the only daughter of Hans the Elder, who, of course, married a mason. He was Stefan Waid von Waldorf, who, with Matthew Boeblinger Jr., completed details of the Frauenkirche (figs. 10-12) and turned over the construction of Köngen to Nisi before he died in 1504. The saga of the Boeblinger family could be paralleled by the even more dramatic history of the Parler family, the legendary *Junker von Prag*, the Ensinger family and others. The role of pattern books in the linear succession of some families must also be considered, for example, the book written by Lorenz Lacher (or Lechler) for his son, Moritz. The Boeblingers in fact formed a sublodge all by themselves. One sees the fatherly pains taken by Hans the Elder to introduce his sons to the art of masonry, and to advance their careers through civic and personal as well as trade connections. His close contacts with Matthew Ensinger who first recommended him and who hired Matthew, the second son, in Ulm, and his prominent attendance at masons' meetings in Regensburg and in Speyer were all part of his public relations activities. As a flexible, talented and thoroughly informed professional he and his wife Ursula easily deserved the family success and succession which was to brighten their old age. As a draftsman and codifier of leaf-work which helped to give late Gothic art its exquisitely improvised character, he can be ranked with the best engravers of the time, including Master E.S. and Martin Schongauer. It is ironic that art historians of the twentieth century might have attributed Boeblinger's booklet to an engraver, had the author not clearly identified himself as *Ich hanns von boeblingen, ain stainmetz.*

Specialized model books

The leaf pattern book was likely to have been one of the required assignments of Boeblinger's last year of apprenticeship. It must, nevertheless, be considered in conjunction with the new genre of highly-specialized model books written and published for students and minor masters intent on acquiring special skills. Scheller gives an excellent survey of model books and Lehmann-Haupt adds to them the Göttingen manual for illuminators which deals exclusively with the patterning of backgrounds, margins and with rather uninspiring semiabstract leaf patterns. The highly technical German text describes the colors used and their chemical production. Hans Hofer's *Ain new formbech'len der weyssen Arbeyt,* published in Augsburg in 1545 contains seventy-two geometric and rinceaux patterns interspersed with images of unicorns, birds, sirens, and a hunt. These were used as models by embroiderers, *briefmaler*, and communal or guild archivists. The already important sketch- and recipe books produced by painters from the sixth century onward became more numerous and popular. They eventually became an art form in themselves and were followed by fundamental treatises on painting and other pictorial arts such as Dürer's *Unterweysung* and Juan de Arfe y Villafane's *Quilatador* of 1572 which addressed itself to gold- and silversmiths as well as jewelers, and his *Commensuracion* of 1585 for sculptors and architects. These treatises reflect an increase in specialized interests. They were designed for the less inventive artists whose talents were more narrowly defined. The originality of the great masters was the result of their inquisitive intellects. Though a mediocre craftsman could earn his living by polychroming figures (see Egbert and Huth), an architect could not. Traditionally, even the most conscientious builder could not find respect among his colleagues nor could he receive any major commissions if he did not master several fields. Aberlin Jörg, discussed previously in connection with Master W.G., was an accomplished builder of spiralling stairs, and from 1498, held a master's diploma from the goldsmiths' guild. In that same year he was known to have carved several stone figures for the Krafft Tabernacle. Landolt has demonstrated that Daniel Heintz, builder of the nave vaults of the minster at Bern, went to Basel in 1575 to build a museum founded by the humanist, Basilius Amerbach, and to become an innovative sculptor. His letters from this period are witty and informative. In the spring of 1588 Heintz returned to Bern to continue his activities as an architect.

The importance of Boeblinger's booklet for the graphic arts

The pattern book reaffirms our repeated stress on the medieval architects' comprehensive interest in the visual arts. An equally strong argument exists in favor of attributing cross-disciplinary activities to fifteenth-century engravers, painters, sculptors and goldsmiths, who were also active as architects, engineers and weapons makers. But architecture remained the matrix from which many principles permeating the visual areas were derived. An almost unified theory or canon facilitated lateral shifts from one profession to another. Brunelleschi's education in goldsmithing, an art largely derived from and related to architectural design theory, made his switch to architecture not only attractive but also relatively easy. Therefore it is not surprising that scholars such as Eduard Flecking and Alan Shestack discuss the varied, yet distinctly chosen professional activities of two of the foremost northern engravers of the fifteenth-century, the Master E.S. and Martin Schongauer. Keeping in mind the number of talented architects who undertook such assignments as the design and construction of altars, fonts, sculpture, and the manufacture of arms, it would seem natural to assume that Master E.S. and Schongauer moved easily between several artistic disciplines.

Master E.S. worked in the area of Constance, Strasbourg, and Bern (Shestack 1967-68). In Constance he might have met Hans Boeblinger. Active as an engraver from ca. 1450 to 1467, Master E.S. depicted a variety of subjects including leaves and vines, and is also credited with the introduction of cross-hatching. We stated that Boeblinger, perhaps influenced by earlier, now lost engravings, had used cross-hatching on pages 3 and 18 of his pattern booklet of 1435. Master E.S. influenced the abstract flower forms and frolicking figures of other engravers. (Shestack, 1967-68). The style of Martin Schongauer from Colmar (ca. 1450-1491), a painter, goldsmith and engraver, is closely akin to Boeblinger's style. His nine prints of ornamental leaves for use by sculptors, woodcarvers, goldsmiths and architects must be considered in conjunction with Boeblinger's booklet of 1435 or another similar predecessor. (figs. 17, 18). Magnificent engravings of a censer, a crozier or a monstrance (Shestack 1967 and 1969) as well as numerous religious scenes, made Schongauer's work highly suitable as a source for the creation of gold objects, bas-reliefs and sculptural groups. His work influenced Veit Stoss and Tilmann Riemenschneider, Dürer, who sought his acquaintance, and a host of other painters, engravers, and sculptors who either used his engravings as models or copied them directly. Schongauer studied at the University of Leipzig in 1465, worked in Burgundy, and died in Breisach, near Basel. In his travels between Stuttgart and Basel it is highly likely that he met Boeblinger, and may have consulted his leaf pattern booklet.

The booklet of Hans Boeblinger must be considered an important and influential work. He systematically set down variations of late Gothic leaf ornamentation which would adorn buildings and portals, works of metal, and would frame or be decorative elements in paintings, frescoes and tapestries. His role within the graphic arts is seminal if his booklet is an original compilation, and not derived from a prototype from which both he and Schongauer took their ornamental leaves. The increasingly secure and sophisticated outlines, the short strokes of parallel hatching which Pause compared to the marks of a chisel, the cross-hatching found on pages 3 and 18, and the increased strength of the sculptural molding indicate an original process of discovery. The young Boeblinger wavered between a career as a painter-engraver and that of an architect, and we know that at the time such indecision was common. Boeblinger, nevertheless, clearly turned to architecture. His drawing of a tower executed in Constance in 1435 (fig. 1) indicates that the formal aspects of the building's variations in scale fascinated him. His drawings of leaves are clearly intended to be cut in stone. In this respect they contrast sharply with a single example of a leaf engraved by "Master W. with the key" (fig. 19), which Joachim (1956-57) dates between 1465 and 1485. This leaf possesses the coiled energy of a spiralling vine and is painterly while Boeblinger's leaves are solidly tectonic and essentially architectural.

In 1435, while still a young man, Boeblinger had already realized that the range of activities offered by the architectural profession would allow him to fully use his creative abilities and graphic talents. Architecture did indeed provide him with a life of artistic richness and great social variety.

BIBLIOGRAPHY FOR HANS BOEBLINGER

Briquet, C. Moise. 1907. *Les filigranes, dictionnaire historique des marques de papier,* vol. 4, Paris.

Bucher, Francois. 1976. Micro-architecture as the *Idea* of Gothic Theory and Style, *Gesta,* vol. 15, pp. 71-90.

Egbert, V.W. 1967. *The Medieval Artist at Work,* Princeton.

Hofer, H. 1545. *Ain New Formbuechlen der Weyssen Arbeyt,* Augsburg.

Huth, H. 1925, 1967. *Künstler und Werkstatt der Spätgotik,* Darmstadt.

Joachim, H. 1956-57. *Prints 1400-1800,* Art Institute, Chicago.

Klaiber, H. 1911. *Der Ulmer Baumeister Matthäus Böblinger,* Heidelberg.

————. 1910. Hans Boeblinger's Entwurf zum Turm der Esslinger Frauenkirche, *Münchener Jahrbuch der bildenden Kunst,* vol. 2, p. 163 ff.

Koepf, H. 1977. *Die gotischen Planrisse der Ulmer Sammlungen,* Ulm.

Landolt, E. 1978. Künstler und Auftraggeber im späten 16. Jahrhundert in Basel, *Unsere Kunstdenkmäler,* vol. 29, Nor. 3, pp. 315-17.

Legner, R. 1971-72. *Rhein und Maas, Kunst und Kultur,* 2 vols., Cologne.

Lehmann-Haupt, Hellmuth. 1972. *The Göttingen Model Book,* New York.

Pause, P. 1973. *Gotische Architekturzeichnungen in Deutschland,* Bonn.

Pfaff, K. 1862. *Die Künstlerfamilie Böblinger,* Esslingen.

————. 1863. Der Bau der Frauenkirche zu Esslingen, und die Familie Böblinger, *Württembergische Jahrbücher,* vol. 2, p. 177 ff.

————. 1863. *Geschichte der Frauenkirche in Esslingen und ihre Restauration,* Esslingen.

Kletzl, O. 1939. *Planfragmente aus der deutschen Dombauhütte von Prag in Stuttgart und Ulm,* Stuttgart.

Scheller, R.W. 1963. *A Survey of Medieval Model Books,* Haarlem.

Shestack, Alan. 1967-68. *Fifteenth Century Engravings of Northern Europe,* National Gallery, Washington.

————. 1969. *The Complete Engravings of Martin Schongauer,* New York.

Shelby, L.R. 1977. *Gothic Design Techniques. The Fifteenth-Century Design Booklets of Mathes Roriczer and Hans Schmuttermayer,* Carbondale.

Supper, W. 1971. *Die Esslinger Frauenkirche,* Esslingen.

Hans Boeblinger's Leaf-Pattern Book of 1435

HB 1

HB 2

HB 3

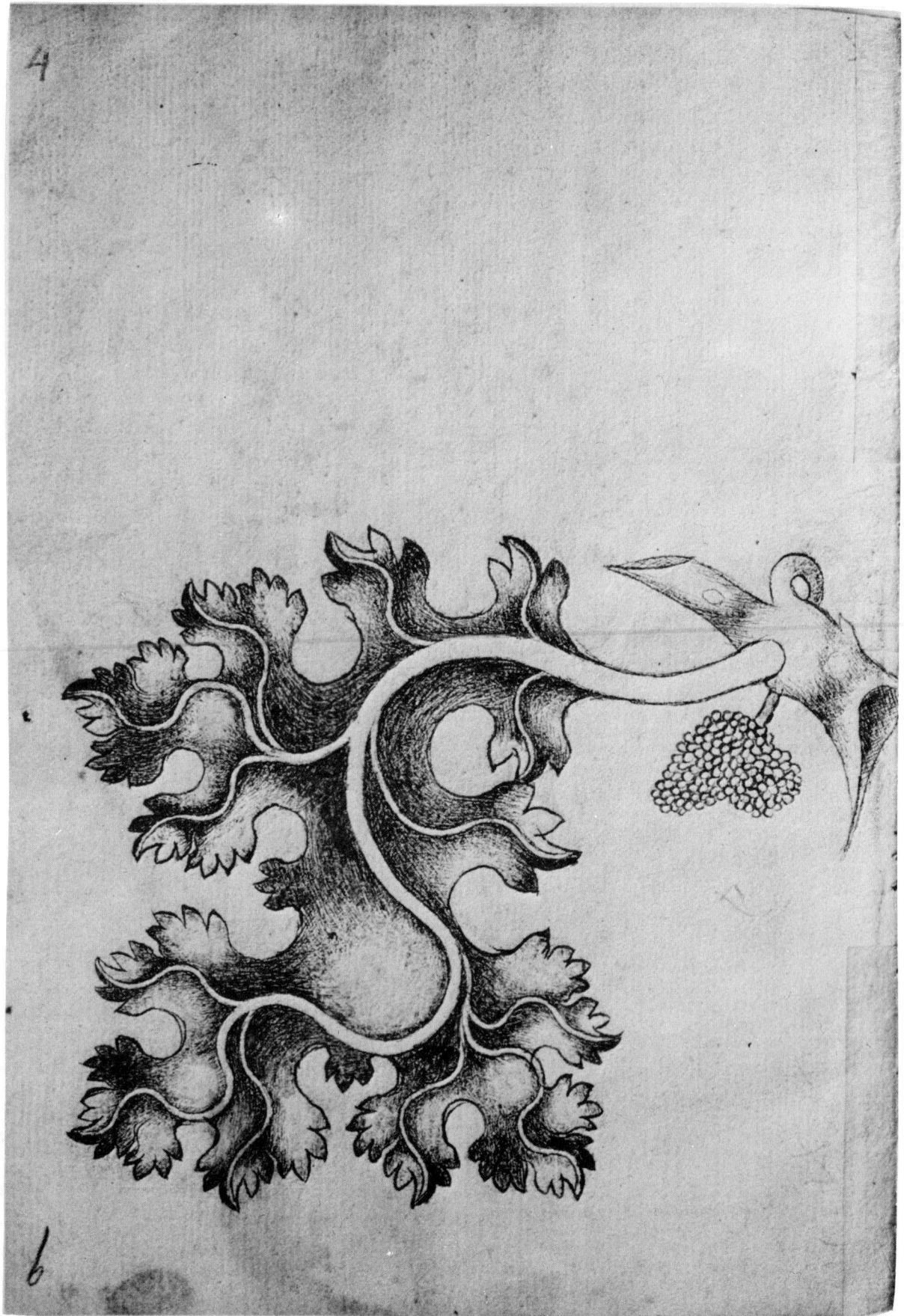

HB 4

HB 5

HB 6

HB 7

HB 8

HB 9

HB 10

HB 11

HB 12

HB 13

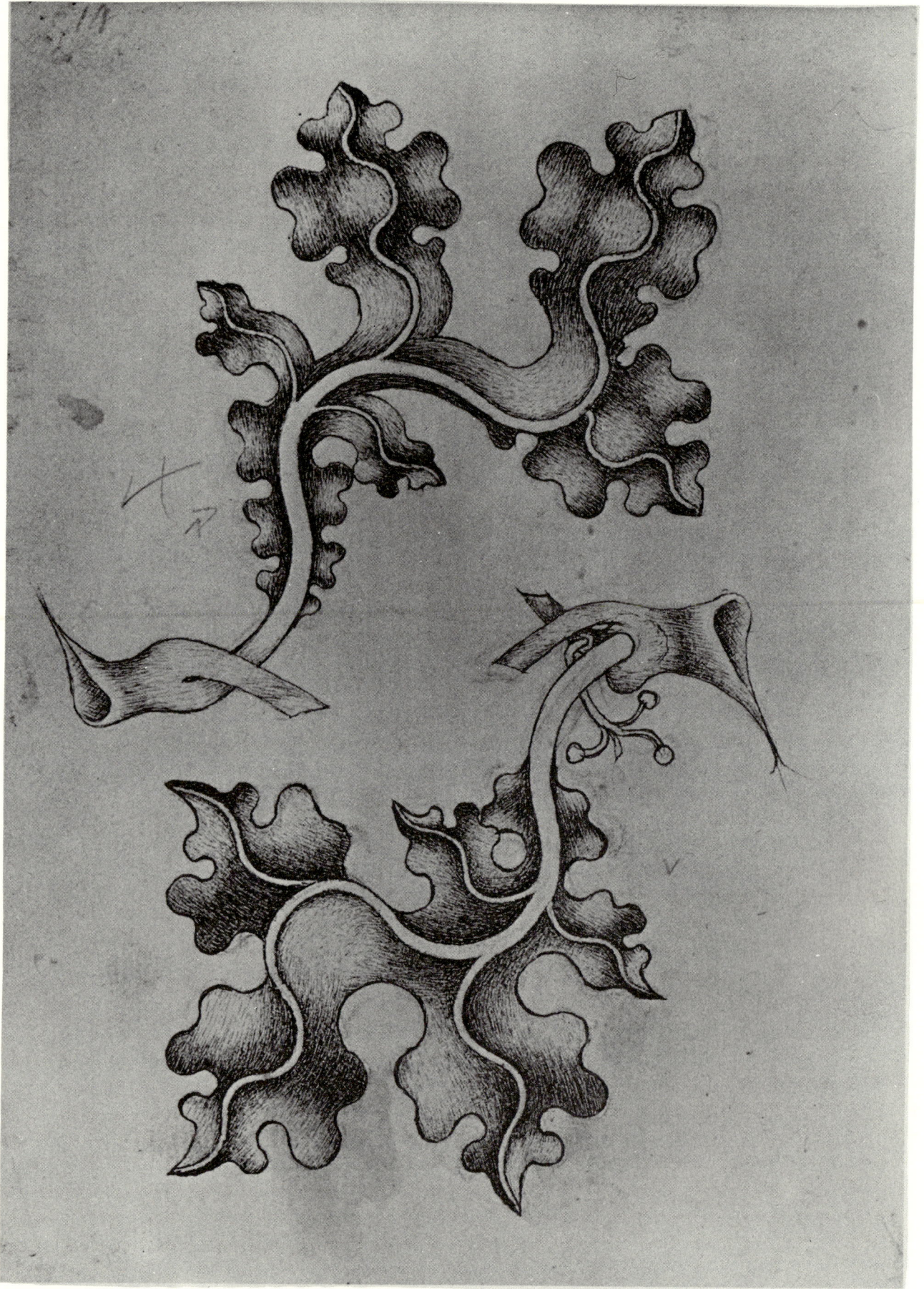

HB 14

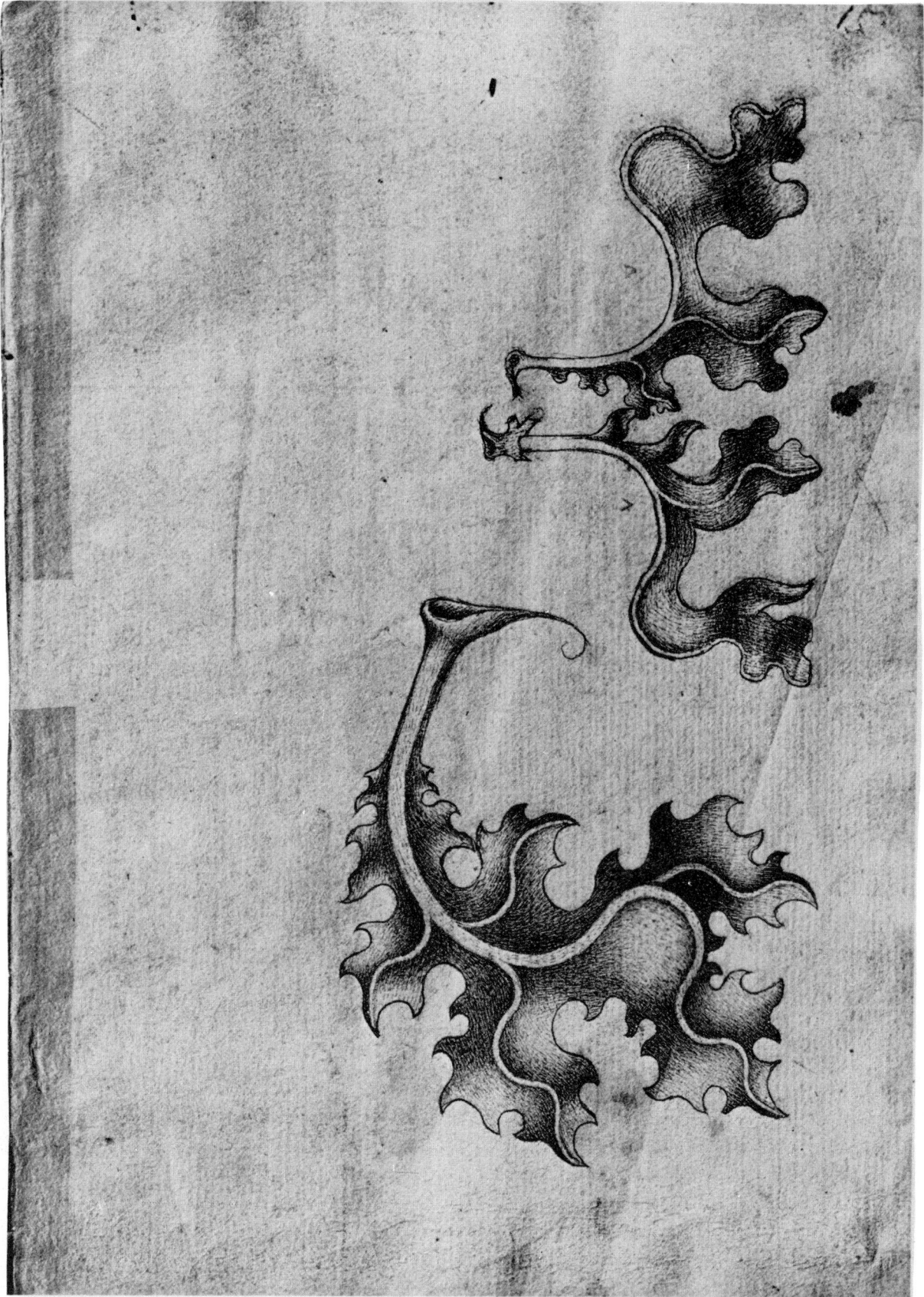

HB 15

HB 16

HB 17

HB 18

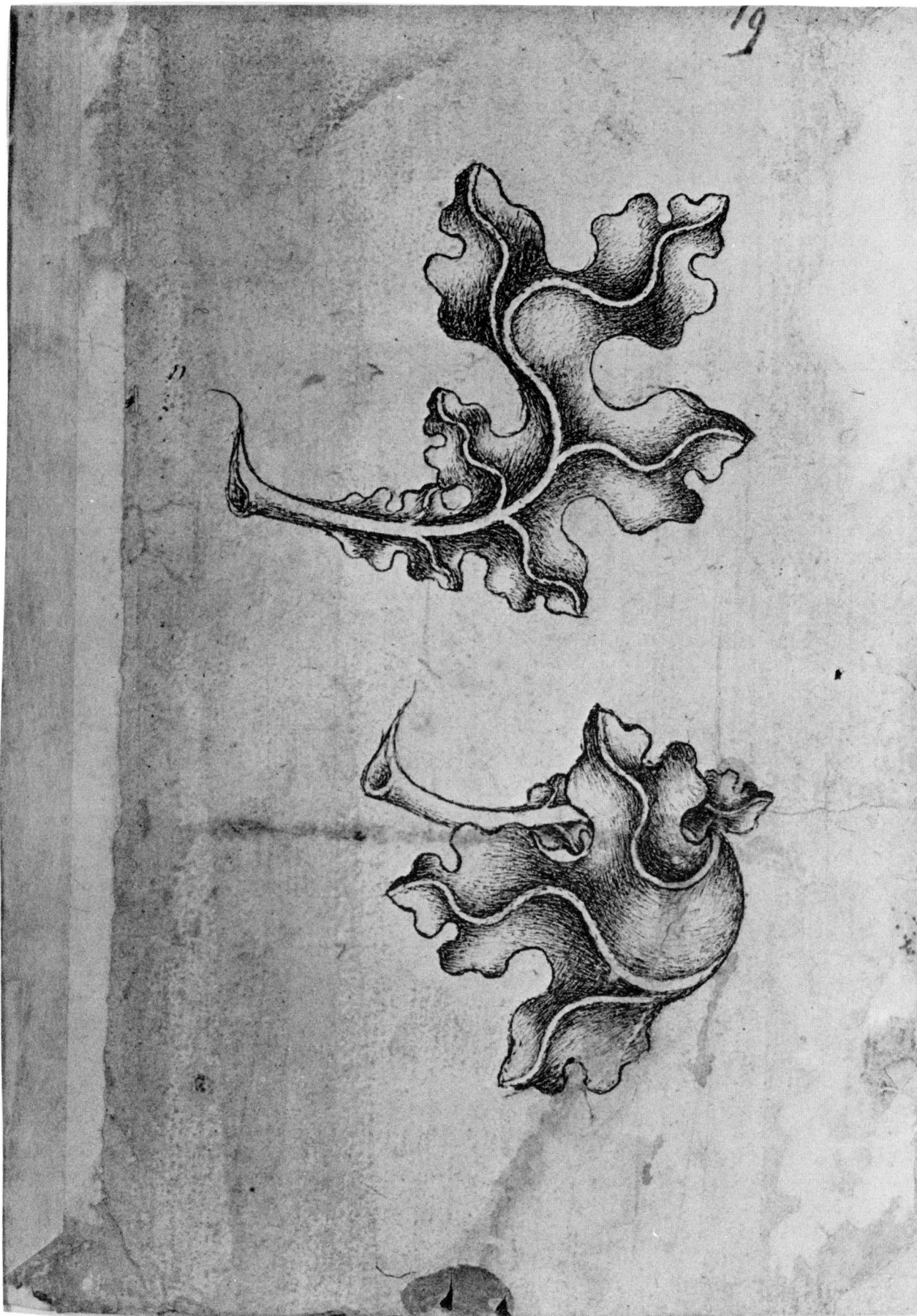

HB 19

HB 20

Illustrations for Hans Boeblinger

fig. 1 H. Boeblinger
Design for
Tower, 1435

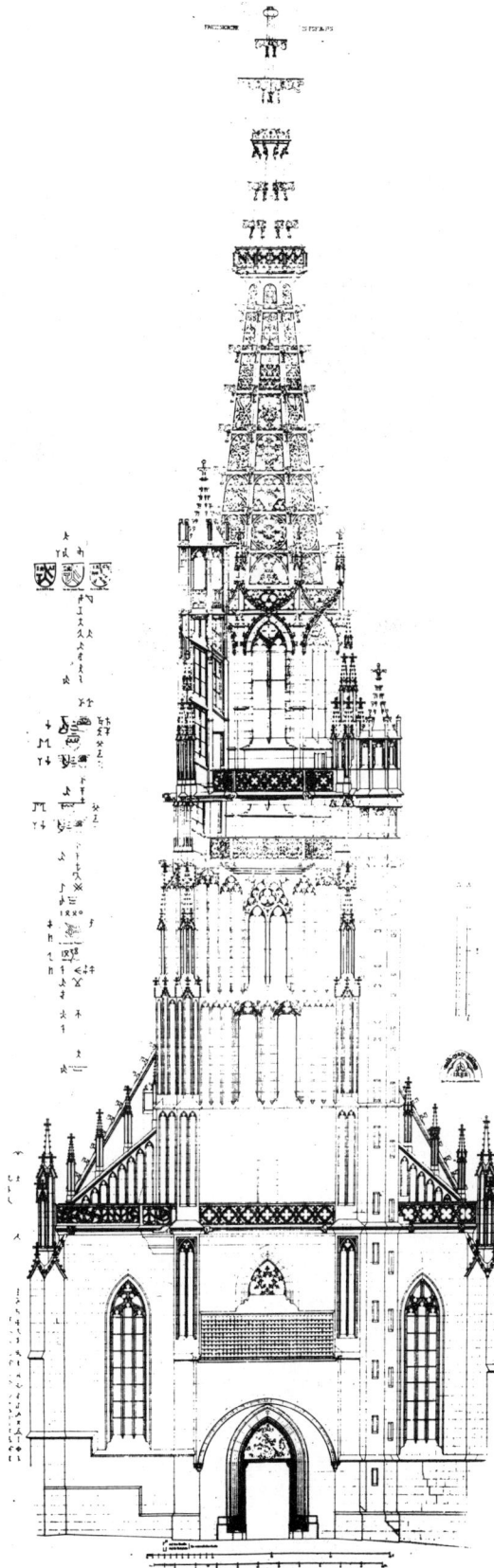

fig. 2 Esslingen,
Frauenkirche.
Elevation of
West-tower

fig. 3 Esslingen, Frauenkirche.
1449. South Facade and
tower by H. Boeblinger (?).
Bayerisches National-
museum, Munich (no.
1028).

fig. 4   Esslingen, Frauenkirche. Spire by H. Boeblinger

fig. 5 Esslingen, Frauenkirche. Interior of Hans Boeblinger's spire

fig. 6   Esslingen, Frauenkirche. Boeblinger's capitals in the spire octagon before restoration

fig. 7   Esslingen, Frauenkirche. Hans Boeblinger's tomb baldachin and capital, 1479

fig. 8   Esslingen, Frauenkirche. Mason's shields of Hans Boeblinger on a nave pier (left) and in the baldachin vault

fig. 9   Esslingen, Frauenkirche. Octagon window by H. Boeblinger

fig. 10   Esslingen, Frauenkirche. Choir finial (restored) by successor of Boeblinger

407

fig. 11   Esslingen, Frauenkirche. Finials from the spire, probably by one of H.
Boeblinger's sons.

fig. 12   Esslingen, Frauenkirche. Finial from South East Ambulatory, probably by one of Boeblinger's sons,
and debased finial design from tower by ⚒

fig. 13 Ulm, Museum. Drawing by Matthew Boeblinger of a Mount of Olives for the Cathedral Square, ca. 1474 (detail).

fig. 14 Langenau, St. Martin. Baptismal font by Matthew Boeblinger; ca. 1470

fig. 15   Vienna, Akademie der Bildenden Künste. Esslingen, Spitalkirche
by Matthew Boeblinger as drawn by his son Hans Boeblinger II in
1501

fig. 16   Constance, Minister, Vault over West
portal by Lucas Boeblinger before 1502

fig. 17   Martin Schongauer, Leaf ornament

410

fig. 18a Martin Schongauer. Leaf
ornament

fig. 18b Martin Schongauer. Leaf
ornament

fig. 18c Martin Schongauer. Leaf
ornament

fig. 19 Bottom right. Thistle ornament by "Master W with the
key"

4232-21
12-96A
138

4232-21
12-96A